HUGO L. BLACK

HUGO L. BLACK

Cold Steel Warrior

HOWARD BALL

New York   Oxford
OXFORD UNIVERSITY PRESS
1996

Oxford University Press

Oxford   New York
Athens   Auckland   Bangkok   Bogotá   Bombay
Buenos Aires   Calcutta   Cape Town   Dar es Salaam
Delhi   Florence   Hong Kong   Istanbul   Karachi
Kuala Lumpur   Madras   Madrid   Melbourne
Mexico City   Nairobi   Paris   Singapore
Taipei   Tokyo   Toronto

And associated companies in
Berlin   Ibadan

Copyright © 1996 by Oxford University Press, Inc.

Published by Oxford University Press, Inc.
198 Madison Avenue, New York, NY 10016

Oxford is a registered trademark of Oxford University Press

Library of Congress Cataloging-in-Publication Data
Ball, Howard, 1937–
Hugo L. Black: cold steel warrior / Howard Ball.
p.   cm.   Includes bibliographical references and index.
ISBN 0-19-507814-4
1. Black, Hugo LaFayettte, 1886–1971.
2. Judges—United States—Biography.   I. Title.   KF8745.B55B298   1996
347.73'2634—dc20
[B]   [347.3073534]
[B]   95–14107

2 4 6 8 9 7 5 3 1

Printed in the United States of America
on acid-free paper

To Associate Justice William J. Brennan, Jr.

We are not an assimilative society, but a facilitative, pluralistic one, in which we must be willing to abide someone else's unfamiliar or even repellent practice because the tolerant impulse protects our own idiosyncracies. . . . In a community such as ours, "liberty" must include the freedom not to conform.

Michael H. v Gerald D., 491 U.S. 110 (1988)

Acknowledgments

First of all, I want to thank some very bright students who worked with me during the 1992–1993 academic year at the University of Vermont. These students wrestled with some difficult questions about Hugo Black and his life and times and, through their relentless questioning, forced me to reexamine, though not necessarily to change, my perspective about Hugo Black. They include Bruce Bernstein, Allison Blew, Matt Byrne, David Donohue, Josh Greenstein, Theresa "Hat" Hand, Laryn Ivy, Mike Kenney, Jason Lillard, P.J. Shafer, Meg Tivnan, Tom Treat, and Karl Von Turkovitch.

Jerome "Buddy" Cooper, Hugo Black's first law clerk and a life long friend of his family, gave me some additional insights about the Judge for which I am grateful. Josephine Black Pesaresi, Hugo Black's daughter, was also very helpful.

The librarians at the University of Alabama Law Library were also very helpful to me as I pored over the books in Hugo Black's library there. Equally helpful were the staff at the Library of Congress's manuscript division, especially its director, Dr. David Wigdor, and his excellent staff including Fred Bauman, Mary Wolfskill, Jeffrey Flannery, Michael Klein, Ernest Emrich, Kathleen McDonough, and Charles Kelly. Finally, the dedicated staff at the Bailey-Howe Library on the University of Vermont campus were extremely helpful in locating hard-to-find books and manuscripts I needed to fully research the Judge's life.

Phillip Cooper, a longtime friend as well as fellow scholar, is another person I wish to acknowledge. I drew upon his dedication to research, love of wisdom, and intellectual prowess as the two of us wrestled, and continue to wrestle, with an understanding of great jurists such as Hugo Black, William J. Brennan, Jr., Thurgood Marshall, and William O. Douglas.

Nancy Poulin, my administrative assistant at the University of Vermont, was of great help to me with research.

My daughters, Sue, Sheryl, and Melissa, were persons I could turn to for kind, reassuring words, and these I greatly appreciated.

Carol, my wife, again understood the need for me to write at home alone and for her love I am deeply appreciative. Thanks also to my friend Sam Conant.

Finally, I want to acknowledge the advice and assistance of a monumental American, the person to whom I have dedicated this book, Justice William J. Brennan, Jr. Like his friend Hugo Black, Justice Brennan is a lover of democracy and, like Justice Black, used all his personal skills, political acumen, and intelligence to move American society closer to the ideal society, one where freedom of inquiry flourishes and where the application of a person's mind and the goodness of a person's soul are the primary human characteristics that determine one's place in our democracy. Unlike his friend, Justice Brennan does not have an overactive thyroid!

Contents

Chronology

1886	Born February 27 in Harlan, Alabama
1889	Black family moves to Ashland, Alabama
1892–1902	Attends Ashland College
1899	Father dies
1903	Attends Birmingham Medical School
1904	Attends University of Alabama Law School
1905	Mother dies
1906	L.L.B., University of Alabama Law School
1906	Private practice in Ashland
1907	Moves to Birmingham and sets up private practice
1910–1912	Police judge, Birmingham
1914–1917	County prosecutor, Jefferson County, Alabama
1917–1918	Captain, U.S. Army
1919–1927	Resumes private practice in Birmingham
1921	Marries Josephine Foster
1922	Son Hugo Jr. born
1923	Joins the Ku Klux Klan
1924	Son Sterling born
1925	Resigns from the Ku Klux Klan
1925	Makes decision to become candidate for Alabama seat in U.S. Senate

1926	Elected to U.S. Senate (November)
1927	Moves to Washington, D.C. (December)
1927–1937	U.S. senator
1933	Daughter Martha Josephine (Jo-Jo) born
1937–1971	Associate Justice, U.S. Supreme Court
1951	Death of Josephine Foster Black
1957	Marries Elizabeth Seay DeMeritte
1971	Retires September 15 from Supreme Court
1971	Dies September 25 in Bethesda, Maryland

HUGO L. BLACK

Introduction

J acob Landynski, among scores of scholars, observed that Hugo L. Black was "one of a half dozen of the greatest Justices in the history of the U.S. Supreme Court in terms of the influence he exerted on the shaping of our law."[1] The challenge for any author writing about Hugo Black is to place him in a context, in a time and in a place. Further, the task is to try to capture *all* of him; to paint a portrait of an *exceedingly* complex man and his times, his family, his contemporaries, both friends and enemies, and to assess his impact on the republic he loved.

Hugo Black thought that such a task would be a difficult one, in part because, as will be shown, he was a very private, very self-disciplined person. When, less than a year before he died, Hugo wrote to his sister-in-law, telling her that, "as a matter of fact I think that [my biographers] are terribly over-estimating the possibility of the success of a biography about me,"[2] it was his acknowledgment of the reality of his largely self-contained, lonely life.

His life, Black believed, would be hard to pierce because he had left little to scholars studying him. In a letter to the author, written two years before his death, he said that "I am not sure that I shall leave my conference papers where anyone else can read them after I leave the Court."[3] He didn't leave them. Just prior to his death, he instructed his oldest son, Hugo Jr., to burn all his conference notes and other private communications between the brethren that he retained in his files. However, there are enough pieces of Black's enigmatic life left, in his personal files and memoirs and in those of his fellow justices, presidents, and others, to put together a clear portrait of a driven and private public person.

Jerome A. "Buddy" Cooper, a close friend of Hugo Black and his family, was the Justice's first law clerk. He loved the Judge, as Black was called by his law clerks. Cooper movingly talked of the Judge's hope for a "world in which men everywhere shall be entitled to walk upright, to enjoy full individual freedom, and to live in peace." In a letter to the author, he wrote that Hugo Black's vision and hope "sprang from a mind and a psyche . . . which miraculously the wings of Destiny must have chosen to dip toward and to touch 'way down in Clay County, Alabama."[4]

Black's life, as Cooper suggested, is one touched by Destiny, to be sure, but it is also the life of a man with an indomitable will, accompanied by an intense drive to excel and to do justice for "the people." Fred Rodell caught Hugo's essence when he referred to the Judge's "greatness of mind and heart, a rare blending of intellectual keenness and courage, with human compassion."[5]

Daddy, his daughter Jo-Jo recalled, "took the greatest pleasure out of living every day." He was a down-to-earth, steak-and-potatoes man who loved gospel songs and disliked opera, high culture, and the fine arts. He hardly ever read novels because they were a waste of precious time. However, Black "loved reading the ancient classics and history texts."[6]

Throughout his life, Black referred to himself, again and again, as a poor, "backward country fellow." But, as Arthur Schlesinger aptly wrote, "if Black was a backwards [sic] country fellow, if he was a hillbilly, he was a special breed characterized as the hillbilly raised to the highest level, preternaturally swift and sure in intelligence, ruthless in action, and grandiose in vision."[7] When the Judge used the "backward country bumpkin" image to describe himself, it was clearly a part of a focused strategy to "set up" the person he was dealing with, whether the person was a legal opponent, a son, or a Court enemy. Black knew he was very intelligent, that he possessed a strength that comes from intelligence and from the capacity to act swiftly with the knowledge he possessed, and he always used his God-given gifts strategically to advance his causes.

It has been suggested that Hugo occasionally chose to be reticent and silent when meeting new colleagues. Tinsley Yarbrough indicates that this behavior was due to Black's sensitivity about his frontierlike Alabama upbringing. When, for example, Justice John M. Harlan II came on the Court in 1957, Black "feared that the aristocratic Wall Street lawyer might be aloof and condescending toward 'a backward country fellow,' as Black often styled himself. He had been both pleased and relieved to learn that those concerns were unfounded."[8] It is doubtful that Hugo ever felt insecure about himself in the company of any man or woman. He was too intent, intelligent, and self-confident to allow a fear about what others thought of him to enter his mind.

The Judge did regularly romanticize about his upbringing in rural Alabama around the turn of the twentieth century. But it was a strategic web he would spin, delivered in his soft, dulcet Southern dialect, complete with a twinkle in his eye and accompanied by his ever-present Southern graciousness. He was fascinated with his family's genealogy. Well into his early eighties, Black continued to gather information and documentation about his early years in farm-country Alabama—visiting the small villages where he and and other members of his family lived and wandering, with Elizabeth, his second wife, in ancient Alabama and Georgia graveyards, revisiting family and relatives, tracing lineage. When visiting Alexander City, Alabama, in the summer of 1966, Black found an old receipt, dated October 30, 1888, for supplies bought by his father from a local merchant,

R. Herzfeld. He was thrilled. Writing his devoted secretary, Frances Lamb, in July 1966, he recalled that the purchase was made when he was 2½ years old— It was probably on this date that I saw my first train in front of the Herzfeld store. While a farmer in Southern Clay County before moving to Ashland to run a store there in 1889, my father traded in Alexander City, going there in a wagon most of the time."[9] Black relished the past because it accounted for his behavior as an adult and provided him with answers to questions about the present and the future.

Hugo Black lived to his eighty-fifth birthday, and his life was very full and active. He was always on the go, using all the time in the day to fulfill some goal and frequently working until the early morning to prepare a legal defense or to draft a Court opinion. He did not waste time. Interestingly, Black, who studied medicine for over a year prior to going to law school, perennially insisted that his overactive thyroid was the primary reason for his constant energy and his successes in life. He refused treatment of the condition, saying to his doctors: "Don't touch that [the thyroid], if it weren't for that, I'd still be plowing in Clay County!"[10]

Black was an extremely successful personal injury lawyer who practiced in Birmingham, Alabama, and who, at one time, dreamed of moving to New York City to practice law among the legal giants. He was also a police court judge and a county prosecutor in Birmingham. He was a lover and a husband and a stern parent to two of his three children, as well as a stern grandparent to his grandsons. With the help of his fellows in the powerful Ku Klux Klan, the major successful pressure group in Alabama and across the South during the 1920s, Hugo Black was elected to the U.S. Senate in 1926.

In the Senate, after a brief, cautious start that reflected the pattern of his learning curve, Black was an absolutely bruising senator, continually speaking on behalf of the poor in his state and across the nation. In short order, he became an aggressive investigator of public utilities, mail contracts, and the maritime industry, as well as a key opponent of proposed national antilynching legislation. When New York Governor Franklin D. Roosevelt became president in 1933, Black immediately saw how important FDR was for the poor in America and, at once, became a vigorous, effective New Deal advocate in the Senate. However, as his legislative proposals during the New Deal showed, the Alabaman was "unbossed and unmanipulated," even by someone he respected and admired.[11] On August 12, 1937, after a tough Court-packing battle in the Senate that the president lost despite Black's vigorous defense, Roosevelt nominated Hugo to fill a vacancy on the Supreme Court. After a quick but controversial confirmation by the Senate, he became the president's first of nine appointments to the high bench.

From the first Monday in October 1937, the traditional opening of the term of the Court, until his retirement in September 1971 (and death just weeks later), Black served the nation as an associate justice for one month shy of thirty-four years. As such, he wrote almost one thousand opinions, more than half of them either majority or concurring opinions. He also played a significant leadership role on the Court in bringing about America's constitutional revolution in the 1960s.[12] As a leading jurisprudential scholar/practitioner on the bench, the Judge also contributed significantly to America as a major philosopher of the Constitution.

What qualities did Black bring to the Court when he arrived on the high bench in the early autumn of 1937? What accounted for his success and greatness on the high bench?

First of all, Black was a dedicated man of the South, who grew up in an Alabama that was barely emerging from a frontier state of existence. Although he spent his childhood in the bleak, rough, scrub-cotton backcountry of the state, an area of Alabama that had few blacks working the fields, Hugo was a racist. Almost all Alabamans were racist and Black "always felt he was one of them." [13] As his outspoken sister-in-law, Virginia "Jinksie" Durr, said: "It's very difficult in the South to be self-righteous. We were all segregationists when we grew up. You can't say everybody else is a son of a bitch or wrong if you were the same way yourself." [14]

Yet this man, who began his national career as the candidate of the Ku Klux Klan, argued forcefully and successfully for an end to segregation in the South while on the Supreme Court. In his correspondence, whether to a former student in his Bible classes in Birmingham who argued for "freedom of choice" [15] or to a still-segregationist first cousin who appealed to Black to "stand by us," [16] the Judge strongly condemned the segregationist Old South and spoke movingly, at law school dedications, of the emergence of the New South. [17]

Black was largely self-taught. From his early years to his death, he was a lover of history who quickly came to view history and human progress as exhibiting patterns of regularity and predictability, patterns that, if understood by political leaders, could minimize human anxiety. Such an understanding of the rhythms of history could allow society's leaders to achieve a homeostasis between the needs and powers of the larger community and the rights individuals possessed in that society. Black came to believe that all persons did have, in the words of one of his major heroes, Thomas Jefferson, unceded rights and liberties that had to be protected by an energetic Supreme Court.

Black's arrival in Washington, D.C., in 1927 was the beginning of his serious reading of history and philosophy. In time, he became an ardent, knowledgable student of history, and his speeches on the floor of the Senate soon were replete with appropriate quotes from the great writers of history, especially America's history. Although some critics insist that Black's interpretation of America's past was inaccurate or "phony," an objective view of his understanding of the constitutional era and of the history of the events and ideas that led to the passage of the Civil War amendments indicates that he was correct in how he perceived these events and chronicled them in his decisions. [18] As Charles A. Reich, a noted Yale Law School professor wrote, the Judge's view on the Civil War amendments, "bitterly denounced when he first advanced it, has stood the test of time." [19]

Black came to believe that only when there was a balance between the rights of the individual citizen and the integrity and powers of the larger community would there be a flowering of human potential. As he wrote to his son, Hugo Jr., "in your associations with people, as everywhere else, it is a question of balance, and the Greeks just about hit on the best doctrine when they adopted as the slogan of life, 'Never Too Much.' " [20]

For Black the historian, the classical example of such harmony was democratic Athens. His personal library, preserved in the University of Alabama Law School, stands as proof of his love of the Greek classics. A visitor picks up books that illustrate Hugo's admiration of Greek writers, philosophers, poets, historians, tragedians. They are worn from repeated use, underlined and replete with marginalia, indicative of the personal conversations Black had with the authors of these books.

He loved Edith Hamilton's interpretive writings about Greece and Rome, especially Greece, and literally coerced his children into reading them, with further admonitions to read Livy or Plutarch when the boys were in college or in the military. Black sent these beloved books to his grandchildren. He had both of his wives—Josephine and Elizabeth—and all his law clerks read Pericles, Aristotle, and other Greek writers, historians, and poets. For all his law clerks Hamilton's *The Greek Way* was their first read when they joined him in the Court. Before the certiorari petitions and the briefs on the merits, these young men and one woman read about the beauty of Greece and about the flowering of the spirit of free inquiry in Athenian democracy.

Black's reading of history, including the history of the American republic, especially the writings of Thomas Jefferson, led inexorably to a vision of a democratic society where men and women achieved their full potential. It was a vision that was a positive one, but with a touch of cynicism.

America was the country he loved with great passion, believing that it could become the biblical city on the hill. However, for that to happen, politicians had to take the responsibility to lead, in order to overcome the darker side of human behavior. History showed that men and women could progress, even though they were not all good, but such progress required great leaders who understood the lessons of history and the fallibility of men and women. "If one views history closely enough," Black wrote to his son Sterling, "there is much evidence that while human progress is slow, it is nevertheless sure."[21] But he also believed that history showed how progress could be overwhelmed by evil tyrannies that, once in power, immediately suppressed and destroyed freedom of inquiry.

He held these views of history and human nature as unreservedly as a religious convert accepts and adopts and lives a new theology. Whether police court judge, prosecutor, senator, justice of the Supreme Court, Hugo L. Black forcefully moved to action in order to actualize his vision to the best of his ability. As he wrote to one of his sons: "Nothing is really disgraceful except that which is dishonorable and it is never dishonorable to fail to achieve something if the person does the best he can."[22]

Although Black was, to many, a pessimistic Protestant, his daughter Jo-Jo spoke about his positive, optimistic outlook on life. She recalled the comments Hugo offered when she told him that her son was born with a serious eye problem that left him without sight in one eye. In a flash, his reponse to her was: "Let see what's possible for a youngster with one eye."[23] Her son's health problem no doubt reminded Black of his son Sterling's serious early-childhood hearing problems. For Black, life proved the efficacy of this optimistic attitude. One had to strive to do the best one could with the tools, both physical and mental, given at birth.

Knowledge of the past, especially the histories of earlier democratic societies, however, was only the beginning for lawmakers in a democracy. Black believed, fiercely and uncompromisingly, that positive law, the man-made law of a society, is the only legitimate way to turn knowledge into policy for a community, to make real the collective ideals and hopes of the people. For him, the making of law and the rule of law were two sides of the same coin. In this process of rule creation and application, the words and phrases of the fundamental law of the nation, the Constitution of the United States, were paramount guidelines. These views of history, human nature, and law were central to his behavior as a public figure, especially in his time as legislator and as justice of the Supreme Court.

At every critical turn in his life, people misjudged Black's character, commitment to enduring principles, and intellect. The initial perception of Hugo was that of an uneducated Alabaman, a rube, redneck, crude country politico who aspired to heights that were simply beyond his reach, both socially and intellectually. The "Big Mules" who ran the Alabama Democratic party and who mocked his temerity when he decided to run for Senate in 1925 had this view of the man, as did the establishment legislators in Washington who greeted the junior senator with disdain when he arrived in 1927. A decade later, when Black left the Senate for the Court, many continued to malign his intelligence and his character. Even the justices of the Supreme Court held a belief, for a few years, that he was absolutely unfit for service on the high bench and that he was an outsider who lacked the intellectual capacity and the judicial temperament to serve as a justice on the highest court in the land.

Black's life disproved every one of his critics. He had to overcome stories in the public press that charged him with incompetence or virulent racism. Some of his critics, throughout his life, accused him of employing crass political, bullying tactics to serve his own ends, whether he was in the Senate or sitting on the Court. For example, the *New York Daily News,* on May 12, 1938, ran the following headline over a feature story: "[CHIEF JUSTICE] STONE DENIES HAND IN ATTACK ON BLACK." Evidently, Stone had given a quote to a *Harper's* magazine reporter, Marquis Childs, critical of Black's legal and jurisprudential abilities. Stone, it was reported, said that Hugo's *"lack of legal knowledge, deficiencies in background and training* have led him into blunders which have shocked his colleagues" (my emphasis).[24] If the Judge was bothered by this notoriety, he did not show it.

His daughter insisted that Black "genuinely didn't care about insults directed at him and held no grudges, period."[25] In fact, Black never showed anger in public at outrageous statements hurled at him by his opponents and enemies, both political and jurisprudential. As he wrote to a law clerk:

> I am not disturbed at all [about adverse comments]. . . . You and I know very well indeed that any man who stands for positions of any advance nature at all is always subject to criticism by those who get most benefit from maintenance of the status quo. No man could ever hold public office who is unable to accept with equanimity the best or the worst invectives that can be hurled at him. Nothing that has been said or done will alter my course.[26]

Black always functioned to the best of his considerable ability. He did not deviate from his vision for America. Black was correct when he said to critics who maintained that, as he grew older, he grew more conservative: Nonsense, I have not changed my views, only the issues have changed and that of course is as it should be.

Perhaps the most appropriate tribute to his greatness came from his oldest son, Hugo Black, Jr., who was terribly hurt by the lectures and harangues to which he was subjected by his "daddy" throughout his life. He wrote to his father's secretary shortly after the Judge's death:

> I have given some thought to whether I should continue the "Jr." at the end of my name and have decided to do so. I understand that most "Jrs." drop the "Jr." on the passing of their father. As you know, however, Daddy was a superstar. As such, I think he deserves to have his number retired, which I have decided to do by continuing the "Jr" after the "Hugo L. Black" in my name.[27]

There are a host of paradoxes that dot Black's landscape. He was the poetic Romantic, a person who loved four women with a fervent intensity and a passion that knew no limits. Yet he was never the jurisprudential romantic. He was disciplined by the words and phrases of the Constitution in all his actions as a justice of the Court. He battled mightily against his brethren, men who were willing to expand the meaning of the Constitution, including the creation of "new rights," in order to do good as they defined it.

Black was never one of those "adventurous, freewheeling . . . reformers who passionately wish to do good and who do not intend to let tradition, law, precedents, or nonromantic readings of the Constitution get in the way."[28] The Judge was forever critical of these "romantic" justices, good friends of his such as William O. Douglas and William J. Brennan, Jr., who "learned to cite 'due process' and 'equal protection' to justify almost any preconceived result . . . [and, in so acting,] imposing their own social agendas" on the community.[29]

Black's life was characterized by his "steely, undeviating, and fighting purposefulness."[30] He was tough and undeviating in his public roles, whether fighting the "do-gooders" on the Court, battling judicial archcautionaries such as his lifelong adversary, Felix Frankfurter, or, as a senatorial investigator, ripping into corporate moguls who unscrupulously pillaged America's vulnerable economy in the first decades of this century. Black was equally steely with his sons and his grandsons, although a soft touch with the women in his life.

Jo-Jo Black reflected on this characteristic of her father. She confessed that although Hugo was hard and steely on the outside, he was a sentimental "softie" inside! It was a well-guarded family secret that Black cried a great deal when watching movies; eventually he refused to attend theaters because he sobbed loudly and didn't want to be seen in public in such a state.[31]

With all his warts and faults, Black was the "superstar" his son revered. He had a moral commitment to his vision of a better America, a nation whose people could achieve the good, free life if they and their leaders would but follow the Constitution's hallowed principles. This book is an effort to capture the intensity of Hugo Black's commitment to the Constitution as well as to describe the manner in which he sought to achieve his goals.

CHAPTER ONE

Hugo L. Black: Cold Steel Warrior

How does one begin the story of a great man, someone whose life was full of ironies and paradox? Hugo Black's eighty-five years were eminently successful ones, although just about each year evidenced discord of some kind for him. Black, however, overcame every crisis in his life in a masterful way. Indeed, Black was outstanding in every role he played—with one exception. He was a harsh, at times cruel, father to his two sons, especially his oldest child, and namesake, Hugo Jr.

To understand Hugo Black is to come to grips with his unique and resolute personality. Almost always, he was in absolute control of his physical, intellectual, social, and emotional self. As a compulsive, driven, singularly focused man, he never lost sight of the particular goal he had set for himself, and more often than not he achieved his objective. Perhaps the best way to understand Black's temperament is to examine one important incident in his life.

The Owen Roberts Letter Incident

It was a steamy, fairly quiet summer's day in the District of Columbia. The U.S. Supreme Court had recently ended its 1944 term. However, Associate Justice Owen J. Roberts, a member of the Court since 1930, couldn't take it any longer. It wasn't the temperature and humidity he couldn't stand, nor was it the Court's workload with its accompanying stress. Rather, what was intolerable was the painful, continuous acrimony generated by some of his so-called brethren on the Court. "Bitter and cynical about his colleagues,"[1]—especially that man from Alabama, Hugo L. Black—Roberts quit the Court on July 30, 1945, after the term's conclusion. He resigned abruptly, immediately.

Waging the relentless, intense "war" that prompted his sudden resignation were Associate Justices Felix Frankfurter and Robert H. Jackson on one side and Associate Justices Hugo Black and William O. Douglas on the other. Harlan Fiske Stone, at that time Chief justice of the United States, a former Columbia University Law School professor, was none too pleased with this continual clash of the opposing forces. Especially irksome to him was the fact that the battlers included the brilliant Bill Douglas, a former law school student of his, and Hugo Black, whom he had hired in 1923 to be a special federal prosecutor during his own stint as U.S. attorney general. Stone remarked to a friend that "I have much difficulty in herding my collection of fleas." The four were "so busy disagreeing with each other" that Stone had to assign himself additional opinions to write.[2]

Everyone in the Court, including secretaries and pages, was aware of these ongoing feuds. At the beginning of every term of the Court, new law clerks were briefed by their bosses about these personal and professional conflicts and concomitant protocols to be observed. When Elliot Richardson clerked for Frankfurter, he was told bluntly by the jurist that "this is a war we're fighting [against Black and Douglas]! Don't you understand? A war!"[3] Richardson never forgot that admonition. After one of his many bitter clashes with Black, Justice Jackson wrote to President Truman that "if war is declared on me [by Black], then I propose to wage it with the weapons of the open warrior, not those of the stealthy assassin."[4]

Black was an immovable and potent player in these battles. He readily acknowledged to his sons the nature of the Court conflict, but in general and very understated terms. "People," he wrote to Sterling, "who are familiar with Supreme Court history know that there has never been a time since it was first instituted that there were not sharp differences among the Justices. As you suggest, it would be bad for any institution of this kind to have men who constantly profess to be of one mind on all issues."[5]

It was not only jurisprudential differences that accounted for the conflicts between the two groups. In addition to these substantive differences on matters of constitutional interpretation and of the role of the Court in the American political system, there was a personal dimension to the tumult in the Court. True, Frankfurter, an Austrian Jew who had immigrated to America at an early age and who had been a brilliant Harvard Law professor and a Roosevelt "brain truster," could not stomach Black's constitutional views, especially the Alabaman's categorical commitment to the primacy of the First Amendment—but he also disliked the Southerner.

And while Black's disagreements with both Frankfurter and Jackson never rose to passionate disdain, the same thing could not be said about the stormy relationship between Douglas and Frankfurter. Douglas believed that Frankfurter was one of the most evil men in public life. Frankfurter, in turn, called Douglas a "mommser," the Yiddish word for "bastard."

Clearly, the brethren were not of one mind on many issues during the first decade of Black's tenure on the Court. On one occasion, Jackson said of the Alabaman that "you just can't disagree with him. You must go to war with him if you disagree."[6] In one of his written attacks on the Southern jurist, Jackson claimed that while he and Stone were standing up for freedoms for minorities before coming to the Court, "Black was getting to the top of Alabama politics by joining the Klan and exploiting racial and religious bias."[7] Friends dissuaded him from releasing the letter publicly, so the draft remained in his files, but this perception of Black's lack of integrity remained with the resentful Jackson until the day he died.

The battles that so disgusted Roberts lasted until the protagonists, one by one, left the Court a decade and more after Roberts tendered his resignation to the president. They became the legal equivalent of a Holy Roman Crusade against the Moor infidels, raging from the late 1930s until Jackson's death in 1954 and Frankfurter's retirement in 1962. (Douglas, alone among the brethren, chose not to attend his bitter enemy's funeral.) This war between four willful advocates was infinitely more rancorous than the clashes Roberts had experienced during the 1930s as a swing justice between the economic conservatives of the Court and those who supported President Franklin D. Roosevelt's New Deal programs. And, while not a direct party to the latest animosity, Roberts was sucked into the turmoil by Frankfurter's friendliness towards him and especially by Frankfurter's willingness to agree with his view that Black was "a rank bully who intimidated his colleagues in judicial conference."[8]

For Roberts, in the summer of 1945, there simply was no relief from the stress brought on by even marginal involvement in these bitter clashes other than the one he finally selected: resignation from the high bench. After his resignation, in early August of 1945, following Court tradition, Chief Justice Stone drafted "the customary letter" thanking the jurisprudentially unpredictable Roberts for his fifteen years of Court work and service to the nation. He circulated it to the justices.

There was a dissenting voice, that of Hugo Black. He had just returned to Washington, D.C., from a trip to Los Angeles with his first wife, Josephine, and was getting ready for a gallbladder operation. He saw the memo and draft letter circulated by Stone and wrote his friend Douglas about the proposal, noting, with his angry humor, "I am ready for the *war* [here in the Court]" (my emphasis).[9] He told his friend that

> on my desk at this moment is a letter from the CJ, enclosed with which is a letter to be signed by *all* the members of the Court and sent to Justice Roberts. I am requested to sign it, and send it to Reed, so that all may have the privilege. . . .
> If the letter is signed and sent to Roberts, he may, and will if he follows the course he did the last years, simply take advantage of the opportunity to say something mean about us. If the letter is not signed, this information is certain to be adroitly passed to the public, together with invidious implications. My first impression was to write to the CJ that I would have no part in it. It would certainly be better however to sign what custom has degraded to almost a formality, rather than to write a separate letter. . . . Perhaps all things considered it is better to sign the "form," though I hate to put my signature on it. If when it reaches you, your inclination is against signing, let me know and I shall stay with you on that position. . . . I shall be greatly surprised if we obtain a *respectful* reply should the letter be sent.[10]

Alone among the brethren (until Douglas joined him), Black selected his first option and wrote the Chief on August 14, 1945, right after he sent the letter to

Douglas, that he would refuse to sign the letter unless two sections were removed by Stone from the draft:

> The announcement of your resignation . . . brings us to a profound sense of regret *that our association with you in the daily work of the Court must now come to an end.*
>
> *You have made fidelity to principle your guide to decision.*[11]

Hugo could not "subscribe to such a loose interpretation" of the English language. From Black's perspective, Roberts, a Hoover Republican appointment, had, from 1933 through 1937, seesawed on critical economic New Deal cases, occasionally voting with the conservatives on the Court to invalidate critical legislative pieces of Roosevelt's plan to end the national economic depression. Furthermore, Roberts also zigzagged in civil rights and civil liberties cases before the Court in the 1940s.

More recently, in correspondence with Frankfurter and in conversation with other members of the Court, Roberts had been contemptuous of what he saw as Black's continued politicking and bullying, especially his behavior in the Court's conference sessions. Furthermore, one year earlier, in February 1944, news stories had appeared that described a "bitter personal feud" between Roberts and Justices Black and Douglas. One such news account reported that

> [there was] an admonition [from] Justice Owen J. Roberts on Monday that unless the Court stops reversing itself it will 'leave the courts below on an uncharted sea of doubt and difficulty.' . . . Justice Felix Frankfurter concurred in this assertion which . . . was particularly aimed at the vacillation of Justices Hugo Black, Frank Murphy, and William O. Douglas in the series of civil rights cases related to Jehovah's Witnesses.[12]

Black was called "Hugo-to-Hell" when he was a twenty-four-year-old police court judge in Birmingham, Alabama, in 1910. As a U.S. senator in the 1920s and '30s, he was called the senator with the "bulldog tenacity."[13] And, in the Roberts resignation matter, he told the Chief that he would not sign a letter of thanks for Roberts's service on the Court unless the two sentences he objected to were removed.

Stone then instructed Black to send the revised letter to Reed for his signature and to pass it to the rest of the brethren. This Hugo did quickly and thought the issue was resolved, believing that his timely directness had avoided an embarrassment for the Court. However, after Black circulated his revision, Stone, upon conferring with Frankfurter changed his mind. The Chief Justice, on August 31, 1945, circulated the Black-Stone correspondence to the other members of the Court so that they would know of Black's disagreement with the "customary" letter. The Chief hoped that the others would try to persuade Black to change his mind. He wrote that "at Justice Frankfurter's request I am appending to this memorandum a draft of a letter which I proposed should be sent to Justice Roberts by his colleagues. . . . While I prefer my own draft, I wrote Justice Black that I would sign the letter with his amendments in order to secure unanimity."[14]

Frankfurter angrily responded to Black's action. And he was not afraid to use dead legal deities to reinforce his view of the Southerner. According to Frankfurter's diary, the late Justice Louis D. Brandeis did not hold Black in high esteem. "Black hasn't the faintest notion of what tolerance means," Frankfurter claimed Brandeis had said about Black, "and," continued Brandeis through Frankfurter, "while he talks a lot about democracy, he is totally devoid of its underlying demand which is tolerance in his own behavior." [15] In a memo to the brethren dated August 30, 1945, Frankfurter summoned the memory of Brandeis in writing: "I could never be party to the denial, under challenge, of what I believe to be a fundamental truth about Roberts, the Justice—that he 'made fidelity to principle' his guide to decision. I know that was Justice Brandeis' view of Roberts, whose character he held in the highest esteem." [16]

Black did not bother to respond to Frankfurter's memo, although he seethed quietly at Stone's effort to force him to change his view. Hugo wrote Bill again, just after the end-of-August Stone note, to bring Douglas up to date on the clash before his return to the Court on September 26 after the summer recess. [17] (Douglas always preferred to remain away from Washington, D.C., until the last moment prior to the opening of the term of the Court on the first Monday in October. Generally, he also left for his summer break as soon as he was through writing his opinions. He never dallied in Washington, D.C., in the hot and humid summer, preferring to head for points west, especially the state of Washington and his Goose Prairie hideaway.)

Douglas, one of the hated "Axis" according to his enemy Frankfurter (the others in the Axis were Black and Justices Frank Murphy and Wiley Rutledge), instantly wrote back in support of Black's revised letter to Roberts, stating that "according to F.F.'s theory, we would be going on record as denying [Roberts] divinity if the first draft had called him Jesus." [18] Furthermore, Douglas noted, "it's all a goddam tempest in a teapot. FF is looking for trouble—some opening so Roberts can let go a blast. I hope we can manage it so that does not happen."

For the Chief Justice, who really did not like Black very much and held little respect for his jurisprudential thoughts, the "Roberts letter" affair was yet another skirmish in the war between the "fleas," a war that he never could control or end, one that led to his untimely death from a massive stroke while sitting in open court hearing oral argument in a case.

Black angrily wrote to Stone, telling him that he was

> still at a loss to understand how it was thought that "unanimity" in Court action would be secured by sending the Memorandum which you prepared at the request of Justice Frankfurter. It seems to me that the Memorandum was calculated to achieve exactly the opposite effect. This Memorandum places the situation in exactly the attitude that it would have been had you suggested one letter to the Court while I suggested another. The Memorandum sent at Justice Frankfurter's request indicates that the members of the Court should pass upon two conflicting drafts. [19]

In his letter to Douglas after Stone's seeming deference to Frankfurter, Black wrote, "I am wholly at a loss to understand why he circulated the second Memorandum, *at Justice Frankfurter's suggestion,* and he did not give me any light on this purpose in the last communication which I received. In the absence of any different information on this subject, I can only surmise the purpose of the Memorandum."[20] (Black's emphasis)

Ultimately, rather than have the "customary" letter signed by only seven of the jurists, it was changed by Stone according to Black's instructions: the letter that was prepared for mailing to Owen Roberts had eight signatures, with the "offensive" language removed. The recently retired Roberts was robbed of the "fidelity to principle your guide to decision" rhetoric. After a few more skirmishes between the antagonists, Stone decided not to do anything. In the end, Roberts received no letter at all from the Court telling how much they appreciated his fidelity to justice. The Justices "divided as bitterly on the issue of complimentary phraseology as [they] ever did on a question of substantive law."[21]

Black, on this occasion standing with only one ally, had won a small battle against some tough adversaries. Such victories happened quite frequently in his lifetime because of his tenacity and resilience.

The Strong Vigorous Temperament

By the time Black was four, he had withdrawn into himself, finding great comfort, joy, knowledge, and strength in the books his mother provided him.[22] Young Hugo enjoyed reading aloud to his mother and listening intently as she read to him. His closest relationships, from his earliest recollections, were with family much older than him, especially his mother and his older brothers and sisters.

While he played outside with other youngsters from time to time, he grew up mostly in solitude. Again and again, exploring the Judge's life from his childhood on, one sees that Black's "outgoing geniality was shot through with a touch of detachment whereby the Justice was, in the most literal sense of the words, a lonely man."[23] This self-imposed solitude, accompanied by the acquisition of knowledge from the books, led to the dramatic growth of self-assurance in the young Black. Long before he found great success as a personal injury lawyer in Birmingham, he exuded confidence in elementary school and at home.

Based on his reading of history, Black developed a grand vision of the good life in his beloved America, one that he valued and tried to implement. His vision was a twentieth-century version of the ancient Greek democratic polis. He "deliberately" committed himself, intellectually and morally, to becoming "a dedicated and purposeful champion of the underdog"[24] in order to achieve this vision. One of the Judge's important behavioral characteristics follows: If a vision was self-evident, then almost any means he could use to achieve it was appropriate.

All of the Justice's opponents would agree with Klan leader James Esdale, a close friend of Black's in Alabama, whose assessment of Black was clear: "Hugo was an opportunist" when it came to acting on his beliefs.[25] He would do almost anything to achieve his goals. Frankfurter sincerely believed this to be true, as did opposing corporate lawyers facing Black in a Birmingham courtroom.

To move America closer to the ideal of the Greek polity meant that Hugo had to act in a very paradoxical manner at times. To achieve even partial success meant that he had to get into politics. In 1920s Alabama, for someone like Black, who was not a "Bourbon" Democrat, joining the Ku Klux Klan was necessary.

He nevertheless was opposed to the Klan's use of intimidation and violence. While Black sympathized with the group's economic, nativist, and anti-Catholic beliefs, however, he joined the Klan because he was a "politically ambitious young attorney [who knew what he had] to do to get ahead in politics."[26] Decades later he acknowledged this "political need to join" the Klan for the sake of his career.[27]

As a candidate for statewide office, Black ran as the "people's" candidate, an opponent of entrenched political and economic power. As he told his sister Ora many years later, he did the right thing to join the Klan; most Klansmen were poor wage earners, members of the economic and political underdog group whose cause he always championed. Toward the end of his life, however, on one of those rare occasions when his self-control momentarily disappeared, he confessed, almost teary-eyed, to a friend that joining the Klan "was a mistake." Even after admitting error, Hugo immediately said: "But I had to do it. I just had to. *I would have joined any group* if it helped get me votes."[28] (my emphasis).

All who knew him said that Black "had about him that indefinable aura of control. . . . His eyes could seem cold." It was repeatedly said by his many adversaries, including his children, his Senate opponents, and his Court enemies, that "in the heat of battle his eyes took on a cold, steely look that could wither distant trees. . . . [Yet] his temper was always under control. He conveyed intensity."[29] He was, as his life indicates, a "personal puritan, unconcerned with appearances but intent on realities," the prime one being to achieve his stated goals.[30]

Black, whether as lawyer, checkers and tennis player, candidate, parent, legislator, or justice on the Court, loved to win. He *had* to win. Life, for him, was adversarial, full of conflict, with winners and losers. He cherished the adversarial process, for it was "the very stuff of life. . . . He did not like to admit he was wrong and he seldom did." Most found his "intellectual stubbornness a source of personal exasperation."[31] He had a "gamecock personality."[32] His son recalled that once while Black, then a U.S. senator, was walking in Birmingham, someone said: "Look at that little sonofabitch. He thinks he's goin' to be President of the United States." A pause, then, "You know, the little sonofabitch just might."[33]

And so, although there was some effort by Chief Justice Stone to try to pressure him to change his mind about the "customary letter" to Roberts, Black's brethren knew that trying to change Hugo's mind—once it was made up—was as difficult as trying to prevent ice from melting in hell. The Judge was, as a law clerk noted, "obstinate and unwilling to explore contradictory viewpoints."[34] His was a temperament honed in the battles he fought and, for the most part, *won* in the four decades prior to his arrival on the Court.

Once more, in the Roberts affair, Black's gritty determination led to a victory that reflected his deeply held views, this time about one of his former "colleagues" on the high bench. Again his tough, no-nonsense behavior angered many of his colleagues, and he was accused of acting on the basis of "political" motives. Finally, once again the Judge's steely immovability on an issue of importance to him led to capitulation by others.

Indeed, even Black's daughter, Jo-Jo, albeit a very infrequent victim of his wrath, sometimes felt the stings of her father's selfish fervor. Felix Frankfurter, married although childless, was Jo-Jo's older "friend" and treated her as the daughter he never had. He once invited her to the Court's private conference session. The eight-year-old responded: " 'Daddy wouldn't like that so I can't come with you. But I wish you would do something for me,' " she asked Frankfurter, "with fierce intensity. 'I wish you would vote against daddy, because he always has to have his way.' "[35]

Black was, as one of his law clerks put it, "a combination of the steel-hard and soft."[36] Self-taught and very learned, Black combined his understanding of history and human nature "with the disingenuous certitude of a backwoods politician."[37]

Books were Hugo's constant companions, from his first years reading a book at his mother's lap to the very last days of his life. Books had an added pleasure for Black, observed his daughter Jo-Jo: they "don't talk back to him!" Black's reliance on the power of the written word was total. So wedded to books and the knowledge they contained was he that his daughter, trying to change her daddy's mind on an issue, would ask him to read portions of books that supported her position. She hoped that the written words would persuade Hugo because her own spoken words often did not.[38]

Black greatly admired persons who exhibited similar grit and determination, whether it was a poor farmer in Clay County, Alabama, fighting the utilities company or the president of the United States, fighting big business and the oligarchs. He especially liked Harry S Truman for his honesty and for his ability to speak *with* the common men and women of America, rather than at them. Black, who had known Truman since the Missourian's first senatorial campaign in 1936, respected him for his integrity, independence, and New Deal liberalism After Truman's surprise victory in 1948, Hugo wrote Harry a short note:

> That was a grand victory—and it was *your* victory. You have proven again that the people cannot be fooled when they are told the truth. I had no doubt that what you had done as a candidate for Senator you could do on a national scale. The people recognize integrity. My best wishes. Take care of yourself, the people need you.[39] (his emphasis)

Black was also a true romantic—easy to cry and terribly in love with his wives, especially his first wife (though not his first love), Josephine. On occasion, the Judge expressed his love with the tenderest of words. Writing to his first law clerk after Josephine died in 1951, Black commented that

> she was sweet, gentle, and kind to everybody—I never heard her speak harshly or angrily to any person in the thirty years we lived together. I believe every person who ever associated with her loved her. She left no enemies in this world—she never had any. Her home was peaceful and restful because her lovely presence made it so.[40]

But Black's romantic nature was evident only in his personal relationships with his wives and in the letters he wrote to them. Publicly, he was the tough tiger in the courtroom, on the Senate floor, and in the battles on the Court. When his mind was made up, whether on a legal issue facing the Court, or in response to a family problem, Black was a daunting, relentless advocate. Whenever confronted with such a situation, and that was very regularly during his long life, Black would work, vigorously, to flatten his opponent. Rising in righteous wrath, well above his modest height, Black briskly, some said viciously, attacked his opponent. It did not matter whether the battle was with one of his sons or a close relative critical of Black's views, a reluctant witness before one of Black's Senate investigating committees, or his arch Court antagonist, Felix Frankfurter.

Elizabeth Black regularly saw her husband turn from a gracious, gentle, and kind person into an "intense man who concentrated all his powers on whatever he was doing at the particular moment." On those occasions, she saw "the County Prosecutor, the Securities Investigator, the attorney Cross-Examiner and the Justice's analytical powers all rolled up into one." There was always the "raw, naked force of Hugo's intellect and will;" however, it was "usually concealed beneath that kind, gentle exterior," she concluded.[41]

Steely Tough at Home

Black married twice. His first wife was Josephine Foster, a shy belle of Birmingham, Alabama, who succumbed to decades of depression, known in the South as "melancholia," and took her life in 1951. The Judge's second wife, Elizabeth Seay DeMerritte, was also from Alabama, having worked in the federal district court there and then in Black's chambers as his legal secretary. They married in 1957 and shared fourteen loving years together.[42] Whereas Josephine was reserved, detached, unhappy in the District of Columbia, and frequently in mental hospitals, Elizabeth had an unquenchable zest for life and was forever the lively and equally strong-willed though gentle and loving partner.

Black was an extremely firm father of three children—two boys, Hugo Jr. and Sterling, and the apple of his eye and youngest child, daughter Josephine, who was soon called Jo-Jo by everyone except her father. Given Hugo's self-assurance and the great store he placed in self-discipline and will power, he became a feared father, especially in the eyes of his two sons. For example, when young Sterling was returned to the house after he "ran away" from home, Black locked the frightened youngster in the attic "for several days of solitary confinement, and warned the rest of the family not to see him."[43]

On rare occasions, the Justice exhibited softness, both inside and out. These occasions were limited to his contacts with his daughter and with his wives, especially Elizabeth. In the late evenings, when most of the world was asleep, including Elizabeth, he would wake her, hold her in his arms, and softly talk to her about his dreams. Occasionally, he read to her one of his opinions, *Chambers v Florida* being his absolute favorite. Or he might read a passage from the Old Testament and discuss how it related to a constitutional or statutory or societal issue he had to confront in a case before him.[44]

The public saw another, much different Black, especially in his role as county prosecutor or as chief legislative investigator. If one crossed the public Black, whether in a wrongful death suit, in front of his investigating committee, on the Court, or at home, invariably one felt pain. "Many times I was hurt by his harsh criticism," recalled his oldest son, Hugo Jr.[45]

During the Second World War, for example, Hugo Jr. frequently ran into money difficulties while serving in the army. The Judge attributed these financial woes to laziness and a lack of diligence on his son's part which angered Black a great deal. He enjoyed reading Cicero's *On Duties,* copiously underlining his well-worn copy, especially the passages on the responsiblities of the young—that is, their duty to avoid surrendering to sloth. It was not enough that his best friend and ally on the Court, Bill Douglas, drove Hugo crazy because the brilliant Douglas was unbelievably lazy;[46] here was his oldest son, his namesake, exhibiting the same behavior.

Consequently, Black's responses to his seemingly wayward son were always stern, warning Hugo Jr. of the consequences of his profligate ways; but, in the end, he always sent the money requested. "I think I should tell you, however," wrote the father to his army son, "that I am disappointed that you have not been able to learn to live in such a way that you can get along from month to month and save something for special occasions." Black then proceeded to tell Hugo Jr. about a fifty-five-year-old man who had been an "outstanding liberal" writer until about ten years before. Because he could not budget his money, for the past decade the man

> has been the paid representative of special interests whose activities he had always detested—he became a slave to them because he was first a slave to his immediate desires. He is a tragic representative of a large group of people who live in each generation who, though they have brilliant minds, finally become the paid employees of men with stodgy minds, fat stomachs and long cigars.[47]

This type of direct, no-nonsense intensity by the father hurt his children, especially his oldest and frailest. Occasionally Josephine would receive soulful letters from Hugo Jr. The message was always the same: complaints about "Daddy's" criticism of the son's behavior and about "Daddy's" lack of understanding.

Hugo was a critical parent, writing, for example, that "[Hugo Jr.] has not at all done what he could have done." He demanded intensity and concentration from his sons when they were at work in school or as lawyers. There was a time when he wrote the president of the University of Alabama to seek advice. Evidently Hugo Jr. had a larger than usual number of unexcused absences, and his father had "no sympathy whatever with unexcused absences from classes." Although advised by some of his law clerks that he "attached more importance to these absences than the College itself does," the Judge wrote to the university president for guidance about the matter. The son, of course was chastised by the father for not attending class.[48]

Black was just as stern with his grandsons. Once, one of them, a four-year-old, was crying very loudly at poolside because his mother was in the water and he was not. After a few minute of the screeching, Black got up, took the grandson by the hand and bought him outside the pool area. " 'Now you cry as much as you please,' he said. 'I never knew anyone to die of crying.' They stood there, Black willing to stand all day if that would help give the child a sense of the uselessness of his noise—unwilling to engage in any of what he would consider coddling." The child continued to howl until an aunt came over and gave the boy a piece of candy. The crying stopped immediately. "Black gazed at the aunt for fully a minute, much as he sometimes gazes at the Solicitor General when he feels the government has won a case that will hurt the country. He then gave his judgment. 'Bribery!' he said, and turned away in outrage."[49]

The Judge was a very traditional, Southern sexist male. As a father he was forever telling his sons and his grandsons how to behave, what to read, and why these books were so important. But he didn't convey this information about the "great books" to his daughter, Jo-Jo. He believed that women should not go out of their way to read the classics. Instead, they should go to finishing school and prepare themselves for the rewarding, nurturing life of mother and wife.

Black tried, without success, to convince his daughter to go to Sweet Briar College, Josephine's alma mater (although his first wife left Sweet Briar after a year to go to school in New York), rather than the coed Swarthmore College. He believed that women should be treated differently from men, that "a real woman cultivated an appearance and personal ways calculated to attract and please men and serve as the hub of the family."[50] He wanted Jo-Jo to go to Sweet Briar because, "according to him, scholarship should never play too big a role in a woman's life. . . . He tried to steer her away from coed, intellectual Swarthmore to Sweet Briar, the school Mama had attended, which Daddy believed to be the finest place in the world for the education of a woman."[51]

Another example of Hugo's sexist behavior: When a class of undergraduates visited the Justice a few years before his death, Black had the young ladies take seats in the front rows and the young men take seats in the rear. He stood at the door to his office and shook hands with all the young ladies, asking their names, and pointing them to their seats directly in front of his desk. And when the meeting was over, he stood again at the door and said his good-byes to the young ladies, who were delighted with Black's Southern-style graciousness. The young men were not too pleased with this behavior, much like Hugo Jr., who wrote that "so strong was Daddy's preference for women that a sensitive male who loved him might feel hurt. As deeply as I know he loved me, sometimes I wonder."[52]

Instead of showing affection for his own sons, Black the teacher was constantly trying to get them to read the classics in order to improve their minds. In 1953, he wrote to Hugo Jr. about the pleasures he found in reading "Milton's Areopagitica; Sidney Smith's Fallacies of Anti-Reformers; Mill's essay on liberty and his autobiography. . . . There are countless other things in those volumes that have given me much pleasure and I am sure that they will give you pleasure as the years go on. Offhand I think of Pliny's letters, Cicero's letters, Meditations of Aurelius, and some of Seneca's writings."[53] In a 1954 letter to his eldest child, the Judge noted his delight that the son "liked the edition of Plutarch." Black closed that letter with a line that illustrated his brand of humor: "Everything here goes on well, that is, provided being in the minority most of the time is well."[54]

Hugo Jr. observed after the Justice's death:

According to today's psychology (and I believe it is right), a parent should en-courage, not discourage, confidence in his child. But Daddy went about raising me just the opposite way. He felt he had to keep me from becoming conceited, and I used to boil with indignation and resentment at his criticism of me. This treatment might have destroyed me had my mother not constantly pointed out, "Love cares and criticizes. Only someone who believes you have something very special would be concerned that you might become conceited."[55]

There were times when Hugo Jr. absolutely hated his father. The senior Black would harshly criticize his oldest son when Junior's grade fell, but Black never complimented the youngster when he received all As for a semester. The Judge, who believed in the virtues of corporal punishment, would use the strap when Hugo Jr. misbehaved. Black never understood why his son read everything he could find about his hero, a Washington professional baseball player named "Hei-nie" Manush, rather than reading about and emulating Thomas Jefferson or some Greek hero. The elder Black also picked on young Hugo because of his acne during adolescence. The son recalled that "Daddy treated it as some sort of disease to run away from. Jo-Jo, my little sister, picked up on his habit and threw it at me. Every morning she reported on the state of my pimpled face, and he encour-aged her."[56]

Sterling's hearing problems, which were seen as quite serious in the 1930s, with Hugo and Josephine worried that Sterling might lose all hearing, seemed to mitigate Black's harshness toward the second-born son. But the solitary-confinement-in-the-attic incident illustrated that the father was on occasion as stern and cruel with Sterling as he was with Hugo Jr.

Viewing the communications between the father and his invalid second son, however, one can see a clear differentiation between those and the often-shrill letters to his oldest boy. There was a softness about Hugo Jr. that seemed to trigger Black's wrath. The Judge's sister-in-law Jinksie Durr commented on this perceived weakness in a June 1962 letter to her brother-in-law, after Hugo Jr. had decided to leave Birmingham to practice law in Miami:

> We do hate to see them move as we enjoyed having them in the same State and we love them very much and especially Hugo who is one of the sweetest spirited boys I ever knew in my life. I am glad he is leaving Birmingham *as I do not think he is made of the kind of iron it takes to live in Birmingham.*[57] (my emphasis)

As Hugo Jr. told it, he was frightened for his family's safety if he stayed in Birmingham. So fearful was he about redneck reaction to his liberalism, the labor union lawyer lied to get out of taking civil rights cases. He wrote:

> As time went on, the pressure didn't let up on me and my family. . . . Things were getting bad. . . . Incidents of violence and oppression were occurring quite frequently—events that turned my stomach. Once, I would have been eager to help the victims, but now I found myself refusing. . . . I was copping out. . . . [and these cop-outs] made me feel more and more unhappy.[58]

Sterling, on the other hand, seemed strong enough to overcome adversity, even during the Second World War, and this greatly pleased his father. "In spite of his very defective hearing," the Judge wrote to Hollis Black, his nephew and former office secretary while Black was a senator, Sterling "was accepted . . . [into] an Administrative Officers' Training School . . . and several months ago he was promoted from a Second to a First Lieutenancy."[59] Hugo Jr., however, failed to become an officer in the military, due to hay fever, asthma, or breaking a leg at an inauspicious time, winding up the war as a corporal stationed in Arizona. Hugo Jr. was phased out of the same type of administrative officers' training school that Sterling successfully completed.

In a 1943 letter to Hugo Jr, the father tried to analyze his son's problems in the military. While Black wrote that "so long as you do your duty in the Army, live so as to keep your own self-respect, and keep your head in the midst of temporary disappointments, I shall be just as proud of you as though you occupied the shoes of General Eisenhower, himself," he did not mind "diagnos[ing] your trouble as timidity."[60]

Black continued the criticism of Hugo Jr. even after he had graduated from law school, had passed the Alabama bar in October 1949, and had begun to practice law in Birmingham. For example, in a three-page letter written on April 1, 1950, to his oldest son, at the time a married, thirtyish parent, Black expressed disapproval of a political speech in support of a local candidate, delivered by Hugo Jr. over the radio. The letter pointed out in detail no less than seven faults. The father began by stating that "my remarks will be rather critical," but he was offering them anyway, "even though they may be wholly or partially wrong, ... as an admonition to get you to walk with caution."[61]

Compare this scolding of Hugo Jr. with a letter the Judge wrote to Sterling after the son served as a member of a court-martial that had imposed a maximum sentence of six years on a soldier charged with being drunk and disorderly. Black sets out to criticize, but "what I say about it [the judgment of the court-martial] will have to be more or less in the abstract. I do have some doubt as to the validity of some of the premises on which you have acted." While Black did criticize Hugo Jr.'s decision-making, e.g., it was "not wise for you to get into this campaign at all," with Sterling, it was "I would be exceedingly cautious about giving the maximum punishment in any case."[62]

If Black was at times a demanding perfectionist regarding his sons' behavior, especially Hugo Jr.'s weaknesses, he also assisted his children through difficult health and personal problems and gave them fatherly advice when confronting professional dilemmas. For example, when Hugo Jr. lost a particularly hard case in the Supreme Court of North Carolina, Black wrote to him: "You had a hard case, one in which the court was not likely to feel much sympathy for your client. . . . It's all in the year's work. . . . It is time to go into Court but I just wanted you to know that you are not the only lawyer who has ever been disappointed at the dumbness of judges."[63]

Clearly, growing up as the son of the cold, steely Black was a painful, searing experience. The two boys often questioned whether Black loved them. Before and after Black's death, they had to deal with the demons released by their difficult relationship with their "daddy." His daughter Jo-Jo reflected on this semi-tragic relationship between father and first-born son. "Hugo Jr. struggles continuously, ninety per cent of the time, with his bad memories of his relationship with his father."[64]

Use of Language

Black's words, often harsh, occasionally gentle, were *always* delivered in clear and simple language—whether in letters or lectures to his children or memos to his brethren. In a letter to his niece, Hazel Black Davis, written in 1941, "Uncle Hugo" confessed that he always was "struggling over what to say and how to say it."[65] Toward the end of that decade, Black knew *what* to say. However, he always struggled over *how* to say it because he wanted his writings to be definitive and understandable to all who read them.

For Black, "simplicity and clarity in the law" were goals from the moment he entered public life.[66] These goals were the consequence of his reading of classical Greeks views about life in a democracy. In Black's favorite book, *The Greek Way,* author Edith Hamilton observed that "clarity and simplicity of statement, the watchwords of a thinker, were the Greek poet's watchwords too."[67]

One of his law clerks wrote that Black believed "that words should be read in light of their plain meaning and should not be subjected to strained linguistic interpretations."[68] Another of the Judge's many law clerks wrote that

> he researched the cases himself, staying alone in his study at home for long days while he read the briefs, facts, law, history, and philosophy until he was ready to draft an opinion. Only after the first draft was completed were his clerks invited to help with it.[69]

Hugo's second wife, Elizabeth, his former office secretary, recalled nights when Hugo would be up until the wee hours of the morning in order to painstakingly draft and redraft his thoughts in longhand on legal-sized notepads. "He didn't often sleep nights through," recollected Elizabeth. "He would get up at two in the morning and go sit at his desk and begin to write on a yellow pad."[70]

Black disciplined himself to write well, which is another example of the Judge's complete focus on the achievement of an objective. When he came to the Court, he "resolved to master the art of writing in such a way as to establish maximum communication with the largest number of people."[71] He tackled the issue head-on, reading articles about correct writing in learned journals, speaking to writers, and using practice exercises in grammar books he purchased. He struggled to find the exact word, always selecting a one-syllable over a two-syllable word. He stayed away from the metaphor and the simile when he wrote. And he never dictated in person or used a Dictaphone. "If you dictate," he said, "it's so easy to let loose too many words. Talking is the easiest thing in the world. But when you've got to write it yourself, your hand and arm muscles make you practice economy with your words."[72]

When Chief Justice Earl Warren arrived at the Court, he asked Hugo to recommend a book for him to read that would improve his writing. Hugo's instant response was to suggest that the Chief borrow Aristotle's *Rhetoric* from the Library of Congress. "If you read Aristotle, you will know all there is to know about good writing," he said. Warren took the book out and, after beginning to read it, went over to Black's office to thank him.

His attention to the proper use of language ultimately led to beautifully written opinions. Black always said to his clerks that his opinions, the Court's opinions, had to be written so that his uncle down on the farm behind the plow would understand them. Writing and rewriting was for Black a lifelong task that enabled the people to more fully understand the nature of their democratic institutions. And he succeeded in crafting opinions that were readily understood by legal authorities as well as the person who worked the fields.

The Human Dilemma

Black's writing reflected his perspective on the drama of human life, his definite views of human nature and human progress. He had what one law clerk termed a "Protestant pessimistic"[73] view of human nature, one that combined his strict Baptist upbringing (and its negative image of human behavior) with his understanding of human history, influenced by the Greek philosophers (which emphasized the inevitability of progress).

In a long letter written to his nineteen-year-old son Sterling in 1944, Black revealed this perspective. Sterling had sent a letter to his father voicing the poignant fears of a new parent about the security of a turbulent, war-filled world. Hugo then tried to cheer his son:

> If one views history closely enough, there is much evidence that while human progress is slow, it is nevertheless sure. While we may have a relapse at any time, I think that this country has during my lifetime moved in the direction of a better distribution of justice, in the large sense of the word, to the advantage of the people of the nation. . . . No one can doubt but that individual human beings have many weaknesses, both physical and mental. It cannot be expected that societies composed of such individual units will somehow achieve perfection overnight. Realization of this fact should not, however, impel a person to conclude to become a member of the Edgar Allan Poe Melancholia Club.[74]

Hugo Jr. wrote him a long letter from army camp in 1945, clearly describing the intense racial hatred of his fellow white soldiers towards black soldiers and displaying his utter helplessness in the face of such anger and bitterness.

> My mind is in a complete state of confusion and turmoil and the world and myself have me perplexed. My ideals are shattered into a thousand pieces. . . . So I'm writing to you, because you have retained such an unbelievable faith in the world and humanity, even though you have seen the things I have seen. . . . I feel that I am lost, that my life has no purpose. . . . Please, Daddy, . . . tell me how you have kept such an unwavering faith in people, such a belief that everything in the world will sometime be all right, such joy and happiness in living, tell me how.[75]

Black answered his pained son with a letter that spoke of the inevitability of human progress that would someday overcome the centuries of racial hatred in America. Drawing upon his almost fifty-nine years of living, Hugo firmly counseled his oldest son. The letter also indicated how the father himself reacted to attacks by news reporters, lawyers, politicians, and his fellow justices on the Court.

Most young men who have a mind and use it sometimes get worried about the state of the universe. . . . Of course, you were bound to be disturbed by the innate or cultivated cruelty of the soldiers who ruthlessly attacked another soldier simply because of his color. If you live long enough, you will see many more evidences of cruel propensities in individuals. . . . You will make a mistake if you think that because some people are cruel and indifferent to social obligations, all people can be so classified. . . . As you go along in life, you will come into contact with many, many kind and gentle persons who try to make other people happy. So the knowledge you have acquired concerning the badness of some human beings should enable you to appreciate more the qualities of others. [Things will get better.] . . . All you have to do is to be philosophical about what you see and hear, enter into no controversies for the single purpose of being controversial, and be as nice to everybody on all occasions (even those whose conduct you detest) as you would like for people to be to you.[76]

Based on his firm, understanding of human history and the unchanging character of human behavior in that history, Hugo Black had a manifestly unshakable assurance in his fundamental views that led him to act toughly and decisively. Justice William Brennan recollected that Black was a "wily son of a gun" who had "learned all the tricks of the trade in the Senate and had no difficulty doing battle with his enemies" on the Court.[77] Power, believed Black, must be used to achieve grand visions, and it had to be employed decisively, using all those tricks of the trade, or else the ends would not be realized. He always used power decisively, whether it was the subpoena, the congressional investigation, the dissenting opinion, or the threat of writing a dissenting opinion.

Another occasion that illustrates Black's views of human nature occurred in March 1963. Erwin Griswold, a conservative Harvard Law School dean who later served as solicitor general for Democratic President Lyndon B. Johnson and Republican President Richard M. Nixon, with "trepidation" sent Black a speech he had presented in Salt Lake City. It was critical of his views of the importance of the First Amendment. The Judge responded in typical "Hugo" style:

As you can guess, I disagree with most of the constitutional principles you advocated in your lecture. As a matter of fact, I am of the opinion that you could not possibly think my constitutional philosophy is any more dangerous than I think is the constitutional philosophy you expressed in the lecture. Nevertheless, . . . my admiration for you—and my respect for your sturdy integrity—are such that I am compelled to admit that the championship of your views causes me to hope that maybe they are not as dangerous as I still believe they are. Sometime, however, when we have time to talk, I would like to discuss with you some of the things you said because they indicated that you are not wholly familiar with the views I think I entertain.[78]

For those on the receiving end of Black's assertive, self-assured judgments and actions, there was often an ill-concealed anger at the perceived cockiness or the bullying of the Alabaman. His sons spoke of their bitterness towards such letters and lectures, as did Black's enemies on the Court. In 1954 Frankfurter wrote a note to his colleague, Justice Stanley Reed, complaining, again, about his brother Black. Said Frankfurter: "Black has reached a conclusion and is not at all bothered about arguments which can be exposed. *You might as well ask him to climb a greased telephone pole as to change his conclusion*" (my emphasis).[79] Justice Reed agreed with Frankfurter's assessment, once telling him that "you can't change people. Black was always a politician and he didn't and can't cease to be one by becoming a judge."[80]

To balance his toughness somewhat, Black had a Southerner's "unfailing courtesy, . . . a total lack of rancor,"[81] as well as a fine sense of humor. He loved a good joke, but it had to be a clean one. His office files contained scores of jokes he clipped from family magazines such as the *Reader's Digest* and used, carefully, in speeches he gave while a senator. Charles Alan Wright wrote about an argument he presented before the Supreme Court, with Justice Black rocking back and forth in front of him. The case involved an issue that had been argued before in the Court, and the Justice had written a clear dissent indicating a total lack of merit in the position Wright was arguing. In a "tone of disbelief," Black put a question to Wright that elicited the expected response. Black then said gently, shaking his head as if scolding Hugo Jr. but "with a twinkle in his eye," that "I think I understand you now."[82] The Judge's humor even found its way into a national magazine. It was a classic Black view of life: "When I was 40, my doctor advised me that a man in his forties shouldn't play tennis. I heeded his advice carefully and could hardly wait until I reached 50 to start again."[83]

Despite the occasional humor and surface gentility, there was an inordinate, almost irrational fear of Black felt by many of his colleagues, in the Senate as on the Court. According to an observer, "by 1945, Hugo Black had become the most feared member of the Court, ready and able to challenge his colleagues on both philosophical and personal issues with a toughness that some Justices found threatening."[84] Justice Sherman Minton, a Democrat from Indiana who worked alongside Black while both were members of the Senate, the friend who conveyed to Black the fact that President Roosevelt was thinking of Black for a seat on the Court, once wrote to Frankfurter that his former legislative buddy "was a demagogue."[85] This characteristic of Black's was noted by one of his early biographers, who wrote that he "was not the first man nor the last figure in American politics to make use of demogoguery for success and survival."[86]

Those who maintained that Black was a demogogue to be feared did not know the man, which is not surprising for very few truly understood his uniqueness. Most of his contemporaries did not appreciate the intellectual intensity of this Southern jurist. Black was always focused on the task at hand, he was "concerned only with his work," wrote a law clerk. "Indeed, there is no Justice more committed to the business of the Court than he."[87]

Love Affair with the Court

Black grew to love the Supreme Court, as he loved the Senate, after starting off his public career as a harsh critic of the institution because he thought that the justices were unconstitutionally intruding into the legislative arena. He became extremely proud of the Court, as he perceived it, and worked hard, facing opposition from brethren such as Frankfurter and Jackson, to change it to his image.

Black regularly clashed with his colleagues on the question of the proper role of the Court and the justices.

Black was always careful to act in a manner that reflected well on the Court. And so when he proposed marriage with Elizabeth, Black felt compelled to discuss the matter in the context of his association with the Court. He said to her: "I have had a prior love affair for almost twenty years now with an institution. It is the Supreme Court. . . . In my personal life, I have to be like Caesar's wife: Above reproach. I have to know that the woman I marry is a one-man woman. . . . [If] you wanted a divorce, I would give you one. But I think it would finish me and hurt the prestige of the Court."[88] Later that evening, Elizabeth received a call from Hugo: he wanted to tell her that he loved her, something he had neglected to say when they were together earlier that day.

For as long as he sat on the Court, Black was critical of his colleagues whose actions brought disrespect to the institution. He would become angry at Douglas because of his penchant for young women; the Alabaman was angry at Frankfurter and Harlan, among others, because of their broad, undisciplined interpretation of due process and their views of the role of the justices. He told Justice Abe Fortas to resign when the press printed stories about Fortas's receipt of money from a financier who had been indicted by the federal government.

As will be shown, Black was a forceful advocate for the judiciary and won more battles than he lost in his efforts to mold the Supreme Court to his perceptions of the institution.

The Cold Steel Warrior's Vision of the Future

While many believe that the Justice was an enigma,[89] a careful view of his life will set aside that assessment. A critic of his was correct when he wrote that Black was an idealist whose "wisdom is the wisdom of the great idea."[90] Hugo "tenaciously (even obstinately) held his ground and would not compromise his principles," wrote a law clerk after his death.[91]

What was the great idea, the "intense moral commitment," the "unwavering vision"[92] of the Justice? It was the evolution of the American experience in democracy, begun in 1776, to the level of greatness of the Greek polis. "Since the earliest days," wrote Black, "philosophers have dreamed of a country where the mind and the spirit of man would be free; where there would be no limits to inquiry; where man would be free to explore the unknown and challenge the most deeply rooted beliefs and principles."[93]

For Justice Black, the Constitution was his legal Bible, the fundamental pathway to the achievement of political and ethical freedom in America. Faithfully following its contours would lead to American greatness. He believed that the nation was slowly progressing towards the goal of freedom. His focused task, as lawyer, judge, prosecutor, senator, and justice, "was to maintain the fragile reality of that [great idea]. . . . To protect and to foster that dream of an open, inquisitive, free, democratic society"—by any means necessary.[94]

This vision ultimately led to Black's unyielding commitment to the virtues of the common man—even when he saw the vices of the common man or read about them in wrenching letters from his army sons. His belief in the concept of democracy, as will be seen in an examination of his life, was premised on the "basis of the Athenian democracy, the conviction . . . that the average man can be depended upon to do his duty and to use good sense in doing it."[95] For Black, a viable democracy meant "the possibility of achieving the full flowering of man: love, trust, reasonableness, fairness, in a word: goodness."[96]

His primary antagonist, Felix Frankfurter, disdained Black's intense commitment to and rhetoric about democracy and regularly ridiculed the Alabaman: "O, Democracy," Frankfurter wrote in his diary, "what flapdoodle is delivered in thy name [by Black]."[97] But if Hugo fumed at such criticism of his vision, he did so in the privacy of his home. At heart, he was an unabashed democratic man, always avoiding "the lure of special privilege"[98] and ever positive, as he wrote his sons, about the inexorable progress of human beings in the American democracy.

Black did see the cruelty of people. From his early days as a police court judge in 1910 Birmingham, to his campaign for the Senate in the mid-1920s, which he won with the help of his fellow Ku Klux Klanners, Hugo saw firsthand the cruelty and the brutality of race discrimination. Even so, he had a sublime faith in the innate goodness of people who understood the obligations of citizenship in a democracy. Even the brutal army rednecks who coldcocked a black soldier in front of a silent Hugo Jr. and laughed about it afterwards, if given the proper tools, especially a good education, would overcome corruption and sloth, and would become the contemporary equivalent of the citizen in the democratic Athens Black loved so much.

For the Justice, as he said in a 1942 "I Am an American" Day speech, "each generation of Americans in turn must dedicate their lives to the realization of freedom's dream."[99] At the very center of Black's unchanging conception of an ennobling democracy evolving in America were the freedoms of speech, press, association, and religion. These First Amendment rights were the most precious principles of citizens in a democracy, whether in Periclean Greece or in twenty-first-century America. "The guarantees of the First Amendment," Black wrote in 1941, "are the foundation upon which our governmental structure rests and without which it could not endure as conceived and planned."[100]

Committed to a set of unchanging principles, Hugo Black forged ahead in the effort to implement them in his many roles. His was a full life, at once defiant and very controlled. It began in the bitterly cold February of 1886 in the northern Alabama hill country of Clay County.

CHAPTER TWO

Alabama Roots

W inter is windstorm and hurricane time in Alabama. On a dreary day in late February 1886, the Black family solemnly walked over a wavering bridge that spanned the Enittechopcho Creek and traveled the narrow road up to Old Mount Ararat Cemetery at Bluff Springs. Perched atop a hill overlooking their small town, the cemetery was the site of the family's burial grounds. They were there that day to bury two-year-old "Little Della," the youngest child of William Lafayette Black and Martha Ardellah Toland Black, who was named for Hugo's mother. The tombstone, still stark over one hundred years later, reads:

> Little Della
> Daughter of
> W. L. and M. A. Black
> Born, February 28, 1884
> Died, February 22, 1886

Martha, mourning the death of her young daughter, was also expecting new life. She was in her ninth month of carrying Hugo. About one week later, on February 27, 1886, on yet another harsh and gloomy winter's day, Hugo Lafayette Black, was born on his parents' farm in Harlan, in rural Clay County. He was named after the famous author Victor Hugo—whose works were read by Mrs. Black and by Leora, one of her daughters—and after his father, whose middle name was Lafayette.

The youngest of eight children, Hugo was born into a frontier environment where the predominantly white and Christian hill-country yeoman farmers worked long and hard trying to earn a bare-bones living off the poor soil. At the same time, the weary women, with wrinkled hands and faces,[1] worked equally hard in the home, bearing and rearing children, cooking for the brood, helplessly watching children die because of influenza and pneumonia, and keeping the vermin out of the wood frame dwellings.[2] As Black would recall, his dead little sister Della "was undoubtedly a victim of the inadequacies of the frontier days, the cold, damp, murky houses."[3] The poor people of Clay County, which was nothing more than "scrub cotton land still devastated from the Civil War,"[4]

> cut and chopped the wood for their own fires, cooked on wood stoves and coals in the fireplace, spun their own wool, wove their own clothes, repaired their own shoes, grew and ground their own wheat, got water out of country springs, . . . and in fact lived as frontier people always have, largely on their own resources.[5]

Black was born at a transitional time in the complex history of his beloved South. It was a region undergoing dramatic change, economic as well as political, moving from rural frontier country to urban, from farming to industry, but it was also a region that held on tight to traditional Southern values as well and harbored a deep, bitter resentment at its cruel fate in the recent War of Northern Aggression.

For example, only ten years after his birth, in 1896, *Plessy v Ferguson* was handed down by a Court that took race and color into consideration in deciding critical cases and controversies (see page 222ff.). Race and racism were issues that Hugo Black and all others from the South could never evade or avoid, regardless of job or career, regardless of whether one remained in Alabama or moved out.

The South

Black entered the world of the South barely two decades after the bloody Civil War ended. At the beginning of the war in 1861, the South was still mostly frontier, with slaveholders making up a small segment of the white population, which consisted primarily of small cotton farmers who owned no slaves at all.[6] The small village of Harlan was an impoverished, isolated crossroads in the rural foothills at the southern end of the Appalachian Mountain range. It had not changed very much since 1861 and would disappear off the face of the Alabama map by the turn of the century.

In 1886, the year he was born, there were two Alabamas: One was the rugged, soil-poor and hard-packed northern hill country, where Hugo lived for his first twenty years, populated mostly by poor white farmers, alongside a very small number of poor black farmers. Southern Alabama, on the other hand, was the soil rich Black Belt, the former plantation section of the state where blacks greatly outnumbered whites and where the "Bourbon" Democrats, also known as the "Big Mules," were in power and firmly controlled Alabama politics.[7] Their platform was a simple one: no government interference in the economy, state's rights, white supremacy.[8]

Black's north country of Alabama—because of the absence of a plantation environment, few blacks, the poor land, and the consequent hardships that generated a fundamental egalitarianism rooted in poverty—produced Andrew Jackson Democrats who fought against secession. After the war the region was home to "tenant farms and the crop lien system defined the world for black and white alike."[9] In 1890, Clay County was home to about fifteen thousand whites, mostly yeoman farmers, and about seventeen hundred blacks, who worked as field hands hired at an annual fixed wage and who did some planting on their small rented lands.

In 1886, the Farmer's Alliance, an agrarian protest movement, began in the South, in Texas, and soon swept across the Southeast. Because of the poverty and the shared misery of white and black farmers, the county of Hugo's birth became the center of agrarian radicalism in Alabama—principally because of the crop-lien system.

The system is easy to understand, and it is especially easy to understand why the farmers in the region hated it. Most farmers in Clay County, whites and blacks, rented their few acres from a white landlord. The landowner—or, in Black's father's case, the merchant who provided tools, seed, draft animals, or the funds to purchase these items—did so with the understanding that one-third to one-half of the farmer's crop would be paid back to lender as payment for the equipment, et cetera. To protect themselves, the landowners or the merchants took a lien "on the crop or a mortgage on the land itself."[10]

The poor farmer, who paid exorbitant prices for the goods and equipment, was always in debt to the landowner or merchant. And if the crop did not come in, there would be foreclosure and forfeiture of the property. In 1890, between 80 to 90 percent of the cotton farmers in Alabama used the crop lien as their basic credit system: the farmer was in "financial bondage to his local merchant."[11] It's no wonder that these poor farmers positively responded to the messages of the Farmer's Alliance people and to the Populists who ranged across the South with a radical message: End the cruel economic system that brutalized life for poor whites and blacks alike by keeping them in debt for life.

By 1892 a People's party of Alabama had been founded that tapped and directed the anger and frustrations of the poor farmers in the state. Although unsuccessful in getting its candidates elected to state office, it was the vehicle through which major political debates took place in Alabama during the 1890s. Because of the brutality of the hated crop-lien system, accompanied by the low prices for cotton, there was political turmoil throughout Alabama, and "it was impossible to remain unaffected by the political turmoil that shook Clay County in the 1890's."[12]

Hugo Black's first decade of life was spent listening to these radical agrarian political speeches. Little Hugo attended all the spectacular rallies, secular tent revivalist-type affairs, featuring outstanding stump orators (mostly Populists passing through), and he was influenced by their speeches attacking entrenched privilege and wealth.

Young Black heard the passionate agrarian pleas for free coinage of silver and an end to the gold standard. The speeches invariably called upon Congress to pass antitrust laws to break up monopolies and spoke to the need for farmers' cooperatives. Finally, he heard shrill cries for restrictive immigration legislation in order to avoid the "tragedy" of America being flooded by immigrants who brought with them alien beliefs and values.

Although he never was a Populist, the ideas of that movement, reflecting the ugliness of life for most of the common folk in the South, did have a major impact on him. The "agrarian battles cries aroused in young Hugo an instinctive and enduring sympathy for the underdog."[13] It was an attitude he carried with him to the Supreme Court. One of his law clerks recalled that the Judge "was an ordinary, democratic man. . . . Whenever Hugo Black saw the lure of special privilege, he actively combatted it. Avoiding the magnificent private dining room reserved for the Justices, he stood in line with his tray in the basement cafeteria that was open to the Court employees and to the public. He told his clerks why—he did not want to be treated differently."[14]

By the turn of the century in Alabama, Populism had faded as a force for change.[15] Power in politics in Alabama during the time Black grew up did not reside with the agrarian radicals. To be successful politically, one had to be a member of the Democratic party. By the 1900s, there *were* "conflicts between up country and the Black Belt, between town and country. . . . The Democratic Party proved too small to contain the ambitions of all the white men who sought its rewards, too large and unwieldy to move decisively." Yet people in Alabama believed that "political machines ran the show [and] that politics was a closed game."[16] To succeed politically, one had to be a good Democrat, a special type of Democrat. The power barons were the "silk hat, Bourbon" Democrats, men from various, primarily industrial, businesses. They included Black Belt cotton planters, railroad magnates, industrial owners, mineral interests, and local office holders.[17]

In 1902, the old-line Bourbon Democrats were able to rewrite the Alabama constitution, thereby effectively disenfranchising black and white reformers. Through such devices and mechanisms as literacy tests, poll taxes, and residency requirements, almost one-quarter of the total white male voting-age population were unable to vote in state elections in Alabama after these 1902 constitutional changes.[18]

These Bourbons controlled politics in the legislature until the 1920s, when the poor whites, buttressed by the organized power of the Ku Klux Klan, defeated the Bourbon Democrats and brought "their kind" of politician into power instead— including Hugo Black who, running as the "poor people's candidate" in 1926, became the junior U.S. senator from Alabama, primarily due to the Klan support he received.

The twin realities of political life in Alabama, the mystical idealism of the agrarian reformers and the reality of knockdown politics, led Black to develop an appreciation of the power of as well as the need for the rule of law.

In the South, "a good trial offered country folk as much entertainment as any tent meeting, the Courthouse was the secular temple of every county."[19] The Blacks had moved to Ashland in 1889, when Hugo was barely three years old, enabling the small boy to take in the courtroom displays. From the age of six, the Clay County Courthouse, located in Ashland, the county seat, was another venue young Hugo visited regularly or hung out in, much like the trial junkies, mostly retirees, one sees in courthouses today. Young Hugo "earned the name of Courthouse pest; he dogged the county lawyers and soaked up their knowledge."[20]

This early exposure to the courthouse, to the lawyers participating in the adversarial system, to the authority of the legal words in the books, and to the majesty of the law, had a dramatic effect on Black. The law was especially valuable in the emergent South. As Black's sister-in-law's husband, attorney Clifford Durr, has written, the "very lawlessness of the frontier tends to generate a respect for law. Its egalitarianism creates a demand that law be equally applied to all. Frontier is a society of individualists. The South was highly personal."[21] Black grew up sitting under the Populist tents and in the upper gallery of the Courtroom, his short rail-thin legs sticking out between guardrails, taking in the arguments of the attorneys below him. Argued again and again were issues that focused on the scope of the concept he heard called liberty.

Alongside the sanctified, sectarian Baptist or Methodist Church (and Black attended both churches on the same day while growing up in Ashland), the secular courthouse was the center of life in the rural South. Black knew church and courthouse very well before he was ten. In 1890s Clay County, life, including play, took place on and around the village square; centrally located on the square were the church and the courthouse.

Religion was a major force molding the mind and values of young Black and his family. Like most others in the turn-of-the-century South, Black's family was an extremely religious one. They were all officially Baptists—except for his father, who was withdrawn from the Harlan church because, in Black's words, "he would now and then become intoxicated."[22] A proper diet, no drinking demon rum, no caffeine, no cardplaying, no cursing, and no dancing, accompanied by a vigorous religious regimen at home and in the church, was the way of life for Black and his siblings.

As a young man, Hugo taught Bible class, in Ashland and in Birmingham, every Sunday until he left Alabama for the national capital in 1927. Although he thereafter occasionally smoked a good cigar in Washington and danced with his wife and daughter, it was not until he became ill in his seventies that Black drank an occasional evening bourbon for medicinal reasons.[23]

Indeed, the major impact of the Southern culture on the young Black, in addition to its politics, was the "character of religion and law"[24] in Southern communities. The Ashland Courthouse Square, with the church on one end facing the courthouse, just across from his father's general store, led to his belief in the centrality of "community."

From these early experiences with religion and the law and politics, as well as from his later extensive reading of history, especially the histories of the ancient Greek and Roman civilizations, Hugo grew to accept a fundamental proposition that remained with him throughout his life: A viable, functioning community, made up of people who could be educated by their leaders and by the media, is the key to achieving a viable, functioning democratic republic.

As was discussed in chapter 1, Black read history and philosophy voraciously, from the time he was barely out of diapers and walking. The Judge's lifelong reading habit is manifest in his record of borrowing books from the Library of Congress from 1927 to 1937, in the extensive library he created in his home, and in the underlinings, marginal notations, and carefully penciled indexes evident in all his books.

From his readings of history, Black grew to see, clearly, a "timelessness about human problems and a relatively unchanging picture of human nature."[25] For the Judge, as a law clerk recalled, "man's life was a straight line. It didn't necessarily go up or down. People were the same today, they had the same problems, that they had 5,000 years ago. That is why he used to send us back to read about the Greeks and the Romans all the time."[26] This perception of human nature, developed prior to his move to the Supreme Court, remained unchanged throughout his tenure on the Court.

For the rest of his life, in light of this view of history and of human nature, and despite his seemingly antagonistic behavior at times, Black sought to strengthen fellowship and community wherever he functioned. While he understood the bitterness that arose in his South after the Court's decisions that ended de jure segregation, he was, however, saddened by the reality. As he wrote to Hugo Jr. in 1950, four years before the *Brown v Board of Education of Topeka, Kansas* decision was announced, "at the present time I rather doubt if it would be wise for me to visit Alabama. High emotions over the segregation cases would be aggravated by my presence. It would of course be very bad for the Court if any kind of public incident should occur on account of these emotions."[27]

Personally, the Judge was heartbroken when, during the civil rights era, he was not welcome in his most cherished community, *his* Alabama. Given a choice between individual freedom and the need for a healthy community, one that does not *unconstitutionally* impinge on the freedoms of the individual, Black "instinctively chose the latter, particularly when it seemed the freedom might not be used with a sense of moral restraint or obligation."[28]

His strong attachment to the concept of community was seen in significant Court opinions he authored, both for the majority and in dissent, regarding the clash of values between community and individual liberty. Whether Japanese Americans,[29] or schoolchildren protesting against the Vietnam War,[30] or blacks taking to the streets to protest against continuing segregation in the South,[31] Black decided controversial legal clashes in favor of the preservation of the community. Community came first, unless there was clear evidence that the person's First Amendment rights were being capriciously abrogated by the community.

Black, unlike Douglas, believed that personal freedom in a democracy was not an end in itself. "It was, however, essential because it facilitated democratic self-government *upon which community welfare depended*" (my emphasis).[32] Throughout his life, Black believed that the "organic unity of the community and the rights of the individual should reinforce each other in harmonious balance,"[33] the same balance ancient Greek poets and philosophers wrote about.

Human nature did not change very much. For Black, the evils addressed by the prohibitions in the Bill of Rights, all human evils, were not timebound eighteenth-century ones. The Bill of Rights was a remedy then, now, and in the future, against wrongs perpetrated by humans against other humans. The Bill of Rights did not have to be informally modified, certainly not by the Justices of the Supreme Court, because it very adequately addressed timeless, unchanging human behavior.

According to Elizabeth, Black believed that history is "a part of life. The history of the world gives you the habits of various times."[34] Modern leaders have to learn from history. And Justice Black believed history to show that only when members of a community respected others did there exist a harmonious balance between majority rule and individual freedom.

The primary function of law in a social community was to act to reduce the tensions that threatened the balance between these two concepts. For Black, the terrible spectre in 1950s America of McCarthyism, whose tentacles reached into the Supreme Court itself, "grew out of human anxieties which had been the problem since the time of Tacitus. Public officials had to work to ensure that the people's higher rather than lower sentiments drove their decisions."[35]

So fearful was Black that individuals, especially the well-meaning, would act in boisterous ways that would only weaken the fragile balance between individualism and community—for example, massing and marching in the streets—that on occasion he tried to get word to the protesters to stop their actions. Jinksie Durr, his very liberal sister-in-law, whose husband Cliff was a lawyer for Martin Luther King, Jr., and the Southern Christian Leadership Conference (SCLC), recalled Hugo telling her "over and over again":

> For God's sakes, tell your friends down there in Alabama, Martin Luther King and the rest of them that you know, to stop marching and to stop having all these demonstrations. That's just going to jeopardize their cause. They should leave it to the Courts.[36]

Jinksie wrote that Hugo "really believed in the Courts. He thought that the marches and the young people coming to Mississippi were just hurting their cause."[37] The Justice was also a historian and a psychologist. His rock-hard commitment to the value of "ordered community relationships"[38] led him to rule against those who threatened this central value—unless it was shown that their First Amendment rights had been violated by the community.

And so, whether the marchers and "sit-downers," as Black referred to them, massing to protest, were blacks or Klansmen made no difference to the Judge. He believed that "no minority can in the long run force its will on the majority. . . . [Black] was fearful that we were going to create a 50- or 100-year backlash by preferring blacks today in what he regarded as violations of the Constitution and so in the long run blacks would be worse off."[39]

More than once, he declared, mostly in dissent, that while he as an individual valued his privacy, that privacy right could be invaded by the community under appropriate, constitutional circumstances.[40] In a lecture Black gave to New York University Law School students and faculty, he said, starkly, that "even though I like my privacy as well as the next person, I am nevertheless compelled to admit that the states have a right to invade it unless prohibited by some specific constitutional provision."[41]

Throughout his life, he firmly stated his views about men and women in history, about the centrality of the community, and about the primacy of the rule of law—views derived in part from Black's experiences growing up in rural, upcountry Alabama.

Race and Racism in Alabama

All social behavior "and every human emotion became entangled in Southern race relations," wrote Edward L. Ayers. "When a [white youngster] referred to a respected black man as 'Mr. Jones,' [his] aunt quickly corrected him. 'No, son. Robert Jones is a nigger. You don't say 'mister' when you speak of a nigger. You don't say 'Mr. Jones,' you say 'nigger Jones.' Children soon learned the lesson."[42] Growing up during the high tide of Jim Crowism in Alabama, Black learned that lesson with everyone else in Clay County. It was not until he was well away from the prejudices in Alabama that he rethought the question of race and concluded that the Court was wrong to have decided *Plessy v Ferguson* the way it did.

"The South breaks my heart," uttered Florida Congressman Claude Pepper at a 1985 meeting commemorating the centennial of Hugo Black's life.[43] Black could just as easily have said these words, for he was painfully aware of the deep wounds suffered by his beloved South as a consequence of its extremist, violent commitment to racial segregation, from before the Civil War well into the twentieth century.

In a poignant response to an angry letter he received from a cousin, Edna Street Barnes, Black addressed the failure of the South's people to address the sickness of racism. Angry about black efforts to integrate "Ole Miss" University, Edna had written about

> this Mississippi University affair. It is deplorable that it had to happen just to please the NAACP crowd. The negro students are not interested in education at these colleges they choose to storm and conquer but only want to tread on the pride and prejudice of the people who have nurtured them and civilized them in such a short period of time.

She ended her letter with a plea to her cousin Hugo to "keep your heart and mind turned toward the South. We need someone in high places to stand by us."[44]

The Judge responded in a three-page letter that carefully tried to educate cousin Edna about the wrongness of a continued commitment to race discrimination by Southerners. While "our affection for the South is probably very much the same," he wrote, "our belief about what would be good for the South, its people and the Nation, may differ some."

> A wiser leadership in the South [is needed.] . . . The Thirteenth, Fourteenth and Fifteenth Amendments to the Constitution have chartered a course that this Nation will follow. They have declared that there must be no discrimination in this country on account of race or color. Ignorant, emotional or prejudicial people who try to persuade the South that they can devise ways to defy and defeat the will of the Nation in this respect can do nothing but once again bring on unnecessary pain and suffering in that area. . . . Our Constitution, and the Amendments to which I referred above, are based on a belief that all people, whatever their color and whatever their history, or whatever their geographical position or origin, are human beings, created by the same Creator, all entitled to have equal opportunities to do their part in helping carry out the great national plan under which all our people must live. . . . I do not recall ever having heard anything contrary to

[these views] in my home, and I am sure that my Sunday School teachers in the little churches at Ashland, Alabama, came very near expressing this same philosophy when they talked to me about the Sermon on the Mount and repeated the story of the Good Samaritan.

Black closed the letter with the following hope. "I only wish that more people who were born in the South, as I was, . . . would realize, as I am sure you do, that this country is a great country because instead of having a Constitution that fosters slavery, hatred and a caste system, it is a country that proudly boasts of its dedication to the principle of 'Equal Justice Under Law.' With my continued esteem and affection, I am your Cousin."[45] Yet Black realized, as a historian of sorts and more than most people, how difficult it was for the South, without strong leaders, to overcome the traditional "pride and prejudice" that enveloped it for hundreds of years.

The brutal reality of racism in the South even after the Civil War is seen in the following dispatch sent to the U.S. Senate by former Union General Carl Schurz:

> Wherever I go—the street, the shop, the house, the hotel, or the steamboat—I hear people talk in such a way as to indicate that they are yet unable to conceive of the Negro as possessing any rights at all. Men who are honorable in their dealings with their white neighbors will cheat a Negro without feeling a single twinge of their honor. To kill a Negro, they do not deem murder; to debauch a Negro woman they do not consider fornication; to take property from a Negro, they do not consider robbery. The whites . . . still have an ingrained feeling that the blacks at large belong to the whites at large.[46]

This was the pervasive reality of Southern racial attitudes in 1886. Black entered the world of the South at a time of "stark, pervasive racial discrimination against the recently freed slaves.[47] When he died in 1971, things had not changed that much. There was racial discrimination present in all kinds of social and political interaction, from birth in segregated hospitals to death and burial in segregated cemeteries.

For example, in the early 1960s, Black gave his oldest son some advice about arguing an insurance claim on behalf of a black man who had been injured while visiting Birmingham from Detroit, Michigan.

> "Just tell your man to act like Southern white people expect him to act and when they start the race stuff, you tell the jury you would rather have a case like this here in Birmingham than anywhere else in America. Tell them to send the message back to *Dee-troit* and Chicago and New York that we take better care of this kind of a plaintiff than anybody else in America." My client reluctantly accepted my suggestion that he act as Jefferson County white people would expect a "good nigger" to act, and then I used Daddy's argument. The jury returned a verdict much higher, I am sure, than a jury would have in Detroit.[48]

Like most white Southerners growing to manhood at the turn of the century, Black exhibited an "unconscious or unreflective racism" in his actions.[49] As Jinksie Durr said, most whites, including those who were not vicious anti-black terrorists who tormented blacks at night, were racist sons of bitches. And, although it is clear that Black "was hardly a racist in the worst tradition of Southern politicians, he nevertheless did not rebel against the racism of the society in which he lived."[50] The citizens of Ashland accepted these racially discriminatory customs and traditions as a matter of course, although there was no rush to incorporate these values into local statutes.

Ten years after Hugo's birth, in 1896, the U.S. Supreme Court placed its imprimatur on de facto as well as de jure racial segregation. *Plessy v Ferguson,*[51] a seven-to-one opinion of the Court, validated state actions that separated the races in other than legal and political matters, provided that the separation was on the basis of equal facilities. The premise of equality was never realized in the South throughout the *Plessy* era (1896–1954).

It was only after Black left Alabama, in fact only after he became a justice of the United States Supreme Court, that he addressed and modified his racial views. By the time of *Brown v Board of Education,* first heard by the Court in its 1950–1951 term and decided in May 1954, Black had turned radically away from his earlier racism.

In 1958, Martin Luther King, Jr., leader of the SCLC, was sufficiently comfortable with Black's actions on the Court to be able to inscribe a copy of his *Stride Toward Freedom* for the Justice thus: "In appreciation for your genuine good will, your perceptive vision, your broad humanitarian concern, and your unswerving devotion to the noble principles of our democracy."[52]

King's respect for Black was based on the Judge's judicial actions in civil rights litigation before the brethren from *Chambers v Florida*[53] to *Brown v Board of Education* to *Cooper v Aaron.*[54] This message of King's was penned before the more controversial "sit-down" cases of the early 1960s came before the Court, cases in which the Judge voted to uphold arrests of blacks for sitting down, praying in, and otherwise participating in *conduct* that Black believed could be controlled and regulated by local law enforcement agencies.

By the late 1950s, however, for all those who followed the goings-on of the Supreme Court, it was abundantly clear that Hugo Black was a leader in the judicial effort to fully implement the concept of equality in America through the legal dismantlement of Jim Crowism. By 1958, he was no longer able to visit his beloved state of Alabama without running into Southerners who cruelly taunted him as "nigger lover."

From Montgomery, Alabama, his sister-in-law Jinksie wrote to Black regularly, over three turbulent decades, to report to him the growing spectre of violence that was a somber, terribly sad reflection of the virulent racism in his beloved South. The stories she told him—about racist politicians catering to the lowest common denominator in those Southern communities, the systemic cruelty directed by the white community towards blacks in Alabama, and the backlash against some federal judges who dared to uphold Supreme Court rulings in the area of race relations—pained the Justice.

Most hurtful to both of them were the messages she sent that described the hatred Alabamans expressed about Hugo himself. She wrote,

> I know that all the Hounds of Hell are after you, and you are the No. One enemy
> as far as they are concerned. . . . You have done a wonderful job and certainly

become the Defender of the Faith, but by so doing you have become the Enemy of all the evil forces that are trying to destroy the country. . . . I have lost my cheerful faith that all of this is silly and now realize how deep and how cruel and how powerful it [the hatred] all is. . . . We can't do a thing."[55]

He knew that the South had to move away from the bitterness, and violence that followed Court orders and national legislation attempting to address the evils of de jure racism. He also knew that the South needed leaders to move the region beyond the irrationality that unrestrained violence generated. Jinksie's letters from the domestic battlefield indicated the absence of such political leadership. In 1962, she told Hugo about George Wallace: "Wallace and 'Bull' Connor [the Birmingham Commissioner of Public Safety] are telling the folks that they will never surrender to the union armies."[56] On another occasion, she wrote: "Politics is just as bad as ever. . . . It looks as if Wallace is a sure thing for either Governor or Senator. . . . [His opposition] will not have have a chance as Wallace can out-seg him by a million miles."[57]

The hatred vented by these citizens, all opposed to integration and equality, had an unfortunate effect on Black's family then living in Alabama. Hugo Jr. had to move out of the state because of the response to his father's actions on the Court and because of his own liberal activities as a lawyer. Jinksie and Cliff Durr had to endure the taunts, ostracism, and the violence against blacks that took place with increasing regularity in Alabama. In 1958, she wrote, poignantly, to Hugo:

> I cannot understand Cliff's almost desperate need to stay here in Montgomery, where we barely make a living, are practically isolated in the community and have to be constantly on our guard to even carry on a casual conversation. . . . I don't even like [the Montgomery white people] very much and besides they frighten me with their suppressed violence and complete irrationality."[58]

Youth is father to the man;[59] Black's growing up in Alabama exposed him to the agrarian radicalism of the Populists, as well as the pervasive racism that was an essential element of the Southern culture. Black's growing up in the confines of Harlan and Ashland, amidst a large, fairly close family also exposed him to a Primitive Baptist upbringing, one that had a lifelong impact on him.

Family History

Hugo's parents, William Lafayette and Martha Ardellah Toland Black, came to Alabama leaving generational family roots in Georgia and South Carolina.[60] His father ran away at fifteen to fight in the Civil War, along with a number of other family members. His father's brother, Columbus, fell mortally wounded in Pickett's charge at Gettysburg.

An amateur genealogist, Black was always tracing his family roots. Given the great value he placed on understanding and learning from the past, the Judge had a need to know his own family history. For example, in July 1968, a little more than three years before his death, he was in contact with the General Services Administration to find out more about his uncle who died at Gettysburg. The National Archives and Records Service uncovered the military service file of Private Columbus M. Black, Company G, Fourteenth Regiment, Alabama Infantry, noting that Columbus "was wounded and missing in action at Gettysburg, Pa., July 2, 1863." A copy of the file was sent to Hugo. He was deeply moved and sent a warm note to the archivist, Dr. James B. Rhoads.[61]

Even in his eighties, the Judge was still interested in his long-deceased uncle because he knew that his mother, Della, was deeply in love with the fallen man. Hugo had heard on a number of occasions that she married William Lafayette "Faet" Black, Columbus's brother, on the rebound, shortly after the death of her true love.

According to Hugo Jr., based on conversations with the Justice, she never respected Black's father, "much less loved him. He had a terrible drinking problem, which didn't contribute anything to an already shaky marriage." Young Black saw this estrangement very early in his life, and he "soon began to regard his father as nothing but a well-functioning spree drinker. His father would go on drinking binges for days at a time, his wife all the while trying to dry him out so he could get back to the store he was running. The only time he was sober, Daddy thought, was when the liquor had run out."[62]

After arriving in Clay County, Alabama, the Black family settled in Harlan. It was little more than a crossroads village where William owned the only general store and supervised the running of a small farm that had, working the land, two tenant farmers. Black's mother was an educated woman who tended the home and their eight children, seven after young Della died in 1886. She was also the U.S. postmistress for the small village. It was, as young Hugo saw, a loveless marriage, in great part because of his father's temper and his alcoholism. From his earliest recollections, Black's attitude towards his father was one of "cold indifference."[63] His male role models were his four older brothers, Lee, Orlando, Pelham, and Vernon.

In a 1963 letter to a dear friend, Black noted that Harlan "no longer exists. . . . It never rose even to the dignity of a 'village.' . . . So far as I know, it may have become a Post Office only for my mother to become a Postmistress. . . . Some time after my father abandoned his storekeeping in that location and moved to Ashland, Alabama in 1889, the United States Government decided it no longer needed a Post Office in Harlan."[64] Three years after Hugo was born, the Black family moved to the county seat, Ashland, a small town of 350, so that their seven remaining children could receive a better education.

As the local merchant, Hugo's father provided tools, seed, provisions, and farming supplies in the early spring to the yeoman farmers—at interest rates that ranged from 50 to 75%. He further protected his loans to these poor farmers "by taking a lien on the forthcoming crop or a mortgage on the land itself."[65] Black was sensitive to the reality that these poor farmers were in "financial bondage" to his drunken father.[66] For as long as he could remember, young Hugo had a strained relationship with him. While respected as a businessman, the father was seen only as a "vital cog in the hated crop-lien system."[67]

Contrary to rumors suggesting that Black grew up poor, the "humble origins in Alabama" story "was grossly overdone," commented a law clerk. "If his father owned the farm and the store, he was probably the richest man in Clay County."[68] The Black family in Ashland grew up in fairly prosperous circumstances. Hugo's brothers became doctors, lawyers, and merchants.

Certainly the senior Black, who prospered from the crop-lien system, never accepted Populism.[69] Although young Black was mesmerized by the orators and grew to understand and feel for the plight of the poor farmers, both father and son were loyal Democrats. "My father was not a Populist," he wrote much later. "In fact he was always much against the Party. He boasted that he was a Grover Cleveland Democrat."[70] The elder Black voted with the downstate Big Mules, the Bourbon Democrats. Years later, Hugo wrote that by the time he was six years old, his political attitudes had developed clearly: "Before I could articulate my syllables distinctly I recall how angry people could make me by saying: 'you are a Populist, a third-party-ite.' My reply in those early days was: 'I am not a t'ird-party-ite. I am a Democrat.' "[71]

Black recalled that "being the youngest [of the Black children], I was the family pet."[72] His brothers and sisters doted on him. At six, in 1892, Hugo began his education at Ashland College, a local school that taught students from kindergarten through what we now know as junior college. He also learned to play instruments and was taking music lessons when he was four years old.

At an early age, with his mother's prodding, he was reading Victor Hugo, Sir Walter Scott, and the Bible. The Judge later recalled that "I read everything that was both readable and available. Along with Nick Carter detective stories, Fred Fcarnots, young and old King Bradys, I remember reading many histories, Walter Scott's poems and novels, Dickens' novels, *Pilgrim's Progress,* and many other books generally thought of as too advanced for children. I read many of these books before I was ten years old."[73]

Black fell in love with his first teacher, Miss Lizzie Patterson, who "guided me like [his beloved] mother."[74] His second-grade teacher, J. H. Riddle, paddled young Hugo for cackling in the classroom. "He believed in school discipline," recalled Black in his autobiography. "It never occurred to me then or since that my fine old Professor Riddle violated the United States Constitution in giving me that whipping."[75]

In this very rural up-country environment, young Black began to exhibit the stubbornness he was to become famous for in his mature years in Birmingham, the Senate, and the Court. During the 1902–1903 school year, when he was about sixteen years old, he courageously, defiantly, battled two of his teachers because he believed that they were treating his older sister Daisy unfairly. Young Hugo told the teacher to let his sister go home. Instead, the teacher

> announced that he was going to whip me. . . . I took the switch away from him and broke it into pieces. . . . Both [teachers] tried to whip me, but I succeeded in breaking all the switches they had. . . . About that time my mother, having been informed of what was going on, came into the school building from across the street where we lived and the whipping stopped. After consultation with my mother and other family members, I never went back to that school again but instead went to the Birmingham Medical College for its 1902–1903 term.[76]

At the urging of his mother, Hugo tried to follow in the footsteps of another successful brother who had attended the medical school and was becoming a promising young physician. His older brother Orlando had received a medical degree from the Birmingham Medical College and was practicing medicine in Wilsonville, Alabama, and so sixteen-year-old Hugo went off to medical school. He was accepted even though he did not have a college education and was younger than others in his class; his brother Orlando's reputation and recommendation enabled Black to enter the medical school.

Although he did well in terms of grades, young Hugo hated the practice of medicine. "He couldn't stand it," recollected one of Black's law clerks. "He said that he assisted his brother in a delivery and all that blood showed him he wasn't going to be a doctor. That's why he went on to be a lawyer."[77] As a consequence of these bad experiences, Black, after one year of medical school, entered the University of Alabama Law School in Tuscaloosa in September 1904.

From his earliest recollections, Black had a lifelong hatred of alcohol, even though he took some nightcaps towards the end of his life, and, during the 1950s, drank many fifths of gin to relieve the pain brought on by a bad case of shingles. When he was five years old, Hugo came down with catarrhal fever. The local doctor told his mother that the child had to drink whiskey to save his life. "My antipathy to liquor had already become so strong at that age that I refused to take one drop of it. My mother stood by me, however; I did not imbibe, and I did not die."[78]

His aversion at that young age was strong for a number of reasons, including his church's prohibition and the alcoholism of his father. Because of Faet's drinking and his exploitation of the crop-lien system, Hugo exhibited a "cold indifference" to his merchant father—a man who died of cirrhosis of the liver, at fifty-two, in September 1899.[79] At his death, William left an estate of twenty-five thousand dollars in cash that was divided among the children.

Young Hugo was only fourteen years when his father died. When he was sixteen, Pelham, an older lawyer brother and Hugo's favorite sibling, drowned at twenty-two years of age as a result of his buggy overturning and throwing him in a shallow stream—after he'd been on a drinking spree.

Almost six years after his father's death, in another wintry February, this in 1905, his mother died of pneumonia. She had instilled in him a love of learning through reading and respected and encouraged his determination to excel. Then, suddenly and dramatically when he was only nineteen years of age, after concluding the first year of law school at the University of Alabama, Black was an orphan.

Black, barely five foot eight and slender, graduated Phi Beta Kappa in 1906 from the University of Alabama Law School—with its complement of two law faculty. He had received at least a ninety in every course he took during his two years in Tuscaloosa. How good a student was Hugo? His law school professor said, cautiously, diplomatically, "I won't say whether Black is the best student in the school or not. I will say he has learned the most. He had the most to learn."[80]

Hugo quickly returned to Ashland and hung up his shingle. But, as Hugo recalled in his memoir, "the people of Clay county saw me not as a lawyer but as the same marble shooting boy they had watched grow up in their midst. Weighing less than 120 pounds, I probably still looked more like a boy to them than like a lawyer."[81] He had grandiose plans for his future: legal practice in Ashland, a seat in the Alabama legislature followed by a successful legal practice in Birmingham. Then, Black imagined, he would go to Congress "and from there go to New York to practice law . . . because it was the nation's largest city."[82] His life didn't fully follow these plans.

In less than a year, in 1907, after a fire destroyed his small law office and his prized law library purchased with funds left to him by his father, Black was off to Birmingham to practice law. What kind of man was he as he moved away from rural Alabama to a different type of life in brawling, booming Birmingham? Who was this young man who thought of going up north to New York City to practice law?

The Complex Man from Alabama

Immediately one sees that Black's life was very controlled, mostly private, and lonely. Hugo, people noted throughout his life, "has a gift for self-containment."[83] Growing up in Ashland, he did not have a great deal of intellectual companionship other than his mother and some of his brothers and sisters. Home alone, he willed himself to learn about law, politics, economics, and religion. Encouraged by his mother, he read at an early age and developed his natural intelligence.

He succeeded beyond his mother's wildest dreams because he had the capacity for unusual intellectual growth. Throughout his life, the Judge, wrote one of his law clerks, was singularly "concerned only with his work."[84] George Freeman, another law clerk, observed that

> Justice Black probably had the greatest control over himself of any person I have ever seen. He controlled when he got up, what he ate, his bodily activities so that he would get the proper amount of exercise. He controlled what he said to you and what he said to other people. And a person that has this much self control also has a little barrier there. It is the barrier of only letting you see him as he wants you to see him. . . . There was an inner core of reserve to the judge that when you finally got down to it was the self-contained, self-assured, self-controlled person. I never felt that I got beyond that and I wonder if anybody ever did.[85]

For example, while awaiting clients in Ashland, he did not sit around the tiny one-room office. Instead, Black walked the woods to practice his speaking techniques and improve his courtroom rhetoric.[86] And he continued to study and read aloud from books on rhetoric, grammar, English, and history. Recalling the characteristics of the lawyers who impressed him when he sat in the courthouse gallery a decade or more earlier, Hugo knew he needed to improve his "talking on his feet" skills—and so he did in Ashland when he was not practicing law.[87]

If Black wanted something, he somehow found a way to get it, whether it was maintaining his health, improving his rhetorical skills, or working to get legislation through the political process. His niece Hazel Black, daughter of the Judge's oldest brother, Lee, recalled that Hugo "led in eating the right foods, in staying thin, and in taking exercise." She also recalled that her uncle Hugo was stubborn and strong. "If Uncle Hugo believes he is right, he enjoys the fight."[88]

His immediate lawyerly success in Birmingham attested to the fact that the year of personal improvement in Ashland was very necessary for him. Black knew that he needed the rhetoric work—and he did it, without deviation and without excuses. That was self-discipline, a rarity in a person who had barely turned twenty years of age. As he wrote years later of that year in Clay County: "I had planned far wiser than I knew."[89]

Black's own family had difficulty getting through to the Judge. Hugo Jr. recalled: "I always had the feeling that Daddy was controlling what he was passing on to me and the rest of his children about his early days in Clay County. He would never confide in me about his boyhood sufferings and joys the way he would talk about his professional life. Perhaps the explanation is, by nature, he believed in keeping more things to himself than I do."[90]

His characteristic well-planned drive towards a defined goal, whether on the tennis court, in the Senate, or in the Court's conference session, bothered some of the people he worked with. Others tried to pierce his secrecy but few succeeded. One example of his willpower involved his love of smoking slim black cigars (Antonio-Cleopatra) all the time. This habit was accompanied by Black's cigarette smoking. In 1935, however, he concluded that smoking cigars and cigarettes was bad for his health, and so he went cold turkey, never smoking a cigar afterwards. He did, however, chew them and, occasionally, he would light up a cigarette.[91]

Many years later, in 1964, he discussed this ability to quit a habit cold turkey with some of his relatives.

> Mr. Justice Black said that when he smoked his first cigarette, he did it with the determination that the habit would not become his master; that whenever he should find that he had a strong urge to smoke, he would quit. He had on several occasions tested himself out and had found that it did not bother him at all to go for an indefinite time without smoking. . . . At one time he was smoking 3½ packs each day. . . . He decided to quit—and—he quit! As far as Hugo was concerned, that was all there was to it. He did not crave smoking. There was no time lost in thinking about smoking, *for after his mind was made up, the matter was closed.*[92] (my emphasis)

Black developed self-discipline much the way he improved his writing or his knowledge of the classics. As he told Hugo Jr., " 'Self control didn't come easy for me, Son. I had to practice it—pick something I liked and quit it. Why,' he said with a twinkle in his eyes, 'I used to give up women for certain periods of time just to see if I could. And I always could.' "[93] Black simply refused to relinquish the upper hand: "when he makes a decision, the matter is finished and no longer bothers him."[94]

After spending a decade in the Senate as a vigorous, dedicated, hard-nosed investigator, Black was described by the press as a "loner" who suffered from an "unpopularity complex" when he moved over to the Court. He left the Senate, as he left Birmingham, with few friends, but there were many who were either angry or envious. As one scholar observed of Black: "He was too ardent a partisan, too zealous an investigator to please the Senate's oligarchs."[95]

From a reading of his autobiography, one can clearly see that by the time Black left Ashland for Birmingham, he had developed a lifelong appreciation and respect for the regularities of history. He also knew that men and women could be cruel and wicked. But the Judge had almost a sublime faith in the impact of education on humankind, and he was always the educator.

If human nature is generally nonchanging, then history will repeat itself "and men are bound to act in the same way *unless* it is shown to them that such a course in other days ended disastrously."[96] Black took on the task of showing others, with a self-assurance born of his total acceptance of this view of history's patterns.

Hugo always preached the value of education to his children, his brethren, and his family. When the many children of his brother Lee were ready for college and he did not have the money for tuition, Black sent four of them—Grace, Hollis (who was to become Hugo's secretary when Black was in the Senate), Mildred, and Hazel—the necessary funds for them to attend college.

And there was a poignant close to this kindness. In February 1964, over forty years later, Hazel Black Davis, married, a high school teacher with two grown children, wrote "Uncle" a letter on the occasion of his upcoming seventy-ninth birthday celebration. In it she attached a check for four hundred dollars, one of five she said she planned to send to the Justice. "My little diary tells me that from 1923 to 1926 you spent $1,971.48 on my education, making a college degree possible for one." After so many years, with her children growing up and going off to college, she had to send her beloved uncle the checks. "Perhaps you might want to add this one to a college loan fund for [your grandchildren]."[97]

Almost immediately the Judge sent the check back to her. Tenderly, he said that "no investment that I ever made in my life paid better dividends than the money I spent to send you through college. . . . My pride in your accomplishments, your character and your personality has never been greater than it was when I received your check and the letter that accompanied it."[98]

In one of his many letters to Hugo Jr., Black told of his "gratification" about his son's pleasure in reading Aristotle's *Poetics* and Cicero's *Nature of the Gods.* And he suggested other Greek writings, including Cicero's *Brutus, Divination,* and *On Duties,* as well as Xenophon's *Memorabilia.* "The reason I mention the study of the above . . . is that I am satisfied that no man can rise to the heights of eloquence merely because he had learning, style, and dialectical skill. To be eloquent or to be happy I think he has to have a great deal more than these things, to keep his language from being hollow."[99]

The elderly Judge was, up to the months prior to his death, ordering books on Greek democracy and on the 1787 Constitutional Convention for his grandchildren.

Hugo Black loved the Greeks because, as Edith Hamilton wrote, they turned full face to life—and aggressively tackled the problems confronting the community with a free mind.[100] Freedom of inquiry and of speech were the hallmarks of democratic Athens. They loved knowledge and were not afraid of the results of the search for the facts.

What especially pleased the Judge was the conviction of the Athenian democrats that ordinary citizens had good sense and would do the right thing when asked.[101] For a century, history showed how beneficial were the results of this harmony between the community and its citizens. Plato's assertion that men find their true moral development only in service to the state was one that Black acknowledged and acted on throughout his life on the high bench. And he underlined and indexed the views of Pericles, including one comment that "liberty is the secret of happiness and courage is the secret of liberty."

Yet, ironically, with regard to the women in his life, he never put into practice what he preached and believed in deeply. Jinksie Durr, Black's free-spirited, liberal sister-in-law, recalled that her sister, Josephine, was "never independent after marrying Hugo [and that] he was one of the most powerful characters that she could have married." She also commented that

> Hugo absolutely worshipped Josephine. . . . He did everything in his power to make her happy, except give her her freedom. She was never free after the wedding, she was Mrs. Hugo Black. That was the way girls were supposed to be anyway. . . . Hugo believed women should stay sweet and feminine and slim. He wanted to send his daughter to Sweet Briar because Sister [Josephine] had gone there. He wanted his daughter to be just like his wife—perfectly feminine and sweet.[102]

Hugo passionately loved Josephine and, after pursuing her for over two years, they were married in 1921. Josephine could not deal with Hugo's dominant personality and his supreme self-confidence. After their 1927 arrival in bustling, political Washington, D.C., she was slowly overtaken with significant bouts of depression and melancholia, the malady that Black the father warned his sons to avoid. In the 1930s and 40s she was periodically hospitalized for depression. During these often lengthy occasions, Black became the housefather to his three children. Ironically, the children, especially little Jo-Jo, were drawn to the uncharacteristic warmth of Felix Frankfurter, their father's bold antagonist.

Josephine, "plagued by doubts [about her] worth in the world, was forced to cope with [an] immensely successful, self possessed husband, who could not understand or help her overcome her depression."[103] It was not until she began to paint that her life exhibited the quality of freedom her husband enjoyed with his typical conviction. But that came too late. Tragically, her life ended when she was fifty-two years old, just beginning to emerge from the emptiness of her life as Mrs. Justice Black.

Jinksie would write, only after Hugo's death in 1971, that

> it was sister's illnesses and depression that were such a source of worry and anxiety to him and that he really dreaded having discussed but now that he is gone, I do not believe any of the children will find that should be left out of his papers, as it was a fact and naturally it was widely known, as she had a lot of friends and went to a lot of doctors. . . . [Sister had] melancholia, . . . a well known Southern Lady trouble.[104]

While he loved the values of free inquiry and the freedom of the mind, Black himself "was a strict disciplinarian at home, domineering everywhere, and conventional in most matters of personal behavior." [105] Given the self-assurance that comes with possession of the truth, "his sense of oneness with ancient values," he was a "stern personality," [106] most especially with his two sons. Indeed, Black's "attentiveness often had a relentless focus that made his two boys run for cover." [107] As Hugo Jr. said years later, "My father liked to teach; he particularly liked to teach me and my brother." [108]

As was mentioned in chapter 1, Hugo was not as strict with his youngest child and only daughter, Jo-Jo. Sterling, the middle sibling, thought he knew the reason for this change: "By the time my sister Jo-Jo came along, Daddy had learned how to be an ideal parent. Hugo and I were his teachers. He practiced on us. Daddy mellowed as a parent just as he grew as a person. Daddy mellowed along the way." [109]

By the time twenty-one-year-old Hugo Black, Esq., went off to Birmingham, Alabama, to practice law in 1907, he had developed a worldview of history, a set of religious beliefs that he retained all his life, a strong commitment to the common man and to the Democratic party, and a deep, abiding respect for the power of the law to assist fallible humans in moving towards a better life in a free society.

Also critically important for understanding Black is the fact that he was controlled and directed in all his activities, all the time. Indeed, the 1906 University of Alabama *Yearbook* wrote of Black, with a great degree of prescience, that he would "use the devil himself with courtesy" to achieve his goals.

Believing in himself and in the power of the ideas he possessed about history, law, and human nature, Black felt ready to enter the legal profession in the boisterous, growing urban environment of Birmingham, Alabama.

CHAPTER THREE

The Birmingham Years

Black arrived in Birmingham in 1907 not knowing a soul. Decades later, he would say that life there "was enjoyable" and that living and working in Birmingham was "the happiest time" of his life.[1] Black, as he liked to say to disarm people, was somewhat of a "backward country fellow" when he arrived. In a very short while, however, he became both a legal legend and a social success story. His acquaintances and friends grew dramatically in number, as did the names in his client roster. Hugo's personal injury practice very soon became the first such lucrative law practice in Alabama. By the time Black went off to the U.S. Senate in 1927, his total worth exceeded $250,000.[2]

In his first year in Birmingham, however, Hugo paid his rent working for the Retail Credit Company of Atlanta, Georgia. He received fifty cents apiece "for reports on the life and habits of life insurance applicants."[3] This job, plus some minor legal work, got Black through his early days.

Success did come fairly soon after Hugo arrived in the big city, for a number of not too surprising reasons, given Black's personal characteristics. First of all, he was an active participant in one of the South's primary social groups, Birmingham's First Baptist Church. Except for his stint in the army during World War I, Black attended services regularly and, every week, taught Sunday school until he left the city for his senatorial work in Washington, D.C. In addition, he met many people because of his growing, well-deserved reputation as a skilled personal injury lawyer. Finally, to meet people, he joined many fraternal groups in the new, bustling metropolis, starting off with the Masons, followed by membership in the Odd Fellows. As he recounted later, "the only ethical way [to build the practice] was to meet as many people and make as many friends as possible. This I proceeded to do immediately after arriving in Birmingham."[4]

Importantly, Hugo came into contact with large numbers of poor blacks because the new city had been a beacon for impoverished people regardless of race. At this time in the South, the first decade of the twentieth century, "people from every level of rural society left the country side for towns and cities. . . . As a result, the South's towns and cities were centers of both wealth and poverty."[5] Because of the crisis in agriculture, with more and more people losing their lands because of the crop-lien system, more poor persons, especially blacks who could not find work in the Black Belt, moved into the city daily. They came to seek employment in the newly developed industries in northern Alabama: the coal mines, blast furnaces, iron foundries, cotton mills, and lumberyards. Traveling from Birmingham to Tuscaloosa, a sixty-mile stretch of dirt roads, a person was in continuous contact with the terrible odors of the wood pulp mills, which were nonexistent a decade earlier.

By the time Black arrived in Birmingham, it had a 40 percent black population, with the men working long days in the mills and factories for low wages and in miserable, dangerous working conditions. Many black workers were also treated brutally by the city's police and prosecutors, as Hugo found out years later when he became Jefferson County prosecutor.

Jinksie Durr, his future sister-in-law, observed that after a brief time, Black "knew Birmingham inside out and upside down—poor folks, black folks, white folks, labor folks. He had become quite a figure, but anticorporation."[6] Hugo was, in the first years, a "complete outsider" who quickly came to function well in the rapidly growing city.

Black began to earn a very good living as a personal injury lawyer whose clients were working men, black and white, and labor unions. By the 1920s, he was making a great deal of money. In 1923, he netted thirty-two thousand dollars. By 1925, the figure had risen to sixty-five thousand dollars annually.[7] Very quickly, given his sense of injustice as well as the guiding hand of history, Black became an energetic proponent and legal champion of the common man.[8] From his first months in Birmingham, he staked his legal and political future on the newly emerging industrial proletariat, the common men in America's age of industrial growth.

Moreover, paradoxically, Black was also emotionally driven to meet the proper people in order to try to overcome the "outsider" label and to become a respected member of the community.[9] Groups such as the Masons, Odd Fellows, Elks, Moose, Civitans, and Ku Klux Klan were "organized grandly,"[10] and, as these groups "were a fact of life in the South, . . . they became a fact of life for Hugo Black."[11] He gravitated to them to find that mystical bond of community between himself and others, a community that meant so much to him as a loyal Southerner, as a citizen of the Southern polis.

Hugo Black in Birmingham was the archetype of the young, ambitious, successful professional who responded well to the anarchic conditions and disputes that emerged from the growing, industrial metropolis. He was a young man who sought more than legal success in the courtroom, a "gregarious Southerner searching for fellowship and power in the company of other men, [searching for] communal bonding."[12] He was seeking to find the intellectual and social comradeship that was lacking in the village of Ashland while representing clients who lived in another world.

After his marriage to Josephine Foster in 1921, Black found himself guardedly accepted into the Birmingham high society he longed to enter. Hugo and Josephine joined the prestigious Birmingham Country Club and were often found golfing and playing tennis, the latter a lifelong love of the Judge's. The Blacks moved into a lovely house on a hill overlooking Birmingham, complete with a garden, a well-stocked library, a baby grand piano played by both of them, and a household staff of "black cooks, nurses, maids, and gardeners."[13]

Even though successful and married to a member of a highly respected Birmingham family, Black believed that there was a great deal of cleanup work to do in Birmingham, for the city was changing for the worse before his eyes. As a student of history, Hugo acknowledged its patterns. He knew that the environment, spiritual and physical, could be turned around. He also knew that his legal assaults against the unfeeling corporations, on behalf of his injured clients, would have an impact on the definition of the community.

But Black felt sadness about the historic reality he confronted—and anger too. The South was moving, rapidly, from a rural frontier, characterized by individualism, to an anomic urban center, characterized by disintegration of the family, crime, labor unrest, pornography, sinfulness, liquor, unfairness of working conditions, industrial injuries and deaths, as well as racial and ethnic clashes. While Black thrived as attorney in this urban cacophony, he sought comradeship beyond the Baptist Church for the solace and friendship it might provide a lonely man.

This seeking ultimately led him, for basic political reasons, to the Ku Klux Klan. But it also led to a marriage that linked Black with one of Birmingham's most respected families, the Foster clan. Always the ambitous advocate, as soon as Black "achieved prominence, [he] began to cement his power in exclusive suburbs, clubs, and marriage."[14] His constant seeking to belong, to be befriended, led to family residence on the fashionable Southside of Birmingham and membership in the established country club, as befitted the family of a successful lawyer. Sheldon Hackney captured these contradictions well, writing that Black somehow managed to balance the principles of the moral, crusading outsider with the behavior of an established Birmingham outsider trying to become an insider.[15]

Practicing Law in Birmingham

Birmingham was called the "Magic City"[16] for good reason. "Born" only six years after Appomattox, the city boasted only 38,000 residents by 1900. However, by 1910, three years after Hugo arrived in town, the population had rapidly expanded to 133,000—largely due to annexation of surrounding subdivisions into the city,[17] the abundance of natural wealth, coal and iron, the existence of a major rail line linking Birmingham to northern industrial centers, and the fact that Alabama industrial capitalists "kept faith and capital in the city." [18] The twenty-one-year-old-Black had moved from a country town of 350 to a growing mining center with all the attendant problems, including homelessness, poverty, homicides, and venereal diseases. [19]

And, in 1907, the year Hugo arrived from Ashland, the huge United States Steel Corporation moved to Birmingham to turn it into the Pittsburgh of the South. That corporation took over a great deal of the town and immediately became a dominant presence in the city, hiring poor whites and blacks at dirt-cheap wages.

Living in the "Murder Capital of the World," Black as an attorney quickly benefited from this ugly reality. [20] With slums populated by many of the white workers and by all of the blacks, such vices as gambling, prostitution and drunkenness, along with the occasional murder, were commonplace and "gave [it] the reputation of the nation's most crime-filled city." [21]

Black reacted in a number of ways. He "saw in Birmingham the drama of helpless people confronting the power of the big, absentee corporations that dominated their lives" [22] and acted aggressively in the courtroom for the poor and powerless. He brought suit on behalf of injured or dead workers against the evil "corporation" and began to represent the newly organized unions in their battles against the local industrial powers, this activity leading to his being labeled a "Bolshevik" by the Birmingham elite. [23]

For a young and somewhat radical lawyer, such legal behavior was the only way Black could move to build up a law practice in Birmingham. Never for a moment forgetting the pain and anguish of the yeomen farmers in Clay County, he quickly became known as the poor laborers' attorney. And, because of his focused preparations while living in Clay County, Black was a crafty, and successful advocate for his clients. Jinksie observed that Hugo "had a passion for the poor. He had a passion for the helpless and the poor." [24] He turned this passion into a very lucrative business, one that eventually propelled him into the world of state and national politics.

For the next few years, Hugo and his boyhood friend Barney Whatley were partners in the law firm of Black and Whatley. In addition to a fine legal mind, his new partner had another valuable talent: "Barney was one of the best mixers I have ever known." [25] Both of them were joiners who made the acquaintance of a great many people in Birmingham who, in turn, brought more and more clients to the firm. Barney, however, contracted tuberculosis and had to leave the area. He settled in Colorado, immediately became involved in the state's Democratic party, developed a very successful law firm, and continued his lifelong friendship with Hugo. [26]

Unlike other barristers in the South, who were poor, Black's singleness of purpose and intelligence led him to become Alabama's most successful civil lawyer in the first decades of the new century. Long after he left Birmingham for Washington, D.C., Black's reputation as a successful trial lawyer did not lose its luster. His behavior in front of juries was legendary, and stories of his successes continued to be told for decades in Birmingham.

Police Court Judge

Black appeared in many trial courts in the area and came to the attention of Circuit Judge A. O. Lane, who was a fellow member of Hugo's Knights of Pythias Lodge when he represented Willie Morton, a black prisoner who had been held in the system beyond his prison sentence, in 1909. This was Hugo's first civil jury trial in Birmingham and he worked hard to prepare his case.

The case focused on the infamous convict-lease system that offended Black so much. He categorically opposed the convict-lease arrangement and defended clients who were victimized by it. (A few years later, as president of the Alabama Anti–Convict Lease Association, he "helped get the State Legislature to abolish" the archaic system.)[27] Willie Morton was a convict leased to a large steel company by the local authorities. Because he had been held over beyond his term of imprisonment, Hugo's complaint was false imprisonment. Masterfully, exhibiting all the confidence and lawyerly skills he possessed, young Black parried all the pleadings that the steel company's expensive lawyer presented to Judge Lane. After presenting his evidence to the jury, Hugo quickly won a verdict for Morton for $137.50 plus costs.

The case had a positive impact on Black's career. His representation of Morton led Judge Lane to offer Hugo the position of police court judge. Black was initially "dumbfounded" by the judge's "proposition."[28] However, after thinking through the offer and its possibilities, he took the tough job in April 1911 (at an annual salary of $1,500), with the provision that the police court work would be finished by 9:30 A.M. each day so that he could continue building up his law practice.

He remained in that position until October 1912, when he resigned to return to his law practice full time. The job itself was a thankless one that more senior lawyers in the city avoided like the plague. The court in the city "was in a state of confusion. The docket was hopelessly congested and bondsmen flourished, while those who were unable to make bail languished in jail until the uncertain day when the court could find the time to try them."[29]

Almost instantly, Black became a local folk hero. Thanks to the creative writing of a local reporter, Charlie Mandy, everybody soon got to read about Judge Black's cases while having their breakfast. Mandy wrote a column for the *Birmingham Sun* that featured the colorful assortment of petty thieves, vagrants, and angry husbands and wives who appeared before the judge. All the stories showcased Hugo's wisdom, fairness, compassion, and humor.

One such story featured a white man who came late to Black's court, after his case had been called. Judge Black told the middle-aged man that he "always insisted on a prompt attendance on this court. It is the only way I can keep the docket clear," and then set aside the forfeiture as to the fine.

The accused visibly brightened, and before the judge could state the fine he smilingly said: "Say, old boy, make the fine as light as you can," his manner indicating a total unconsciousness of any flippancy. The request brought a covert smile from his honor and a broad grin from Clerk Bill. "You see, judge," he continued,

"I live with my old mother, she is over 80 years old and I am her only support." At the word "mother" Judge Black's rather stern expression softened, and the pen that was about to write $25 skipped the figure 2 and in his mildest tones the judge said, "Five dollars." The man dug down in his jeans and handed the clerk five silver dollars and departed.[30]

Thanks to Mandy, the good folk of Birmingham who read the paper also learned of "a colored belle named Lucy King" who appeared before Black, "Clara Williams, a member of the colored 400," and "John Glover, a tall, husky negro" charged with trespassing on a railroad. After letting Glover go with a ten-dollar fine, Black warned him that the next time "[I will] sentence you to life imprisonment, and if you outlive the sentence you will be hung. Next case."[31]

Black's police court work brought out a bias he had against homosexuals. As the Judge himself told Hugo Jr.,

> This fella had charged another fella with beating him up. The one charged admitted that he beat the stuffing out of the one who swore out the warrant, but said, "Judge, sir, this fella made advances to me." I took one look at the other fella's face and said, "Is that so?" He just dropped his head. So on my own, I threw out the charges and found the pervert guilty of disorderly conduct and gave him the maximum sentence. That kind of thing will destroy a society, Son.[32]

Junior wrote that the Judge "was always very reserved in his physical contact with the males he loved most. . . . He and I limited ourselves to handshakes. I never embraced him or kissed him on the cheek, because I knew that such demonstrations of affection between man and man made him uncomfortable."[33]

His work as a police court judge at these "morning matinees,"[34] while entertaining to readers who came to know him as "Hugo-to-Hell",[35] was an emotional experience, one that never left Black's mind. The work brought him into daily contact with poor, predominantly black prisoners. His view of criminal justice was a principled one, i.e., that people should be arrested for real crimes and not harrassed and arrested for questionable actions. For uninhibited Birmingham, it was a very radical one. The work also exposed him to clear violations of due process and to almost-daily examples of practical injustices.

Judge Black immediately impressed the legal community because he insisted on clearing the docket rapidly; there were no delays in his courtroom. When he stepped down in 1912, a decision supported by Judge Lane, the court's docket was clear and he had established "some healthy principles of elementary justice."[36] Hugo himself noted that the job was "a valuable experience and afforded me a broad insight into human nature."[37] A more mature Black recalled in 1971 his police judge experience: "I learned much about life in that position."[38]

As a result of the positive publicity surrounding his police court activities and his growing visibility as he continued to join more organizations, the Black and Davis law firm prospered. David J. Davis, a Yale Law School graduate, joined his friend Black in 1910, after Barney Whatley's poor health forced him to leave Alabama for Colorado. The young trial lawyer found himself arguing cases with greater frequency and with great success.

In his memoir, Hugo probably understated the reality when he recalled that "I had acquired a reputation for winning lawsuits, which brought me cases—some of them from other lawyers."[39] With this growing success, Black moved into new offices and, two years later, in 1914, made another important career decision. Although he was making over seventy-five hundred dollars a year, Black began to think about reentering public life in Jefferson County, Alabama, as its county prosecutor. After consulting with his friends, he decided to make the run because he felt strongly about the need to reform the then-weak and corrupt system of law enforcement there.

Birmingham's Prosecutor (Jefferson County)

After announcing his candidacy for the office of Jefferson County prosecutor, Black found himself in the middle of a four-man race for the position. The campaign itself raised a major and difficult issue: whether convict labor and the fee system, which was an integral element of local justice administration in the South, would continue in the county. Officers of the court, including police, received a salary generated from the fines paid by those arrested and convicted.[40]

However, the twenty eight year old lawyer developed a successful campaign strategy attacking the fee system. It was a grassroots technique that Black would use again when he ran for the U.S. Senate in 1926: He would travel about the county in an automobile, visiting every precinct in Jefferson County, meeting, face-to-face, as many voters as possible "in lodges, picnics, basket suppers, stores, basketball games."[41] Black talked with them about problems like the fee system that he as prosecutor could resolve. Attacking the system as immoral, Hugo stumped the backwoods, stating that "the people were tired of having hundreds of negroes arrested for shooting craps on pay day and crowding the jails with these petty offenses."[42]

On primary day, in the spring of 1914, he outpolled his three Democratic opponents and, in late November 1914, Black became the prosecutor of Jefferson County. His comments about his unexpected victory reveal a great deal about his intensity of purpose:

> "Lest someone think, 'How easy,' I hasten to add that this victory, like every one I have ever had, *was the result of hard, concentrated work, not only during eight and one half months of active campaigning but during all of my first seven years in Birmingham."* . . . Only seven years after the young hillbilly from Clay County arrived, almost a total stranger in Jefferson, Alabama's most populous county, he was elected its Prosecuting Attorney by the people."[43] (my emphasis)

On taking office, Black immediately confronted the problems of the fee system and convict labor. Convict leasing replaced slavery in many towns across the South after the Civil War. Because of the large number of blacks in jails, "mines, cotton mills, and steel companies leased convicts from the state, taking on the problems of feeding, housing, and discipline in return for cheap labor."[44]

In addition to dealing with convict leasing, when he moved to the courthouse with his small staff, Black found another problem: a clogged docket. There were over three thousand criminal cases awaiting trials; nearly one hundred of them were murder cases. He also found that incarceration fees, called "turn key" fees, were charged for everything: entering and exiting the jail, arrest, bond, and even sleeping and eating. Because he had pledged to dismiss all cases "against honest-to-goodness working payday crapshooters,"[45] the new prosecutor released five hundred prisoners who had been charged only with this offense. To quickly dispose of the murder cases awaiting trial, Black had judges from other parts of the state assigned to Jefferson County. Within a year, all the capital cases had been tried, including one that was ten years old.

In 1915, Black uncovered the brutal third-degree measures used by the police in Bessemer, a suburb of Birmingham, to obtain confessions from black suspects. Although the Bessemer district was outside his county jurisdiction, Black presented information to the grand jury, who adopted his report and ended the abuse.[46] And he vigorously pursued bootleggers, brewers, and distillers. As one of his Alabama supporters wrote, these groups "hated Black . . . because they could not corrupt him as they have bought a large proportion of law enforcement officers in every city across the United States."[47]

While he had run as an antiestablishment candidate, "nothing he ever did was very far away from the [Birmingham] mainstream."[48] A resident of the city for barely seven years when he became solicitor, Hugo was still an outsider who "accomplished what the legal establishment and the general public wanted him to accomplish."[49] Seeking community, Black was nevertheless still outside the magic circle because of his roots and his values.

By the summer of 1917, the prosecutor had run afoul of some special interests in the state, especially the liquor and brewery industries, newspaper owners, and the downstate Bourbon Democrats. Vigorously prohibitionist, loathing alcohol ever since he saw what it did to his father and brother, Black ran into the monied interests who were in favor of keeping Birmingham very wet and thus very supportive of the freedom of the press to accept liquor ads.

For many months, he had to fend off his opponents' efforts to curtail the power of his office. Evidently, Joe Tate, the circuit solicitor and an enemy of Hugo's on the liquor issue, began to challenge the constitutionality of the county solicitor's office's jurisdiction. In Jefferson County, the jurisdictions of the two offices overlapped, and Tate began to "attack [Black's] authority."[50] Finally, confronted with a state supreme court ruling that he had to use some of Tate's staff attorneys on his staff, Black resigned in August 1917.[51]

Why would a defiant young prosecutor uncharacteristically abandon a fight with his enemies? According to his son Hugo Jr., his father backed off in great part because of his personal unhappiness over a love affair that he had to end at that time.

Black had fallen in love with a girl whose parents were orthodox Jews.[52] Evidently they wanted to marry, but when her parents found out he was not Jewish, she was forbidden ever to see Hugo again, or the parents would sit shivah[53] in memory of their "departed" daughter if she married a goy (a non-Jew). Distraught, the young man left for the army shortly afterwards. For Black, who did not like war, leaving the prosecutor's office and entering the army was an escape. It was the only occasion during his life that he "escaped" a painful reality in such a manner.

Clearly, the experiences as police judge and prosecutor were searing ones for Hugo. He saw the seamy, ugly real-world life of poor people in the new industrial society and tried to remedy some of the wrongs and injustices, sometimes succeeding. As William O. Douglas later observed, both he and Black "were exposed to raw-boned experiences" due to the growth of industrialization, and those experiences left indelible marks on these brilliant, shrewd jurists.[54]

The Army, Loves, and Marriage

At the time of Hugo's resignation as county prosecutor, America was formally involved in World War I. He was opposed to our entering the European conflict. "There is to me no glamour in war," remarked Black later.[55] However, once war was declared and although he was overage, he enlisted in the U.S. Army. Assigned to the field artillery, Black learned trigonometry from a high school text and spent three very hard months at officers' training school.

He was commissioned a captain in the army field artillery and was stationed near Chattanooga, Tennessee. During the war Black remained Stateside, training soldiers, while his regiment, the Eighty-first Field Artillery, traveled to France. The day they arrived in the trenches, November 11, 1918, the Armistice was signed.

With the end of the war, Black returned to his law practice in Birmingham. As soon as word got around that he was back in legal business, "clients began to hire me immediately," he recalled in his memoir.[56] Black also retained one of the army officers who had trained him, Major Crampton Harris, "taking him into [his firm] as a partner."[57] Harris, who soon became the Cyclops of the Birmingham Ku Klux Klan Klavern, persuaded Hugo to join the Klan in 1923.

Black was an aggressive trial advocate who used all the skills of the profession to win cases. A view of trial transcripts featuring Hugo representing a poor, injured plaintiff, black or white, gives one the picture of a well-prepared advocate who, like a grand chess master, plotted out his moves five moves ahead of his opponent. And if it was a black person he represented, Black did not think twice about use of the vernacular in front of the jurors: "Was he standing at the door where this nigger woman [Black's client, Mary Miniard] came in?"[58]

Black was wealthy, making about sixty thousand dollars annually, a "phenomenal salary for a lawyer in 1920's Alabama."[59] He was successful because he was innovative, energetic, and outgoing—too much so for some of his acquaintances and legal rivals, who nicknamed him "Ego" Black.[60] As his son commented, "no matter how much one of them [fellow lawyers in Birmingham] might have disliked Hugo, everyone conceded that he was practically unbeatable in the courtroom. 'Old Ego had a way in there. You can't take that away from him.' "[61]

"Ego" Black had so much confidence in his ability to persuade an Alabama jury that he seldom asked the judge to discharge a juror. Invariably, he would look over the potential jurors, turn to the judge, say that he would " 'take the jury in the box,' and turn around and smile at them. Cockiest lawyer ever I seen," said Jake Taylor, a contemporary of Black's during his halcyon trial lawyering days in Birmingham.[62]

On his return to Birmingham after the War ended, walking up a steep incline, Hugo "saw a beautiful young lady struggling up the hill."[63] That was his first sighting of Josephine Foster, daughter of a prominent member of the Birmingham "landed aristocracy,"[64] Dr. Sterling J. Foster. Although thirteen years older than Josephine, Hugo fell in love immediately. He was smitten "by her beauty and charm."[65] As he said years later, she "just seemed to have a sweet nobility about her. . . . She just seemed to reflect a spiritual quality."[66] However, Josephine, a lovely, popular young woman who, at one time in her social life, had three dates in the same day, "was not stricken with love for Hugo at the very beginning."[67]

After aggressively courting her for over two years, competing with two other suitors during this time, Hugo married Josephine on February 23, 1921—without her parents' approval. They believed that she married below her station; her husband was seen as a radical Bolshevik of sorts, an outsider who did not belong in the company of families like the Fosters. Ironically, after Hugo married Josephine, he found out that Dr. Foster, while outwardly the picture of Birmingham high society, was actually bankrupt. Black, the dutiful son-in-law, immediately developed a scheme to provide the Foster's with funds so that they could continue to live in the style of the Birmingham establishment. This compassionate largesse continued for decades until the Fosters died.

Josephine, years later, confided in Hugo Jr. about his father's self-confidence in those stressful times: "I have never seen any man before with so much confidence. He assumed that I was fated to marry him and that everybody else was out of the picture. He was like an irresistible force; he just kept coming at me. . . . He seemed so sophisticated yet somehow so youthful. . . . Nobody *looked* at me with such total adoration"[68] (my emphasis)

Hugo Jr. was born in 1922, a year after the wedding. Sterling Foster, the second son, was born in 1924. Their only daughter, Martha Josephine, or Jo-Jo as she was called by all except her father, was born in 1933.

Josephine, a dutiful and sensitive spouse, always remained two paces behind her husband throughout their married life. Disappointed in having to leave the comfortable confines of Southside Birmingham, Josephine was unable to cope with Hugo's assertiveness and success in national politics.

Although she became quite popular in Washington and was asked to serve as the chair of various women's groups on Capitol Hill, she was deeply unhappy and unfulfilled until the end of her life. She began to write poetry and then tried her hand at short stories, sending out essays under assumed names. She even took creative writing classes at a local university. However, she always received rejection slips from editors.

After their arrival in Washington in 1927, Josephine drifted in and out of melancholia and depression throughout the 1930s and '40s. Ironically, while going through her own personal hell, she was sought out by many others, wives of senators, Supreme Court justices, "even the wife of a future President," who were troubled.[69] They knew her capacity to offer advice that enabled them to cope with their own problems. Hugo would ask Josephine if he caused her bouts of depression and she gently dissuaded him from that notion. As his son recalled, "occasionally tears came into my father's eyes because he could do nothing, . . . he could only say, 'I am helpless.' "[70]

But no one was able to lift her spirits, and "she continued to suffer real torture"[71] until she began painting. That outlet enabled her to express herself in a wonderfully positive way, and a studio was built in their new Alexandria home. She won prizes and, for the first time in her life, was praised for her creative talent. Josephine did seem to shake the bouts of depression after she began painting, but then, tragically, she took her life on December 7, 1951. A few months before her sudden death, at the young age of 52, she confided to her oldest son: "I have worked through this thing. I have worked through it. I have never felt such peace in all my life."[72]

Her daughter Jo-Jo did not and still does not believe that Josephine committed suicide (there was no note). Although Josephine was melancholy and was diagnosed and treated for clinical depression, she died, Jo-Jo believes, because of two inter-related facts: Josephine's increased reliance on sleeping pills and her growing insomnia. Jo-Jo insists that Josephine unintentionally took a fatal overdose of sleeping pills, for her insomnia.[73]

The letters written by the Judge to Josephine, his sons, and close friends were often poignant and valiantly tried to disguise the malady his wife experienced throughout their married life. In a letter to his wife, hospitalized at the time, immediately after Japan's attack on Pearl Harbor, Black gently informed her of the attack, told her about the boys and "little Josephine" and "how much we miss you, but also how much we want you to do that which is best for your complete recovery. . . . Devotedly, Hugo."[74]

During these regular, extended bouts of depression that led frequently to Josphine's institutionalization, Black became a doting single parent. Furthermore, he continued to inform his children of "Mother's" condition even when they were grown. "Mother is still better," he wrote to Hugo Jr. in 1946, "but I hope you write her a short note right away. It is important that you do this, and that you mention her in any letter you write to me. This is a good booster for her."[75] In another letter to his eldest son, Black asked him to write Josephine because "she has not been feeling well for several weeks." In August 1944, Black thanked Hugo Jr. for the letter he had sent to his mother: "For the first time in a number of years she has been able to sleep without taking medication of any kind."

During World War II, when not being treated by physicians and psychologists for melancholia, Josephine served as a Grey Lady, visiting wounded soldiers in local hospitals. That was not very helpful because she saw in the wounded soldiers her two sons. "She evidently thinks of you and Sterling every time she sees anyone of them," wrote the father to his oldest son. "This has demonstrated the fact that failure to hear from you is very injurious to her. When I arrived home Friday night, before you were expected to call—I found her in tears. . . . I have told you this not in any spirit of criticism, but because I was sure you want to know about it in order that you might not give her pain by your failure to write."[76]

In another letter to his oldest son, Black informed him that Mother "has not been doing quite so well the last two or three weeks and has now gone to spend the weekend, probably including Monday, at Dr. Katzenelbogen's country place. In her present condition you will agree that it is necessary that she have the fewest possible burdens."[77]

But the Justice wrote joyfully to his oldest son in 1949 that Josephine "was swimming on the high tide of her painting achievements. She entered pictures in three contests—two in Washington and one in New York. . . . Yesterday she was somewhat astonished to receive a notice to 'Miss Josephine Black' stating that her picture had been accepted in the much larger and more highly competitive New York contest." Yet, typically Black closed the letter by lecturing Hugo Jr. on the importance of a "generous business practice" rather than a narrow labor law business. And, of course, there was the Greek classic that Hugo Jr. had to pick up, or else Black would buy him a copy. This particular letter featured a short essay on the *Annals* of Tacitus.[78]

Jo-Jo claimed that her father was terrified only once in his life. Hugo know Josephine's suffering but was hopelessly frustrated because there was, in that era before Prozac, little that could be done to minimize her depression. Black tried a number of experimental medical "cures," including hospitalization and electric shock therapy, but nothing worked. These continual failures, over twenty five years, "drove Black apoplectic with anger, frustration, and terror."[79]

Tragically, in December 1951, Josephine was dead. Her suicide profoundly affected the Justice. He could not imagine her gone. Hugo Jr. wrote about the instant he saw his surviving parent when he arrived at the Black home in Alexandria after her death: "[My father had] sunk into [a] pitiful state. . . . The figure there looked like nothing I'd ever seen before. He just sat staring straight ahead, tears shining on his face, his teeth grinding together."[80]

It was a heartbreaking period for the Judge, and colleagues on the Court on infrequent occasions saw Hugo visibly burdened with the extreme sadness of his wife's illness and her death. Everybody knew of Josephine's "sparkle and vivacity that made her seem so young."[81] As the distraught Black told his oldest child, "Son, there's no such thing as natural justice. That's the best human being ever I ran into, the best, sweetest, most thoughtful, most unselfish. She ought to be the last to die of her generation—not one of the first. Life is wrong—it's just wrong."[82]

After his 1921 marriage, Black continued to be the state's most successful attorney, and that success extended to a few scandalous cases won by him. The most sensational was his firm's defense of Edwin Stephenson, a lay Methodist minister charged with the murder of a Catholic priest, Father James E. Coyle, who had been the leader of the Birmingham Catholic community since the turn of the century.

Stephenson had admitted killing the priest in a fit of rage because Coyle had married Stephenson's daughter to a young Puerto Rican Catholic. Even though the confession was a valid one, "thanks to the strong anti-Catholic sentiments which pervaded Birmingham and to the courtroom tactics of his counsel," Black's partner, Crampton Harris, Stephenson was freed. The jury accepted Harris's "temporary insanity" defense as well as racist comments in closing argument, where Harris "urged the jury to show the world, by their verdict, that Birmingham's Protestants would not allow their daughters to be proselyted by Catholics."[83]

Hugo also continued to join organizations after his army stint in order to develop new clients, to keep his name in the minds of his fellow citizens, and to partake of the communal fellowship associated with such fraternal associations. Despite the fact that many of the Birmingham elite continued to "snub" Black while he resided in the city,[84] he did join the American Legion, the Praetorians, the Fraternal Order of Moose, and the Odd Fellows. And, in a fateful moment in 1923, after his firm's Stephenson victory, Hugo Black joined the Birmingham Ku Klux Klan Klavern in which his law partner, Crampton Harris, was an officer.

Joining the Ku Klux Klan

"Raw ambition" drove Black to join the Klan.[85] Because of his anticorporation beliefs, opposition to economic monopolies,[86] and defense of the little men, black and white, in personal injury lawsuits against the large corporations, he was cut off from the political support of the Big Mules, the downstate Bourban Democratic leaders. For Hugo Black to make any move politically, certainly a run for statewide office, he needed strong political support from groups that could counterbalance the political strength of the monied interests in Alabama. The Klan was that counterbalance, said Buddy Cooper, Hugo's first law clerk and a close friend of the Black family. Black's joining the Klan "simply was a politically inspired instance of when Jove nodded."[87]

Unlike the first Klan that arose after the Civil War when Union troops were the occupying power in the South and the Klan terrorized in the night, the second Klan marched down Main Street, "voted for Klan-endorsed political candidates . . . [and were] less interested in the lynchings that were performed by the criminal element than in winning elections."[88]

The second Klan of the 1920s did not have a great many "men of property and social power who made up the local economic elite." Rather, the Klan after World War I, for the most part consisted of Hugo's kind of clients, almost three million "clerical workers, small-business owners, independent professionals, and farmers."[89] The second Klan was, as well, a "protest movement of poor, marginal whites."[90] What Hugo perceived in 1920s Alabama was the Klan as a powerful electoral force, more powerful than the Bourbons because of the large numbers of people who listened to the Klan's leaders and voted as they were told. He saw a Klan consisting of men like his former army major and law partner Crampton Harris, as well as poor workers, impoverished farmers, and lower-middle-class entrepreneurs. What Hugo saw were people he had worked with and represented all his professional life since arriving in Birmingham.

So Black quickly concluded that, if he wanted to move—successfully—into politics and public service, he had to get the support of the Klan's leadership and, through them, the Klan's rank and file. While never overtly supporting the raw, brutal violence of the Klan, Black nevertheless saw the Klan as a group that reflected the needs and the visions of his most natural voting constituency, poor and middle class whites who populated both the rural areas as well as the new cities in Alabama like Birmingham and Bessemer and Montgomery.

The second Klan was built upon a "fund of folk memory and reverence for the 'Lost Cause,' a set of emotions and passions more intense than those that inspired allegiance to the Elks or Moose."[91] These new Klansmen and Klanswomen, sought to revive and glorify the past through electoral victories, for, in the 1920s, they had sufficient voting strength in the state to send Hugo Black to the U.S. Senate.

Hugo Black, born of the South, whose father and other relatives were wounded or killed for the South in the Civil War, must have been touched by the Klan's revival of community memories. The Klan, however, also reflected the miseries in the South of the 1920s, miseries keenly felt by poor white Alabamans, the men who visited Hugo's law offices and made Hugo the most successful trial lawyer in Alabama.

In post–World War I Birmingham, the revived Klan and the Anti-Saloon League were very powerful politically active pressure groups. "In Alabama," wrote a newspaper editor at the time, "it is hard to tell where the [Anti-Saloon] League ends and the Klan begins."[92] In this decade, a person running for statewide political office in Alabama could not offend either group without risking a loss at the polls. The Klan in Birmingham, the center of Klan power in the state, controlled eighteen thousand of the city's thirty-two thousand registered voters.[93] Support from the Klan meant sure victory for a candidate in Alabama in the years after the First World War; opposition by the Klan meant sure defeat.

Black's joining the Klan in 1923, in front of over seventeen hundred other Klansmen who were members of the Robert E. Lee Chapter, at a time when that group was doing a "booming"[94] business in the state, was nothing but "an act of purest expediency."[95] Although the Judge in later years said that he believed he was "doing the right thing even though I don't like the Klan," there is evidence that he marched in Klan parades in 1923 and 1924. And dressed in his full KKK regalia, he gave a rousing speech at a local Klavern meeting in Greensboro, Alabama, as reported in the press.[96]

Hirem Evans, the Imperial Wizard of the regional Klan, was a longtime friend. William Simmons, one of the founders of the second Klan, was a Clay County buddy. Hugo's two closest friends in Birmingham, Ben Ray and Hugh Locke— the former one of the first assistants Black brought into the county prosecutor's office and the latter to become an aide to Senator Black in Washington— were Klansmen. Finally, Alabama's Grand Dragon, James Esdale, was a friend and confidant who managed Black's succcessful 1926 campaign for the U.S. Senate.[97]

Hugo told his wife that "the main reason he joined was so that he would have an equal chance in trying cases before jurors who were largely Klan members in Alabama at that time and because most of the defendants as well as most of the lawyers who represented corporations and who opposed Hugo were also members."[98] And the Judge later told a *New York Times* reporter that "he was trying a lot of cases against corporations, jury cases, and I found out that all the corporation lawyers were in the Klan. A lot of jurors were too, so I figured I'd better be even up. . . . I wanted that even chance with the juries."[99]

Even Black's liberal colleague on the Court, William O. Douglas, maintained that, "like all trial lawyers, Hugo Black depended heavily upon the favor of local people who made up juries. The Klan was the biggest, most powerful club in the South and Hugo Black joined it."[100] But for sixteen years, from 1907 to 1923, Black saw no need to join such an organization and was never-the-less the most successful personal injury lawyer in the state. Joining the Klan was clearly a strategic political move.

When Black did run for the U.S. Senate, James Esdale, the Grand Dragon of the Alabama Klan, took control of the day-to-day management of his campaign. Through Esdale's efforts, Hugo received the full voting support of the Klan in that election,[101] and won easily, defeating the organized interests backing the Bourbon, Big Mule candidate. Black's involvement with the Klan, in the years prior to his move to Washington, D.C., was obviously "extensive and ardent."[102]

Interestingly, again as a matter of expediency, a month after Black decided in June 1925 to run for the U.S. Senate seat of Oscar Underwood, who had announced his retirement, he formally resigned from the Klan. "In a deliberate act of political strategy, he resigned as secretly as he had joined almost two years before."[103] Black silently resigned after meeting with a small group of Klansmen friends to plot his political future,[104] and then proceeded to work with Esdale for over six months, speaking at Klavern meetings, making political speeches in the local courthouse square as Klan members in the crowd passed word that Black was "their candidate."[105]

If, towards the end of his life, the Justice admitted that joining the Klan was his biggest error, a younger Black in 1923 felt it was an imperative move if he wanted to win a primary election for public office. Unlike his good U.S. Senate friend, Harry S Truman, who hated the Klan and turned down Klan support, thereby losing an early election in Missouri, Hugo did not reject the Klan. Indeed, he courted their support, and the Klanners' votes gave him his 1926 senatorial victory.

Running for the U.S. Senate

During the winter of 1925, Black told his former law partner, David J. Davis, who had left the firm in 1913 but remained a close friend, "I've got an idea I'd like to run for the Senate."[106] The incumbent, Oscar W. Underwood, who was extremely vulnerable due to his economic conservatism and his "open defiance of the Klan,"[107] announced his retirement from the Senate in early July 1925. On July 9, 1925, Hugo wrote a letter to J. W. Hamilton, Kligrapp of the Robert E. Lee Klan No. 1 in Birmingham: "Dear Sir Klansman: Beg to tender you herewith my resignation as a member of the Ku Klux Klan, effective from this date on. Yours, I.T.S.U.B. [In The Sacred, Unfailing Bond], Hugo L. Black."[108] He then announced a campaign for the Senate seat that would be waged "along the line of merit and principle alone."[109] Black began his "underdog" campaign a full six months prior to the other Democratic candidates.

It was a truly unusual campaign, for Hugo was bucking traditional politics in Alabama. The state "had not seen anything like the Black race. Candidates were customarily members of the established ruling class, elitists who *stood* for office" (my emphasis).[110] Here was an outsider, a very successful trial lawyer to be sure, but still an outsider *running* for elected office! Further galling to the Birmingham and Bourbon establishment was the fact that Black (although quite wealthy) was running as the candidate of the "poor people," the only one who had the support of the Klan in Alabama.

His announcement focused on his close association with the common man in Alabama:

> We are in this fight to the finish, and will wage an aggressive campaign in every county of the State. This office is the highest honor within the gift of our people, and should be given only to one who best represents the sentiments and welfare of the people of Alabama. This office must not be purchased. . . . Our organization will be devoted to presenting honest principles and policies to the people, and a candid exposition of the questions affecting public interest. In this cause we are enlisted to win. This campaign will be conducted on our part entirely by voluntary workers, and carried directly to the people of the State.[111]

With his announcement out of the way, along with his secret resignation from the Klan, Black implemented a strategy for a statewide race in which he would be in a competition with four other Democratic candidates, all well known across the state and all wealthy Bourbon Democrats, for the seat vacated by Underwood.

Other than his successful race for the county solicitor's position, Black had no electoral experience, certainly none at the statewide level. "Not many people considered him a serious contender," said his oldest son later of Hugo's 1925 announcement.[112]

His opponents were John Bankhead, the son of a former, very popular U.S. senator; Thomas E. Kilby, a respected former governor of Alabama; Breck Musgrove, a wealthy coal mine owner/operator, and James J. Mayfield of Birmingham, a highly regarded Alabama Supreme Court judge. For the unknown outsider/underdog Hugo Black, it was to be a campaign by him, the "poor people's" candidate, against the candidates of privilege and wealth. "I am personally of the opinion that there have been so many millionaires and corporation lawyers in the U.S. Senate that the people rarely ever have a representative," wrote Black to a family member at the time of his announcement. His hopes, he wrote, rested with the "DRY PROTESTANT-PROGRESSIVE VOTERS of the State of Alabama."[113]

The Black senatorial campaign strategy was similar to that of the campaign he ran in 1914 for prosecutor of Jefferson County; it was based on Hugo's "extraordinary charisma."[114] He conducted a largely one man race and traveled extensively across the state, into the smallest towns and hamlets, with his "common man" theme. On many of these automobile swings throughout Alabama, Black would take his two sons with him but not his wife, so that everyone he met knew that he was a good Christian family man.

He spread his message with outstanding stump speeches and in conversations with locals while playing checkers with the village champion. Nearly always,

Black would beat the person handily, but during the game, he would be talking to the onlookers, handing them his cards, and asking them to give him their votes. As Hugo Jr. noted some years later, his father "knew that most rural Alabamians thought that excellence in checkers signified excellence of mind and character."[115]

When Hugo returned to Birmingham, his pocket was full of the names of men whom he'd met and beat in checkers. Like clockwork, he would send them a personal letter and additional cards for them to hand out, always thanking them for helping him beat the monied interests in the state. And, as a perusal of the Black files in the Library of Congress will attest, he recorded every name in the dozens of little black books he always locked up in his small black safe.

Hugo answered all letters sent to him, stuffing the envelopes with campaign literature, including cards and stickers. Writing a Mr. D. C. Arthur, of Bon Secour, Alabama, a newly announced Black supporter, the Judge reminded Arthur of his leanings:

> I know the needs of the people and if elected to the U.S. Senate I can work in behalf of the whole people without having any strings attached to me by any selfish corporate interests. Since beginning my practice of law in Birmingham I have had the opportunity of representing practically every big utility corporation which does business in this city and vicinity, but have always fought on the other side, preferring to be always on the side of the people.

Black closed the letter by asking Arthur to circulate the auto windshield stickers, placards, and small cards enclosed. He also asked him to send a letter "stating the situation with reference to the Senatorial race in your community as you see it."[116] In his effort to capture all information and control as much as possible the environment around him, Black kept detailed lists of persons who supported him—as well as those who vigorously opposed him.

Decades later, Hugo was interviewing Elizabeth Seay DeMeritte, who would become his secretary and then, a few years after Josephine's death, his second wife. When she sat down, the Judge opened his old black safe, unlocked a small compartment, and took out a little black book, one of his dozens of old campaign volumes. After opening the worn book, Black thumbed through it and announced to the dumbfounded woman that her daddy had campaigned against Black. The Judge told her that he "knew her father very well. I also knew his brother in Pratt City, Dr. Cleveland Seay. Your uncle was one of my warmest supporters in my race for county solicitor and later for the U.S. Senate. Your father never was for me; we were on opposite sides of the fence politically. I was a strong prohibitionist and he was anti-. However, I liked your father."[117]

Elizabeth took the job immediately after this incident. Leaving the Judge's chambers, she was warned about him by the exiting secretary: "He gets very involved with people. He'll take over and try to change your life, your personality and everything about you."[118]

Black controlled the 1926 election and kept detailed records of the campaign, which take up yards of space in the Hugo Black collection in the Manuscript Division of the Library of Congress. He collected these records in alphabetical order by county. Names were on slips of paper, with a notation that the person "offered their assistance to Hugo."[119]

When he was in the Senate, he obviously kept up with the creation of these records, including lists of school board trustees and bus drivers, alphabetical by county. All sixty-seven Alabama counties were covered in his lists, which grew literally day by day as letters came in to Black from constituents offering their support. The Judge's compulsive list-making efforts paid off at election time. Planning, as he said, was everything, and Black was the consummate recorder of names and deeds.

Black traveled back to Clay County on March 20, 1926, to formally open up his campaign and to inaugurate his "speech" to former friends and neighbors, reflecting the strategy he would use throughout the campaign. "I am," he said, "happy to be home again." He pointed out that the "times cry aloud for men in public office who have not lost the common touch." He talked of power concentrations and of "blocs and cliques and rings" wielding power in Washington. And he spoke of the people electing public officials who would not be in control of these powerful forces. Those interests, he said,

> have never shaped my ideals, fashioned my political creed, nor helped me in my aspirations for public office. They have not been a part of my environment. I am not a millionaire. . . . My father was a farmer. I have no hereditary claim to office, but is there any clause in our Constitution which says the son of a Senator shall be Senator, but the son of a farmer must always be a farmer?

Black then talked about the major planks in his campaign. "I am now and have always been a prohibitionist in theory and in practice"; in other words, he was not "politically dry and personally wet." On the question of tariffs and taxes, he noted that "the Democratic party has always opposed high tariffs. . . . Tariff and taxes alike, when imposed, should not unduly burden the toiling many for the idle few." He also supported the improvement of roads, rivers and harbors, "fully realizing the[ir] absolute necessity." Hugo spoke strongly on behalf of cheap fertilizer, for its availability would mean "profit and prosperity to the farmer." In that context he was supportive of the Muscle Shoals electricity project providing such inexpensive material to the farmers and against having it sold to the Alabama Power Company (see page 76).

Black's nativistic sympathies emerged when he spoke of the immigration problem: "The greater proportion [of immigrants] however, are ignorant, illiterate and wholly incapable of appreciating, during a lifetime, the ideals and duties of American citizenship," said Hugo. "The melting pot idea is dangerous to our national inheritance," he concluded. "I oppose further immigration, and always believe our nation would be greatly benefitted by closing the gates until such time as we can Americanize and educate those already here. This nation has cost too much in sacrifice, toil, and blood to jeopardize its safety in order to swell the profits of Millionaire Coal Operators, Millionaire Mill-Owners and the Millionaire Steel-Makers."

Turning to veterans' issues, Black recognized the "debt of gratitude to the boys who left their homes to serve in the World War." He, too, was concerned about their economic well-being after their sacrifice, and he bitterly lashed out against the tragedy of the growing pauperism of veterans. "If I am your United States Senator, and it is in my power to do so, no Honorably Discharged soldier shall die a *pauper's death.* [his emphasis] It is a tragic generosity that extends the debts of Italy for 62 years at 1½%, and lets loyal American soldiers die neglected paupers."

Black closed with a reminder about his campaign finances. The law limited him to an expenditure of ten thousand dollars. Declaring he would run a clean campaign in this regard, he commented that "what I cannot do directly, I shall not do indirectly. You will, therefore, receive no multitudinous literature and advertisements in my behalf, from imaginary Clubs." He could not and would not compete with millionaire opponents; he would be bought by no one, he concluded. "If you want a United States Senator who is willing to buy the help of political parasites and machine politicians, you do not want me." [120]

It was an immensely popular speech. People loved the rhetoric, especially when he said that "no living man will receive one penny from me for his support." One of his slogans, presented in that first speech and used continually as a basic campaign theme in his effort to defeat the Bourbon Big Mules, was "Does a son of Senator always have to be a Senator and the son of a farmer always have to be a farmer?"

His second wife, Elizabeth, told of how the slogan came about. It was a typical Black story. Hugo had been traveling the backroads of Alabama when he stopped his car and approached a farmer tending his fields. He introduced himself and gave his card to the farmer, who returned it to Black and said he couldn't vote for him, he was voting for John Bankhead because Bankhead's father was a good Senator, "so I thought I ought to vote for the son."

Hugo asked the farmer if he had a son; finding that the man did, Black asked: "Do you plan to educate him and try to see that he gets opportunities in life?" The farmer answered yes, and then Hugo asked him if his son might become probate judge of the county someday. Again, the farmer answered affirmatively. "He can't do that!" Black retorted, because "Wilbur Nolan is the Probate Judge and he has a son. According to your theory, his son should get the job. Wilbur has made the County a good Probate Judge." The farmer paused, asked for Hugo's campaign card and for "spares" to give "to all his friends." The campaign slogan emerged from that chance encounter in a cotton field between Black and a poor farmer: "Does the son of a Senator always have to be a Senator and the son of a farmer *always* have to be a farmer?" [121]

Running as the "poor man's candidate," Black's primary campaign slogan, spoken in that first Clay County speech, was "I am not now, and have never been a railroad, power company, or a corporation lawyer." [122] At rallies in Courthouse squares across the state, with Klansmen in the crowd whispering their support, Hugo continued to argue in favor of veterans benefits, Prohibition, better roads, cheap fertilizer, and limits on immigration to the United States.

He was considered by most observers of the 1926 primary to be an outsider, an underdog. But Black toiled tirelessly to attract voters—and he was ever so clever in this task. For example, the popular Bankhead and Kilby held a two-person debate, one that obviously excluded Hugo. And so he developed a plan to capitalize on the matter. Black hired "an old colored man" to sit on a stationary carriage attached to an old mare. The rig was parked outside the city hall where Bankhead and Kilby were debating. There were two signs, identical, attached to the rig. They said, in bold letters: "BANKHEAD SAYS THAT KILBY WILL NOT DO. KILBY SAYS THAT BANKHEAD WILL NOT DO. THEY ARE BOTH RIGHT. VOTE FOR HUGO BLACK." The ploy was a huge success, embarrassing both Bankhead and Kilby while attracting additional votes for Hugo.[123]

Black's secret association with the Klan meant that he was a welcomed speaker in almost 150 Klaverns across the state of Alabama. Esdale, his campaign manager and the state's Klan leader, "arranged for Black to spend six months speaking at Klavern meetings on topics of general interest," including his views on immigration and Catholics.[124]

And these efforts succeeded—much to the surprise and chagrin of his more well known opponents. The underdog candidate visited fifty-seven of the sixty-seven Alabama counties and won forty-two of them in the Democratic primary. Hugo's total of 84,877 votes, 32 percent of the votes cast in a field of five candidates, "came uncannily close to the estimated total of Klan membership in Alabama in 1926."[125]

Weeks after winning the Democratic primary, Black spoke at a victory rally attended by thousands of hooded Klansmen. He thanked his Klan friends for their steely commitment to

> American manhood and womanhood, revering virtue of the mother race, loving the pride of the Anglo-Saxon spirit—and I love it—true to the heaven born principles of liberty which were written in the Constitution of this country, and in the great historical documents, straight from the heart of Anglo-Saxon patriots.[126]

There were, however, many people in Alabama who could not vote for Black in the Democratic primary. The state's black citizens were unable to participate in primary elections at that time. Hugo received a poignant letter from one of them, the Reverend W. H. Hunt, of Birmingham: "I regret very much that I cannot cast a vote for you, in the primary election tomorrow; as the state of Alabama does not admit colored voters in the primary."[127] (Years later, as an associate justice of the U.S. Supreme Court, Black had the pleasure of overturning state voting laws that prohibited blacks from participating in primary elections because of their race.)[128]

In November 1926, Black won the general election with a margin of seventy thousand votes (ninety-two thousand votes to twenty-two thousand votes). The big winner in Alabama elections in 1926, however, was the Ku Klux Klan. Their candidates for U.S. senator and governor, Black and Bibb Graves, won handily. The new senator-elect was to join another official long supported by the Alabama Klan, Senator Thomas "Tom-Tom" Heflin. Noted one political observer: Alabama was "the most completely Klan-controlled state in the union."[129] However, times change; within a year, due to growing revulsion evoked by the Klan's increased use of violence, membership dropped precipitately.

And so Black and his family—at that time consisting of his wife Josephine and his two very young sons, Hugo Jr., and Sterling—packed up and went off to Washington, D.C., to reside for a few years in a white ivy-covered bungalow home on Cathedral Avenue. He was forty years old. The first twenty years of his life had been spent living and learning in a rural village and in a modest law school. The next twenty years were spent, for the most part, in Birmingham, Alabama, where Hugo learned about the horrors of life in a laissez-faire industrial America. He brought both sets of experiences with him as the "poor people's candidate" to the nation's capital. Black had staked his future on that theme and, as the next phase of his life unfolded, became a forceful advocate for a variety of public policies that would aid "his" people.

CHAPTER FOUR

Senator from Alabama

ewly elected junior U.S. Senator Hugo L. Black faced a number of serious problems. First of all, he had never served a day in his life as a state legislator! With no experience, Black was soon to march off to enter the nation's most elite legislative club.

Another problem Black had to address was the manner in which he was presented in the media to the world beyond the Alabama borders: as a country buffoon and a Klansman with little native intelligence. After all, if Black's campaign battles over such issues as the availability of cheap fertilizer, improvement of the mud roads in rural Alabama, the evils of industrialization and monopoly, and keeping Alabama dry were any indication of the breadth of his concerns, then the Senate would have to put up with another Southern redneck, another "Tom Tom" Heflin, Alabama's senior U.S. Senator, who was known only for his hatred of blacks and his stereotypical Southern political oratory.

After the election results were in, the always-focused Black knew he had to prepare for confronting yet another "outsider" scenario, much like the reality that confronted him when, in 1907, he arrived in Birmingham to open a practice of law. This confrontation, however, would be more intense and much more public, for he was entering the halls of the U.S. Senate, the most powerful of "inside" clubs in America.

Initially seen as an crude outsider, a rural backward lawyer from Ashland, Black, through continuous, gritty determination, preparation and hard work overcame that image after joining the Senate. But in 1927 as Senator-elect, he was again an outsider, a largely self-educated Southerner about to enter the inner sanctum of political power in America.

Black was elected in November 1926 to serve in the Seventieth Congress. Because President Calvin Coolidge did not convene an extraordinary session of that Congress, the national legislators did not formally meet until December 1927—thirteen months later. The clerk of the Senate informed the newly elected Black of that fact, ("Unless there is a special session called by the President, you will not take the oath of office until the regular December session in 1927")[1] along with information about staff he would need to hire and their salaries. Hugo responded in December 1926, thanking the clerk for the information, saying also that "I was somewhat surprised however to learn that it would not be necessary for me to take the oath of office until December 1927."[2]

Always in control of himself and his environment, and infinitely smarter than his peers thought he was, Hugo Black did not waste a moment of that free time. Much like his use of time in Ashland, when Hugo took "educational" walks in the forests surrounding Ashland while awaiting new clients, he used every moment of the thirteen-month delay as preparation for a new life in the Senate including self-education through late-night reading. Between November 1926 and December 1927, Black learned all he could about the rules and procedures of the U.S. Senate. In addition to reading about parliamentary processes used generally in legislatures and particularly in the U.S. Senate, he continued to read history, political theory, economic theory, American history—especially the records of the 1787 Constitutional Convention and Thomas Jefferson studies, and the history of the French Revolution.[3]

When the Black family finally moved into a small house in the national capital, the senator was fully prepared to participate in the legislative process. Within months of the opening of the Seventieth Congress, Black's behavior was forcing his fellow solons to change their perceptions of the junior senator from Alabama; he was not a younger version of the tragicomic, avowedly racist Senator Heflin. Hugo was articulate, he cared intensely about issues before the national legislature, and he sprinkled the ideas of Aristotle, Pericles, and Thucydides, among other Greek philosophers and historians, into his speeches and debates.

By the time of his 1932 reelection campaign, Black had become, by virtue of Heflin's losing his 1930 senatorial reelection campaign, the senior senator from Alabama. He had skillfully survived the 1928 Al Smith presidential campaign and had begun to openly fight monied interests in America through his work as a senator on a number of important Senate committees. Recalling the pain and agony of the poor in his state, both the rural farmers as well as the urban workers who slaved away in coal and iron mines, Black vigorously and relentlessly attacked monopoly and its progeny as well as the consequences of an out-of-control economic system that tyrannized the American nation. Whether it was the holding company or the highly paid executive of a corporation, Black criticized, analyzed, investigated, and attacked the evil.

In 1932, Senator Black vigorously supported Franklin Delano Roosevelt's successful presidential effort. Hugo was to become an important player in the New Deal, in great part because of his perception that Roosevelt was committed to a resolution of the abysmal economic dilemmas that beset America and that led the nation into the 1929 Depression. "As a Senator," observed one scholar, "Black was an uncompromising liberal on economic issues."[4] But, in the Senate as in Birmingham, Alabama, Black marched to his own drumbeat; on a number of occasions on important legislative proposals, he openly disagreed with Roosevelt and his New Deal brain trust, including one of Roosevelt's leading advisors, Felix Frankfurter, then a well-known professor at Harvard Law School.

Beyond his lawmaking and debating skills, the instrument that he used to gain wider popular support and power on Capitol Hill was his skill as the grand inquisitor, or, as a newspaper labeled him, the "Chief Ferret" of the Roosevelt Senate. By 1932, the Alabaman had "sloughed off a considerable portion of his Southern parochialism . . . and became a flamboyant congressional investigator."[5]

Black continued to be the consummate politician. Using the lists of supporters, potential supporters, and constituents that he amassed over his career, he periodically wrote to them, offering information, showing interest in their work, and attaching to some of the letters recent speeches he'd made about the economy and his respect for the workers. And he had his staff carefully review all his correspondence. When a letter writer wrote something like "Any time I can be of service to you, command me," that person's name went into one of his famous black books, the letter went into the "Thanks" file, and the appropriate letter asking for help was sent to the person at the right time.[6]

The Legislator from Alabama

Black's first term in the Senate was an extended learning experience for him. Between congressional sessions, he traveled back to Birmingham, rented an apartment, and went on speaking tours that hit most of Alabama's sixty-seven counties. In Washington there was a sign on his door telling his Alabama constituents who needed to see him but had missed him to "go to elevators, ask boy to show you phones where you can call and ask for extension 17 and state your business."[7]

During this time, from the winter of 1927–1928 through his reelection campaign in 1932, Black had to cope with a difficult presidential campaign that featured, at the top of the Democratic ticket, the "wet" Catholic New Yorker, Al Smith. This trinity of characteristics in their presidential candiate created havoc for Alabama Democrats and created some serious fissures within the state Democratic party. And Hugo, by virtue of his winning the 1926 senatorial election, was a major figure in the state Democratic party.

In addition, Black along with other elected legislators, had to deal with the first responses, by newly elected President Herbert Hoover, to the stock market crash and the onset of the Great Depression. Hugo very quickly saw the impact of the Depression in Birmingham when U.S. Steel closed some of its plants. More than 25,000 of the city's work population of over 108,000 lost their jobs and could not find employment.

As a representative of the poor farmers and small businesses in Alabama, Black was also concerned about providing electricity—at reasonable prices—to his constituents as well as trying to find ways to get cheap fertilizer to them. This concern led him, inexorably, to fights with power and utility companies and to an examination of the public utility lobbyists and their practices. By 1930, Hugo was invited to participate in a Senate investigation of Muscle Shoals and had his first taste of the potential power of a congressional committee (see page 80ff.).

Within a short time of his arrival, Black developed an economic legislative agenda that was positive and imaginative, even radical in character. However, on social issues touching on race relations, he was defensive, protective, and conservative. Probably nothing typified Black the economic radical more than his 1932 call for a thirty-hour work week, a demand that led to the passage of the Fair Labor Standards Act in 1938. On the other hand, his participation in the opposition to the anti-lynching bill was Black the Alabama states' rights conservative at work in the Senate.

The 1928 Presidential Campaign

Black's first serious problem, as newly elected Democratic senator, was how to survive, politically, the actions of the national Democrats when they chose Al Smith to be the party's standard-bearer in the 1928 presidential election. In the spring of 1928, it became clear that Smith would be the candidate. It was equally clear that Black, the dry, Baptist, nativist U.S. senator from Alabama did not, for a single minute, cherish that reality. In a lengthy letter to an old friend, he expressed himself in no uncertain terms.

> Smith signed a bill passed by the Legislature of New York while he was Governor, permitting in that state by legal enactment, the sale of beers and wines. This was in the teeth of the Prohibition Amendment and in effect placed New York in the position of defying the Federal Government. . . . [Smith would appoint] a large number of Catholics . . . to office. . . . [As a Catholic, Smith may use troops to aid Catholics in other nations.] He would be no more than human if a persecution of his fellow churchmen played no part in his decision with reference to the nation persecuting his church. . . . It is also . . . well known that most of the Catholics favor foreign immigration. . . . Due to the immense power which a president is frequently able to wield in bringing about the passage of laws, a man's religious faith . . . might be important. . . .
>
> I oppose the nomination of Governor Smith. . . . [He is] too small to hold the exalted position of President of the United States. . . . I consider him to be the most over-estimated man in America, as to ability. I think him to be the living exponent of the predominating sentiment of the foreign element in the City of New York, and the ideals of that element are totally at variance with the traditions and sentiments of the people of the South. . . . I believe the Democratic Party would be almost committing suicide to select him as the standard bearer of the followers of Jefferson and Jackson.[8]

However much he deplored the Smith candidacy, Black, the good Democrat, could not and would not bolt the party. In letter after letter to his constituents, who wrote demanding to know who he was going to support in the presidential election, he responded: "Due to the fact that I was elected by the Democratic Party to the office which I hold, I do not believe there is any other course for me to pursue, except to vote the straight Democratic ticket."[9] For him to leave the party would have meant political suicide. He knew that and did what he had to do: Black prudently walked a tightrope in his state.[10]

His support of the party's candidate for president in 1928 was very mixed, to the point that the media in Alabama wondered where Black was during the campaign. Indeed, in late March 1928, the Washington correspondent for the *Alabama Journal* had to write Hugo to find out whether he favored the nomination of Al Smith. "I greatly appreciate a prompt reply from you."[11] The following day, Black responded to the newsman. In a two page letter, he stated, unequivocally,

> "I am opposed to the nomination of Governor Smith for President by the Democratic Party. . . . It is illogical, unreasonable and wholly unjustifiable to assume that Governor Smith is the only man among the many able Democrats, who is qualified to be our Democratic Standard Bearer. His views on law enforcement, immigration, and [prohibition] . . . do not appeal to the patriotic and law abiding citizens of this Nation."

Hugo closed his letter by predicting that Smith's "nomination would destroy party solidarity."[12] Black's prediction was accurate: For the first time since the end of the Reconstruction era in the South, the solid Democratic vote in the region broke, and a number of Southern states, but not Alabama, voted for the Republican candidate, Herbert Hoover.

During the 1928 campaign Black was caught between a rock and hard place. He was a Democrat but also a prohibitionist, a public figure supported by the Klan and the Anti-Saloon League, two then-powerful groups in Alabama who opposed anyone who supported the sale of beer, wines, and liquor. And so Black became very busy, too busy, in fact, to campaign for Smith in Alabama.

In a July 1928 letter to his political friend William "Bill" McAdoo, Black, "strictly confidentially," told McAdoo that "my staunch friends advise me that the less I can say [about Smith], the better it will be. . . . At present I am making a tour of the State, speaking on non-political subjects. My time is fully taken up between now and September 15th." Although the "situation is bad," and the "privileged few have a throttle hold on the present leadership," observed Hugo, he urged McAdoo not to bolt the Democrats. Drawing upon his understanding of history's rhythms, he pointed out that "sometime, however, in order to do that which will accomplish the most good in the long run, it is necessary to make a temporary sacrifice. . . . Personally, I would hesitate a long time before I would renounce the Democratic Party."[13]

The Reverend J. P. Morgan of Speigner, Alabama, wrote to Black in September 1928, complaining about the senator's non-disavowal of Smith, and recommending that he resign from the Democratic party. Black immediately wrote to let the minister know of the terrible consequences that would fall on the senator and the citizens of Alabama if he bolted. "I consider it my duty, either to support the party, or to resign my position," Black told him. However, "a man without a party in the Senate is a man without influence in that body. . . . I cannot . . . follow the course which you seem to think now that I should." By following the course he was on, avoiding public support of Smith while remaining in the Democratic party, "I am absolutely convinced that . . . I can do more to carry out the principles in which you and I believe."[14]

Black successfully maneuvered himself during the 1928 election debates, refraining from backing the presidential candidate of his party in public. After Smith lost the election, Black wrote to a colleague expressing his views about the state of the Democratic party and how it had drifted far from its Jeffersonian and Jacksonian heritage. If the Party continues to push for an end to prohibition, warned Black, "it will be impossible to fight reaction and special privilege. What this country needs today above all things is a Party devoted wholeheartedly and exclusively to the betterment of the masses of the Nation."[15] That day for the Democrats was to come soon, in great part as a consequence of President Hoover's inability to deal with the stock market crash of 1929, bringing on the Great Depression and Roosevelt's New Deal.

First Term, 1927–1933

Hugo Black was generally low-key during his first term as junior senator from Alabama.[16] But he answered every letter he received from his constituents. In this response to constituent letters, Hugo was following the advice offered by successful politicians: Answer your mail. Tip O'Neill, late Speaker of the House of Representatives, spoke Black's thoughts in his recommendation to "always send them something."[17]

There was one exception to Black's correspondence rules: Letters from local NAACP chapters and black ministers in Alabama and other Southern states asking Black to take actions that would end the lynchings of blacks in the South went unanswered. The senator jotted a stock notation to his secretary on such letters, to which were sometimes attached photos of the lynch victims: "Propaganda: No Reply."[18]

When he was later nominated by Roosevelt in 1937 to serve on the Supreme Court, Senator Black's stock with the black community was as low as it would ever be. He had participated in successful filibusters of the Costigan-Wagner antilynching legislation introduced in the Senate in 1935. The bill would have punished local law enforcement officers if prisoners in their jurisdiction were dragged out of jail and lynched by an angry mob.

Although Black drew on his understanding of the patterns of history—in this debate, drawing on Macaulay's *History of England*—to argue that the Costigan-Wagner type of remedy did not work in post-Norman-conquest England and would not work in America, he was seen by the press as one of the group of bigoted yet successful Southern "redneck" senators who were able to table the legislation.[19]

While Black was horrified at the lawless practice of lynching blacks for any real or imagined breach of law or Southern "codes" of honor, he did not believe the congressional legislation would effectively reduce the horror of the lynch mob. For Black, eradication of the monstrosity of lynching was the states' obligation, not that of the national government. Led by local Southerners who had the courage to challenge their communities' lawlessness and violence, the South would resolve the lynching madness.

To the end of his life, Black argued vigorously for what he referred to as "Our Federalism." A viable federal republic had to consist of a strong national government as well as an equally strong set of state and local governments. Black always maintained a healthy respect for the capacity of the states and their local communities to deal with very problematic issues involving the health, safety, and well-being of all citizens, whether the issue was illegal lynching, laws concerning marital privacy,[20] or responsibility for ensuring fairness in voting.[21]

The former Alabama police court judge and county prosecutor as a senator was a sharp-tongued defender of the justice system in his Alabama. It was a problematic task for him; that system produced the 1931 guilty convictions of the nine "Scottsboro" boys, a travesty of justice that went on in the state for many decades.

Scottsboro was an American racial tragedy. From the moment nine itinerant black youths riding the rails in Alabama were arrested in late March 1931 and charged with raping two white women (both poor prostitutes known to "service" white and black men), until 1976—*forty five years later*—when the last of the young men was pardoned for a crime they did not commit, the Scottsboro incident has illuminated the harshness and the terrible cruelty of America's racial dilemma. For the nine black defendants, accused falsely as it turned out, there were no less than four state trials (all four juries returning guilty verdicts), two Supreme Court opinions setting aside two of the verdicts as violative of the youngsters' Fourteenth Amendment due-process rights (*Powell v Alabama,* 287 U.S. 45 in 1932 and *Norris v Alabama,* 294 U.S. 587 in 1936).

However, after each Supreme Court opinion and order to the state, Alabama simply went ahead and retried the youngsters. Each time juries found them guilty and, on most of these occasions, sentenced them to death. A third certiorari petition to the U.S. Supreme Court, filed by the black defendants' attorneys, after the third set of convictions in state court was upheld by the Alabama Supreme Court, was denied by the Court at the beginning of its October 1937 term. This denial occurred just weeks after Black joined the Court. When denying certiorari petitions, the Court never gives reasons. It did not offer an explanation for not hearing the Scottsboro litigation in 1937.[22]

When his membership in the Klan surfaced again after Black was confirmed by the Senate to be an associate justice of the Supreme Court, the black community was anguished, truly fearful that the Alabaman would bring his prejudices with him onto the Court. It took a conscious effort by the chief justice at the time, Charles Evans Hughes, a jurist who did not receive the senator's vote when he was nominated by President Hoover in 1930 for the center seat, working with newly appointed Justice Black, to change the black community's view of him.

Black Thursday, the day the stock market crashed, left Democrats in Congress shocked, pained and frustrated. The disaster of October 24, 1929, led to a variety of economic crises that the national leadership, Herbert Hoover and the conservative Republicans in the Congress, could not effectively address.

The economic problems that accompanied the crash were allowed to fester without focused national treatment until the Roosevelt New Deal program was given a mandate by the voters in the 1932 presidential election. In the meantime, Black, like many other Democratic senators, tried to pass piecemeal legislation that would assist the poor in America. That meant discussions about farm relief and whether high tariffs would benefit American workers and farmers. The onset of the Great Depression led him again into a debate about the future of the Muscle Shoals project, with Republican presidential vetoes of Democratic legislation.

Black and other Democratic senators believed that the Muscle Shoals electricity project, on the Tennessee River, should be taken over by the federal government and operated by the government to produce cheap electricity and fertilizer, as well as providing flood control to the farmers working in a large region in the South. Republican Presidents Warren Harding and Herbert Hoover wanted to place the Muscle Shoals project in the hands of private business.

It was not until the Roosevelt New Deal that the proposals introduced by Democratic senators, supported by Black, were passed into law and the Tennessee Valley Authority (TVA) was created. Until its passage, Black continued to receive letters from the folks back home, either supporting the expansion of the project or arguing that "widows and orphans of Alabama have in good faith invested in the preferred stock of the Alabama Power Co." and that their savings would be lost if the TVA were created.[23]

Newly elected President Franklin Delano Roosevelt, during his first hundred days, in a special message to Congress on April 10, 1933, called for the development of Muscle Shoals and the entire Tennessee River. In the message, Roosevelt summoned Congress to pass legislation creating a Tennessee Valley Authority, an independent regulatory agency that would be "charged with the broadest duty of [regional] planning for the proper use, conservation, and development of the national resources of the Tennessee Valley drainage basin, . . . clothed with the necessary power to carry these plans into effect."[24] Senator Black's vision of a government-operated facility on the Tennessee River that could provide cheap fertilizer for the poor farmers of Alabama would be more than realized by Roosevelt's grander vision.

Second Term, 1933–1937

Since Heflin's defeat in 1930, an election in which Black avoided campaigning because of the volatility of the issues—in particular Prohibition and the clashes between the two Democratic candidates, Heflin and Bankhead—Hugo was the state's youngish senior senator. His nephew Hollis Black, who was serving as Black's office secretary, along with many political friends of the senator, had urged him not to enter the 1930 fray:

> You will be forced upon the stump, speaking for the whiskey element against the dry element, for the Catholic domination of your party and your country, against the Protestant traditions of your country, your state, and especially your following who elected you in 1926 and gave you the office you now hold.[25]

Black took this advice and, much like his action in the 1928 Al Smith presidential campaign, lay low during the 1930 election. It was one that sent Bankhead to the Senate, replacing the vulgar Tom Heflin. Hugo was pleased with the electoral outcome: for one thing, he was the new senior senator; for another, the embarrassing Heflin was no longer in the Senate.

Black won reelection to the Senate in a landslide in 1932. He returned to the capital as a part of the emergent Democratic administration's New Deal legislative team, although still very much the outsider in the early halcyon days of the New Deal.

There appeared a story in *Barron's* that showed him at his decisive political best as he "silenced the loudest speaker south of Detroit." In doing so, Black "showed the Senate how to regain control of its own actions; how to rewin its self respect, how, in other words to shut up Hollering Huey Long."[26] The Louisiana Senator was, again, tieing up the work of the Senate with his long-winded, mini-filibusters. His goal: to get a compromise on the legislation in order to get him to shut up and sit down.

Black, however, closed Long down by using something called the Thunders of Silence. This strategy, accepted by Alben Barkley, the Senate's majority leader, was to let Long talk and talk, without compromise. Black promised to

> object to every motion for unanimous consent agreement until Long has con-
> cluded and yielded the floor. . . . It's time right now to decide whether this
> Senate is a Senate or whether it's a one-man side-show. If Huey's the dictator
> boss and leader, then I'm for packing up and going back to Alabama. . . . Word
> of Black's blow-up spread like a blaze. Within fifteen minutes 30 Senators had
> gone to Black and said: "We're sticking, too." From that moment on, Huey
> was beaten.[27]

Although Hugo hated liquor and was a "strict prohibitionist,"[28] he participated in the repeal of the Eighteenth Amendment almost immediately upon his return to Washington, because "he felt that though prohibition worked pretty well in Alabama, it didn't in the rest of the country."[29]

His radical proposal for a thirty-hour work week was a prime example of his outsider status, as well as another portrait of his intensity when he believed he was right on an issue. The bill was introduced because of the terrible impact of the Depression on working men and women. During a congressional recess, he returned to Birmingham and set up an office in the Federal Building to meet people and hear their stories. At 9 A.M., the hall was so filled that Hollis suggested that numbers be given to them to avoid a riot in the building. Black sat and met every one of the people, until 5 P.M., and he returned for three more days. "Some people were threatening suicide if they didn't get a job." They were all kinds of people—farmers, court clerks, business men—and their fears and anger had a dramatic impact on the senator.[30] For the Alabaman who had seen suffering of poor people since his childhood days in Ashland, there was a critical need to redistribute wealth in America. "What we need to do," he wrote to a constituent, "is to prevent special privilege in this nation and thus bring about a proper distribution of the income produced by all of the people. Income is what counts in our economic system."[31]

Even before the new, Democratic Congress led by FDR could convene, Black introduced his thirty-hour bill. At the insistence of the surprised new president, it was defeated in the House, but Hugo stayed with the effort to shorten the work week to five days and the working day to six hours until the enactment of the Fair Labor Standards Act in 1937.

He argued, in the Senate and at home in Alabama, that the existing wage structure and working conditions were essentially unfair. Big industry was taking undue advantage of the poor working men and women of America and their children, especially in the South. National legislation, using the Congress's power to regulate commerce, was the answer to the economic dilemma for workers.

"This nation," Black said, "must choose between a dole and shorter hours of work. . . . Business in America can give jobs or doles." A shorter work week for the next four years he insisted, would "create an actual scarcity of labor, thereby causing employers once again to bid for labor[, and] would be a wholesome economic tonic for America."[32]

Black believed, fervently, that the most effective way to stimulate the economy and increase production was to enhance demand, which could be done by providing more jobs to the unemployed. Workers with salaries would immediately spend their wages, increasing the demand for goods.

The legislation introduced by Black was based on the use of the congressional power to regulate commerce. If passed, his bill would have excluded goods produced "in any mine, quarry, mill, cannery, workshop, factory or manufacturing establishment" from interstate commerce if employers violated the law's thirty-hour weekly work limit for employees. "It would," argued Hugo, "greatly increase production."[33] Although the bill "had great immediate popular appeal,"[34] especially with organized labor, and very rapidly made it through the Senate, FDR "personally opposed the measure"[35] and succeeded in blocking Black's legislation in the House.

However, in response to the manner in which the legislature and the public at large responded to Black's initiative, Roosevelt called in his advisors to produce what eventually became the National Recovery Act (NRA). The Alabaman, from the beginning of the debates on the NRA, opposed the new legislation. Roosevelt's proposal would have stabilized prices and limited competition through the creation of codes written by businessmen themselves. Essential to any such program was suspension of the antitrust statutes, and it was this provision of the NRA bill that became the focal point of opposition by congressional populists and progressives like Black. As he later recalled, "it created committees of business men at various parts of the country to set up commissions and draw what I considered to be laws. And it also provided for the suspension of the anti-Trust Act . . . and [would] leave the control of prices to business men meeting in common." Black also said to Joe Robinson, the Senate majority leader who had asked him to sponsor the NRA legislation.[36] "If you let a group of business men get together even for a dinner to talk among themselves, then the public's going to suffer. And that's the way I feel about this NRA."

The Alabama senator correctly predicted that the legislation, if enacted, would be struck down on constitutional grounds by the Supreme Court. It was passed over vigorous opposition but was overturned by the U.S. Supreme Court in 1935.[37]

Black did not, however, give up his idea of the thirty-hour work week. On February 23, 1937, he was reintroducing his bill "to establish a six hour day for employees of carriers engaged in interstate and foreign commerce, and for other purposes."[38] As he wrote to a constituent, although business and organizations representing business, such as the Chamber of Commerce, distorted the merits of the bill, and "people have been misled by the propaganda," his task was to battle for passage of this legislation, which would provide America with a "system of fair and decent wages for our working people."[39]

Once again his proposal failed, but, as before, his initiative generated an important response from the White House: the Fair Labor Standards Act, a major piece of legislation that set minimum wage and hour restrictions for American workers. The importance of Black's role is indicated by the fact that the FLSA came to be known as the Black-Connery Act (for the Democratic Congressman from Massachusetts, William P. Connery, who introduced identical legislation in the House of Representatives) even though the legislation was actually drafted by the White House.[40]

The Public Utility Holding Company Battle

In one of his early Senate speeches, the "poor man's" candidate-now-senator said that

> Monopoly should be discouraged. . . . Chain groceries, chain dry goods stores, chain drug stores, chain clothing stores, here today and merge tomorrow, grow in size and power. Railroad mergers, giant power monopolies, bank mergers, steel mergers, all kinds of mergers, concentrate more and more power in the hands of the few. In the name of efficiency, monopoly is the order of the day. . . . We are rapidly becoming a Nation of a few business masters and many clerks and servants. The local business man and merchant is passing, and his community loses his contribution to local affairs as an independent thinker and executive.[41]

After battling unsuccessfuly for a thirty-hour work week, Black's next battle against big business found him allied with the president in 1935. It was the struggle for control over public utility holding companies, financial entities that used the assets of their subsidiaries to underwrite the parent firms' investments; they were huge conglomerates. A congressional committee that investigated these operations found the following:

> In 1925 holding companies controlled about 65 percent of the operating electric utility industry. By 1932 thirteen large holding companies controlled three-fourths of the entire privately owned electric utility industry, and more than 40 percent was concentrated in the hands of the three largest groups—United Corporation, Electric Bond & Share Co., and Insull. . . . In 1929 and 1930 twenty large holding-company systems controlled 98.5 percent of the transmission of electric energy across State lines.[42]

Black had campaigned in 1926 against "power systems [that] spring up in one state and spread their wires over many states in a titanic web that entangles the destiny of our children and our children's children."[43] By the time of the New Deal, then, Black was more than ready to support legislation aimed at wiping out the holding companies. When asked whether he would be satisfied with regulation as opposed to prohibition of them, Black replied: "I have no more sympathy in the attempt to regulate [holding companies] them than to regulate a rattlesnake."[44]

As he wrote in a letter to an Alabama banker in 1935, the proposed holding company legislation, while eliminating holding companies, "will not destroy a single street car, nor a single generating plant, not a single electric line." He also stated, "It is my own belief that the *intrinsic* value of stock even in holding companies, will not be reduced one penny below the *intrinsic* value today."[45] (his emphasis)

Black's bitterness about the secretive, nondemocratic practices of holding company lobbyists led him to turn the congressional investigative weapon on them in the effort to reduce their unfettered power in Congress. Very quickly, he became the Senate's most vigorous investigator, uncovering the unscrupulous and illegal dealings of the monied interests in America—and their shills, paid lobbyists. As he wrote in a *Harper's* magazine article: "There is no power on earth that can tear away the veil behind which powerful and audacious and unscrupulous groups operate save the sovereign legislative power armed with the right of subpoena and search."[46]

"Go for the Jugular" Senate Inquisitor

In 1929, Senator Thaddeus Henry Caraway, Democrat of Arkansas, invited Black to become a guest assistant on a Senate committee investigating the lobbyists in Washington, D.C. Black instantly fell in love with the legislative investigation, a mechanism for uncovering skullduggery among the rich and the famous, leading to corrective legislation. By the summer of 1935, Black, who was now senior senator from Alabama was dubbed the Senate's "Chief Ferret" by the *Washington Post*. The newspaper further stated that "he has been widely commended for his attempts thus far to unearth the influences at work trying to shape or block legislation before Congress by lobbying for selfish purposes. The inquistorial mantle of the late Senator Thomas Walsh of Montana seems to have fallen upon Black's shoulders."[47]

Being called the "Chief Inquisitor" of the Senate greatly bothered the Alabama senator, although he seldom showed his distaste. For Black the historian, that was an inappropriate title because he was doing the job his people had elected him to do: Root out special privilege in America. The labels were the result of a number of investigations by Black-led committees—between 1933 and his 1937 departure from the Senate—that produced nationwide publicity and important legislative action.

Senator Black's initial investigations involved subsidies to the merchant marine shipping industry in the form of mail contracts and expanded into an even more careful examination of the administration of airmail contracts. In Black's mind, the investigating committee of Congress was neither a criminal trial nor a fishing expedition. Instead, it was a vitally necessary and constitutional legislative technique that led to new legislation, the savings of millions of dollars in public funds, and the collection of back taxes by persons whose illegal behavior was exposed during the hearing.[48]

The investigations began in September 1933. Black's name was soon on the front pages of newspapers across America, and he was called a "useful Torque-mada" by *Newsweek* magazine.[49]

He was subpoenaing to his investigating committee some of the biggest names in the industry. Testimony pried out of reluctant witnesses by Black showed that forty-seven of fifty-two ocean mail contracts were obtained without competitive bidding and went to firms whose ships were built or refinished at governmental expense, over four hundred million dollars in toto, and then sold to shipping companies at below-cost prices, leading to enormous profits with little or no capital invested by the owners. One of the shipping magnates, fearful of Black's questions, brought his personal physician with him to check his pulse while he testified.[50]

The merchant marine findings "astounded the public and the Committee"[51] and quickly led to legislative action, the Merchant Marine Act of 1936. However, Senator Black's investigation of the airmail contracts was much more shocking. The airmail hearings ultimately provided evidence of abuses that simply had to be dealt with, even if the consequences were severe—and they were.[52]

Black was extremely critical of the behavior of American business in this issue because the airmail scandal showed business in its most base behavior. "The control of American aviation," he said during the hearings, "has been ruthlessly taken away from men who could fly and bestowed upon bankers, brokers, promoters, and politicians, sitting in their inner offices, allotting to themselves the taxpayers' money."[53]

Black acquired information from a young Hearst reporter, Fulton Lewis, Jr., about an airmail contract scandal involving President Hoover's postmaster general. William Randolph Hearst, the owner of the chain of papers for which the journalist worked, "flatly refused publication of Lewis's reports" and Lewis took the information to the "redoubtable" senior senator from Alabama.[54]

The Lewis data showed that Hoover's postmaster general, Walter F. Brown, had, since 1930, avoided competitive bidding procedures, deliberately using the mail contracts to close out small air carriers and support the development of those commercial companies, especially American, United, and TWA, that were emerging as the leading airlines in the industry.[55] The subsequent overpayments had totalled forty-seven million dollars between July 1930 and January 1934. As a consequence of the discovery of these fraudulent contracts, Roosevelt acted decisively—and erroneously. The Roosevelt postmaster general, James Farley—after speaking with the army air corps commander, Major General Benjamin Foulis—cancelled all of the mail contracts[56] and directed the U.S. Army Air Corps to fly the mail.

Unprepared for this responsibility, six army fliers died in less than a week[57] dozens more army airmen died in crashes later, and there were more than fifty crashes of planes where the pilot survived. By May 1934, the Roosevelt decision had been termed an unmitigated "major, tragic blunder." After losing army pilots due to foul weather and improperly equipped planes, Roosevelt allowed all airmail once again to be transported by the commercial carriers.[58] However, Black's investigation of the airmail contracts did lead to legislation, the Air Mail Act of 1934, which provided for true competitive bidding on all airmail contracts.

The merchant marine and airmail hearings conducted by Black demonstrated two elements of his investigative technique: his immense skill as a questioner and his strategic use of subpoenas and other techniques for acquiring evidence for the committee. He drew upon all his experiences as successful attorney and county prosecutor. While in Birmingham, Black had "perfected an insidious cross examination technique: the soft question which provokes the wrathful answer and mires the witness in his own welter."[59]

As congressional examiner, because the Congress could not find quality private attorneys to act as questioners for only $255 per month, Black served as a piercing, dramatic, direct questioner. "Courteous, smiling, puffing gravely on his cigar, he undertook to 'refresh' [witnesses'] memories, leading them imperceptibly into admissions which enabled him to conclude with incisive and damaging summations of their testimony."[60] As the *Washington Post* noted,

> Black, always courteous with witnesses, relies a great deal more upon finesse and shrewd questioning to make his point and bring out the desired testimony. The Alabamian is also equipped with a ready sense of humor which sometimes proves most uncomfortable to a pompous or arrogant witness who seeks to impress the committee with his importance.[61]

George Creel, a critic of Black's investigatory techniques, wrote in *Colliers* magazine in 1937 that Black would be an outstanding Senator "were it not for the fact that he still thinks in terms of the time when he was prosecuting attorney. . . . Almost everybody, to Hugo's gimlet eye, is a potential defendant."[62]

The most spectacular of Black's investigations, one in which he chaired a special Senate Lobby Committee, was called "Chairman Black's Three Ring Circus" by the press.[63] It was his 1936 investigation of public utility lobbying practices, which he initiated to respond to sleazy efforts by corporate leaders and their lobbyists to defeat the 1935 Public Utility Holding Company Act. The opponents of the legislation had hired many hundreds of persons to send thousands of telegrams and letters from fictitious "constituents" opposing the legislation.

This investigation pitted the Southern prosecutor/solon against some of the nation's toughest cohort of experienced political fighters, the nation's lobbyists. But Black did not shy away from this confrontation with the enemy. In the investigation, he proceeded "as a prosecuting attorney or a muckraking journalist bent on exposing and convicting malefactors, using questionable tactics to uncover wrongdoing."[64]

In one of his most controversial moves, Black demanded that Western Union surrender records on all of its telegrams that came to the nation's capitol during the utility company battle and enlisted the aid of the Federal Communications Commission (FCC) in enforcing the subpoena. One of those who challenged the legality of Black's committee action was the controversial William Randolph Hearst. Hearst brought suit against Black and the FCC, seeking an injunction to block the commission and the Senate committee from acquiring the telegraph records. He also asked for an order requiring that those documents already in the committee's possession be returned, claiming that the committee had seized telegrams unrelated to the investigation sent by Hearst to his Washington-based news staff.

The district court refused to grant the injunction and the case went on to appeal. The court of appeals found that the court was without authority to compel the legislature to return the records.[65] In the case, *William Randolph Hearst v Hugo L. Black,* the federal judges concluded that the seizure of the documents was a violation of the Constitution and that the FCC was "without lawful authority to coerce the telegraph companies, over which it has supervisory control, to make the contents of appellants' telegrams available to the Senate Committee."

However, the federal appeals court panel concluded that because the documents were "now physically in the hands of the Senate," the court was without "authority" to interfere. To do so would violate the separation of powers concept. "The universal rule, so far as we know it, is that the legislative discretion in discharge of its constitutional functions, whether rightfully or wrongfully exercised, is not a subject for judicial interference."[66]

Black defended his actions vigorously, charging that critics were using attacks on the investigative process to divert attention from their own culpability. When an Alabama paper wrote an article about his "polecat committee," Hugo quickly responded. He wrote to Warren Roberts of the *Mobile Times.*

> You are probably sufficiently familiar with efforts to counteract committee exposures to understand that such efforts are frequently made. Charges are made against the investigators. A vigorous effort is now being made throughout the country not only to handicap the work of our Committee but to cripple the activities of Senatorial and Congressional Committees. We intend, however, to continue our exposure from time to time.[67]

Black charged against the utility lobbyists with letters, speeches in the Senate, and radio broadcasts. On one broadcast, he said:

> Contrary to tradition, against the public morals, and hostile to good Government, the lobby has reached such a position of power that it threatens Government itself. Its size, its power, its capacity for evil; its greed, trickery, deception, and fraud condemn it to the death it deserves. You, the people of the United States, will not permit it to destroy you. You will destroy it.[68]

Black was moving directly to the center of the lobbying problem in America, and his harshest opponents knew it. Senate Democrats who broke with the president by not supporting the public utilities legislation were "beginning to squirm" because of the Black committee's revelations of fraudulent and illegal tactics used by the power trust and their lobbyists to defeat the bill. "Some of the shady activities of the power trust already have been brought into the light, but the worse is yet to come," editorialized the *Alabama Herald.*[69]

The utility brokers realized, too late, as so many had before and after, the fortitude, skill, and ingenuity of Black. As David Davis, his former law partner, said to him: "Even those who strongly sympathize with the power interest concede your ability. Frankly you have uncovered a great deal more than I ever dreamed you would. . . . [Your work] should convince the people that the only way to regulate the great web of corporate organization is to break them down into simple, responsible, reachable units."[70]

Black quietly seethed when "liberal" pundits such as Walter Lippmann warned of the danger of Black's investigative excesses: "[W]hen lawlessness is approved for surprisingly good ends, it will be used even more viciously for bad ones."[71] For Black, the hearings were not lawless actions; the congressional investigation was there to fight abuses against the body politic by greedy corporate special interests. "It is never possible," he wrote,

> to uproot any kind of special privilege without continued fighting. It is also true that those engaged in the fight will have all kinds of invectives hurled at them by those who fear that they will lose some of their unjust privileges. It is really an honor in this country to be abused by newspapers such as those operated by Mr. Hearst and the Chicago Tribune.[72]

And Black's committee was using techniques that earlier congressional committees had employed in the effort to expose wrongdoing and to pass legislation in response to the evils exposed by the investigations. Unlike the congressional committees investigating Communism and other forms of subversion in America in the 1940s and 1950s, Black's committees typically produced legislation that was passed by the Congress and signed by the president. Hugo's investigations did lead to legislation, including a bill to require the registration and regulation of all lobbyists. That bill, introduced by the senator himself in March 1935, was passed a year later by the Congress.

The Alabaman was sly and sneaky tough, although very rarely was he brutal, in these investigative hearings. His cajolery and his firmness underscored his primary motivation: to attack and rid America of the hated special interests. Black saw "greedy groups" fighting to end the congressional investigation. Why? He answered, directly, sharply: "Special privilege thrives in secrecy and darkness and is destroyed by the rays of pitiless publicity."[73]

When Black received letters from innocent people who were hurt because of their appearance before his committee, he was sympathetic but unyielding in his defense of the congressional investigating committee's work. Daniel Willard, the president of the Baltimore and Ohio Railroad Company wrote Black in February 1936, complaining about the treatment he received in a hearing involving his actions during World War I and wondering whether the action he described "was necessary in order to protect the public interest."[74]

Black responded by indicating that "it is undoubtedly true that mistakes have been made in connection with investigations," and he acknowledged that "it is wholly and completely impossible that all of the people connected with investigating committees, covering a long period of years, would, without exception, act with that tolerance, fairness, caution, sincerity and patriotism, which should rightfully accompany all human conduct." And Black admitted that Willard had been unjustly treated. However, Black concluded that, having watched investigations "at close range, . . . *as a whole, however, I consider their work to be most useful and most necessary, if graft, corruption and privilege are to be exposed and punished for the public welfare.*"[75] (my emphasis)

Sara Eldridge, Kansas's American Civil Liberties Union representative, wrote Black to complain about the deprivation by the committee of the liberties of the companies and individuals "whose activities are under investigation." The senator immediately responded by denying her allegation.

> Our committee has in no way encroached on the constitutional rights of any individual. . . . It is to be regretted that a group that claims to stand for the liberties of the people should unite with a group that recognizes no right of liberty except for themselves. Our committee is acting in accordance with the principles that have been carried out by the Senate and Congress since Congressional investigations began.[76]

The editors of the *New York Times,* no friends of Black during his early Senate days, talked of Black's militant opposition to "malefactors of great wealth."[77] His energetic investigative actions that targeted these malefactors, pleased the news editors.

A. A. Berle, well-known public servant, New Deal economist, and friend of presidents, also believed that Black was doing the right thing. He wrote to tell the solon "how much I have admired and appreciated your services to the whole country in this matter. The use of money and other improper influences to secure harmful legislation is, in my judgment, one of the most important issues now before the people of this land." The "brevet, We love him for the enemies he has made," wrote Berle, belonged to Black, and the senator should continue "to hammer the iniquitous crowd in spite of the gangsters who are attacking you. . . . Few brave men are really defeated in such battles as yours."[78]

There were some jarring moments for the Alabama senator. For example, in the summer of 1935 Black received a critical letter from a Birmingham constituent, W. G. Bruce. He wrote to complain that Black should be helping big business, which "made this country of ours," and not be "playing to the galleries, making mountains out of molehills, and looking out for your own selfish interests."[79] Surprisingly, Hugo did not respond; instead, he wrote a letter to the Birmingham district attorney, Jim C. Smith, asking the local law enforcer to look into Bruce's activities. Concluded a suspicious Black: "There is something strange about his writing me as he did and there may be a story behind it."[80] The matter was quickly dropped by Smith.

By 1934, in addition to his visible role as chief Senate interrogator, Black had become a national Democratic, much like his predecessor, Oscar Underwood. Hugo was an outstanding and very popular stump speaker for the national democratic party, even better than Underwood in this role. As national spokesperson for his party, the senator was given his assignments by Jim Farley, the President's postmaster general and one of FDR's chief political advisors. And Black prepared for his speeches like an A student preparing for examinations.

The Alabaman received data, especially economic and unemployment data from the Department of Labor and wove into his speeches the bleak reality for workers in the states he visited. And he traveled to a number of them, including but not limited to Indiana, Pennsylvania, West Virginia, Missouri, Minnesota, and Vermont to campaign for Democratic senatorial candidates in 1934 and 1936 and for the president in 1936. He met and helped win elections for Senate newcomers such as Harry S Truman of Missouri and Sherman Minton of Indiana.

And Black was greatly appreciated by state Democratic leaders and was encouraged to return to the state's in the future. Harry Witters, the vice chairman of the Vermont Democratic State Committee, wrote Hugo a letter informing the senator that the Democratic candidate came within thirty-nine hundred votes of defeating Warren Austin for heavily Republican Vermont's U.S. Senate seat. Hugo's "splendid addresses contributed materially to our success" in closing the gap.[81] Another Vermont Democrat writing to Black thought that if the senator had been able to give just four more talks in the state, the Democrats could have defeated the popular Austin.[82]

The President's Court-Packing Plan

As national legislator, Black was extremely critical of the U.S. Supreme Court. A student of the Constitutional Convention of 1787, he believed that the sitting Court, a majority of the justices laissez-faire jurists, was acting in an unconstitutional manner, usurping the powers of the legislature by striking down legislation that tried to address the economic ills of the society. As he wrote to a constituent: "A study of the cases [decided by the Court] has convinced me that a majority of the judges for a number of years have been usurping powers that were never intended to be given to Courts by the Constitution. This is dangerous and jeopardizes Constitutional Government itself."[83]

In another note, Black wrote that he was "convinced that the majority of the judges have usurped so much power that they are actually threatening the existence of our Constitution and shackling the government in exercising its ordinary function both in the states and throughout the Nation."[84]

In 1935, from the floor of the Senate, an angry Black, asking "whose government is this?" suggested the introduction of an amendment to the Constitution that would have the justices of the Court directly elected by the people. "If I had my way," the future Justice of the Court said, "the Constitution to the United States would be amended so as to provide that the federal judges should be elected, because I believe in a democracy, and I believe in the election of judges by the people themselves."[85]

By 1937, Black was angry enough to propose some structural changes in the Court, changes that were anathema to him when he became a Justice.

> Personally, I have thought for some years, that there should be additional members of the Supreme Court, and that the Court should function in divisions as does our Supreme Court in Alabama. It is my belief that this would not only relieve a part of a very heavy burden resting upon the present Members of the Supreme Court, but that it would make it possible for them to give more careful consideration to the hundreds of petitions for certiorari that are filed in the Court every year. Under the existing system, when a petition for certiorari appears in the Court, the Court only considers those that *it believes to be of most importance.* This deprives some litigants of a decision by that Court *even though there may be plain, palpable error in the record.* This I believe to be a *denial of justice.*[86] (his emphasis)

Black's critical views on the Supreme Court mirrored the president's frustration and were voiced at a time of great political and legal excitement in the nation in response to a bold move on FDR's part: his plan to "pack" the Supreme Court. "In the first week came a surprise" from the president.[87] It was a plan that would have permitted him to appoint one new justice for each sitting justice who reached age seventy, up to a maximum of fifteen justices, and was based, so the president argued, on the need to help the aging brethren of the Court deal with their heavy caseload.

It was a plan, however, submitted by Roosevelt without consulting the Senate leadership in the new Congress. FDR evidently believed that, because of his landslide victory in 1936, "which gave him the largest majority in Congress ever enjoyed by a President,"[88] he didn't need to seek counsel about his radical proposal from his loyalists in Congress. Roosevelt was to be proven wrong, for the opposition to his Court-packing plan was, from the very first day, "fierce."

The real reason for the plan was that the president was frustrated with his inability to change personnel on the Court. Since Roosevelt took office in 1933, there was not a single High Court vacancy. He had to find a way to take action against the Court that had struck down vitally important economic New Deal programs. He ultimately dropped the superficial justification and argued that the United States had "reached the point as a Nation where we must take action to save the Constitution from the Court and the Court from itself."[89]

Roosevelt miscalculated badly, however. First, the four arch conservatives on the Court—if they were to continue to succeed in blocking, voiding, Roosevelt's legislation—needed at least one additional vote for a majority. The fifth vote usually came from either Chief Justice Charles Evans Hughes or Justice Owen Roberts—sometimes both. But both Roberts and Hughes began to shift their voting patterns in late 1936 in opinions that were announced just as the president began his assault on the Court.

Second, Hughes proved to be a particularly able adversary who took on the president and beat Roosevelt decisively. Hughes delivered forceful and successful arguments in his now-famous letter to the Senate Judiciary Committee. The basic claim was a response to the president's ostensible justification for the legislation, that of workload. The Chief Justice accurately observed that the Court was "fully abreast of its work. . . . There is no congestion of cases upon our calendar."[90]

A few loyal Democratic senators stood by Roosevelt, including Black, Alben Barkley, Sherman Minton, and Harry S Truman. Truman, however, unlike the much more vigorous and aggressive Alabaman, "took no part in the debate."[91] He had just been elected in the 1936 Democratic party national landslide and was, much like Black a decade earlier, just getting settled into solon work when the Court-packing plan was unveiled.

Black "earnestly, wholeheartedly, and aggressively"[92] supported the president. Hugo had long advocated change in the Supreme Court and had introduced legislation in 1935 and 1937 to check the Court's powers. Just days before Roosevelt introduced the Court-packing plan, Black wrote to him advocating a change in the structure of the Court, arguing that it should be expanded by two justices and that the larger court could sit in two panels.[93] Upon announcing his Court-packing proposal, FDR wrote back to Black, indicating, "We seem to have been thinking along the same or else parallel lines."[94]

The senator spoke out for the president's plan at every occasion, including on the floor of the Senate, and also wrote many letters about it. For Black, Roosevelt's plan was a "much needed reform" of the judiciary.[95] He argued that "the President's Program is a wise one, both in the interest of expeditious and efficient administration of justice and in order to protect the people of this nation from judicial usurpation."[96]

Black even appeared on the popular radio show *America's Town Meeting of the Air* on February 11, 1937, to defend the president's plan. He did so vigorously, arguing that FDR had the power to act in such a manner. Those attacking Roosevelt, Black stated, "are thereby attacking the wisdom, the integrity, or the patriotism of our Founding Fathers who wrote and established the Constitution itself."[97] He also commented on the radio about the Court: "A majority of our judges should not amend the Constitution according to their economic predilections every time they decide a case."[98]

The bill was reported out of the Senate Judiciary Committee unfavorably, with several Democrats defecting. Roosevelt's vice president, John Nance Garner, among many other Democrats, was critical of the plan. There was little public support for it because it was seen as a crass political gambit by a frustrated president.

Black's efforts were not enough to persuade his fellow senators. On July 22, 1937, by a huge fifty-vote margin, the bill was sent back to committee, effectively defeating the measure. The senator was one of the few who stood with the president until the July action that killed the plan. Less than one month later, Hugo Black was a member of the United States Supreme Court.

CHAPTER FIVE

"I Nominate Hugo L. Black of Alabama"

The Court-packing debates in the Senate and across the country raged throughout the spring and early summer of 1937, and during that time, many people forgot that Justice Willis Van Devanter, on May 18, 1937, had given President Roosevelt his letter of retirement from the Court at the end of the 1936–1937 term. Van Devanter was one of four extremely conservative jurists on the Court, the others being James McReynolds, George Sutherland, and Pierce Butler.

This extremely cohesive conservative quartet, with occasional voting support from Owen Roberts or Chief Justice Charles Evans Hughes, dominated the Supreme Court for over two decades. Justice Van Devanter was appointed by President William Howard Taft in 1911, after serving as a federal appeals court judge in Wyoming. On the Court for over twenty-five years, he wrote fewer opinions than any of his brethren who served with him—averaging three a term during his last decade on the Court.[1] He was a very remote, reserved, tightly disciplined, and inner-directed person who suffered from a severe case of chronic writer's block.[2]

Justice McReynolds, President Woodrow Wilson's attorney general, was appointed by him to the Supreme Court in 1914. A recognized trustbuster prior to his elevation to the Court, he became the most strident Court critic of Roosevelt's New Deal programs.[3] A virulent anti-Semite, McReynolds did not speak to Justice Louis D. Brandeis for three years after Brandeis, the first Jewish Supreme Court justice, was appointed in 1916.[4] McReynolds was, to all who had contact with him, a "lean and sour"[5] jurist.

Justice Sutherland, appointed by President Warren Harding in 1922, had served as U.S. senator from Utah when Harding was also a senator. After appointment to the Court, he became "the lucid and articulate spokesman for the Court's solid Darwin-Spencer wing."[6] (See below.)

Justice Butler, holder of the "Catholic" seat on the Court, was appointed by Harding in 1923. Called the "most doctrinaire" of this quartet of conservative justices, Butler grew up in Minnesota and was a millionaire railroad attorney at the time of his appointment to the Court.[7]

Hugo Black, ever since his 1927 arrival in the national capital, had nothing but bad words for these conservative jurists. They were men who incorporated into the U.S. Constitution a "substantive due process" philosophy. It was the substantive economic concept, one that defined the Constitution as a laissez-faire document. As a consequence, efforts by government, both national and state, to protect labor against the power of the corporation were regularly invalidated by the conservative Court majority.[8]

These four conservative Supreme Court justices, incorporating into the Constitution Herbert Spencer's survival-of-the-fittest tome,[9] were viewed by Black and Roosevelt as the "direct descendents of Darwin and Spencer," [men who] were totally antagonistic to the "New Deal" with its "radical" view that government, both the states and the national policy-makers, had to intervene in the economic affairs of the nation.[10] Bitterly opposed to the policies created by New Deal legislators to end unemployment and encourage economic recovery, the conservative quartet caucused each day in the car that drove them to the Supreme Court from their separate Washington, D.C., residences as well as on the golf course where they were a regular foursome.[11]

These justices, with the votes of Roberts and, on occasion, Chief Justice Hughes, "made mincemeat"[12] of the Roosevelt New Deal strategy for economic recovery from 1933 through 1937. The National Industrial Recovery Act's Petroleum Codes were invalidated by them in 1935,[13] the Federal Farm Bankruptcy Act was invalidated,[14] as was the Railroad Act,[15] along with the National Industrial Recovery Act itself,[16] in 1935. And, in 1936, the Supreme Court invalidated the Agricultural Adjustment Act[17] and the Coal Mining Act.[18]

By invalidating these federal statutes, as well as a spate of state laws that tried to eliminate unfair treatment of labor by big business, the conservative Supreme Court majority, led by the Four Horsemen (as they were labeled by their critics), created a "no-man's-land" in which government, whether the national Congress or state legislatures, was prevented from expeditiously acting to regulate the economy. These reactionary actions of the Court through 1937, accompanied by the fact that Roosevelt, since his election in 1933, had not yet named a person to the Court, led to the surprise introduction, on February 5, 1937, of Roosevelt's Court-packing plan. By the end of July 1937, however, FDR had been decisively beaten by his own party in the Senate. Angry, he turned to the task of selecting someone from his own party to replace Van Devanter.

The President Nominates, the Senate Confirms

Washington, D.C., in July 1937, "was a sweltering, half-dead city, from which the Congress and the President desired to get away as soon as possible."[19] The defeat of the Court-packing plan on July 22 had left President Roosevelt "sore and vengeful."[20] That crushing defeat had followed by eight days the sudden death of the Senate's majority leader, sixty-four-year-old Joseph Robinson, who was a close ally of the president. Many believed that the Arkansas senator's stressful lead role in the vain effort to rally Senate Democrats behind Roosevelt's Court-packing plan had contributed to his death. Furthermore, Robinson, although somewhat conservative, was a shoo-in to become FDR's initial appointment to the Court. With Robinson's unexpected death, Roosevelt had no immediate replacement for Van Devanter ready for submission to the Senate.

Consequently, Roosevelt turned to his attorney general, Homer Cummings, for a list of possible nominees to replace Van Devanter. Sixty names were produced, including federal judges, Solicitor General Stanley Reed, law professors such as Felix Frankfurter, and strong congressional defenders and advocates of the New Deal, including Senators Hugo Black of Alabama and Sherman "Shay" Minton of Indiana.

At a White House meeting, Roosevelt and Cummings agreed upon four criteria that the nominee had to meet: First, the nominee needed solid New Deal credentials; he had to be a "thumping, evangelical New Dealer," said Roosevelt (and Black was certainly that, having voted for all twenty-four of Roosevelt's major New Deal programs).[21] Second, he had to be confirmable in the Senate. Third, he had to be reasonably young. And finally, he had to come from a region of the country unrepresented (on the Court)—the West or the South.[22] Using these criteria, by August 1, 1937, the two men had cut the list to seven names.

The seven included four federal judges (quickly dropped because they were not economically liberal enough), Solicitor General Reed (Kentucky), Senator Minton (Indiana), and Black. However, Reed, according to Roosevelt, "had no fire" and was dropped from consideration. Minton became the leading candidate "because he was closest to Cummings, the President's sole advisor in the matter."[23]

Minton did not want the job at that time; he had, in his aggressive advocacy of Roosevelt's Court-packing plan, "attacked the justices of the high bench with an intemperate fury."[24] On August 9, after his name was removed (and at the request of Cummings), Minton raised the question of Court membership with Black.

Hugo recalled, many years later, the events that led to his nomination. Josephine, who was in Birmingham with their son Sterling, had just been told that he was going to lose his hearing, so she put him on a train back to Washington for further medical tests in the capital. After Black had brought Sterling home from the station, Minton spoke to the boy's father in a Senate cloakroom about the Court vacancy. According to Black,

> I would think about it more because I had just learned that one of my children was liable to lose his hearing entirely. I explained to Shay that, if he did, he would need all the home companionship he could get from members of his family, including his father. . . . I explained to Shay, as he knew, that [Senate work] consumed all of your time—it took seven days a week for me. And even then I couldn't keep up with it. And I told him that my wife was coming home the next day, and after she got home I would talk to her about it and see how she felt.[25]

Josephine had no difficulty with the idea of Hugo joining the Court. She "hated" the cacophony of Senate politics, and their son's ill health would cause enough stress in her life in the future; she didn't need the added pressure of Senate goings-on. That evening his wife persuaded a much more reluctant Black to leave the hurly-burly of the Senate and take the seat on the Court if it was offered to him.

Josephine really wanted the Black family to return to the comfortable and friendly environs of Birmingham, where Hugo could once again enter the legal business, make a lot of money, and have the time to play golf with her at the Birmingham Country Club. That, however, was not to be, for Black became excited eventually at the prospect of sitting on the Court.

Franklin Roosevelt, according to Harold Ickes, a Roosevelt Administration figure, liked Black very much. FDR thought Hugo was too liberal for his own state; while he was not as good a lawyer as others,[26] he would make a good justice because of his support of New Dealism. According to Bill Douglas, at the time the newly appointed chairman of the Securities and Exchange Commission (SEC), Roosevelt was attracted to Black for three reasons: his use of the investigative role of the Senate to shape the American mind on reforms, his strong voting record in the Senate, and his early support for FDR in 1933.

Douglas insisted that President Roosevelt chose Black because he wanted "to throw a 'tiger,' as he put it, into the Court—an outstanding opponent of all that the old Court had done."[27] It is clear that the president "longed to give the Senate a bitter pill to swallow, yet make the rebellious legislators gulp it down."[28] Douglas, concluded, "Happily, Black had greatness as well, but Roosevelt could hardly be expected to know that."[29]

Black had initially been lukewarm about the idea of going to the Court. "I had no desire to get out of the Senate, and I really wanted to run the next time just to show some people down there that they couldn't beat me, as they were threatening to do."[30] He was a vigorous, aggressive Democratic politician and, like other politicians who thought of service on the Court after being asked to consider such a job, Hugo believed that a life on the high bench might be too sedate for an energetic politician with an overactive thyroid. Besides, he really "preferred the rough and tumble and the opportunity for real policy-making of a senator's place to the important but secluded eminence of the high bench."[31]

There was yet another possibility that crossed Black's mind at this time. He knew he would win reelection to the Senate in 1938 and looked forward to the 1940 presidential election. Roosevelt would be seeking a new vice presidential running mate in 1940 and Black thought he might be tapped by FDR for the second spot. Hugo's belief "was based on an insight that he stood as good a chance as any man in the Democratic Party to move to the other side of the presidential desk."[32]

Black pondered that possible future overnight. However, Josephine was insistent on his taking the Court seat if the president offered it to him. The next day, therefore, Black informed his friend Minton that he would accept the nomination to the Supreme Court if Roosevelt nodded to him. Word finally got to Cummings, who informed FDR of Black's decision. Hugo could not meet with Roosevelt on Tuesday because the Democrats were giving newly designated Senate Majority

Leader Alben Barkley a banquet, and so the meeting was set for Wednesday, early evening.

On August 11, 1937, Roosevelt received the senator by himself as a guest at the White House for an early dinner. It was a momentous time for Hugo and Josephine. She could not stand to sit and wait at home alone; while Hugo was with the president, she went off to see the film version of Pearl F. Buck's best-seller, *The Good Earth.*

For what seemed an eternity to Black, the president talked about everything but the appointment to the Court. Then, in the Oval Office after dinner, Roosevelt reached into his desk, opened a drawer, and pulled out a roll of parchment paper. It was a blank, though very official nomination form.[33]

"Hugo," he said, "I'd like to write your name here [on the presidential commission sent to the Senate]. But I want to tell you that it hasn't been without some protests that I am appointing you. Hugo, I wish you were twins because Barkley says he needs you in the Senate because you are the best floorman he has. But I think you'll be more useful on the Court."[34]

After listening to the president, the Alabaman said, "That settles it, I'll go to the Court."[35] Roosevelt then wrote Black's name on the commission. The senator, after seeing the president inscribe his name, then quickly left the White House.

The only people who knew of Roosevelt's decision prior to the Thursday message to the Senate were the president, Cummings, Minton, and Senator and Mrs. Black. James Farley, Roosevelt's close advisor and then U.S. postmaster general, had visited the White House later that Wednesday evening and the president did not mention the appointment even to him.[36] At no time did his former membership in the Klan come up in any conversation FDR had with Cummings and others—except, evidently, in his conversation with Black Wednesday evening.

Toward midday on Thursday, August 12, a messenger from the White House arrived at the Senate chambers with the Roosevelt nomination in hand. As a contemporary news account observed, he arrived "in an atmosphere taut with revolt and raw with the wounds of the court-plan battle."[37] When the nomination was read, "it produced the effect of an explosive shell."[38] The chief clerk of the Senate had gotten no further than "I nominate Hugo L. Black" when the chamber exploded. Incredulity and then "a dark and fruitless irritation" spread throughout the hall.[39]

Black was in his seat in the Senate chamber. Josephine, in a black dress, sat ramrod stiff in the gallery above the tumult, watching the disruption. As a contemporary reporter noted, "slumped in his seat, [Black] twisted a sheaf of papers into a slender roll and then rent them to bits" as his erstwhile colleagues shouted their outrage at Roosevelt's selection.[40] *Time* magazine reported that "the nomination fell as a bombshell to the press" as well. The Senate's anti–New Deal clique, the article continued, "saw the [Black] appointment as a Roosevelt trick to ram the furthest Left-winger available down the Senate's throat."[41]

Henry Ashurst, Hugo's Senate colleague, tried to break the tension. The outburst clearly suggested two realities. Many senators still viewed Black as an uncultured, very common redneck who had been supported by the hated Klan. Other senators disliked him because of his highly publicized legislative role as a vicious interrogator/inquisitor who had, they claimed, intentionally violated the constitutional rights of witnesses appearing before his investigating committees. Ashurst asked for immediate confirmation, consistent with the practice of senatorial courtesy.

Objections to the Ashurst proposal were immediately heard, and there were harsh criticisms of Black's competency to serve on the Court. Senator William King remarked bitterly that "it's a good thing the President didn't have six nominations to make." A Georgia representative, Eugene Cox, said bluntly about Black: "Why, he's nothing but an anarchist." Others, however, supported Black's nomination and urged confirmation immediately, without a hearing.

The popular press was very critical of the president's choice. Raymond Morley, for example, writing for *Newsweek,* said that "there have been worse appointments to high judicial offices, but with Rodgers and Hart, I can't remember where or when."[42] After the story of Black's Klan membership broke in mid-September and became the political scandal of the year in the nation, Morley, certainly not alone among reporters, livid with anger, wrote that "Black represents class hatreds. . . . He is a bigot!"[43]

The Senate, however, elected to schedule a hearing conducted by the Judiciary Committee on his nomination. For the next five days, the Senate awakened to the realization that one of their own, someone not loved by most solons, would have to be confirmed by the senators. Hours were spent, for the very first time since 1853, discussing the competency of one of their own kind.

It's important to note that during these heated discussions in the Judiciary Committee and on the floor of the Senate, there was no public mention of the Alabaman's possible membership in the Klan in the 1920s, and certainly Black was not going to volunteer that information, for it would have jeopardized any chance he had of sitting on the Court. Although there was conversation about the significant support he received from the Klan during his 1926 Democratic primary campaign, there was nothing said about his *being* a white-robed Klansman.

When asked by the reporter Duncan Aikman of *Newsweek* during this period of intense debate whether he was ever a member of the Klan, Black immediately said "no comment."[44] On another occasion during this five-day period, he stated that he was "not now" a member of the Klan and urged senators to vote against his confirmation if any of them were "concerned lest he might have been a Klansman in the past."[45]

Evidently the president took delight in the dispute in the Senate during these five days: he saw the "open discomfiture of his senatorial enemies."[46] The Senate's Judiciary Committee reported Black's nomination favorably, on August 16, by a thirteen-to-four vote, and his name went to the floor of the Senate.

"Floor consideration brought out some of the most acrimonious debate of the session. Charges that the Alabama senator had been a member of the Ku Klux Klan were denied and reiterated. . . . In the end, a motion to recommit was rejected, 15 yeas to 66 nays."[47] The next day, August 17, 1937, after the debate—during which the Senate barely hinted about Black's possible membership in the Klan—Hugo's colleagues confirmed (sixty-three to sixteen) his nomination to the Court. Ten Republicans and six Democrats voted against "one of their own."

On August 19, Black took the oath of office and submitted his resignation from the Senate to Alabama's governor, Bibb Graves; then immediately he and his wife sailed for a short European vacation. Hugo later told his second wife, Elizabeth, that he took the oath very quickly because "I wasn't taking any chances. I knew that my enemies in big business and the press would inflame the public against me so much that they might get a judge to enjoin me from taking the oath. After I had taken the oath, my enemies would have to impeach me for something I had done *since* taking the oath of office."[48] It was, like Black's other crucial actions, a prudent move.

Membership in the Klan: Sit or Quit

In Robert Penn Warren's *All the King's Men,* Willie Stark, the archetypical Southern redneck politician, tells one of his workers to

> dig up some dirt on an opponent, a judge who is seemingly above reproach. "There is always something. . . . Man is conceived in sin and born in corruption and he passeth from the stink of the didie to the stench of the shroud. There is always something." Soon the investigator discovers that Stark was right, that the judge, years earlier, took a bribe. He says to Willie, "nothing is ever lost. There is always the clue, the canceled check, the smear of lipstick, the footprint in the canna bed, the condom on the park path, the baby shoes dipped in bronze, the taint in the blood stream."[49]

The writer who cited this Southern literary classic in a *Newsweek* piece, however, was not reflecting on Black's Klan dilemma that emerged full blown within weeks after he was confirmed. He was commenting on the political scandal of 1991, the Clarence Thomas Senate confirmation hearings after Anita Hill testified that President George Bush's Supreme Court nominee had sexually harassed her ten years earlier. The magazine writer could well have been commenting on the scandal that surrounded Hugo Black after it was revealed in the national media that he had been a member of the Alabama Klan in the 1920s.

While the Blacks were trying to vacation in Europe, the *Pittsburgh Post-Gazette,* in mid-September 1937, ran Ray Sprigle's articles about Hugo over five days. Sprigle was the archconservative paper's "eccentric, middle aged ace political fact-finder, [who was sent] to Alabama to investigate the [Klan] story as soon as Hugo Black was nominated."[50] The articles charged that Black was a member of the Ku Klux Klan from September 11, 1923, to July 9, 1925, and that, on September 2, 1926, he accepted a gold-card life membership in the Klan. Letters and documents were printed in the paper illustrating Hugo's membership in the Klan. The story exploded across the nation and became, swiftly, the "prize political scandal of the year."[51]

Senators, including Millard Tydings of Maryland, William E. Borah of Idaho, and Edward R. Burke of Nebraska, argued that had they known of Black's membership in the Klan in 1925, they would have voted against confirmation.[52] *Commonweal,* a liberal-Catholic weekly, noted that "the first issue is not one of the Klan at all but of Mr. Black's personal integrity." The editorial concluded by stating that "there remains only the powerful force of public opinion which will not tolerate, we believe, a Klansman on the Supreme Court bench and the personal conscience of Mr. Black himself."[53]

The *New Republic,* a friendlier newsweekly, had more difficulty criticizing Black in light of his impeccable New Deal credentials. After indicating that any person who wanted to get elected in Alabama in the 1920s had to have Klan support, and that joining the Klan then "was much like what joining Rotary or Kiwanis or the Lions is in some small midwestern town," the editorial went to Black's New Deal record. "His record in the Senate," it concluded, "shows no signs whatever of Klan leanings. . . . Let him remain on the Bench and continue the fight against special privilege and on behalf of the rights and interests of the common man in which he has played so fine a part in his years in the Senate."[54]

There were, however, many more voices in shrill opposition to Black's sitting on the Court. The *American Mercury* called him a "vulgar dog," while *Time* magazine wrote that "Hugo won't have to buy a robe, he can dye his white one black."[55] The *New York Herald Tribune* called Black a "coward," and the *New York Times* editorialized: "At every session of the Court, the presence on the bench of a Justice who has worn the white robe of the Ku Klux Klan will stand as a living symbol of the fact that here the cause of liberalism was unwittingly betrayed."[56]

There were claims that these attacks on Black were attacks on Roosevelt, that the Alabaman was a surrogate and therefore fair game for these vituperative New Deal attackers. Others argued that he was attacked because of his vigorous support for New Deal policies, his investigations that led, for example, to the Public Utility Holding Company Act, and his support of the Fair Labor Standards Act.[57]

Black, not surprisingly, agreed with these assessments. In late October, shortly after the hysterical criticism dropped off and the Supreme Court's 1937 term began, he wrote to an acquaintance, Hugh G. Grant, that

> there was nothing strange about the fight against me. It was waged by the same old crowd. They brought out no new facts that have not been thoroughly brought out in campaigns in Alabama. With their practically united press, however (which is chiefly against the President), they had no difficulty in making the public believe that they had broken a startling piece of news.
>
> On Sunday, however, the Gallup poll showed that they had accomplished nothing. A previous poll indicated that immediately after the news broke, the public was 59% against me and Sunday's poll indicated that the public was 56% with me. Whether there is anything to these polls or not, I do not know, but I am sure that the campaign against me proved to be a dud. Thousands of letters have come to me from every part of the United States and I have no doubt but that the people know the causes for the fight. I am now at work and gradually getting settled down.[58]

One of the letters Black received was from Hazel Black Davis, his delightful niece. She was saddened by and concerned about the attacks on her absolutely favorite uncle. In his reply letter, he said, in part, to comfort her:

> Just do not let all this stuff worry you. I have never missed one single minute's sleep, and have never had a single fear as to what would occur. . . . The conspiracy to ruin me has not worked. . . . Your letter was sweet and I appreciate it. . . . In the meantime rest assured that my enemies have not caused me to suffer. I have followed my course and my conscience approved it. This armor has protected me and will continue to guard me from their poison shafts.[59]

President Roosevelt's reaction was, for some observers, "the oddest of all the extremely violent [reactions] which the proofs of Black's Klan membership provoked."[60] FDR suggested, through his aides, that he had been deceived by the Alabaman. For example, on September 14, 1937, he told a press conference that "he had not known of any Klan link when he appointed Black to the Court. 'I know only what I have read in the newspapers.' "[61] Roosevelt left it up to Black to deal with the dilemma as he left for a political trip out west just as the new Justice and his wife were returning from their European vacation.

They had been harangued by the press all during their trip. Upon their return, over one hundred news reporters at the boat dock greeted them. Black had to seek refuge in his sister-in-law's home in Alexandria. He had, by this time, decided to use a national radio broadcast to address the Klan question. He wanted Americans to hear him speak about the matter directly, rather than having them rely on the print media's reporting. He just didn't trust them, in great part because of the extremely conservative bias of the publishers and many of their investigative reporters.

William O. Douglas, who would become Black's Court colleague, provided a juicy target for the media in future years because of his predilection for marrying very young women (three), insisted that this lengthy, unhappy run-in with the angry press influenced Hugo's views on the limits of the right of assembly and petition. Douglas wrote that Black's "house was picketed en masse, an experience that I think colored his decisions in all subsequent cases involving picketing, mass demonstrations, protest marches. . . . [Black] was seared by the experience."[62]

Finally, at exactly 9:30 P.M. on the evening of October 1, 1937, in the dining room of the home of his close friend, Claude Hamilton (who worked as a lawyer in a federal agency in Washington, The Reconstruction Finance Corporation), Justice Hugo Black spoke on national radio for about eleven minutes. All the national radio networks carried the unprecedented broadcast. "There was practically nothing else on the air throughout the U.S."

Like the 1991 televised Clarence Thomas–Anita Hill coverage, where millions of people across America were glued to their TVs for three long days and nights, over 50 million people were glued to their radios in 1937, to hear Justice Black respond to the Klan story. In the street outside Hamilton's home, there were no less than four newsreel cars and over 250 persons: "reporters, cameramen, and bareheaded neighbors were lined up" to record or simply observe history in the making.[63]

Armed with two packs of Chesterfield cigarettes, even though he had stopped smoking cigarettes a few years earlier, Black got ready for his latest crucible. Sitting in a plush, high-backed, dining room chair, with a glass of water nearby, a number of microphones facing him, and a cigarette resting in an ashtray, he was ready to present to the nation the 1,054 words he'd prepared about his membership in the Ku Klux Klan in the 1920s.

He said softly, in his mild Southern accent, that "I did join the Klan. I later resigned. I never rejoined." He charged that the issue raised by his critics was part of a "concerted campaign" to fan the flames of religious prejudice. "If continued, the inevitable result will be the projection of religious beliefs into a position of prime importance in political campaigns and to reinfect our social and business life with the poison of religious bigotry." Addressing the Klan membership issue directly, Black said,

> The insinuations of racial and religious intolerance made concerning me are based on the fact that I joined the Ku Klux Klan about 15 years ago. I did join the Klan. I later resigned. I never rejoined. What appeared then, or what appears now, on the records of that organization I do not know.
>
> I never have considered and I do not now consider the unsolicited card given to me shortly after my nomination to the Senate [in 1926] as a membership of any kind in the Ku Klux Klan. I never used it. I did not even keep it.
>
> Before becoming a Senator I dropped the Klan. I have had nothing to do with it since that time. I abandoned it. I completely discontinued any association with the organization. I have never resumed it and never expect to do so.

Claiming that he had many Catholic and Jewish friends, Hugo ended the brief broadcast by stating, "When this statement is ended my discussion of this question is closed."[64] Hugo lit yet another Chesterfield and put his text away. And it was a closed question until after his death, when a *New York Times* obituary was published that included Black's remarks about his Klan membership.

Even this dark, ugly moment in his life had a humorous side for the Supreme Court Justice. According to his second wife, Elizabeth, Black "started to disclose his secret membership in the CMA [Coming Men of America, an organization he joined after clipping their ad from a pulp magazine when he was eleven years old] when he made his 1937 radio address about the Klan, showing that, along with the Knights of Pythias, Eagles, Masons, Doakies, and so forth, he had joined all sorts of secret societies."[65]

Although he never publicly challenged Roosevelt's assertion that the president had not known about his membership in the Klan, Black did leave a May 1968 statement about their relationship in the Virginia van der Veer Hamilton file, a Southern historian, in his papers in the Library of Congress. In the note to the file, he said:

> President Roosevelt, when I went up to lunch with him, told me that there was no reason for my worrying about my having been a member of the Ku Klux Klan. He said that some of his best friends and supporters he had in the state of Georgia were strong members of that organization. He never in any way, by word or attitude, indicated any doubt about my having been in the Klan nor did

he indicate any criticism of me for having been a member of that organization. The rumors and statements to the contrary are wrong.[66]

Representative Claude Pepper, then in the Senate, also commented that Roosevelt "might even have known at one point [that] Hugo Black had played footsie" with the Klan, but he "put his faith in that man."[67]

A renegade cousin of Black's, a convicted felon named J. C. ("Curry") Toland, provided a novel twist on the Klan episode. In December 1938, after the anger toward Black had diminished somewhat, the Justice received a letter from his cousin asking if Hugo could provide "one little bit of justice," in particular, some legal help in an estate matter as well as some cash from the Justice to "right a grave wrong." And, in a postscript, Curry Toland told Black how he had denied a reporter from the *Dallas News* any information about the Judge's membership in the Klan. He "wanted to find out the truth about this KKK business from a member of the family, feeling sure the family would know. I declined to give him the information which my father gave me concerning your membership in the Lodge."[68] Hugo never answered the letter, nor did he send any funds to his cousin.

October 4, the First Monday in October, marked the beginning of the Supreme Court's October 1937 term, the 148th term of the Court. It began just three days after Black's unprecedented broadcast. By the opening of the term, it was quite clear that Hugo was not about to resign. He was on the high bench for the rest of a lifetime.

On that first day of the term, Black entered the Court through a rear entrance. Accompanying him was his first law clerk, Jerome "Buddy" Cooper, a twenty-four-year-old Birmingham native of the Jewish faith who had recently graduated from Harvard Law School. The Justice took his seat with the brethren on the extreme right side of the long, straight bench.

He did not repeat the judicial oath in open Court, as was the custom because, recounted Black, "Chief Justice Hughes said it was completely unnecessary. I would have repeated the oath in the courtroom had the Chief Justice not decided to the contrary. Fear of 'a sensational challenge' had nothing whatever to do with the Chief Justice's decision."[69]

That first day of the 1937 term, there were two petitions filed, by Albert Levitt and Henry Kelly. They challenged Black's eligibility to sit on the Supreme Court. Both lawyers claimed, in light of Article I, Section 6, of the U.S. Constitution, that the Alabaman was ineligible to sit as a justice. This was so, they insisted, because, as a senator, he had voted to increase the salaries of justices when he voted for the Supreme Court Retirement Act. Levitt had shown Black a courtesy by forewarning him on August 18, 1937, that Levitt was filing a motion that would try to remove him from the Court. "May I assure you that my action is taken without any personal unfriendliness or bias," he wrote in a letter, sending along a copy of his motion and petition for Court action.[70]

Lawyer Levitt, at the appropriate time on opening day, rose and announced: "May it please the Court. I have a motion in reference to the seating of Justice Black." Chief Justice Hughes grimly intoned, "Is it in writing?" Levitt indicated that it was, and Hughes then closed the matter by stating that "you may submit it to the Court and it will be taken under advisement."[71] The petitions were quietly dismissed by the Court later that month. On October 11, 1937, the Court ruled that Levitt and others did not have "standing to sue" in federal court. The immediate crisis had ended; now the Judge had to deal with the bitterness the Klan revelation had triggered in the hearts and minds of thousands of people across the nation, especially black citizens.

Friendship with Walter White of the NAACP

Still very angry, many civil rights groups continued to severely criticize the Black appointment. The Independent Young Democrats, for example, ran an ad, complete with a black mourning trim, referring to the opening of the Court as Black Day and a day that will

> be so mourned each year as the **Blackest Day** in the history of American Justice [because of] Hugo Black['s membership in the] Ku Klux Klan, which organization is dedicated to racial and religious intolerance, bigotry and class hatred [and because he has taken a seat on the] Supreme Court of the United States, highest Tribunal of our Democracy and safeguard of equity, justice and liberty.[72]

The anger and dismay of blacks due to the revelation of Hugo's membership in the Klan led to a minicrisis for Walter White, the highly respected executive secretary of the NAACP. He had to respond to hundreds of letters from angry members of the organization, all demanding that the NAACP vigorously oppose the Black appointment and call for his impeachment, resignation, or whatever so long as the former Klansman left the high bench.

The problem for the senior leader of this major black organization was a simple yet profound one: White and Black had become friends, and the NAACP official knew that Hugo was a decent, vigorous New Deal liberal. They became friends when Black served as chairman of the Senate Committee on Labor and Education. There was, noted one biographer, an "extraordinary reciprocal respect [between the two that] bridged the gulf that separated them."[73]

Ever since 1935, the two men, usually accompanied by Charles Houston, the legal director of the NAACP, had been meeting privately to share philosophies and discuss educational issues affecting the races in the South. But they soon went beyond political issues and developed a close personal friendship. When, for example, Black's daughter, Jo-Jo, was injured in an automobile accident, White wrote two letters to Hugo inquiring about her health.

In his autobiography, White wrote that he saw Black as fundamentally different from the other racist Southern senators, men such as Theodore Bilbo of Mississippi, Tom Connally of Texas, "Cotton Ed" Smith of South Carolina, and Kenneth McKellar of Tennessee.

> I was convinced that [Black] believed what he said. His superiority of intellect and character over most of his colleagues from the South was so apparent that he seemed to me to be an advance guard of the new South we dreamed of and hoped for when that section of the country emancipated itself from the racial, economic,

and political bondage which fear, prejudice, and a regional inferiority complex had created.[74]

White also acknowledged the sincerity of Black's opposition to the federal antilynching bill, even though he did not agree with Black's legal and political arguments against the legislation. However, in their discussions White indicated to the senator that the NAACP's "constitutional authorities have been making certain changes in the bill to prevent its being used in labor disputes." White told Black that, when the redrafting was done, "I should like very much to take advantage of the invitation you extended . . . to come in and talk with you and get your advice upon it."[75]

The NAACP executive secretary was also in close communication with Hugo regarding federal aid to education, especially how *Plessy*'s continuing validity would impact aid to schools in the South: "From our conversation I am sure you will agree that some sort of safeguards should be included in the measure to prevent gross disparity in expenditure of school funds for whites and Negroes in those states where there are separate schools." White sent Arthur Raper's book, *Preface to Peasantry,* to Black and asked the senator to read the chapter that focused on white and Negro schools, "in which you will see how unfair has been the distribution not only of state and county funds for education but of [federal] funds as well. We fear that the same disproportion would be true under the bill which you and Senator Harrison have introduced."[76]

Discussing the federal aid to education bill with Black led to the development of White's great respect for the Southern legislator.

> I had learned that he was not only capable of intellectual growth but was one of the ablest men in the Senate. The dead hand of tradition was anathema to him, although he combined a very shrewd and realistic expediency with his belief that many American concepts had to be revised because of changing world conditions.[77]

And, although Hugo was opposed to placing safeguards into the aid to education legislation because these would alienate the other Southern senators and the bill would never get out of committee, he spoke of the importance of education in changing the South. "Education," he told his NAACP friend "is the answer to the race question, not legislation. When white Southerners are educated and given economic security there will be less prejudice against the Negro—fewer lynchings, more jobs, greater justice for the Negro."[78]

By the time the Klan membership firestorm broke in September 1937, the two men had worked together for almost two years to deal with the concerns each had about the other's position on public policy matters, especially antilynching, protection of labor, wages and hours legislation, and aid to public education. Clearly, the revelation about Black's membership in the Klan upset White, as it did all blacks. However, White had, by that time, developed an understanding of Hugo's true liberalism and did what he could to minimize the NAACP's condemnation of Black.

As soon as his name was presented to the Senate by Roosevelt for the Court opening, White was inundated with letters from NAACP affiliates expressing deep concern about the nominee. J. L. LeFlore of the Mobile (Alabama) NAACP affiliate wrote that Black, in 1923, when he was a special federal prosecutor,

> inadvertently referred to Negro witnesses and defendants as "niggers," showing the utmost of contempt for colored people with his scurrilous and insulting remarks. His record in opposing federal anti-lynching also shows obviously that Negroes need not expect a fair, unbiased and impartial consideration of any case involving our rights as citizens that must be passed upon by him.[79]

White's initial response to Black's Supreme Court nomination, for the NAACP, was to send Hugo a telegram, on August 16, 1937, asking his friend to

> advise us what your attitude will be if your nomination to the Supreme Court is confirmed by the Senate with respect to the full enforcement of all the guarantees of the federal constitution particularly in respect to a broad interpretation of the Fourteenth and Fifteenth Amendments to the end that minority groups will have full citizenship and actual equal protection and due process of law guaranteed by these amendments.[80]

Walter needed a reply in order to "answer telegraphic and other inquiries with respect to your nomination which pour in upon this office." Black, however, had left the country for his European vacation and did not provide the information to his friend.

There were requests made by the NAACP affiliates to have the confirmation process delayed so that the Senate could examine carefully the rumors about Black's possible membership in the Klan. This did not happen. Thurgood Marshall, then the NAACP's assistant special counsel, wrote to a member that "as you know, however, the judiciary committee did not vote for an open hearing but quickly recommended confirmation of Senator Black."[81]

Within a few weeks of the nomination and confirmation, just prior to the Sprigle stories in the *Pittsburgh Post-Gazette,* White sent Hugo's secretary and nephew, Hollis Black, himself a member of the Alabama Klan, a short letter, with accompanying copies of some of the mail he had received from irate blacks: "I want you and the Justice to get this taste of the pummeling the NAACP in general and its secretary in particular are getting for our attitude. I hope you are now getting some rest, and I also hope to be seeing you in Washington some time this fall."[82]

White had indeed been battered for his defense of his friend Black. As he wrote in his autobiography, "the position I took . . . brought down on me a considerable deluge of criticism, the most acrimonious of it coming from a Negro politician who declared to an annual convention of the Negro Elks that 'Walter White has sold out his race and ought to be driven out of the race.' "[83]

Then the Klan story broke with all its fury, followed by the national protest. When a reporter asked whether Black believed in the Klan's credo, Hugo noted that his secretary was a Catholic, his law clerk was a Jew, "and one of his closest friends was 'Walter White of the NAACP.' "[84] Although White knew of Black's admirable qualities, he had to speak for the membership and interests of the

NAACP. On September 16, 1937, a telegram was sent to President Roosevelt from the organization demanding that FDR

> call upon Black to resign his post or take other appropriate action in the absence of repudiation and disproof of the charges by Senator Black to relieve himself and the nation of the embarrassment of having upon the highest court a man pledged to uphold principles inimical to true Americanism. It seems to us impossible that any man can uphold the doctrines of the Ku Klux Klan and at the same time keep his oath to uphold the Constitution of the United States."[85]

At the same time, White sent a three-page letter to all branches of the NAACP informing them of the telegram to the president. However, FDR did not respond, and the matter seemed settled on October 4, 1937, when Black took his seat on the Court.

Their friendship, although tested, nevertheless continued. Indeed, after this crucible, it was enhanced. When asked about Black's assertion about their friendship, White, at the time of intense black anger directed at Hugo, nevertheless responded by stating that his "firsthand acquaintance with the new Supreme Court Justice's views on racial, economic, and political questions convinced me that Mr. Black would prove to be one of the most valued and able members of the Court."[86] White's statements about the Justice were courageous ones, words that angered his fellow workers in the NAACP.

As early as October 16, 1937, White received a letter from Hollis Black. It was a letter of appreciation, for the new Justice and his secretary realized the dilemma for their friend Walter:

> I can fully realize your situation and what you have been through. Knowing Justice Black as I do, however, I do not hesitate to state that the time will come when every true [American] of tolerance and real Americanism will applaud you for your foresight and your courage. . . . I also know that Justice Black would be glad to see you, and hope you can call at his office when you are in Washington.[87]

White never lost his confidence in Black. At the time of his nomination to the Court, the NAACP official wrote to a friend that the Judge would be on the "spot" whenever a civil rights case came before the Court. Hugo confided in Walter "frankly and soberly that he realized this and that he hoped that he would be able to measure up to what I and others of his friends expected of him."[88]

The two friends did continue to meet and discuss philosophy. Indeed, by May 1941, White had the pleasure of inviting Justice Black to address the delegates attending the thirty-second annual conference of the NAACP, and they met to plan on such a presentation together.

In 1948, Hugo sent Walter a gracious letter after the Justice had received an autographed copy of White's autobiography. White, who had a bad heart, was admonished by Black to "take care of that heart. When its beat stops, the world will lose something that it needs."[89] When the Court heard oral argument in the school segregation cases in 1953, Hugo set aside a number of reserved seats for

Walter. After the *Brown* decision was announced in May 1954, an obviously delighted White wrote his friend a letter, "expressing my deep appreciation for the great contribution to democracy you participated in making through Monday's decision."[90] The two men had weathered a terrible challenge to friendship and had, afterwards, become much, much closer friends.

Within a few years, certainly by the time of his majority opinion for the Court in *Chambers v Florida* (1940),[91] the very shrill criticism of Black as Klansman died down. After one of his opinions was announced in 1938, Black received letters applauding his behavior from blacks across America. Reverend P. T. Hughes, writing from Pennsylvania, told the Justice of his "pleasure" with Black's actions from the bench. "God bless you, Justice Black. Our people are singing your praises throughout the east. . . . The Negro as such in this country is not seeking favors, but justice. I wish to assure you that you have my prayers and I beg that you will [continue] to remember our down-trodden race."[92]

Chambers raised the spectre of racial discrimination in the criminal justice system in the South. It was a notorious example of denial of due process to four black defendants, young men accused of murdering an elderly white man. Questioned without stop for over five days and nights, they confessed to the murder during the final day of questioning. While the men were not physically assaulted by the police, the argument of the NAACP in the appeal was that the confessions were involuntary because of the fatigue factor and psychological stress, as if the confessions were beaten out of them. (Sadly, Isiah Chambers, one of the four blacks who had been convicted for the murder, "lost his mind" because of those five days of psychological pressure and was committed to an insane asylum a year after the 1940 arguments in the Court.)[93]

Black heard the arguments of Thurgood Marshall, who was chief counsel for the defendants and presented the case to the Court in briefs and in oral argument. For a unanimous Court, the Justice wrote a clear, moving opinion setting aside their convictions and ordering a new trial, concluding that to "permit human lives to be forfeited upon confessions thus obtained would make of the constitutional requirement of due process of law a meaningless symbol." In *Chambers,* Black penned words that, when he read them in subsequent years or had Elizabeth read them to him, always brought tears to his eyes.

> Under our constitutional system, courts stand against any winds that blow as havens of refuge for those who might otherwise suffer because they are helpless, weak, outnumbered, or because they are non-conforming victims of prejudice and public excitement. Due process of law, preserved for all by our Constitution, commands that no such practice as that disclosed by this record shall send any accused to his death. No higher duty, no more solemn responsibility, rests upon this Court, than that of translating into living law and maintaining this constitutional shield deliberately planned and inscribed for the benefit of every human being subject to our Constitution—of whatever race, creed, or persuasion.[94]

Chief Justice Charles Evans Hughes strategically had Black, for the Court, announce the opinion in *Chambers* on Lincoln's birthday, Monday, February 12, 1940. It was received with the highest praise by blacks across America. For example, the president of the Fort Worth (Texas) NAACP, wrote to Hugo shortly afterwards, extolling his "superb statesmanship" and "recording our most sincere thanks to you for the strong, timely utterances" in *Chambers:*

> When your name was submitted to the Senate for confirmation, . . . Negroes throughout the country were greatly horrified and at once sent up a mighty howl of protest to your appointment and confirmation. When nothing could be accomplished by their best efforts, . . . Negroes everywhere were a sad, disappointed, sickened group. If it were possible, Negroes all over the nation would recall every word of derision heaped upon you and smother you with the glory of their praise. We thank you and congratulate you for the unprecedented decision, not because Negroes are involved, but rather because it rings true to the tone of justice and fair play. . . . *Chambers* is a "2nd emancipation" for it not only affects the immediate victims, but it equally forcefully thousands of Americans, both White and Black.[95]

At about the same time, Hugo received a letter from Mary McLeod Bethune, one of the black leaders in America. In 1940 she was the director of the Division of Negro Affairs of the Federal Security Agency's National Youth Administration. She wrote because she wanted

> to join the great throngs in extending to you our congratulations and gratitude for your decision in behalf of the four Negro boys in Florida who were condemned to death. God bless you. Our prayers are that you may live long enough to render such just decisions. The Negro race has been waiting for men like you on the bench for many years. May He give you courage, vision, and a growing spirit of justice. We need you in a day like this.[96]

There were many hundreds of such letters from Negroes across the nation, thanking Black and telling him how the Court's actions, on Lincoln's birthday, had abated their "bitterness and resentfulness,"[97] and had given them renewed hope for justice from the Court. Almost all the writers "apologized"[98] for their initial enmity directed at the former Klansman, and many saw his actions as the "opening of a new day for real democracy in America. A thing which we Negroes have long since wanted to happen."[99]

Finally, Hugo began to see change in the attitudes of black leaders in the form of laudatory editorials in black newspapers that had been, until *Chambers,* suspicious of the newly appointed Alabaman. For example, in December 1938, the black-owned *Informer,* a Houston newspaper, had editorialized about Black after the Court handed down the *Gaines* case. Entitled "JUSTICE BLACK COMES THROUGH," the editorial said that

> to our great surprise and infinite relief, our good friend, Justice Hugo Black, was found with the majority, which upset a tradition of the South [prohibiting blacks from attending white-only state law schools] that is as old as the freedom of the Negro. Not a Negro in America would have been surprised if Justice Black had been found on the minority mumbling nothings with Justices Butler and McReynolds, two old men still actuated by the tenets of slavery days. Along with thousands of other Negroes, we fought confirmation of Justice Black and were loud in our wailings after he was confirmed. But we want to hasten now to join that

ever-increasing group who are beginning to suspect Hugo L. Black as a sincere liberal, who is for the elevation of the underdog. To say truth, the action of the justice is too good to believe, and we are still waiting for another occasion to see if our ears and eyes are deceiving us.[100]

Because of Black's essentially powerful and just judgments and values, by the beginning of the Second World War, by the time of *Chambers,* he had overcome the outraged cries of many minorities in America. Black newspapers across America, including the *Informer,* went from writing about the horror of a former Klansman sitting on the Court to editorial huzzahs and hurrahs about the Alabaman.

Once again, however, as was the case when Black moved to Birmingham and when he arrived in Washington, D.C., he was the outsider in the Court's hallowed halls. He was perceived by his new Court colleagues as the uneducated, unwashed, radical political appointee of an angry, frustrated president—ill-prepared and temperamentally ill-suited to serve on the Supreme Court. Called "Alabama's Hillbilly" by many and ridiculed by most, Hugo began the 1937 term "surrounded by doubts as to his training and intellect. . . . Indeed, Justice Stone asked Professor Frankfurter to lecture Black on what a Supreme Court Justice was expected to do!"[101]

Harlan Fiske Stone, who as attorney general had hired Black in 1923 to prosecute rum runners in Mississippi, in 1937 wrote to Felix Frankfurter, then teaching at Harvard Law School: "Do you know Black well? You might be able to render him great assistance. He needs guidance from someone who is more familiar with the workings of the judicial process than he is."[102] Frankfurter responded to Stone in what was his imperious, characteristic style: "Black means nothing to me—I have never laid eyes on him."[103]

At about the same time, the highly respected Supreme Court Justice Louis Brandeis, a close friend of Frankfurter's, also asked the professor to help the Alabaman as much as possible.

In this unfortunate manner, under the Klan cloud, did Franklin Roosevelt's initial appointee, Hugo Black, join the Court. In a matter of months, he would be joined by other Roosevelt appointees. Ultimately, Roosevelt appointed nine justices, including Felix Frankfurter, William O. Douglas, and Robert Jackson, to the Court. The Supreme Court, and the nation, would soon see Black's jurisprudential impact. Sadly, the nation would also be party to a series of public clashes involving the Justice and his brethren.

CHAPTER SIX

The Supreme Court Justice from Alabama: The Role and Functions of the U.S. Supreme Court

Hugo Black was the seventy-fifth person to sit on the high bench since the beginning of the U.S. republic in 1789. When he retired thirty-four years later, he had worked with five chiefs and twenty-eight associates, almost a third of all the men and women who have sat on the nation's high bench.

When Black joined the U.S. Supreme Court for the start of its 1937 October term, he had already developed a strong commitment to a society based on the rule of law, one in which all citizens, rich and poor alike, regardless of status or power, would be treated fairly. By 1937, he had been engaged in an intense, self-paced reading program that, for over a decade, enabled the Judge to absorb the great lessons of history.

Black had a clear political perception of the role of the Supreme Court and its justices in a representative democracy. In speech after speech while in the Senate, he spoke of the importance of the fundamental instrument of governing, the Constitution, and of the limited interpretative role of the federal judges, acting in light of the Constitution's general principles. For example, just prior to his move to the Court in 1937, Black rose and addressed the matter of judicial usurpation of power in a democracy:

> Most of the Framers believed in popular government by the people themselves. Like Jefferson they were not willing to trust lifetime judges with omnipotent powers over governmental agencies. They were familiar with the lessons of history, and they knew that the people's liberty was safest with the people themselves or their properly elected representatives.[1]

By the time Black joined the Supreme Court, he had developed and presented on the floor of the Senate articulate, although abstract, criticisms of the high tribunal. Quickly, he saw the realities of judicial usurpation from the inside out. Just as quickly, he knew what had to be done to curb what he judged to be judicial excesses. And, as was the case throughout his life to this point, Black did not hesitate to enter the fray, battling for a much more limited role for the Court.

The institution he joined was, because of existing internal conflict and fragmentation "no longer a Court."[2] By the middle of the fourth decade of the twentieth century, a bare majority of the justices of the Court, in their zeal to curb the economic and social policies of the Roosevelt administration, were deciding cases and controversies totally "animated by aversion to the New Deal."[3]

This narrow Court majority interposed their economic and social views for those of state legislatures and the Congress, overturning legislation passed by large majorities in the Congress and signed into law by an energetic president.

The judicial intervention was based on their substantive interpretation of the due process clause in both the Fifth and Fourteenth Amendments to the Constitution. The anti–New Deal Court "construed 'liberty' [in the due process clause] in such an expansive way as to make it impossible for the government, whether the Congress or a state legislature, to enact legislation that interfered with the freedom of an owner of a business—corporate or otherwise—to run it as he chose."[4]

Interestingly, the Court was somewhat racist and had to confront segregation at the very moment Black entered the spanking new building. Because of the sitting justices' reluctance to move into the new Court building, Black was its first occupant. A. Leon Higginbotham, a highly respected African-American federal appellate judge, noted in a 1990 letter to Thurgood Marshall that the Court's cafeterias did not allow any blacks to enter, whether visitors or lawyers arguing cases before the brethren. Evidently, Higginbotham had been told that

> in the late 1930s, when Thomas E. Waggaman was Marshall of the U.S. Supreme Court, . . . there were a variety of incidents by which it was obvious that Waggaman had only contempt for blacks. . . . Waggaman complained to Chief Justice Charles Evans Hughes [about the blacks]. Hughes told Waggaman to go outside of the building and look at the portals of the Supreme Court, where there is emblazoned the words "Equal Justice Under the Law," and if even reading these words he did not know what the policy of the Supreme Court should be, the Chief Justice would appoint a new Marshall to replace Waggaman. From that date on, . . . there were no further attempts made to discourage blacks from using the cafeteria of the United States Supreme Court.[5]

It is clear, as Black and other justices found out once they relocated to the national capital, that Washington, D.C., was still very much a Southern city and that racial segregation pierced even the court itself.

From the very beginning of Black's work there, he was committed to redirecting Court behavior. Immediately, Black was to play a key role in the implementation of doctrines of judicial self-restraint that worked to move the Court away from interposition in social and economic matters of state. Grounded in history, Black tenaciously argued for the primacy of the Constitution's plain meaning. Furthermore, he vigorously defended the essential principle of the supremacy of the legislature in the American political system and strongly argued for a much more limited, constitutionally prescribed role in American politics for the Supreme Court and its nine justices.

The Constitution as Fundamental Law

At the very core of Black's view of life in a constitutional republic was the document itself. The fundamental law, the Constitution of the United States, was the essence of freedom and liberty in a democratic republic. It spelled out how laws were to be made and how they were to be implemented by government. The Constitution also provided protections for all persons with respect to political participation in the making of laws and procedural fairness in the implementation of the laws.

Anything else in America's political philosophy was merely commentary on the Constitution itself, including the encrustations on the Constitution written by court majorities over the generations. Black believed it imperative to remove these unnecessary words and to judge cases based on the historical meaning of the terms of the Constitution as well as defining the intent of the Framers of the 1787 fundamental law. He had an unshakable commitment to ridding the books of gratuitous and erroneous precedent by goal-oriented "substantive due process" Court majorities. It was a commitment that was never compromised in his thirty-four years on the Court.

Black's jurisprudence, as it finally emerged by the end of the 1940s, was comprised of three essential components: history, literalism, and, ultimately, absolutism.[6] All three concepts were "intertwined" in it.[7]

First, he understood the impact on policy makers of a good understanding of history—of their own society and of societies in antiquity, especially the history of ancient Greece and Rome. Without this comprehension, men and women might have to repeat past errors and tragedies of human existence. Understanding the past was the way to move to a more positive future.

Second, his commitment to literalism involved his "employing standards—the Constitution's words—for determining constitutional [powers of government and the] rights" of litigants before the Court.[8] Doing so meant, practically speaking, restricting judges, especially the justices of the Supreme Court, to the correct usage of the document's words. Black insisted that judges rely on the intent of the Framers as well as the "plain meaning of the Constitution's words and phrases (drawing on the history of the period) when reaching judgment in a case.

The type of judicial behavior that Black recommended called for a degree of self-restraint generally not in evidence in Court decision-making. But by acting with self-discipline, the justices would validate the supremacy of the legislature in public policy-making in the republic, unless of course the legislature itself was denying people the freedoms they have in America—and embodied in the First Amendment of the Constitution.

Finally, for Black, there was the commitment to an absolutist jurisprudence, absolutism being "a standard for enforcing the rights in the Constitution, not a method for exacting the meaning, scope, or extent of those rights."[9] The rights in the Constitution, argued Hugo in many hundreds of cases over his tenure on the Court, were absolute and "legally binding" on the brethren.[10]

When hearing cases that called for constitutional interpretation, the challenge for Black and for all the brethren was drawing upon *history,* to try to "decipher" the *literal* meaning of the constitutional clause and then to enforce the phrase *absolutely,* "against competing counter-claims" brought by other parties to the dispute.

This was not, however, a slot-machine jurisprudence. Black knew that constitutional clauses, for example, "due process" and "equal protection," were not static and were not, in themselves, absolute. Judgment meant choosing among a variety of constitutional interpretations of the meaning of the phrases, most not grounded in historical accuracy. Black believed that the brethren were "required to confine [their choices] to the words and phrases contained in the Constitution" and to the historically correct understanding of those words and phrases.[11]

The Judge's jurisprudence simply underscores his lifelong ardor for the Constitution. It was his legal Bible and, like the most dedicated religious fundamentalist, he knew its passages by heart. Hugo regularly communicated with the Founders, through extensive readings and rereadings of their essays about the Constitution and about constitutional government, and through readings about the history of the period. One of his law clerks, Chuck Lace, once told the Justice's wife Elizabeth that "Hugo is up on Mount Olympus communing with the Constitution."[12] Black always transmitted his "findings" through his opinions on the Court, whether for the majority, concurring, or in dissent.

For most of his life, Black was an education junkie. He borrowed more books from the Library of Congress than any other senator or congressman in the entire history of the library in a similar time frame. He haunted his favorite bookstores in Washington, D.C., Alabama, and Florida (when he and his wife took their annual winter vacation in Miami). He ordered books through the mail for himself, his family, his law clerks, and others. In addition to the baskets of grapefruit or oranges he sent from his vacation locale in Miami, Black loved to send books, especially those written by or about about the Greeks. And, in the 1960s, when he was in his eighties, he and Elizabeth would get up early mornings to watch the popular *Sunrise Semester* on CBS, whether it was a course on Greek tragedies or one on the Fourth Amendment.

At a moment's notice, in front of visiting students or a clutch of legal dignitaries from another nation visiting the Court, the Judge would whip his tattered copy of the Constitution from his coat pocket, flip through it to a particular passage, and then read the passage *con vivace.* "More than just a faith," commented one of the Judge's clerks, Black "had a true passion for the Constitution."[13]

Reading voraciously about the debates that took place during the summer of 1787 and carefully examining the arguments of the defenders of the new constitutional framework in the *Federalist Papers,* the Alabaman saw how crucial it was for elected and appointed public officials to act in accord with the Constitution's language and its plain intent. A law clerk commented on Hugo's understanding of the Framers and their document, "They perceived a whole series of issues from their reading of history and proceeded to solve those issues [of power and the needed restraints on power]. In particular, Black believed in a written Constitution and felt that that imposed very severe limits upon judges and governments."[14] For him, every word in the Constitution "represented a command" for some kind of action or, equally important, inaction on the part of government.[15]

For the newly appointed Justice of the Court, there was the imperative for balance, the Greek "balance" discussed by Aristotle and other Greek authors, between the rights of the person and the needs of the community. The Constitution's language gave the community both a representative policy-making process as well as an essential core of public values, found in its preamble and throughout the document and its amendments, that would, if kept on track by federal judges, balance the power of the government with the freedom and rights of the individual.

Without the checks and balances that the Constitution provided for American society, centrifugal forces, the *factions* James Madison feared and wrote about in *Federalist* no. 10, would move the society to either a tyranny of the majority or a state of near anarchy where rights and liberties overrode a legitimate societal need for orderliness. These possibilities, absent the constitutional balance, meant, ultimately, constraining the liberties of persons. For Black the historian the dominance of factions in America, such as those of business he had fought against as senator, could lead only to the destruction of democratic freedoms and the onset of a tyranny, albeit an industrial, commercial one.

Denying citizens absolute freedom was a controversial position for the Justice to take. However, he firmly believed that balance would strengthen the public value he called orderliness. Black once received a letter from someone who had been in the Judge's Birmingham religion classes a half century earlier; that correspondent complained about school integration plans approved by the federal court in Mississippi. Black wrote back:

> You worry about citizens being denied their "freedom of choice." Government is bound to deny citizens freedom of choice at some time to some extent and on certain subjects. *That is one of the great objects of government so that we have a country of law and order instead of one of anarchy and riot, and I believe in having the former kind of country as I always did back in the days when you were in my Sunday School class in Birmingham.*[16] (my emphasis)

There was, Black insisted, the categorical and constitutional need for government to be strong enough to provide for common defense and public order, but not so strong as to deprive persons of inalienable rights they possess in a representative democracy. The Constitution provided the guidelines for such a society. Its words had to be followed, absolutely and literally, by the public's policy-makers and by the Justices of the Court.

All these persons, whether legislators, members of the executive branch of government, or bureaucrats working in quasi-independent regulatory commissions; whether at the national, state, or local levels of decision-making, took an oath to follow the commands of the Constitution. The positive law they created, whether in the form of statutes, regulations, or treaties, all commanding a certain kind of societal behavior, to be enforced by the "sovereign" state, was for Black the "only relevant law"[17] in America.

Lawmaking in America is a supreme legislative function, maintained Black again and again, as a senator and as a justice of the Supreme Court. Legislators, freely elected by the citizens, had the constitutional responsibility and authority to legislate for the common good. This notion of legislative supremacy was the essential bedrock of Hugo's views about decision-making in a democracy. The legislators were to be constrained only by the words and phrases of the Constitution and its amendments. They were not to be constrained by the justices of the Court, unless the Court found palpable, capricious error in the actions of the lawmakers, either in the drafting of the law or in its application.

Constitutional Powers of Government

On the Court, Black had heated battles with his colleagues over how much power governments have to limit the actions of persons. After one such heated argument in conference, he told his son, Hugo Jr., waiting in his office, that "he thought that Felix was so mad at me that he almost hit me."[18]

Black knew that the Constitution, the fundamental charter of society's powers and rights, "sought to strike a lasting balance between the individual and the government, one that would guarantee that the nation was both strong and free," wrote his friend, William O. Douglas.[19] Federal appellate judges had to act in light of this constitutional axiom. They had the critical responsibility to "maintain the original constitutional protection of the freedom of the individual against the constitutional grant of power to regulate."[20] Further, he expressed his fear of the misuse of "the awesome power of the Supreme Court [as well as] the need to confine that power within precisely defined boundaries."[21]

The primary responsibility of the elected leaders in a representative democracy, wrote Black, is to "develop definite and precise laws under the authority of a written Constitution."[22] He had been taught at Alabama's law school that "legislators, not judges, should make the laws."[23] In addition, the Justice believed that a "legislature can do *whatever it sees fit to do* unless it is restrained by some express prohibition in the Constitution"[24] (my emphasis). The Constitution permitted legislators "to do virtually anything [they] wished in controlling the economy." The legislature, Black always insisted, "was fully clothed with the power to govern and to maintain order."[25] As Hugo said to an interviewer a few months before he died, legislatures, whether state or national, have the fundamental "right to invade an individual's privacy unless prohibited by some constitutional prohibition."[26] Judges had to determine, in cases before them, whether the legislators "stay[ed] within their proper constitutional limits" or whether, when making or implementing policy, they went beyond the legitimate scope of their powers.[27] The Justice carefully "search[ed] the record in every case that charged [legislative] overreaching to make certain that officials had acted responsibly and within bounds."[28]

Furthermore, he believed that administrative agencies, whether state or national, had sufficient power to make rules and regulations to effectively implement the law. Minimally, Black argued in dissent, federal agencies had the power to make regulations that implemented substantive legislation prior to judicial review of agency action.[29]

The Japanese exclusion cases, coming to the Court during the height of the Second World War, clearly illustrate Black's belief in the supremacy of legislative-executive lawmaking for the national community.[30] During the conference sessions in the Court, Black was categorically committed to supporting, validating, the legislative and executive actions that led to the forced evacuation of Japanese-Americans and other alien Japanese residing in America. For Black, the military orders, issued in accord with legislative and executive mandates, were the consequence of military judgment and "it is unnecessary for us to appraise the possible reasons which might have prompted the order to be used in the form it was."[31]

His last words on these cases underscored his belief that individual liberties had to be set aside, on occasion, for the national security and for the maintenance of orderliness in the community:

> I would do precisely the same thing today, in any part of the country. I would probably issue the same order were I President. We had a situation where we were at war. People were rightfully fearful of the Japanese in Los Angeles, many loyal to the United States, many undoubtedly not, having dual citizenship—lots of them. They all look alike to a person not a Japanese. Had they [the Japanese] attacked our shores, you'd have a large number fighting with the Japanese troops. And a lot of innocent Japanese-Americans would have been shot in the panic. Under these circumstances, I saw nothing wrong in moving them away from the danger areas.[32]

For Black, popularly elected leaders and the appointed federal or state administrators charged with the task of implementing legislation had almost unlimited freedom to act in the economic and social arena. They could do so as long as the legislation or its implementation did not interfere with the liberties of the people that were protected by the Constitution. The central question for judges hearing these cases was also their most difficult one: At what point does preserving community values through the creation of law violate the uncedable rights of persons living in that community?

Constitutional Limits on Governmental Uses of Power

Given his understanding of history and its discovered rhythms, Black saw how easily people lost their liberties. Democracies survived only when the fundamental freedoms of speech, press, religion, and the right of assembly were maintained. For the Justice, as one of his law clerks said, "the only security for the maintenance of a democratic society under law" were the "absolutes" of the First Amendment.[33]

According to Black, implementing these First Amendment absolutes would enable the people to productively participate in democratic decision-making. Combining his religious beliefs with his passionate love of the Constitution, he saw

America moving inexorably, as he said to his sons so many times when they were depressed, toward the ideal free society. In 1960, he described his vision of such a place:

> Since the earliest days, philosophers have dreamed of a country where the mind and the spirit of man would be free; where there would be no limits to inquiry; where man would be free to explore the unknown and challenge the most deeply rooted beliefs and principles. The First Amendment was a bold effort to adopt this principle—to establish a country with no legal restrictions of any kind upon the subjects people could investigate, discuss, and deny.[34]

For Hugo, "the right to think, speak, and write freely without governmental censorship or interference is the most precious privilege of citizens vested with the power to select public policies and public officials."[35]

As he commented to another First Amendment philosopher, Professor Alexander Meiklejohn, free speech is absolute. Likening his views to those of his hero, Thomas Jefferson, Black wrote that "it is time enough for government to step in when speech evolves into conduct or as some might say when speech evolves into 'other kinds of conduct than speech.' "[36]

For Black, Thomas Jefferson's views on the centrality of freedom of speech, press, religion, and assembly were appropriate in the eighteenth century and, indeed, were timelessly valid ones. Jefferson's philosophy was a "dynamic one," thought Hugo, one that, at its core, was premised on educating the people, who would then be "left wholly free to think, formulate opinions and openly discuss them." The Justice said, of Jefferson, "he declared that 'opinion, and the just maintenance of it shall never be a crime in my view, nor bring injury on the individual.' . . . To preserve and protect free opinion, [Jefferson] fought unremittingly for the addition of a Bill of Rights to our Constitution."[37]

For most of his years on the Court, Black was an ardent advocate for these absolute, Jeffersonian views of the centrality of the First Amendment.[38] At a Town Hall meeting in New York on May 15, 1955, in honor of Albert Einstein, Black spoke about the transcendent value of the First Amendment's guarantees:

> People in this country must have an *undiluted* right to speak and write about public matters and . . . the exercise of this right cannot safely be made to depend upon the bad or good judgment of any agency of the United States Government. Maybe that view is wrong. Maybe it is wrong to give the language of the First Amendment its *literal* and *unequivocal* meaning. . . . For myself, I think it was our great fortune to have a man like Dr. Einstein remind us once again that in preserving inviolate freedom of speech, press and assembly lies the security of our Republic. (my emphasis)

Like his hero, Thomas Jefferson, Black was an "*unapologetic and unafraid* advocate of the right of the people to speak their thoughts and write their views without any governmental interference or censorship."[39] (my emphasis) For the Judge, there was absolutely no governmental interference with a person's use of the first Amendment practices until the speech evolved into *conduct,* action that can be constitutionally controlled, restrained, or restricted by government—local or national. Whenever and wherever he could, Hugo always argued that "the

United States was without power to pass laws that abridged discussion of public questions at all" while sadly noting that, in 1953, "no group seems to be advocating such a [Jeffersonian] view today."[40]

Black harshly criticized his brethren when some of them sought to create and then employ their own judicially created "tests" to resolve cases involving the First Amendment that had the effect of weakening its absolute protections. For the steely Alabaman, there was no need for any judge-made devices or tests such as "clear and present danger," "bad tendency," "gravity of the evil," "reasonableness," or, worst of all, "balancing," because the First Amendment spoke in commanding terms. The opening words of the amendment, "Congress shall pass no law," were not subject to judicial watering down! When other Justices argued for such a judicial amending of the words, Hugo argued vehemently against such a substantive change.

By the 1950 term, Black had developed a well-articulated theory of the centrality of the First Amendment, from which he never deviated. In *Smith v California* (1947), he expressed his belief in clear, unambiguous terms. For him, in direct opposition to Felix Frankfurter's position, the First Amendment was

> wholly "beyond the reach" of federal power to abridge. No other provision of the Constitution purports to dilute the scope of these unequivocal commands of the First Amendment. Consequently, I do not believe that any federal agencies, including Congress and the Court, have power or authority to subordinate speech and press to what they think are "more important interests."[41]

Black "drew the line," however, "between speech and conduct" somehow associated with speech.[42] While the former was, in his view, always protected from governmental interference, conduct was something else—whether it was picketing, or marching in the streets, or participating in sit-ins and teach-ins, or other action. All his life, he was, as he said, "vigorously opposed to efforts to extend the First Amendment's freedom of speech beyond speech."[43]

He was mortally afraid, as he said to his sister-in-law Jinksie Durr, of the street protesters! His reading and understanding of history, from the destruction of the Greek city-state to the rise of Hitler in Germany barely a generation earlier, led him to conclude that marching, singing, demonstrating, picketing, tramping street protesters for "good causes" today would soon lead to the jackboot protests of marchers who supported evil causes tomorrow. Black also believed, absolutely, that such violent conduct would threaten the very essence of representative democracy and would, if left unchecked, lead to the destruction of freedom.

The Justice greatly feared the consequences of the loss of societal orderliness. His fear of uncontrollable disorder was well known. It became a profound visible concern of his as members of organized protest movements in the 1960s, especially the civil rights groups and the opponents of the Vietnam War, took to the streets and began burning draft cards and flags, protesting in schools, and sitting down in private businesses. Clearly, these actions of the protest groups was "speech plus conduct" and the state had the right to control such activities. As he said in a 1965 dissent, in *Cox v Louisiana,* a case involving civil rights demonstrators arrested for marching in the streets, "the crowds that press in the streets for noble goals today can be supplanted tomorrow by street mobs pressing the courts for precisely opposite ends."[44]

While the Court majority invalidated the convictions of the noisy street protesters, Black dissented in part because he felt that the convictions were appropriate.

> A state statute regulating *conduct*—patrolling and marching—as distinguished from *speech*, would, in my judgment, be constitutional. [The First and Fourteenth Amendments do not] grant a constitutional right to engage in the conduct of picketing or patrolling, whether on publicly owned ground or on privately owned property. . . . Picketing, though it may be utilized to communicate ideas, is not speech, and therefore is not of itself protected by the First Amendment.[45] (Black's emphasis)

From the earliest picketing cases Black heard in the 1940s to the shopping center picketing and the sit-down cases of the 1960s, he insisted on treating speech-plus-conduct cases separate and apart from the pure speech cases. The former type of litigation did not have the full protection of the First Amendment; the latter always did. This division of pure speech from speech plus conduct led to significant battles between the Court "liberals" and Black. Given Black's insistence on the appropriateness of distinguishing speech in that fashion, his disagreements with his liberal friends on the Court were never resolved.

Due Process of Law

Black had serious problems defining operationally the due process clause in the Fifth and Fourteenth Amendments. It was a clause that, along with the Fourteenth Amendment's equal protection clause, limited the use of governmental power against people in a significant manner. Yet, he said periodically, in some frustration, "No one ever has marked its [the due process clause's] boundaries, . . . it is as elastic as rubber."[46]

The Court was continually at loggerheads over the meaning and scope of due process, and there was no consensus about it while Hugo served on the Court. Due process was one of the clauses in the Constitution that regularly kept him awake at night. Elizabeth recalled one such instance.

> He woke up at 3:00 A.M. and got up and talked. He said his mind was racing and he was "writing" an opinion in his mind. It must be, he said, the Holmes-type opinion—short, classic, citing no authorities—about "I am fearful that the Court goes farther and farther on the Due Process Clause."[47]

Finding the correct meaning of due process was essential for an appellate judge, because there was the need for a standard with which to decide the due process cases that came to the Court.

Resolution of this constitutional-interpretation dilemma meant, for the Judge, going to historic antecedents, in particular, twelfth-century England and its Magna Carta. Reading history led Black to a definition of due process that he used for most of his three-plus decades on the Court: Due process meant that all persons were to be tried in accordance with the procedural guarantees in the Bill of Rights (Fourth, Fifth, Sixth, and Eighth Amendments) and in accordance with "laws passed pursuant to constitutional power, guaranteeing to all alike a trial under the general law of the land."

All persons must be given equal treatment by government, according to "the law of the land that already existed at the time the alleged offense was committed."[48] The limit on the powers of government was the constitutional requirement of equal treatment in the legal process for all persons, regardless of wealth,[49] age,[50] or race.[51]

Black's was a restrictive understanding of the meaning of due process, premised on equal *procedures* for all persons caught up in the criminal justice system. In his absolutist, literal, historical determination of the meaning of due process, Black was at odds with many of his brethren for most of the terms he served on the Court.

Black's major antagonist during his first two and a half decades on the Court was Felix Frankfurter, their disagreement continuing until Frankfurter left the high bench in 1962. The former Harvard Law professor urged a substantive, "natural law" interpretation of due process that was based, at bottom, on the individual judge's sense of outrage at the challenged state practice. If the challenged action did not "shock the conscience" of the jurist, or somehow go against the British concept of fairness there was no violation of due process of law. John M. Harlan II, who came to the Court in 1954 and became close friends with Black, nevertheless agreed with Frankfurter about due process.

Black was in disagreement on the matter of due process with his liberal friends on the Court as well. By the middle of the 1960s, the liberal majority of the Court—including his good friends William Douglas and William Brennan, joined by Thurgood Marshall, Earl Warren, and Abe Fortas—were giving due process a much more substantive meaning than Hugo was ever able to accept. It was a definition of due process that began to paint new *judicially created* rights for persons, especially the right of privacy.[52]

These new and subjective "natural law" definitions of due process, which enabled the majority to strike down legislative statutes and governmental actions believed to be unfair, or unreasonable, or that shocked their consciences, was simply maddening to Black. There were times, according to Bill Brennan, when the Alabaman would visit him and vent his anger at the way in which the court majority was rewriting, *unconstitutionally*, the Constitution. Clearly, Black despised such loose interpretations of the due process clause, whether crafted by liberals such as Douglas and Brennan or by the more conservative justices such as Frankfurter and Harlan.

The Equal Protection Clause

The equal protection clause in the Fourteenth Amendment was even more troublesome for Black than was the due process clause. By the late 1940s, after a number of years of reviewing the historical context of that clause, he concluded that it was a constitutional prohibition on state governmental actions that invidiously or capriciously discriminated on the basis of race. For Black, race and the related characteristics of alienage and national origin were the only "suspect" categories addressed and protected by equal protection.[53]

His view was that, aside from civil rights litigation involving state action or racial discrimination matters, the equal protection clause could not be introduced in an effort to have a court invalidate state actions. Unlike his liberal friends on the Court, especially Douglas, Brennan, and Marshall, Black insisted that equal protection could not be interpreted broadly to invalidate state actions that did not have a nexus to race. Equal protection, he said in an interview shortly before he died, "should not have been allowed to creep out beyond race."[54] He believed that race discrimination litigation had to be strictly scrutinized by the brethren but that all other state-action litigation had to be examined by the Court using a less burdensome test.

Epitomizing the clash between Black and the liberal judicial activists on the Court over the extent of the equal protection clause's prohibition on state action was the 1966 poll tax case, *Harper v Virginia State Board of Elections*.[55] In *Harper,* the Court majority, in an opinion written by Douglas, called an "egalitarian activist" by some,[56] invalidated Virginia's poll tax statute as being in violation of the equal protection clause. Hugo wrote a dissent in which he criticized the liberals for giving "equal protection a new meaning."[57] In part, he said,

> I have heretofore had many occasions to express my strong belief that there is no constitutional support whatever for this Court to use the Due Process Clause as though it provided a *blank check* to alter the meaning of the Constitution as written so as to add to it *substantive* constitutional changes which a majority of the Court at any given time believes are needed to meet present day problems. Nor is there in my opinion any more constitutional support for this Court to use the Equal Protection Clause, as it has today, to *write into* the Constitution its notions of what it thinks is good government.[58] (my emphasis)

Congress or state constitutional conventions, not the justices of the Court, have the constitutional power to change the meaning and the scope of due process and equal protection, maintained Black. Unless there was an invidious or capricious use of governmental power that discriminated on the basis of race, ill-advised or merely stupid legislative actions could not be overturned by federal appellate judges, including the justices of the Supreme Court, simply because they believed the statutes to be unwise.

Black delivered his dissent in *Harper* in open Court, with a self-discipline that kept his anger under control. He did not want to be seen by the reporters as "shaking with anger" as they had described him when he read another dissent earlier in that term. Hugo was angry about the Douglas opinion for the majority, but also because he had split with Black on this important case. Douglas was "writing new law" by enlarging the plain meaning of the equal protection clause. He had "pushed Hugo unmercifully on this case all week and Hugo was relieved after it came down."[59]

The Judicial Function in a Constitutional Government

Black knew, of course, that lifetime-appointed federal judges were not directly affected by the election returns; neither were they restrained by the impact of pressure groups. Once appointed, the federal judge had the capacity to roam far beyond the confines of the law's framework; she was limited solely by her sense of the proper role and function of the federal judiciary in a system framed by a written Constitution.

The judge's awesome power, interpretation of the Constitution and the statutes, can be held in restraint only by "requiring 'strict construction' of the Constitution and legislative acts."[60] Unfortunately, Hugo also knew that one did not give a federal judge such instructions and "order" her to follow them. Judicial self-discipline came only as a consequence of understanding the basic constitutional principles of governing and abiding by the conclusions drawn from such understanding.

Throughout his life on the Court, therefore, Black became an intense proselytizer for judicial restraint and a fierce opponent of judicially created legislation. He preached from the bench, he "ranted and raved" in conference sessions,[61] he tried to persuade in the memos to the conference written by him. His written opinions, whether for the majority, in concurrence, or in dissent, were always efforts to educate future jurists about the appropriate, constitutional, behavior of judges in a democratic republic.

His harsh, occasionally shrill retort to his less constrained friends on the Court whenever they roamed jurisprudentially was always the same: You are acting unconstitutionally. As he wrote, "I deeply fear for our constitutional system of government when life-appointed judges can strike down a law passed by Congress or a state legislature with no more justification than that the judges believe the law is 'unreasonable.' "[62] As his friend and "friendly enemy," John M. Harlan II said of Hugo: "No Justice has worn his judicial robes with a keener sense of the limitations that go with them."[63]

Whenever Black spoke about the power and responsibilities of federal judges, he always made reference to the British jurist Sir William Blackstone's aphorism about the corrupting influence of power, even on lifetime appointed jurists. Hugo wrote, in 1968, that "power corrupts, and unrestricted power will tempt Supreme Court justices just as history tells us it has tempted other judges." He strongly believed, and always acted on the belief, that federal judges, especially his brethren on the Court, "have not been immune to the seductive influences of power, and given absolute or near absolute power, judges may exercise it to bring about changes that are inimical to freedom and good government."[64]

The judges in America had to be restricted to a narrow interpretive role in American political society: They are interpreters of the Constitution and statutes and regulations written in accordance with the Constitution, not social engineers or unilateral rewriters of the Constitution. There must not be any judicial enlargement of constitutional liberties beyond their literal or historically intended meaning. For Black, "civil liberties in the Constitution had a ceiling as well as a floor."[65] Douglas, Brennan, and other liberal justices, however, believed that there was no ceiling for civil liberties and that federal judges could "dynamically enlarge the scope of individual freedoms against government."[66]

Judges must read the words of the Constitution in light of their "plain meaning," and not have them "subjected to strained linguistic interpretations to carry out the will of the judges."[67] "A judge untethered by a text is a dangerous instrument," he observed again and again.[68] Laws properly made, that is, passed in accord with the powers given to legislators by the Constitution, must be validated by the Court, *however unwise they might appear to be to the judges*. Judges were not social engineers, contrary to what his Court friends Douglas, Brennan, and Marshall believed.

The Constitution prohibited appellate judges, especially justices of the Supreme Court, from putting their gloss on the statutes produced by legislators and from substituting their values for those of the legislature when the judges disagreed with the social or economic views of legislative majorities. Black spoke out, in his classic 1965 *Griswold v Connecticut* dissent, against his colleagues' use of "subjective considerations" to invalidate legislation they did not like. "Many good and able men have eloquently spoken and written, sometimes in rhapsodical strains, about the duty of this Court to keep the Constitution in tune with the times. . . . For myself, I must with all deference reject that philosophy."[69]

Black possessed an unending fear of these unrestrained judges, either sitting next to him on the high bench or on one of the federal appeals courts. He categorically rejected the concept inherent in their behavior, that federal appellate judges were left "completely free to decide constitutional questions on the basis of their own policy judgments."[70] He

> rejected the open-ended notion that the court sits to do good in every circumstance where good is needed, and insists that federal judges are contained by the terms of the Constitution, no less than all other branches of governmental authority. He consider[ed] himself to be a judge of cases, not of "causes," and unhesitatingly set himself against federal judicial intervention whenever he was unable to find in the Constitution or valid legislative authority the basis for such action.[71]

His dissent in the 1947 case of *Adamson v California*[72] reflected his strong disapproval of judges interposing, without any effort at judicial self-discipline, to strike down legislation they did not like. For Black, *Adamson* was his "most significant opinion written."[73] According to the Alabaman, the Bill of Rights was a set of protections against governmental mischief, both national and local varieties. It is a document that must be vigorously defended, through rigorous enforcement of its guarantees, by the judges, regardless of the popular passions of temporary majorities of the day.

> I cannot consider the Bill of Rights to be an outworn 18th century 'strait jacket.' . . . Its provisions may be thought outdated abstractions by some. And it is true that they were designed to meet ancient evils. But they are the same kind of human evils that have emerged from century to century wherever excessive power is sought by the few at the expense of the many. In my judgment the people of no nation can lose their liberty so long as a Bill of Rights like ours survives and

its basic purposes are conscientiously interpreted, enforced, and respected so as to afford continuous protection against old, as well as new, devices and practices which might thwart those purposes. . . . I would follow what I believe was the original intention of the Fourteenth Amendment—to extend to all the people the complete protection of the Bill of Rights. To hold that this Court can determine what, if any, provisions of the Bill of Rights will be enforced, and if so to what degree, is to frustrate the great design of a written Constitution.[74]

At bottom, Hugo feared for America if the justices of the Court acted without any self-discipline as they went about their judicial business. Black was very friendly with his liberal brethren, good men like Brennan, whom he might try to persuade to his view during barbeques at his Alexandria house. "He was a steak and potatoes man," recalled Brennan. "He used to take a special pride in his ability to broil steaks. Actually, he sometimes overdid it. He had a terrible voice, but he used to love to sing. He knew all the words to many old songs,"[75] including songs of the Civil War such as "I Am A Dirty Rebel," one of Hugo's oft-sung favorites! (In fact, words from this song found their way into Black's opinion in the Pentagon Papers case, *New York Times v United States* [1971]; see page 196ff.). Brennan's mind remained unchanged, however, on the role and functions of a Supreme Court justice.

And Black was concerned because not all the substantive jurists sitting on the Court were as admirable and as committed to individual rights and liberties as his friend Brennan. As Hugo noted, ruefully, in 1968, "to people who have faith in our nine Justices, I say I have known a different court from the one today."[76] He remembered well the Four Horsemen of the 1920s and '30s, and how they rode roughshod over critical pieces of legislation they did not like.

His anger toward these constitutional expansionists was always deep and unrelenting, accompanied by profound fear, about the use of "natural law, shock the conscience" language of his brethren. Black wrote concurring opinions rather than join a majority opinion that cited one of those "natural law" opinions he despised so much.[77]

The Role of the Supreme Court in American Politics

When Hugo's daughter, Jo-Jo, graduated from Swarthmore College in June 1955, he gave the commencement address. It was, in America, a difficult time for liberty. Black, along with William Douglas, had been fighting on the Court, and losing,[78] in defense of absoluteness of First Amendment rights for those accused of Communist party membership or who were suspected of supporting Communism.

It was the time of Senator Joseph McCarthy, the Republican senator from Wisconsin who made a reputation searching for Communists who, he alleged, were in government agencies, the entertainment industry, the military, and all walks of American life. His self-created task it was to root them out before they destroyed America from within. It was the time of the House Un-American Activities Committee (HUAC), the congressional committee that ranged far and wide to uncover and present to a startled America alleged Communist traitors, including

Black's sister-in-law, Jinksie Durr, and her husband, Clifford, who was, at that time, one of Martin Luther King's lawyers and who in 1955, were accused of being Communist sympathizers by HUAC.

It was an era that called for strong, courageous political leadership on behalf of individual rights. "We desperately need today a new Jefferson," Black told the assembled Swarthmore students, "and a new baptism in his sane and sound faith in complete freedom to think, speak, and write."[79] He warned the young graduates, the future leaders of America, of the need for all virtuous citizens of the American republic to act vigorously in order to retain liberty.

"Our Constitution shows one thing pretty clearly," Black said to the young graduates. "While the Founders wanted a stable government, they were also afraid of it. . . . . Those who established our new government decided to try to safeguard individual liberty with what was then a novel experience—a written Constitution and an explicit Bill of Rights." He also voiced his own beliefs about the first nine amendments to the Constitution:

> In my judgment, the very heart of the Bill of Rights is the First Amendment. Unless people can freely exercise those liberties, without loss of good name, job, property, liberty, or life, a good society cannot exist. *That is my faith.* I believe that without the liberties of that Amendment your commencement here would be a very sad one indeed—if you had any.[80] (my emphasis)

Implicit in this message to his daughter's classmates that hot June day was the critical role of the Court in defending the absolute protections in the First Amendment. The role of the Supreme Court in American politics was a dual one, Black argued over and over again for more than half a century. The Court, first of all, had to aggressively protect individual rights in the Bill of Rights from governmental attempts to usurp them. Second, the Court had the responsibility to validate actions of a state legislature or the Congress if the statute did not conflict with an express prohibition against legislative action in the Constitution itself. "Government at all levels," wrote Black, "was fully clothed with the power to govern and to maintain order."[81]

The fiery Southerner did not believe that this was a complicated agenda for an appellate judge in America. It was a simple but profound framework for judicial decision-making. "This approach" of the Judge, observed a law clerk after Black's death, "can easily be seen as naive, but is in fact extremely complex, with deep philosophical and jurisprudential roots."[82] Hugo, the student and chronicler of history, the Judge with a vision of an America that rivaled the democracy of city-state Greece, believed "that the only way to steer this country toward its great destiny is to follow what our Constitution says, not what judges think it should have said."[83]

Appellate judges had to bravely defend the liberties of the people whenever and wherever they were challenged by state authority. The maintenance of liberty, as he knew from his study of history, depended on the ability of men to remain free citizens of the community. When freedom was deprived, because of excessive state action not invalidated by passive federal courts, then liberty was lost. For Black, this was the basic lesson of history, from the ancient Greeks to the rise of

Hitler to America's grappling with the paranoia of anti-Communist hysteria in the middle of the twentieth century.

Throughout his time on the Court, but especially toward the end of his life, Black was continually "driven by a burning evangelical need to persuade his colleagues of his views." He "worked intensely at his job,"[84] knowing that his time was running out and that he would have to leave a Court packed with unrepentant subjective interpreters of the Constitution. As his colleague Byron White observed, "the longer judges [like Black] have been on the bench, the less they give. The longer they're on the Bench, the more they accumulate issues on which they won't give in."[85]

Black never gave in on these fundamental issues of governmental power and the limits on that awesome power, of the role and functions of the justices on the Court, and, most important, of the centrality of the Constitution in American life. Alexander Bickel, one of the many professorial surrogates used by Felix Frankfurter in his never-ending battles with Black, was one of the lawyers for the *New York Times* in the famous 1971 *Pentagon Pagers* case before the Court. He wrote in his book, *The Least Dangerous Branch,* that the "Constitution is merely words—deathless words." The Judge's comment, written in the margin of the book, was classic Black: *"The Constitution is not deathless; it provides for changing or repealing by the amending process, not by judges but by the people and their chosen representatives"*[86] (my emphasis).

An examination of the Judge's views, as seen in a variety of cases and controversies, reveals his insistence that in America, as Thomas Paine said in the eighteenth-century, the Law, the Constitution, is King.

Looking at his actions on the Supreme Court, one quickly notes Black's courage as he fought, at times savagely, with his colleagues in the effort to bring into practice his idea of jurisprudence, one based on the value of history, literalism, and absolutism. He continued to teach this lesson until his death. His words still teach the virtue of judicial self-discipline in constitutional adjudication

CHAPTER SEVEN

Friends, Enemies, and
Legal "Children"

Ⅰn his entire life, Black never had difficulty generating fierce opposition to his
ideas and his behavior. His work on the Supreme Court did not prove to be
an exception. While he was greatly admired by a number of his brethren and
by the community outside the Court, Hugo was also hated and despised by some
on the Court. Black's relationship with Justice Robert Jackson had dramatically
"deteriorated" over time because he "was appalled by what he viewed as Black's
partisan, nonjudicial approach to cases." [1]

Again and again, Felix Frankfurter said, with derision, that Black was a damn
politician and would always remain one. He was correct, for the Alabaman was
someone who interacted successfully with others involved in public policy-
making, whether in Congress or on the Court. He never apologized for his behavior, for he believed that it was appropriate and necessary in his line of work. Many
years later, Associate Justice Harry A. Blackmun had a more benign memory of
Black. The Judge, said Blackmun, was a "canny, lovable manipulator, ever the
politician, ever the U.S. Senator still, a man who thoroughly enjoyed the manipulation in the old fashioned Southern way." [2]

Interactive work on the high bench is an art form grounded in the intelligence,
vision, strength of commitment, and temperament of the jurist. Felix Frankfurter
did not have such a capacity to interact. History has already noted Black's impact
on American jurisprudence, but for all Frankfurter's intelligence and love of the
judiciary, he is not considered anything more than a brilliant, brittle, and petulant
federal judge. For most of Frankfurter's tenure on the Court, he was an angry
man, almost an outcast.

Just prior to joining Black on the Court, in December 1938, Frankfurter wrote
to Black to "instruct" him that Court justices were political and indeed had to be
such if they were to be effective jurists. He did not know Black at all, and so

Frankfurter lectured at him from his office in Cambridge, Massachusetts. He wrote that

> the problem is not whether the judges make the law, but when and how and how much. Holmes put it in his highbrow way, that "they can do so only interstitially; they are confined from molar to molecular statements." I used to say to my students that legislators make law wholesale, judges retail. In other words they cannot decide things by invoking a new major premise out of whole cloth; they must make the law that they do make out of the existing materials and with due deference to the presuppositions of the legal system of which they have been made a part. Of course, I know these are not mechanical devices, and therefore not susceptible of producing automatic results. But they sufficiently indicate the limits within which judges are to move.[3]

As was typically the case when Black was confronted with such condescending behavior, however subtle and ingenious, he did not become enraged. Instead, in his most gracious Southern manner, he thanked Frankfurter for these instructive lessons in judging. Hugo, however, continued to fine-tune his own jurisprudential thoughts about the role of the justices sitting on the Court.

Developing an intellectual framework for doing constitutional interpretation and identifying the "presuppositions of the legal system" is only one aspect of Court work. In addition, being a Justice means working closely and harmoniously with and on one's colleagues on the Court in the continuing effort to convince some of them and then marshalling them to act in ways one believes the Court should act.[4] In his thirty-four years on the high bench, Black met with a wide variety of justices.

One cohort of justices included such men such as Stanley Reed, Tom C. Clark, "Shay" Minton, and Charles Whittaker. Not very gifted intellectually, and certainly no match for the intelligence of Black and Frankfurter, Hugo accepted their jurisprudential limitations quietly, patiently. There was no open rage or assault on them because of their inability to act as Black believed federal judges should act in a constitutional democracy.

In this regard, the Judge was unlike the more intemperate and, at times, cruel Frankfurter, who did this judge-bashing indirectly for the most part, in letters to close friends such as Judge Learned Hand, in comments to his law clerks, and in his diary. However, there was the occasional mean-spirited note from Frankfurter directly to some of his brethren whom he considered less intellectually gifted.

He was particularly cruel to Justice Frank Murphy, another of Roosevelt's appointees, a man who had been governor of Michigan and, prior to his appointment to the Court, Roosevelt's attorney general. The bitterness between Frankfurter and Murphy grew over the years. He became a "special target" for the barbs of Frankfurter,[5] who called him "the Saint" or "the stooge," among other crude names, and who joked about many of his colleague's weaknesses, including medical and personal.

Once Frankfurter wrote to Justice Reed, saying that "you would no more heed Murphy's tripe than you would be seen naked at Dupont Circle at high noon tomorrow."[6] He also ridiculed Murphy's alleged fondness for showgirls. "Us

Girls call him Murph," Frankfurter was heard to say to one of his friends in the Court. Murphy, who was very self-conscious about his abilities as a justice, was made extremely uncomfortable by these sarcastic public insults and found Black's friendship to be a great comfort.

The Alabaman was surprisingly gentle with his brethren. For example, in the debates surrounding the *Bartkus v Illinois* case,[7] Hugo was trying to mold a majority. While Frankfurter went after the indecisive Whittaker's vote with abandon, Black backed off the lobbying effort. Whittaker had joined the Court in 1957 and stepped down because of the terrible stress five years later, in 1962; he had been a fine trial lawyer in Kansas but turned out to be an extremely weak, vacillating jurist on the Court. He was courted by the two cliques on the Court because his vote was generally up in the air and typically went to the group that made the last, but not necessarily the best, argument. Hugo refrained from proselytizing Whittaker, even though it was an important civil liberties case and Frankfurter was working the weak justice very hard. As his law clerk, Guido Calabresi recalled, Black "saw Whittaker's agony of decision. Finally, he said, 'I cannot destroy a man.' "[8]

Once, after a difficult time with a complicated civil case, Justice Clark wrote to Black, thanking him for his advice: "I'm sorry about the FHA case—I never studied the claim frankly—From what I've read of the brief since you called my attention to it, I believe you are right—I may change my vote tomorrow."[9] Although Hugo did not show the same patience with his sons or with witnesses before one of his Senate committees, he had infinite forbearance when working with this special group of colleagues.

Then, of course, there was a second group of justices Hugo worked with—or more accurately, fought with—on a regular basis. These brethren included his nemesis, Felix Frankfurter, along with Owen Roberts and Robert Jackson. For the most part, these jurists were bright, literate, and absolutely at odds with Black's views of judicial role and his beliefs about the primacy of the First Amendment. The Judge often succeeded against these antagonists in the conflicts that took place continually over disagreement on jurisprudence as well as on constitutional doctrine.

A third group of jurists Black worked with were men such as Frank Murphy, Bill Brennan, Jr., Thurgood Marshall, Earl Warren, Arthur Goldberg, Abe Fortas, and his closest friend on the Court for many years, William O. Douglas. These men were, of course, the well-meaning "liberals," jurists who loved to produce justice through very broad interpretations of constitutional phrases such as due process of law or equal protection of the laws. For a brief period of American constitutional history, the "Warren Court" era, these men constituted, with Black's participation, a strong voting majority on the Court and, indeed, engendered a constitutional revolution between 1957 and 1969.[10]

Much as he liked these men with their humanistic, individual-oriented policy agendas, and even though Black worked with them to secure strong majorities on some substantive civil liberties litigation (largely through his concurring opinions), he raged against their seemingly carefree meanderings in the rhetoric of the law in order to do the right thing, by any means necessary! His son recalled Black saying that

> the Chief [Earl Warren], Brennan, Bill Douglas, Arthur [Goldberg], Thurgood [Marshall] are usually going to do the right thing. . . . While they're around, we'll generally get just judgment. But when they're gone and we get a McReynolds type, he's free to let go with his bad sense of right and wrong. I believe we've got to tie the judges of this Court and the subordinate federal courts to something lasting, even if we've got to sacrifice doing some good through the federal courts. We don't want this Court to be like one of these agencies—one law when the Republicans are in and another when the Democrats are in. This Court's got to have some enduring principles.[11]

Black always asserted that if the Justices selected would always be such liberty-loving jurists as the men in this liberal cohort, he would not argue for tight reins on Court members. Of course one could not make such a promise because of the intensely political nature of the Supreme Court selection process.[12] Equally important for the Judge was his understanding of the reality of the Court's past history. Black had seen the institution he had come to love behave as the arch defender of economic and socially conservative values, beliefs that more conservative justices led by the Four Horsemen had poured into the due process and equal protection "containers" by a majority.

There was also a fourth, very special, cohort. It consisted of one person, Black's gentle, virtually blind colleague and, as it turned out, distant cousin, John M. Harlan II. Even though Harlan was usually a member of the Frankfurter camp in the Court's constitutional wars, Black interacted comfortably with him until both were forced, due to their precarious health, to retire from the Court within weeks of each other in September 1971. It was a genuinely respectful association, even though on many issues, including the role of the judges, the two men differed dramatically.

The Fur Begins to Fly: Conflict in the Court

Conflict was a basic part of life on the high bench, just as it was in the Senate. But, for the most part, the conflicts of the Supreme Court were played out in secrecy, unlike the public battles that occur frequently in the Congress. Black always participated fully in the give-and-take of politics and policy-making thoughout his career in Washington, D.C. The conflicts with his Court colleagues were primarily professional, internal ones that emerged from differences of opinion about the role of the federal judiciary and how the brethren went about the task of constitutional interpretation.[13]

In these mostly behind-the-scenes clashes, Black was gentlemanly, forceful, direct, and, on infrequent occasions, aggressively confrontational, as he had been in his prior prosecutorial and legislative work in Birmingham and in the Senate. Once Black engaged in a constitutional battle, he was an immovable force. One of Black's chief "enemies," Robert H. Jackson, once said that "you just can't disagree with [Black]. You must go to war with him if you disagree."[14]

When Black arrived in the Senate in 1927, he had already developed and incorporated into his value system a fundamental understanding of the relationship of the people to their elected representatives. By 1937, he had come to accept uncritically the enduring value of Thomas Jefferson's ideas about the absolute necessity of maintaining First Amendment freedoms in order to insure democratic electoral politics.

As judge, prosecutor, and legislator, he experienced and reacted to the abuses of public power—especially excessive, illegal, unconstitutional uses. When he came to the Supreme Court in 1937, Black knew what political power was, including its limits, how power should be used, and how it was abused by officials in and out of government.

Black argued relentlessly that the Constitution was the people's document. The *sovereign people,* and Hugo always underscored the importance of that phrase, can amend the Constitution if they choose to—but not the judges, especially not the justices of the U.S. Supreme Court. "The people and their elected representatives, not judges, are constitutionally vested with the power to amend the Constitution. Judges should not usurp that power in order to put over their own 'views,' " wrote Black in dissent in *Boddie v Connecticut* in 1970.[15] He fought repeatedly with his brethren over this fundamental axiom. Judges, he insisted, must be bound to the words of the Constitution because a runaway judge is dangerous.[16]

Justices always are in disagreement with some of their brethren at any given moment in time. Most of the time there is no personalization of professional disagreements among them. Some justices, however, with Frankfurter as a classic example, "took the refusal of the brethren to follow his lead as a personal affront, and unfortunately allowed full play to his considerable talent for invective."[17]

Always concerned about taking actions that would tarnish the public's image of the Supreme Court, Black, even when publicly pummeled by one or more of his brethren (Stone in 1938 and Jackson in 1945 and 1946), insisted on remaining silent in public. With the exception of the publication of his New York University Law School lectures that presented his view of the Constitution (published as *A Constitutional Faith*) and a television interview he gave on the same subject, Hugo never took his clashes with his brethren beyond the confines of the Court.

Black fought tenaciously, however, within the Court. According to Brennan, Hugo was a wily son-of-a-gun who had no difficulty doing battle within the confines of the Court's house, the marble palace.[18] In these internal Court conflicts, the Alabaman did not give very much. More often than not, Black would tell a colleague that the opinion the person wrote was "excellent [but] you know darn well I can't join you."[19]

Within the Court, the weapons of choice for battling brethren included the conference debate, the withheld vote, individual lobbying, threatened dissent, or the effort to build factional support or opposition. Black used this set of battle instruments very well. His threats were credible; his threats to dissent were unshakable unless the majority made serious attempts to address his concerns. He invariably took great care to study the opposition's position on an issue and then to craft a response aimed directly at the key elements of the opponent's argument.

Black's tactics were those of the strategic jurist. He actively sought out adherents for his constitutional views. He was not above the use of threat and, as Frankfurter suggested, blackmail to persuade his colleagues to act in a certain way. He used the dissent in a rapierlike manner to pierce the arguments of opponents, whether Frankfurter, Brennan, or his close friend, Douglas. Black asked no quarter and gave none; it was too important a set of conflicts to back away from principle.

During conference sessions, Black could be a tough and occasionally threatening negotiator. Many hundreds of times his argument would find its way into the majority opinion. If not, it would form the basis for a concurrence or dissent. In those instances, and through the memorandum to the conference device, Hugo, as some of his brethren admitted, did threaten them. In the *Alexander* case,[20] for example, Black wanted an "Integrate Now" result from the Court and threatened his colleagues with a sharply worded dissent if such an order was not announced by the Court.

> While a dissent at this time may seem premature, this procedure has been followed only to avoid further delay. . . . There has already been too much writing and not enough action in this field. Writing breeds more writing, and more disagreements, all of which inevitably delay action. The duty of this Court and of the others is too simple to require perpetual litigation and deliberation. That duty is to extirpate all racial discrimination from our system of public schools NOW.[21]

In the end, Black did not have to use the dissent. Following a lengthy conversation with him, in which Black told Brennan what language should be used in the Court's order, Brennan wrote a short per curiam order, incorporating all of the Alabaman's suggestions.

> Continued operation of segregated schools under a standard of allowing "all deliberate speed" for desegregation is no longer constitutionally permissible. Under explicit holdings of this Court the obligation of every school district is to terminate dual school systems at once and to operate now and hereafter only unitary schools.[22]

Black clashed hard with his colleagues on cases as well as on other matters that, for him, affected the credibility and image of the institution he loved so much. He sent them memos and notes from the bench, the conference, and his chambers in order to persuade them to change their positions to agree with his. So insistent was Black that Douglas referred to him as one of the major proselytizers ever to serve on the Court.

Black was occasionally alarmed at the public utterances and indiscretions of his brethren. Bill Douglas, who married four times, each time to a younger woman, caused Hugo great consternation because of the poor publicity each succeeding wedding received from the press. When Douglas announced his final marriage to a college undergraduate forty years younger, Black sarcastically told him that he should have kept his fly zippered. Fortas's involvement with the Wolfson Foundation (which led to that justice's resignation from the Court) troubled Black as much as Douglas's romantic interludes, and the Alabaman told Fortas to resign for the good of the Court.

Even when very harshly (1945) and very publicly (1946) attacked by Jackson, Black remained publicly silent at a time when the headlines screamed out the story of the "SUPREME COURT FEUD"[23] between these two brethren and their allies on and off the Court.

Although Black did not necessarily cultivate those outside the Court while serving there, there were some outside who pursued him, seeking advice or help to land a job in the federal judiciary. He responded positively to many of their pleas.

Jerome Frank, a friend and New Deal SEC commissioner, wrote to Hugo in 1939, indicating that FDR had promised him a seat on a federal appeals court in return for his service on the SEC. He was concerned because he was Jewish; Frankfurter, a fellow Jew, had just been appointed by the president to the Court. Frank commented: "I learned this morning that there is some reason to believe that, because of Frankfurter's appointment, the President feels hesitant about appointing me. Perhaps you would be willing to say something to Tom [Corcoran, a Roosevelt counsel] which he could report."[24] The Alabaman contacted FDR personally, recommending Frank for a seat on the Second Circuit U.S. Court of Appeals. Roosevelt soon appointed Frank to that federal court.

Others—like Sherman Minton (a decade after turning down the seat given to Black) and Wiley Rutledge—also came to him for counsel and assistance in their efforts to gain a seat on a federal appellate court or on the high bench.[25] Over time, some justices on the Court came to Black hoping that he could help with different professional and personal problems. He was asked by Warren and Douglas to speak to Fortas's wife in order to convince her that her husband should take the seat offered to him by President Lyndon B. Johnson. Frank Murphy would write short, plaintive notes to Black asking the Alabaman to listen to his "troubles."[26] Evidently, Black took pleasure in intervening for and consoling people he felt strongly about and who were, in addition, good New Dealers.

Friends and Enemies

While the Judge interacted with almost one-third of all the men who had served on the Court between 1789 and 1971, there were some significant relationships that developed during his thiry-four years of service on the Court.

The men who argued with Black were mostly men he knew from the New Deal era. William Douglas, Felix Frankfurter, Robert Jackson, and Abe Fortas were men he had known, admired, or worked with during his years prior to his appointment to the Supreme Court. Once they joined him on the Court, there developed antagonisms between Black and Frankfurter, Jackson, and, much later, Fortas.

On the other hand, the Alabaman had a close relationship with Douglas, about as close as anyone could get to Douglas. Because of their different views about the role of the judges and their differences over constitutional interpretation, however, their friendship cooled somewhat in the mid-1960s.

In addition to these substantive interactions with his New Deal colleagues, Black had warm relationships with two men who joined the Court in the 1950s: William J. Brennan, Jr., and John M. Harlan II.

An understanding of Hugo's decades-long relationships with these men, friends and antagonists, is an important introduction to an understanding of the creation and development of his doctrinal position on significant constitutional issues.

William O. Douglas

When Black's book, *A Constitutional Faith,* was published, he gave a signed copy to Bill Douglas. The inscription summed up the Judge's views of his colleague:

> To my good friend Bill Douglas, my close-working colleague for nearly thirty years, a genius in his own right, a man of indomitable courage, unexcelled energy and to whom I am indebted for his contribution to the formulation of many of the constitutional principles expressed in this book.[27]

Cathy, Douglas's fourth and last wife, recently remarked that Black and her husband were really "two country boys." One came to the Court from rural Alabama and the other from equally rural Washington state. They turned out to be similar yet so very different. One was an outstanding, self-taught politician who never lost his strategic political skills after moving to the Court. The other, her husband, was a maverick professor, a scholarly loner, an academic mountain climber who continually stated that "the only soul he had to save was his own." Black, she claimed, was loved by many while Douglas was not liked by brethren and clerks alike.[28]

Interestingly, while both were New Deal Democrats, they really did not get to know each other until both were appointed to the Court by their mutual friend Franklin D. Roosevelt. Black was the vigorous elected New Dealer in the Senate, while Douglas was a New Deal appointee to the Securities and Exchange Commission in February 1936. Although they took different paths to the Court, both had overcome a number of obstacles in their lives, including some serious health problems when they were young, and brought these experiences with them to the Court.

Different Backgrounds, Close Friends

"If any student of the modern Supreme Court took an association test, the word 'Black' would probably evoke the response 'Douglas' and vice versa. For more than thirty years," noted Hugo Jr., "the two sat together, and the odds are that in any given case, even toward the end of [Black's] career, the two would have voted together."[29] Black declined an invitation to write a law review essay about his friend, saying that "you perhaps know without my stating it that I have the very highest regard for Justice Douglas as a friend and as a member of this Court. In fact, our views are so nearly the same that it would be almost like self praise for me to write what I feel about his judicial career."[30] The Alabaman was, in Douglas's words, "my closest friend on the Court and my companion in many hard judicial battles."[31]

Even before they became colleagues on the bench, Douglas had come to respect Black's work on the Court. In a letter he wrote to the Judge while still the chairman of the SEC, Douglas said: "I have just read with great interest your dissenting opinion in the case of *Connecticut General Life Insurance Co v Johnson*.[32] It is a perfectly swell job. An awful lot of people will agree with you. I congratulate you on your courageous stand."[33]

Instantly, after Douglas joined the Court, the two men developed an easy, comfortable relationship. They did not disagree with each other at all for the first three terms they served together on the Court. But they were, as Cathy Douglas recalled, very different men, although both were "quite feisty." Furthermore, they were not in each other's chambers or meeting on golf courses or tennis courts to plot out Court strategy. They worked independently and communicated, as did so many of the brethren, by notes from on the bench and off. The two rarely called each other up on the phone to chat about a case or a personal matter.[34] Most of their communication, both very personal as well as Court business, was written, and is preserved in their files in the Library of Congress.

An "unconscious teamwork existed" between the two men, recalled Douglas's widow. They worked almost automatically in response to cases that came to the Supreme Court during their tenure as justices. Their unique relationship was eerily brought home to Douglas after Black's death. He quickly realized that some of the written dissents from the Court's denial of certiorari were not published in the *U.S. Reports*. They were missing because his friend of over thirty years on the high bench was no longer there to write them. Until that revelation, which occurred during the 1971 term of the Court, Douglas "hadn't realized the degree to which they had this unspoken communications [between the two of them] in terms of areas where they agreed."[35]

Hugo Jr. suggests that the relationship between Black and Douglas led to an important role for his father. "For most of their service together, Hugo acted as liaison between Bill Douglas and the Court, and this function must be considered one of [Black's] important contributions to his country; talent like Bill Douglas's should not be allowed to go to waste."[36] Black commented that "when [such a creative person] is required to work with others, he will be lost without a sympathetic person within his particular field of activity."[37] The Justice was that "bridge" between Douglas and the world. He recognized Douglas's special strengths and told his son: "The fella is a genius, Son, and he's got right instincts on social and political issues."[38] This was especially true in the area of First Amendment freedoms, where they shared the belief that Courts had a responsibility to ensure that minorities had complete protection from majority oppression. "Douglas," said Brennan, "would say what Black had said [in this area of constitutional law]."[39]

Although their Court "enemy," Felix Frankfurter, argued again and again to all his close friends and associates that Douglas was a "mommser," an evil person who was "shallow" and "cock-sure of himself,"[40] Black categorically rejected those negative views of his friend and simply chalked such comments up to Frankfurter's extreme bitterness in general.

From their first days together on the high bench, the two men shared personal information regarding wives, children, parents, political gossip, and their health problems in the letters and notes they wrote to each other throughout the year—before, during, and after the term of the Court for a particular year. When Douglas's mother was dying, Black wrote his colleague: "I hope your mother will improve, but anyhow it will be a great comfort to her that you can be with her."[41] And after her death a month later, he wrote again to his colleague: "I am very happy that your mother lived long enough to see her son on the Court. The greatest joy and satisfaction that can come to any mother is to see her children move to high positions of trust by reason of innate ability and integrity. That is what your mother saw. If her life had not been rich before your career would have made it so."[42] Clearly, Black would have given anything to have shared his successes with his mother, who died in 1905, many years before Hugo, her youngest and her favorite son, succeeded in law and politics. Black's note to Douglas was from his heart, reflecting his sadness while at the same time cheering up his friend.

In their letters Black and Douglas also discussed politics in general and national political opportunities for Douglas that, had he accepted any of them, would have meant his leaving the Court. On September 8, 1941, in a letter marked "Confidential," Douglas wrote Black that Roosevelt had talked to him over the telephone and "he wants me to be the top guy in the defense work—to take it off his neck; to be his 'alter ego.' He apparently visualizes the present defense set-up continuing. Apparently, I am to be the top holding company, so to speak. I have not said yes nor have I said no. He's put it on a personal basis—that I was the only one who could swing it; that he needed me badly, etc, etc. I would have to resign from the Court. I have no enthusiasm for the project. . . . I can think of nothing less attractive—except practicing law in New York City. . . . Of course, there comes a time when all bets are off and every man has to shoulder a musket or do some chore for his country."

But Douglas was not too optimistic about the possibility of success at the defense job. "I think that as a member of the Court I can knock out a base hit once in a while. In the defense job, I would go to bat with 2½ strikes on me." Douglas then speculated about political payoffs in the future: "Some of the President's inner circle whisper that this is a big chance. That it will lead to the 1944 nomination. But that leaves me cold because I am not a bit interested in running for any office." He closed: "I am quite sure that F[elix]. F[rankfurter]. has inspired this offer—at least that he has been influential. . . . If he could get me there and you back in the Senate I am sure he would be happier." Roosevelt was really pressuring him to accept—even though he recognized the wisdom of declining. "It's hard to say no. . . . He is a hard one to get away from."[43]

Black, who was in Colorado at the time, wrote a long letter back to Douglas, pleading with him not to leave the Court.

The prospect that you might leave the Court disturbs me greatly and I have been strongly tempted to cut my visit short, return home, and discuss the question with you personally. And I would do this were I satisfied that I could be of help to you in making your decision. . . . You and I know that the Court has the last word on questions of law which are determinative of questions of public policy upon which the course of our republic depends. [It would be very unwise to leave the Court] unless you would perform more infinitely needed work and unless further, no one else is able—I doubt if the position you have been asked to take, under conditions already existing, is so important as that of membership on the Court, and it would require much to prove it to me that no one else is available.[44]

On September 20, 1941, Douglas sent Black a short note. He appreciated Hugo's letter. He had not yet spoken to the president about the job but Douglas "expected to have it out with Roosevelt the first of the week. . . . I think I can wiggle out this time."[45] He did.

When Truman became president in 1945, the issue of high political office (and ambitions) again arose. By 1949, Douglas had turned Truman down twice: in 1946 when the president had asked him to become secretary of the interior[46] and in 1948[47] when Truman had asked Douglas to run with him as the vice presidential candidate of the Democratic party.[48] Recently retired Justice Owen Roberts, no friend of either man, in July 1948 wrote his friend Felix Frankfurter a letter:

Haven't these developments re Little Billie been exciting? He's too damned smart to risk a licking with Truman! I guessed that was where he'd come out, if he was asked to run with Harry. What luck it would have been if he'd left the Court to run and then been licked! . . . We'll never know the truth about the whole business. Maybe F.M. [Frank Murphy] will have the story straight."[49]

Light moments on the Court were shared by the two men. During oral arguments in the *Everson* case in 1947, while sitting on the bench, Douglas sent the following note to Black, a few chairs away: "Hugo/ I think if the Catholics get public money to finance their religious schools, we better insist on getting some good prayers in public schools or we Protestants are out of business. WOD."[50]

And there were also occasions when the two worked on sensitive, personal Court matters. In early August 1965, Douglas wrote Black: "Abe Fortas's wife is very upset over Abe's appointment. It is apparently a very serious crisis. I thought maybe you and Elizabeth could think of something to do."[51] In Elizabeth's journal entry for Tuesday, August 10, 1965, she wrote: "We had invited Carol and Abe Fortas for dinner in answer to an sos by Bill Douglas, saying they were having a serious crisis about Abe's going on the Court. Carol told me . . . that they can't live on the small Court salary and may have to give up their new home. Later, Hugo talked to Carol in that dear, straightforward way of his. . . . It did have a great softening effect on Carol, I could tell. . . . I do believe Hugo's advice helped. They stayed until after midnight."[52]

Douglas beat the drum for his friend Black when the center seat opened up while they were serving on the Court. In 1941 when Chief Justice Hughes retired, then in April 1946 after Harlan F. Stone suffered a fatal heart attack while sitting on the high bench, and again, for a third and last time, in 1953, Douglas touted

Black for the chief justiceship. To no avail. Given the political context of each of these openings—that is, war and the need for national unity (which meant the elevation of Republican Stone to the chief justiceship by FDR, the Democratic president), stress and fighting within the Court (which forced Truman to appoint a peacemaker, Vinson, to the center seat), and, finally, Republican control of the White House (which led to the appointment of Warren by Eisenhower)—Black's move to the Court's center seat was not to be.

Black and Douglas quickly grew together as colleagues and as friends, only to seriously fall apart during the mid-1960s due to differences of opinion over the breadth of the due process and equal protection clauses. Although they were different in many ways, there was a true affection between them. As has been mentioned, in Douglas's mind, Black was his "closest friend on the Court." And the Judge, for the most part, "reciprocated Douglas's affection and trust."[53]

Doctrinal Disagreements between Friends

The two, however, had some serious disagreements on significant doctrinal issues.[54] They fought over free speech, civil rights, criminal justice, and "new rights" matters occasionally bitterly and painfully. And, in the mid-1960s, Black sadly told Bill Brennan and Harry Blackmun that Douglas had "left him" because of conflicts over the right of privacy concept Douglas had crafted in *Griswold* and other controversial matters that the Court was wrestling with at this time, especially the sit-in cases.

For Hugo, simply put, the Bill of Rights protections were enough! Douglas, however, firmly believed that those protections were not enough and must be broadly expanded by judicial interpretation of their great principles.[55] According to Black, the protections in the Bill of Rights covered all the known evils a person, representing government, could inflict on another person. For Douglas, the Bill of Rights "do[es] not cover all of man's idiosyncrasies" and evil actions and therefore the justices had to read rights broadly to deal with these new wrongs perpetrated on men and women.[56]

Black always distinguished between a person's freedom to speak and publish, which was, for the Judge, categorically protected by the Constitution, and speech plus conduct (picketing, sit-downs, pray-ins, flag and draft card burning, or wearing a jacket with FUCK THE DRAFT written on its back), which he always maintained could be regulated by public officials under certain circumstances. A picketer, according to the Alabaman, was "not only communicating ideas . . . but pursuing a course of conduct in addition to constitutionally protected speech and press. [Such a person] has no constitutional right to appropriate someone else's property to do so."[57]

Douglas, too, distinguished between pure speech and speech plus conduct. He differed, however, from Black as to when speech and peaceful protest become subject to regulation by state authorities. These jurisprudential differences were most visible when the Court, in the 1960s, had to deal with litigation involving Vietnam War protesters and black civil rights demonstrators in the Deep South who sat down, prayed in, and protested in other ways against segregation.

These cases forced Black to distinguish his belief in free speech from his strong commitment to the sanctity of private property. For the Justice, the conflict arose when he confronted the black protesters' quest for the right to peacefully assemble and to petition for a redress of grievances. A property owner does not have to turn his place into a forum for people to protest by sitting down, or singing, or praying in his store. "We have a system of private ownership of property [and an owner can] tell people he doesn't want to get out. Therefore, he can call the police to help protect that right. If that right is in the owner, the law must enforce that right."[58]

Douglas disagreed with his friend. If Black's narrow views prevailed, Douglas believed, the nation would return to the segregation of the 1896 *Plessy* Court and society. "Retail stores can't discriminate and therefore state proceedings to help them are unconstitutional. . . . I would make the store owner a public utility."[59] Black became apoplectic whenever Douglas spoke in such a radical manner about private ownership of property. These radically opposing views of the two strong-willed men were clearly enunciated when the Court heard cases involving civil rights groups protesting against both official and custom-based racial segregation by sitting down in private establishments such as Penney's and Woolworth's.

By the end of the 1962 term, their relationship was under increasing strain due to the sit-in cases they had heard that year. The 1963 *Bell v Maryland* case worsened the tension between the two men. Their differences in this area of constitutional jurisprudence became permanent in 1966 with *Adderley v Florida*.[60]

Adderley involved black students who were arrested for trespassing on the grounds of the county jail in Tallahassee, Florida, where they were protesting the arrests of other students who had been demonstrating against racial discrimination in local movie theatres. The Judge, writing for a very narrow Court majority, upheld the trespass convictions while Douglas, joined by Brennan, Fortas, and Warren, dissented. Brennan complained, in a letter to Douglas, that "Hugo's whole treatment of the facts reflects a distorted picture of the actual situation."[61]

Black successfully argued that the "singing and clapping" demonstrators did not have a "constitutional right to stay on the property, over the jail custodian's objections. . . . Such an argument has as its major unarticulated premise the assumption that people who want to propagandize protests or views have a constitutional right to do so however and wherever they please."[62] Douglas's dissent suggested another view. For protesters, the jailhouse, much like the statehouse, the executive mansion, a courthouse, or a legislative chamber, "is an obvious center for protest."[63] *Adderley* and other sit-in cases "marked Black's constitutional divide"[64] with his friend Douglas.

Black and Douglas also clashed over the meaning of due process. Even when they agreed on a case's outcome, they often arrived at their judgments by very different conceptual routes. Black the constitutional literalist believed that the due process clause was a dangerous provision in the Constitution because of its open-endedness. As Justice Brennan recalled: "He used to get so steamed up about due process questions. We'd often say: 'There goes Hugo again.' "[65]

Douglas, like his other liberal colleagues who constituted the Warren Court majority in the 1960s, had a much more expansive view of due process. Unlike former police court judge and county prosecutor Black, he saw the police, whether local or national, historically as dangerous persons. "If law enforcement were the chief value in our constitutional scheme, then due process would shrivel and become of little value in protecting the rights of the citizen. But those who fashioned the Constitution put certain rights out of the reach of the police and preferred other rights over law enforcement."[66]

However, nothing divided the two jurists as much as their conflict over demands for new constitutional rights. If Black saw Douglas changing in this area, so, too, did Douglas think he saw a change in Black. Douglas's wife Cathy recalled some very poignant conversations she had with him about Black. He confided to her that a younger Hugo would have acted differently in deciding these constitutional matters. "Hugo, at the end, was not quite that well," commented a sad husband to his wife.[67]

Douglas was incorrect, for Black's views about substantive due process and "new rights" in 1971 were very similar to his comments on the floor of the Senate in 1930. At that time, as senator from Alabama, Black railed against the Supreme Court's usurpation of legislative powers.

An incident surrounding the effort of Republicans to impeach Douglas in 1970 reveals the true depth of their friendship. Black, by this time, was suffering the ravages of old-age health problems and was in Bethesda Naval Hospital. Hugo Jr., visiting his "daddy," told the Judge of the impeachment trial that Douglas was facing, instigated by President Nixon and Attorney General John Mitchell.[68] Hugo, the very successful Alabama trial advocate, informed his son, boldly and defiantly:

> I have known Bill Douglas for thirty years. He's never knowingly done any improper, unethical, or corrupt thing. Tell his detractors that in spite of my age, I think I have one trial left in me. Tell them that if they ever move against Bill Douglas, I'll resign from the Court and represent him. It will be the biggest, most important case I ever tried.[69]

Black never had to get off a sickbed to defend his friend Douglas. He would have done just that if it had been necessary.

Felix Frankfurter

"History has not been kind to Justice Frankfurter, . . . there is now almost a universal consensus that Frankfurter the justice was a failure, a judge who . . . became 'uncoupled from the locomotive of history' during the Second World War, and who thereafter left little in the way of an enduring jurisprudential legacy."[70] Felix Frankfurter was nominated in January 1939 by Roosevelt to fill the seat of a man Frankfurter greatly admired, Benjamin N. Cardozo. His appointment met with the wholehearted approval of the nation's legal community. There was the great expectation that Frankfurter, who was both a scholar of the Court as well as a close friend of a number of Supreme Court justices, would assume the mantle of leadership once he began to work in the marble palace.

Black, then sitting on the Court and already a recipient of Stone-instigated

Frankfurter lectures and essays on jurisprudence, wrote a generous letter to his new colleague, welcoming him to the Court and signed with the affectionate "sincerely your friend" closing that he reserved for persons close to him:

> You know, of course, how very happy I am that you will soon sit by me on the Court. One regret, however, is that you were not here this week, and could not participate in the Conference I left a few minutes ago. . . . I am looking forward with unusual pleasure to our association in the important work—work which my experience here has convinced me, more than ever, is vital to the causes in which we believe. With kindest regards to your wife, I am sincerely your friend, Hugo Black.[71]

Black and the nation expected Frankfurter to decisively utilize the legitimate powers of the Court in defense of individual liberty. That did not happen. Frankfurter, once on the high bench, was a conservative jurist. And fairly soon after Frankfurter joined the Court, the warmth between the two men quickly dissipated and was replaced with enmity and bitterness, which characterized their stormy relationship until Frankfurter's departure from the Court in 1962. Frankfurter simply could not accept Black's Bible-thumping rhetoric about democracy, a style born out of Black's political background and fine tuned during his Senate days.

Frequently, Frankfurter would enter crude remarks into his diary about Black's polemics, such as "Black indulged in a harangue worthy of the cheapest soap-box orator," after one conference session.[72] On yet another occasion, in a letter to his jurisprudential ally, John M. Harlan II, Frankfurter complained that Black and his law clerks probably did not read briefs in certain cases:

> I wonder how many of those who are reversing out of hand [i.e., Black] have read the record and not have relied merely on the memoranda of their law clerks. And since my curiosity is very alert this morning, I wonder how many of the law clerks have read the whole record in these [FELA] cases. Reasonably or unreasonably yours, whichever I appear to you to be. FF[73]

Frankfurter was, like Black, a New Dealer—but he had been more the insider than was the Alabaman. He was one of FDR's chief recruiters of young legal talent, called Felix's "hot dogs," for the Roosevelt administration's numerous agencies, bureaus, and other federal programs. Felix founded the liberal journal the *New Republic,* was on the legal panel of the NAACP, and fought over the decades for liberal causes while teaching law at Harvard.

He came to the Court after twenty-five years as a professor at Harvard Law School and a confidant of Justice Brandeis. As early as 1940, Black and Frankfurter had drawn the line in the sand and, from the hectic wartime years until Frankfurter's retirement from the Court in 1962, they were bold antagonists.

There was disagreement between the two men over the role and function of judges in a democracy. There was also the dissonance between Frankfurter and Black with respect to fundamental doctrinal matters, especially the primacy and scope of the First Amendment as well as the meaning of the Constitution's due process clause in the Fifth and Fourteenth Amendments.

Ironically, their enduring conflict arose "from a premise both men shared—the premise that judicial authority depends for its legitimacy on its clear differentiation from the judge's 'merely personal' views, that a judge must stand for, and stand within, some transcendent authoritative social entity."[74] For Black, this "transcendent" authority was the Constitution with its "univocal commands." For Frankfurter, it was his reliance on what he termed a "supertextual judicial conscience,"[75] one that would enable a judge, drawing upon British legal customs and traditions, to dispassionately find the appropriate judicial response to a legal question that confronted her.

A Fundamental Clash of Wills

Frankfurter was foreign-born; an Austrian Jew who immigrated with his family from Vienna to America at the age of twelve, he went to public schools in New York City, then to City College of New York, and, finally, to Harvard Law School. Frankfurter and millions of immigrants who entered America during the first three decades of the twentieth century were the very people the nativists in Alabama, including Black, wanted to keep out, trying to have their representatives in Congress pass restrictive immigration statutes. These immigrants possessed, believed the Klan and other nativists, an alien set of values; if they were allowed to enter America without any constraints, the old, traditional American values would be destroyed.

While Black loved America because, in its constitutional values, he saw the potential contemporary democratic polis where human nature could flourish, Frankfurter loved America and its democratic institutions with a passion that emerged from his immigrant status. America provided him with the opportunity to reach his full intellectual potential and he was forever in its debt.

Frankfurter's payback, as a Supreme Court justice, was an almost categorical deferral to the actions of its elected leaders. Shedding all loyalties to his religion and to his former nationality, he embraced America wholeheartedly. A few days before his death, Frankfurter urged his biographer: "Tell the whole story. Let people see how much I loved Roosevelt, how much I loved my country." He truly loved every institution he associated with, from the Court, "which comes nearest to having, for me, sacred aspects," to Harvard Law School which, he said, he had "a quasi-religious feeling about."[76]

At a conference session in 1942, Frankfurter told his colleagues: "I am saying what I am going to say because this case[77] arouses in me feelings that could not be entertained by anyone else around this table. It is well known that a convert is more zealous than one born to the faith. None of you has had the experience that I have had with reference to American citizenship."[78]

The professional differences of Black and Frankfurter were magnified by their dramatically different personal styles. Black was forever the Senate politician, able to build coalitions and, with his allies, fight for specific goals. Frankfurter never ceased his professorial style of lecturing down to his brethren, thereby alienating many potential soldiers.

Even after Frankfurter left the Court due to ill health, he continued to rebuke his brethren. As was typically the case when he acted in this fashion, it was criticism raised behind their backs. In December 1964, shortly before he died, Frankfurter wrote to his friend Harlan about Byron "Whizzer" White's opinion for the Court in a Florida miscegenation case.[79]

> Is your colleague [White] such a man of the world that he does not know that when a couple cohabit, I don't know for how long they did so in the Florida case, they certainly fornicated.* Indeed the only definition the Oxford Dictionary gives for cohabit is to live together as husband and wife, in short being married and has he ever heard of Taft C.J.s famous sentence that what everybody knows judges are also supposed to know. And how brazenly some of the brethren disregard the elementary principle of their job not to decide what is not before them indeed specifically, if I am correctly informed, withdrawn by counsel. Other times other ways.
>
> Ever yours, F.F.
>
> *or did the Whizzer assume they . . . read Plato's *Dialogue* to one another ?????[80]

Frankfurter once wrote to Justice Charles Whittaker, "I have an incorrigibly academic mind."[81] Another colleague of Frankfurter's, Justice Potter Stewart, recalled that "Felix, if he was really interested in a case, would speak for fifty minutes, no more or less, because that was the length of the lecture at the Harvard Law School."[82] He often openly acknowledged his intention to continue to play professor in critical notes sent to his colleagues. In a letter sent to a new colleague on the Court, William Brennan, who was a former law school student of his at Harvard, Frankfurter confessed,

> You have had, I am sure, ample proof by now of my predominantly academic-minded way of dealing with issues before this Court, by which I mean my interest in the intellectual process by which we reach decisions and not merely the results that we reach. Therefore, I can count on you to believe me when I say that in making comment on your concurrence . . . I am not seeking to argue you out of your statement but merely indulging in the freedom of telling you what I think of it.[83]

In the Court's biweekly conference sessions, Frankfurter had the knack of infuriating thereby alienating many of his colleagues because he lectured to them "with his notes and records on a book rest."[84] This habit of a lifetime drove almost all his colleagues to distraction. Black, who generally did not show much anger and passion when with his brethren in conference sessions, on a number of occasions stalked out of the conference room while Frankfurter was lecturing. The Judge simply could not stand to listen to any more of Frankfurter's pontificating and, dramatically, left the conference session while the Harvard professor held the floor.

Douglas opened his mail while Frankfurter droned on. Others grew impatient with Frankfurter's incessant talk. Douglas wrote, in 1974, that "we were always twitting our brother Frankfurter over his long and dramatic performances in Conference. He was an artist as well as an able advocate and his Conference presentations were dramatic and lengthy. Most of us thought the function of the Conference was to discover the consensus. His idea was different: he was there to proselytize and to gain converts."[85]

If not interrupted by the Chief, Frankfurter would lecture for forty five minutes. He eagerly challenged his brethren to engage him in discourse because he felt very strongly that conferences should be more than vote-counting sessions. And the chiefs, especially Stone, could do little to rein him in in order to get on with conference session business. Frankfurter, was insistent about the need to have full dialogue on the cases that came before the Court. In a memo to his brethren, Frankfurter said:

> Some twenty-five hundred years ago—and not even referring to judicial action—Pericles said that "Acts are foredoomed to failure when undertaken undiscussed." To decide cases with inadequate discussion is to disregard the conception of a Court. If we just decide as individuals then we ought to have, as the English have, opinions seriatim by the individual judges. And so, for me it had always been a postulate of the work of this Court that we should have full and candid collective discussion . . . by fresh and not fatigued minds.[86]

Frankfurter, sadly, did not have the personal qualities that were vital for Court leadership, building consensus, presenting ideas in a fashion that would lead to change. Rather, his behavior irritated and angered most of his brethren. Black's oldest son wrote,

> With all his brilliance, charm and stratagems, however, FF could not really match [Hugo] in picking up converts. Even though their passionate conviction of the righteousness of their positions was equal, there was one important difference that gave Hugo the edge. FF had gained his reputation in an academic system, where he was mainly concerned with instructing, not persuading. But Hugo had gotten ahead by convincing ordinary citizens . . . as well as congressmen and judges, that his view was right.[87]

Some have suggested that Frankfurter's was a "willful isolation," one brought about when his Court colleagues brusquely rejected his intellectual and spiritual leadership of the Court. Their abandonment of Frankfurter came shortly after the 1940 *Gobitis* decision[88] (which was written by Frankfurter). His colleagues' rejection was seen by him as a "stinging personal rebuke, a wholesale repudiation of his leadership." As a consequence, Frankfurter "was virtually consumed by a vitriolic anger toward his brethren. . . . Frankfurter acted the leader abandoned by his followers, the lover spurned, the exile in his own country."[89]

By the 1939 term of the Court, Black was in fundamental disagreement with Frankfurter on a variety of key constitutional issues. In a letter to the Alabaman, written on December 15, 1939, Frankfurter critiqued an opinion of Black's, "in the same spirit and for the same academic purpose as I would were I writing a piece as a professor in the Harvard Law Review."[90] Black, said the professor, was a Benthamite who was overly concerned about protecting "judicial legislation."

As has been mentioned, Frankfurter's position was one of utmost judicial deference to the judgments of the popularly elected branches of government, especially the legislative branch. While he yielded to no one in his respect for the legislature, Black could not disagree more with Frankfurter on this matter. "I think it is the business and the supreme responsibility of the Court to hold a law unconstitutional if it believes that the law is unconstitutional, without 'deference' to anybody or any institution. In short, . . . I believe it is the duty of the Court to show 'deference' to the Constitution only." Black thought Frankfurter's view "both an exercise in judicial hypocrisy as well as a refusal of judicial responsibility," while Frankfurter condemned Black's views as "constitutional heresy."[91]

There were those occasions when Frankfurter's attacks on Black lacked grace and were spiteful. In 1945–1946, Justice Jackson, while serving as chief American prosecutor in Nuremberg, Germany, during the war crimes trials, had charged that the Alabaman and others had gone to Truman and threatened resignation if Jackson were appointed to the center seat. In 1950, a news column revealed that Frankfurter had written to Jackson while the latter was serving in Germany as U.S. Prosecutor. The story indicated that Frankfurter had told Jackson of Black's efforts to block Jackson's appointment.

Frankfurter wrote Black a letter denying the allegations:

> [The story] is so unqualifiedly unfounded in fact that I am greatly tempted to sue both the publishers and the authors . . . for libel. . . . I want you to know that nothing is further from the truth than the quotation from the [article] in question to the effect that I wrote to Jackson in Nuremberg about an alleged visit of yours to the President threatening to resign from the Court in case Jackson were named to be Chief Justice. Neither directly nor indirectly did I send any communication whatsoever to Jackson regarding the vacancy created by Stone's death.[92]

Black sent a "Dear Felix" letter on October 2, 1950. It said, in part, "I had neither seen nor read any part [of the article] until you sent me extracts from it. So far as I am concerned, it is the same as though it had never been written. For it too will pass away."[93]

The truth is that Frankfurter did send Jackson a letter, but *after* Vinson had been nominated by Truman, reflecting on the fact that Black's "skullduggery" had not succeeded! Frankfurter's letter to the Alabaman was correct, but in the narrowest sense, for Frankfurter was not discussing the "vacancy created by Stone's death" when he wrote to Jackson: he was, however, commenting on Black's alleged behavior when he wrote to the disappointed jurist in Germany. Frankfurter used the old lawyer's tricks with Black: Be precise in retelling an incident, even if the truth was ignored by the "truthteller." What probably galled Frankfurter more than anything was the fact that Black seemed impervious to these little mindgames and half-truths that Frankfurter sprang on him from time to time.

Jurisprudential Clashes

On one occasion, in a fit of anger over Black's insistence that the First Amendment freedoms were absolutes that could not be placed in jeopardy by the government, Frankfurter sent to his brethren, with his "compliments," a poem entitled, "A Dialogue (with apologies to Gertrude Stein)." It went as follows:

L(ibertarian) L(ads):
  Speech is speech is speech.
F(rivolous) F(rankfurter):
  Crying-fire-in-theatre is speech is speech is not "speech."
  Libel is speech is speech is not "speech."
  Picketing is speech is speech is not "speech."
  Pornographic film is speech is speech is not "speech."
                                               —Anonymous [94]

Frankfurter claimed to be the Court's only rationalist: "She who knows me best often tells me that I have an incurable faith in reason and in exchanging views as a means of attaining reason. Well, that which is incurable cannot be cured—and I plead guilty to the charge of trying to understand things that are profoundly the result of a reasoning process." [95] Black's firmly worded reactions to Frankfurter's pleas for reasonableness led to angry comments by Frankfurter, such as that found in a 1954 letter to Stanley Reed, in which Frankfurter wrote: "[Black] has reached a conclusion and is not at all bothered about arguments which can be exposed." [96]

Frankfurter viewed the Alabaman with utter disdain: Black was an unprincipled, "self-righteous, self-deluded part-fanatic, part demagogue, who really disbelieves in Law, thinks it essentially manipulation of language." [97] The professor saw Black as a scheming, manipulative politician in Court robes, a former representative of the Klan, who had shrilly called for a halt to American immigration to prevent Frankfurter and millions of other foreigners from coming to America.

After Frankfurter left the bench due to ill-health in 1962, he continued to lecture, by mail and by private courier, his Court foe. On a number of occasions, their mutual friend, John M. Harlan II played the role of courier! When, for example, Black dissented in a sit-in case, *Bell v Maryland,* [98] Frankfurter, through Harlan, sent a number of letters to the Alabaman. While he was "brought up to believe that it is not proper to congratulate a judge on the views he expresses in an opinion, because presumably a judge's views are the compulsions of his conscience, . . . [this letter] is, I believe, the first time I have departed from my deep conviction on this subject to tell you of my pride in you for your dissent." [99]

Black's response in December 1964, shortly before Frankfurter died, was the typically gracious response from the Southerner. "Our differences, which have been many, have rarely been over the ultimate end desired but rather have related to the means that were the most likely to achieve the end we both envisioned. Our years together, and these differences, have but added to the respect and admiration that I had for *Professor* Frankfurter even before I knew him—his love of country, steadfast devotion to what he believed to be right, and to his wisdom." [100]

A friendship of sorts emerged after Frankfurter retired from the Court. It came about a year before Frankfurter died, and it was "the friendship of foes." [101] But these foes were primarily intellectual battlers. In a book of Frankfurter's papers given to Black, Frankfurter had written a note to his intellectual adversary. It summed up their stormy quarter-century relationship: "For Hugo Black, whose fault it won't be if my mental veins harden." [102]

Black fought Frankfurter especially hard regarding the nature and the breadth of the First Amendment. Frankfurter argued, again and again, that the First Amendment rights did not deserve to be placed above other constitutional clauses. In a 1958 letter to his ally Harlan, Felix was critical of Harlan's views about the First Amendment in the *NAACP v Alabama* litigation then before the Court.[103]

The case involved an effort by the state to acquire the membership list of the civil rights organization. The NAACP refused to turn the list over and was held in contempt by a state judge and fined one hundred thousand dollars. The Court, ruling nine to zero, in an opinion written by Harlan, concluded that the organization could successfully argue the constitutional, First Amendment rights of Alabama members of the NAACP not to be revealed to Alabama authorities. Freedom of association, protected in the First Amendment, sheltered these men and women from being revealed to the state.

Frankfurter was battling the influence of what he called Black's "loose rhetoric" in this case and expressed his bitterness to Harlan in an effort to persuade him to write a moderate opinion for the Court.

> Little did I dream in my early days when we were dealing with explicit curtailments of speech that loose rhetoric in the service of recently discovered doctrinaire views by members of this Court would be snowballed into a talismanic mouthing (what mixed metaphor!) of "First Amendment" in dealing with state action, which only by the most indirect argumentation could be made to relate to utterance or refusal to utter. . . . [This] loose talk of this Court is responsible for . . . flannel-mouthed talk dished up to us [by lawyers in this Court] in the confident belief that they have to get only one more "vote" to win their case. . . . And so I have become strongly allergic to all this loose talk and the loose notions about "First Amendment"[104]

Black, on the other hand, as early as the 1940 term of the Court, in the case of *Milk Wagon Drivers Union v Meadowmoor Dairies,*[105] expressed what would become his view about the high preferred place, and, later on, the absolute protections of the First Amendment in the hierarchy of constitutional rights and liberties.

Furthermore, Frankfurter, to Black's anger and chagrin, continually drew upon principles of natural law and his favorite Anglo-Saxon concepts to define the constitution's "due process of law" language found in the Fifth and Fourteenth Amendments. The professor-turned-jurist's "affinity for British common law . . . made him comfortable with legal interpretations of a rather sweeping sort. . . . He was willing (unlike Black) to decide issues arising under the due process clause according to his understanding and love of English law and values associated with decency and fairness."[106]

While Black kept these clashes with Frankfurter within the Court's confines because he felt it inappropriate for the brethren to argue in public, Frankfurter was never disposed to limit the conflict he had with Black to internal notes and diatribes in conference. Consequently, their battles spilled beyond the Court. They were read about in law review articles, popular essays in magazines, and national gossip columns. While there was, in Frankfurter's last year, some effort at pleasantries between the two of them, the Judge and the Professor were bitter judicial adversaries from 1939 to Frankfurter's retirement in 1962.

Their profound differences were delightfully captured when a visitor from Israel spoke with the two men in their Court chambers. Chaim Cohen, the young nation's attorney general, was in America to study its constitutional foundations and he spoke to the two justices about that general theme. "Mr. Justice Black began our discussion by saying, 'The first thing you should do, young man, is write a constitution.' Cohen went next door to see Frankfurter: 'The first thing you should not do, young man, is to write a constitution. Good and courageous judges best protect civil liberties.' "[107] Black and Frankfurter never resolved the differences that made them the major protagonists on the Court for over two decades.

Robert H. Jackson

Robert Jackson was an associate justice of the Supreme Court appointed by Roosevelt in 1941 who served until his death in 1954. In 1949 he wrote an incredible forty-six-page document about his strained relationship with the Judge. Written in the third person and shared with a small number of readers, it has become a part of the Jackson collection in the Library of Congress.[108]

It is an angry piece, for Jackson was still filled with a hatred of Black that went back to the 1945 *Jewell Ridge* "portal-to-portal" case and the tragic events that followed that legal clash between the two men, with Frankfurter siding with Jackson over the question of recusal by a sitting justice. He began the document by noting that while the two campaigned for Roosevelt together in 1936, he did not know Black personally prior to his service on the Court. However, he had heard of the Alabaman's reputation as a senator. Black was, according to Jackson, "one of the most persistent patronage seekers in the Senate, and one whom a subordinate better not cross and the heads of departments rarely offended for fear of reprisal. I had known of his ruthless conduct of Senate investigations with little regard for the constitutional rights of persons he was pursuing."[109]

Black's appointment to the Court, wrote Jackson, "was a surprise and shock to Jackson, as it was to most others in the Administration." He did note that Hugo generally supported his arguments made before the Court when Jackson was attorney general. But there never developed a friendship between the two men.

Black and Jackson "had little common background or experience." One was a man from the "Deep South," the other was a Yankee born in Pennsylvania and a resident of New York state for most of his life.

The extended criticism of Black pointed up the differences between the two that also characterized their careers: Black's crude politicking versus Jackson's nobility of spirit and action. There is this assessment of the two jurists' experiences.

> Black had waged a successful campaign all his life for popularity and masses of votes by conforming to the view of the most numerous group, joining rather than resisting even those organizations he claims to have disagreed with. Jackson's life was a long defiance of the political sentiments of the majority of his neighbors, for whose votes or favors he never asked except in one place—when they

sat on the jury. . . . The most striking difference between the two grew out of their different lives. Black appears to have endured a hard economic and political struggle, one which left scars and bitterness against the successful and well-to-do, made him uneasy among them. . . . Jackson, however, moved in such circles with easy familiarity and self-confidence. Often at their faces, he assailed their reactionary views.[110]

Black had extensive political experience "in appealing to popular support," whereas Jackson, by his own admission, "had no legislative experience and was regarded as somewhat inept politically."[111] Jackson's self-assessment in this respect tragically proved to be correct. His public tangles with Black in 1945 and again in 1946, while Jackson was in Germany as America's chief war crimes prosecutor, showed a shocked Washington community as well as an unbelieving public a view of the Supreme Court rarely seen outside the marble palace.

Jackson, who had worked for Roosevelt when the latter was governor of New York, came to Washington with the new president and was a vigorous defender of the New Deal, including Roosevelt's Court-packing plan of 1937. By the mid-1930s, Jackson was in the Department of Justice as assistant attorney general (antitrust), then as solicitor general of the United States, and finally as Roosevelt's attorney general. In June 1941, Jackson was nominated to take Harlan F. Stone's seat on the Court when Stone was moved to the center seat.

When he met Black, it was "doubtful if either of them recognized their latent antagonisms."[112] Jackson, who was the last of the Court justices to receive law training by apprenticing for a lawyer in New York rather than going to law school, was described by Douglas as a "lawyer of great versatility. . . . He had a sharp pen and an incisive mind. He was a lone wolf on the Court, having no close friend except Frankfurter. . . . His ambition to be Chief Justice truly poisoned his judicial career."[113]

By 1943, Black and Jackson "typified the rival polarities" that had emerged in the Supreme Court since 1939 on issues other than economic and social engineering by governments.[114] On the one side, there stood the dreaded "Axis," which included Black and Douglas, regularly joined by Murphy and Rutledge. On the other side stood Frankfurter, Jackson, and, on occasion, Roberts. From Jackson's appointment to his departure for Germany in June 1945, he and Black were at odds over process and jurisprudence. When he was in Germany, their relationship grew even more difficult because of actions taken by Jackson against Hugo.

Clashes between Enemies

The tense, stressful environment in the Court was the reason Jackson took the overseas assignment in 1945, even though it meant that the Court would function as an eight-person tribunal for at least a term. Jackson's absence for such an extended period of time, however, led to criticism from the brethren, including Black, who showed an "open hostility" towards Jackson for his temporary departure.[115]

Douglas speculated that Jackson took the prosecutor's position because "he was planning to run for governor of New York and perhaps for President, so from

A Charles Mandy column about police court judge Hugo Black. (*Birmingham Sun, 1911*)

Josephine Foster, the first Mrs. Hugo Black, circa 1927. (*Collection of the Supreme Court of the United States*)

PUBLIC SPEAKING

Judge Hugo L. Black
Candidate for
United States Senate
Will Make the Opening
Speech of his Campaign
At the Court House in Ashland
Saturday, March 20th, 11 a.m.

Let everybody come out and let's give Clay County's Distinguished son an enthusiastic hearing. Ladies especially invited.
Local Campaign Committee

(Paid Political Advertisement. Authorized by Hugo L. Black. Birmingham, Alabama.)

Hugo Black senatorial campaign flyer, 1925.

Announcement for a 1935 speech by Black. (*Collection of the Supreme Court of the United States*)

"Lobby Investigation"

+

Speech

of

Hon. Hugo L. Black
United States Senator From Alabama

Hugo L. Black

+

Arranged by
THE WASHINGTON STAR

And Broadcast Over a Nation-Wide Network of
THE NATIONAL BROADCASTING COMPANY

Thursday Night, August 8, 1935

Compliments of
The Evening Star
The Sunday Star
WASHINGTON, D. C.

Above: Josephine Black
with the three Black
children, Hugo Jr., Jo Jo,
and Sterling, 1936. (
*Courtesy of Josephine
Black Pesaresi*)

Right: Senator and Mrs.
Black at the time of his
confirmation as justice of
the U.S. Supreme Court,
August 1937. (*Collection
of the Supreme Court of the
United States)*

Above: Justice Black addressing a nation wide radio audience to explain his membership in the Ku Klux Klan, October 1937. (*Associated Press*)

Right: Justice Hugo Black, October term 1937. (*Collection of the Supreme Court of the United States*)

Black and his children, circa 1957. From left to right: Sterling, Graham (Hugo Jr.'s wife), Jo Jo, Hugo Jr., Hugo Black, and Charlotte (Sterling's first wife). (*Courtesy of Josephine Black Pesaresi*)

Black and some of his former law clerks in his Alexandria, Virginia, home, with his daughter Jo Jo sitting next to the Justice, circa 1957. (*Courtesy of Josephine Black Pesaresi*)

Elizabeth Seay DeMerritte,
Black's second wife, circa 1960.
(*Collection of the Supreme Court
of the United States*)

An informal portrait of the Supreme Court's justices in the mid-1960s. Front
row: Tom C. Clark, Hugo Black, Earl Warren (Chief Justice), and William O.
Douglas; rear row: Byron "Whizzer" White, William J. Brennan, Jr., Potter
Stewart, and Arthur J. Goldberg (not shown, John M. Harlan ll). (*Collection of
the Supreme Court of the United States*)

Black's eightieth birthday party at the White House, 1966. Black is shown with "Lady Bird" Johnson and William O. Douglas. (*Collection of the Supreme Court of the United States*)

Memo to the Conference, *Alexander v Holmes County* (1969), with Black threatening to dissent.

Above: Black with one of his grandsons, circa 1970. (*Courtesy of Josephine Black Pesaresi*)

Left: Black's letter of resignation to President Richard M. Nixon, September 1971.

a political viewpoint it was desirable for him to be our Nuremberg prosecutor, since the Jewish vote is important in many parts of our country." [116] Truman himself, in a conversation with Clark Clifford in the spring of 1946, "mentioned that there was one man—Associate Justice Robert H. Jackson—whose experience and talents seemed to make him presidential timber." [117] However, because of the long-simmering feud between Jackson and Black that was to soon become a major public scandal, Jackson was to become a truly tragic figure on the Court. If he harbored any thoughts about running for high political office, these quickly evaporated as a consequence of his totally inopportune actions in 1946.

While Jackson was serving as war prosecutor in Germany, Chief Justice Stone died and, after false allegations in the press that Black and Douglas had gone to Truman to threaten resignation if the president appointed Jackson to succeed Stone, Fred M. Vinson, Truman's close friend and his secretary of the treasury, was appointed to the center seat. Truman evidently hoped and prayed that Vinson's political experience, as congressman and as a member of the Truman administration, might help control and direct the Court's two contentious blocs.

Black never commented on these scurrilous allegations. Douglas, however, categorically rejected these news accounts: "Truman never broached the matter with us [Black and Douglas], and neither of us sent any message to Truman." [118] The Alabaman's son also categorically rejected the view that Black went to Truman. "It was a plain lie. [My Father] had said no such thing." [119] However, within four days of the announcement of the Vinson nomination, an angry Jackson took an action that shocked the community of Washington, D.C.—as well as the country. He publicly condemned Black in a telegram sent to Truman, with copies to the Judiciary Committee chairs in Congress and to the media.

In his angry letter, Jackson cited feuds within the Court, including a major one that had been brewing between Black and himself for some time. The issue was whether Hugo should have disqualified himself in the so-called portal-to-portal pay case of *Jewell Ridge Coal Corp v Local 6167, UMW.* It was a closely divided case in which Frank Murphy—according to Frankfurter, "stooging" for Hugo—wrote the majority opinion in May 1945. Jackson wrote the dissenting opinion.

In *Jewell Ridge,* union miners had argued that they should be paid for their travel to and from mine work and had brought suit under the provisions of the Fair Labor Standards Act. The case was argued on March 9, 1945. In the conference session the following day, the justices voted five to four against portal-to-portal pay—with Jackson assigned to write the opinion for the majority. However, over the weekend, Justice Reed changed his mind, which shifted the decision of the Court in favor of portal-to-portal pay.

Black was the senior justice in the new majority, and he assigned the opinion to Murphy. Jackson's dissent angered the Alabaman because the dissenter had quoted *Senator* Black when he took a position on the scope of the Fair Labor Standards Act—the Black-Connery Act—in 1937 contrary to the position Justice Black was taking in the 1945 case. Hugo wrote a memo to the conference, complaining that Jackson was misquoting him. "The very page from which the [Jackson] dissent quotes negatives the inference. . . . If the dissent does go down as now printed, it will not be a fair representation of the true facts."[120] Jackson did not modify the dissent. The draft opinions were circulated in early April 1945. The strike at the mine was settled before the opinion came down in May 1945. A petition for rehearing was filed at the end of May and was denied on June 18, 1945, the day the Court adjourned for the term and Jackson flew off to Germany.

The clash was not on the substantive portal-to-portal issue per se. Rather, Jackson and Frankfurter were angry with Black because he did not recuse himself from the case. One of his former Birmingham law partners (and the Cyclops of his Ku Klux Klan chapter there), Crampton Harris, was the attorney for the United Mine Workers local. The Black-Harris partnership had ended twenty years earlier, although they had worked together on a congressional investigation when Hugo was chair of a Senate investigating committee.

The coal company petitioned the Court for a rehearing on the ground that Black should have disqualified himself because of his prior association with the attorney for the miners. This set off a rancorous debate within the Court as to whether or not the Court should directly respond to this question raised by the company lawyers.

Frankfurter and Jackson were unwilling to give "blind and unqualified approval"[121] to Black's participation in the case. They felt that some statement should be appended to the denial of rehearing order indicating their concern about Black's participation in the case. To simply deny the petition for rehearing without commenting on the fact that the Court had no power to pass judgment on the question of qualification, they felt, was not correct. It would give the impression that the Court condoned Hugo's action. The two Black enemies did not want to leave that impression.

Jackson drafted a statement, in the third person, that said, in part:

> Because of this lack of authoritative standards [upon which a justice of this court may be disqualified in any case], it appears always to have been the responsibility of each justice to determine for himself the propriety of withdrawing in any particular circumstances. . . . There is no authority known to me under which the majority of this court has power under any circumstances to exclude one of its duly commissioned justices from sitting or voting in any case.[122]

Frankfurter then wrote another of his classic, gratuitous "Dear Hugo" letters to try to explain his support of the Jackson statement.

> By silence I would impliedly be denying the truth of what he stated—that as to qualification I have no right to sit in judgment on my Brethren any more than they have a right to sit in judgment on my qualifications in a particular case. . . . I had no share in creating the situation whereby Bob felt it to be his duty to make clear the issue of qualification. But since he has done so, I could withhold joining him only by suppressing my belief in the truth. I do not propose to do that—and that is the sole reason why I join him. Needless to say I greatly regret the whole incident.[123]

And once again, Black did not respond to the missive from his Court antagonist.

On May 16, 1946, just about one year after *Jewell Ridge* was decided and shortly after Stone's death, Doris Fleeson's column in the *Washington Star* appeared. Its catchy headline, "SUPREME COURT FEUD: INSIDE STORY OF JACKSON-BLACK BATTLE LAID BEFORE A HARASSED PRESIDENT," stunned most readers. The story discussed the *Jewell Ridge* clash in detail and quoted at length from the Jackson comments on the denial of a rehearing. Included in the story were quotes from Truman himself who, it was claimed, confided to a Southern Senator that Black and Jackson threatened to resign if the President appointed the other to the center seat on the Court.[124]

On June 7, 1946, Jackson sent the ill-thought-out telegram to Truman, legislators, and the press. For two weeks, just about every paper in America carried stories about the feud. After congratulating Truman on the nomination of Vinson to the center seat, Jackson in the telegram addressed the rumors he had been hearing, from Frankfurter and from reading the Fleeson column and other news columns, that Black had threatened to resign if Jackson were named to that position.

He then wrote about the *Jewell Ridge* case because it reflected the existing clash of wills and values on the Court.

> Mr. Justice Black has apparently made good his threat of "war." He followed it by threatening the President if he dares to make a court appointment which is not to his liking. . . . Protection of my own name lies in disclosing the facts heretofore suppressed. I cannot discharge my duties . . . if I allow the impression either that an Associate has "something on me" which is disqualifying in your eyes, or that my opinion in the *Jewell Ridge* case was a "gratuitous insult" to an Associate.[125]

Throughout June, the press had a field day with this dirty linen displayed by one of the brethren. The *Washington Post* headline read: "JACKSON'S CHARGE AGAINST BLACK SPLITS SUPREME COURT WIDE OPEN." The *New York Times* ran the story under the following banner headline: "JACKSON'S ATTACK ON BLACK STIRS TALK OF COURT INQUIRY," "JACKSON ATTACKS BLACK FOR JUDGING EX-PARTNER'S CASE." Lewis Woods's story in the *Times,* dated June 10, 1946, began: "The national capital was stunned tonight to read of the bitter denunciation of Associate Justice Hugo Black delivered at Nuremberg by Associate Justice Robert H. Jackson." Drew Pearson's *Washington-Merry-Go-Round* syndicated column of June 13, 1946, focused on the feud, supporting Black's position in the dispute. Journals such as the *New Republic* and the *Progressive* featured stories on the clash. Congressmen discussed the possibility of investigating the Supreme Court.

Black received many letters of support, including one from Charles Grove Haines, a professor of political science at the University of California, Los Angeles.

> It is difficult for the general public to realize or understand, when an attack of this kind is made, the underlying forces and factors which are at work in the interpretation of the words and phrases of our fundamental law. My chief concern is that the publicity which has been aroused through this incident will in no way affect the constructive and extremely important work which you and the other liberal-minded Justices have been doing to restore something in the nature of

democratic simplicity, fairness and balance in the process of Constitutional interpretation.[126]

Black's response was revealing, for it reflected, once again, his strong-willed personality:

> When I decided to enter public service, I did so with the belief that public servants who stand and fight for principles are likely to create powerful antagonism. Consequently, I have always viewed personal attacks as incident to my work. As a result, none of them have ever caused me to deviate from the fundamental purposes of my life. Nothing that has recently occurred has shaken this resolution.[127]

Shay Minton, who was Black's Senate colleague in the 1930s, and, at the time of the Jackson telegram incident, a federal appeals judge in Chicago, also wrote to Black. Minton's letter, like so many the Alabaman received, was a consoling one, urging Black not to do anything rash in response to the Jackson attack. Hugo wrote back to his friend, saying in part:

> The recent statement made by my colleague has undoubtedly done great injury to the Court as an institution. You can rest assured, however, that I am not at all disturbed or bothered as to its ultimate effect on me personally. . . . Long ago I became convinced that the only way a public man could escape smears was either to actively espouse or acquiesce in conditions and practices abhorrent to his sense of justice. Since I could not follow this course with any inward satisfaction, I concluded that the only thing to do was to accept criticism as an incident of my work. I sincerely hope that you will not let this matter disturb you any more than it has me.[128]

The Jackson telegram was unique in the annals of American jurisprudential behavior. The Supreme Court justices were as much shocked and saddened by these strange events as anybody in America. Frankfurter was saddened because of his friend Jackson's turmoil. Wrote Douglas: "The weapon Bob used against Black was forged in passion and intemperance."[129] And Justice Rutledge stated: "Too bad, but it's just like Bob. I'm not surprised."[130] Even Jackson, in a personal memo written for his files, indicated that the telegram was intemperate, because he sought no outside advice on either the idea of sending it or the quality of the contents: "This seems a capital blunder; for, accepting the policy of making a statement, some minds not so close to the events it dealt with could have clarified and strengthened the document. . . . There were deeper defects."[131]

Jackson resumed his duties on the Court in October 1946. For some time, he and Black did not speak to each other. However, "after their passion had been spent,"[132] they resumed a respectful, although cool relationship. They grew further apart on issues of constitutional interpretation, especially in the area of First Amendment freedoms and national security. As the Jackson memo notes, "it always was naive to think that men of the type of Black or Jackson could be jollied out of their differences and convictions. Their disagreements are intellectual matters, fundamental to their respective characters. They are not likely ever to be reconciled to each other's viewpoint, however much each respects the other's ability." [133]

Doctrinal Disputes

Jackson, like his ally Frankfurter and all other New Dealers, wanted a more deferential judiciary when governments passed economic and social legislation. Jackson, however, wanted a more deferential Court in almost all other areas as well, especially in regard to curtailing political enemies in America. Prior to his year (1945–1946) at the Nazi War crimes trials in Germany, Jackson had supported the Black-Douglas perception of courts as protectors of civil and political rights of persons and groups such as the Jehovah's Witnesses who really did not threaten the nation's security with their religious fervor.

He joined Black and Douglas in deciding a number of these kinds of cases involving civil and political freedoms and the rights of observant religious persons. In *Barnette,* one of dozens of Jehovah's Witnesses cases heard by the brethren at this time, Jackson, writing for the Court majority in 1943, said:

> If there is any fixed star in our constitutional constellation, it is that no official, high or petty, can prescribe what shall be orthodox in politics, nationalism, religion, or other matters of opinion or force citizens to confess by word or act their faith therein. . . . The very purpose of a Bill of Rights was to withdraw certain subjects from the vicissitudes of political controversy, to place them beyond the reach of majorities and officials and to establish them as legal principles to be applied by the Courts. One's right to life, liberty, and property, to free speech, a free press, freedom of worship and assembly, and other fundamental rights may not be submitted to vote; they depend on the outcome of no elections. [134]

However, when Jackson returned from his year in Germany prosecuting Nazis and experiencing firsthand the duplicity of the Communists, he was a changed jurist. Perhaps the reason was his misfortune in not getting the center seat, or his public feud with Black, or Frankfurter's support of Jackson before and during Jackson's absence, or his profound experience serving as chief prosecutor at the war crimes trials. Whatever the reason, Jackson "became a markedly conservative interpreter of the Bill of Rights [and] more often than not sided with the Frankfurter wing of the Court." [135]

Jackson always had a sympathetic listener in Frankfurter. A law clerk of Jackson's recalled that the two jurists "were in and out of each other's chambers often; they tended to agree on most legal issues, and enjoyed discussing them between themselves." [136] An entry in Frankfurter's diary notes the following exchange between them.

> Jackson . . . again reverted to his own very great unhappiness on the Court. He said, . . . "It is an awful thing at this time of the Court's and country's history, with the very difficult and important questions coming before this Court, to have one man, Black, practically control three others, for I am afraid Rutledge will join the Axis [Douglas and Murphy]. But on the other hand, I say to myself it

would be rather cowardly to leave the field to them. But I can tell you it is very sad business for me and it isn't any fun to be writing opinions to show up some of their performances." I did the best I could to soothe him.[137]

Jackson again penned a memo to his file, once more written in the third person, about his disagreements with Black: "Their disagreements are intellectual matters, fundamental to their respective characters. They are not likely ever to be reconciled to each other's viewpoint, however much each respects the other's ability."[138] He was, in the end, correct in his observations. Jackson was never able to counter Hugo's intellectual and political skills. He was uncomfortable with politics and that discomfiture turned Jackson into a very bitter jurist on the Court for the last decade of his life.

Abe Fortas

Abe Fortas was another Democratic New Dealer who sat on the Court, but he joined it long after Roosevelt's administration ended. In 1965, Fortas replaced Justice Arthur Goldberg, who had resigned, at President Lyndon Baines Johnson's urging (accompanied by a great deal of arm-twisting), to become U.S. Ambassador to the United Nations. The son of immigrant Jews who settled in Memphis, Tennessee, Fortas had been Douglas's protégé when he attended Yale Law School and after graduation. He worked briefly with Douglas at the SEC and then joined the Department of the Interior during the Second World War. After the war, Fortas entered private practice in Washington, D.C., and was a founding partner in the prestigious law firm of Arnold, Fortas, and Porter.

During his New Deal activities, Fortas befriended LBJ, then a young, lanky, savvy, and ambitious congressman from Texas. It was their friendship that brought Fortas into direct contact with Justice Black in 1948, although they had known each other slightly while the Alabaman was in the Senate and Fortas was with the SEC.

Johnson was in the race of his life for the U.S. Senate in 1948. In August of that year he was in a Democratic party runoff primary, complete with allegations of voter fraud by both candidates, which he won by eighty-seven votes. Coke Stevenson, the loser, challenged Johnson's "landslide" win in federal district court. The judge issued an order that temporarily set aside the election returns and then ruled Stevenson to be the winner. Johnson immediately called his friend Fortas to help him overcome the federal ruling in a timely manner so that Johnson's name could get on the ballot.

Fortas's strategy: Get the appeal directly to the Supreme Court, for, he said, "Hugo Black will handle it expeditiously."[139] He took LBJ's appeal to Hugo, who "rode circuit" and heard appeals in the Fifth Judicial Circuit during the summer. Fortas's argument: A federal judge should not enjoin a state-run election.[140] Obviously, and the very intelligent lawyer Fortas knew this, such an appeal would strike a chord with Hugo, who was forever defending "Our Federalism," especially states' rights in the federal system.

Fortas took the appeal directly to the Justice, who was still in Washington, D.C. After hearing four hours of argument, Black ruled in Johnson's favor and quickly set aside the federal district court judge's restraining order. With that ruling, Johnson was rapidly certified as Democratic candidate and won election to the Senate in November 1948. Although it took two decades to repay the enormous debt he owed Fortas, Johnson was to repay his friend with a seat on the Court when Goldberg became UN ambassador.

Fortas's appointment to the Court in 1965 was greeted warmly by Black, who had been on the Court for twenty-eight years. Potter Stewart believed that "both didn't like each other, I think, beginning at the word go."[141] And, shortly after Fortas was appointed, Jinksie Durr quizzed her brother-in-law about the new member of the Court.

> How do you get on with Abe and Carol? I know you will never answer this question so I might as well not have asked. Abe is smart, but we never have known if either he or Carol had any heart at all. We used to see so much of them through Tex and Wickie Goldschmidt, but never really got to be friends.[142]

Early correspondence and diary entries by the Blacks clearly indicate, however, that during the first year there were efforts to "get on" with the Fortases. At the time LBJ asked him to serve on the Court, Fortas was making almost $200,000 annually from his law practice. He was, naturally, troubled by the potential impact on his family's lifestyle if he became a Justice of the Court. Although his wife, Carolyn Agger, was a very highly successful Washington attorney, his salary would decrease dramatically, to $39,500 annually.

When Fortas was asked by Johnson to take the seat of the departed Goldberg, he called Hugo and Elizabeth a number of times to talk about the matter. Elizabeth remembered a critical conversation "Abe called again and said the President said, 'Now look, Abe! They need you on the Court. You may never have this opportunity again. *Take this job!*' So Abe felt he had to accept. We are all glad"[143] (her emphasis).

Hugo and his wife, along with Douglas, were asked by Warren to try to encourage Fortas to accept the nomination. Shortly after the subject of Court service was raised, the Blacks had the Fortases over for dinner in order to persuade Abe to join the Court. The following day, he wrote Hugo: "I cannot adequately tell you how much the evening meant to me—and, I think, to Carol."[144] Evidently, the Alabaman was delighted that Fortas would be joining the Court.[145] Although it took some persuading by Warren, Douglas, Black, and the president, Fortas finally agreed to serve. Elizabeth wrote about a critical meeting she and Hugo had with Abe and Carol at the Blacks' home in Alexandria.

> Carol told me they had several big things going that now have to be given up, that they can't live on the small Court salary and may have to give up their new home. Later Hugo talked to Carol [about] how a man needs a wife. . . . Carol asked indignantly if he was suggesting that she give up her practice which was her life, and Hugo said, "Certainly not." . . . They stayed until after midnight.[146]

Fortas's wife, Carol, continued to be extremely unhappy with the president's pleas to her husband to take the Court job. "I could shoot Arthur Goldberg for taking the U.N. job," she said in a letter to Bill Douglas, dated August 12, 1965, after Fortas was appointed. She was "very upset about Abe's being forced into this at this time." As one of her "oldest friends," she wanted Douglas to "understand the reasons for my profound concern and unhappiness about this."

> I can only hope that you are right in your thoughts about this business because Abe is giving up an awful lot—a firm he built, a tremendous reputation as a lawyer—to say nothing of a reduction in income to about 1/5 of what he is used to and upon the basis of which we made financial commitments which will not now be easy to fulfill. In fact, they could not be fulfilled except for my earnings—which I hope will stand up.[147]

Once on the Court, in the first year, Fortas and Black quickly became estranged. The elderly Hugo, uncharacteristically, soon began to bitterly attack Abe on numerous occasions, including angry outbursts directed towards him in open court.

A Very Bitter Clash of Strong-Willed Men

Laura Kalman, Abe Fortas's biographer, noted that Fortas, who had been a very successful legal practitioner, always "retained a lawyer's perspective." He acted, in oral argument, "as if he wanted to remind the audience that Attorney Fortas would have done a better job of arguing the case than the lawyer standing before Justice Fortas."[148]

Furthermore, Fortas, as a lifelong aggressive legal advocate, "remained ambivalent about his job" and referred to himself not as justice but as a "government clerk."[149] Abe also had to acclimate to the slow pace, the ceremony, and the monasterylike secluded setting in which the Supreme Court decided cases and controversies. "The pomp of the Court," wrote Kalman, "tickled Fortas."[150]

In addition, even after his appointment, Fortas continued to serve as a close personal advisor to President Johnson, providing counsel to LBJ regarding the terribly painful Vietnam war. This Asian conflagration had dramatically expanded by the time of Fortas's appointment to the Court. The war's costs, in American lives and matériel, had escalated precipitately. Fortas, who was considered a military "hawk," supported LBJ's moves to escalate the war. The war, however, was ripping society apart. Johnson, confronting dissent and hatred in America because of his actions, sought advice from his longtime friend, and Fortas provided it whenever LBJ called him up and invited him over to the White House.

Finally, it became very clear to Black, soon after Fortas joined the brethren and began participating in Court decision-making, that he—unlike Hugo—was a believer in the broadest possible interpretation of the due process clause.

These characteristics and behaviors infuriated Black; Fortas's constant proffering of counsel to LBJ irritated most of his colleagues on the Court as well. Initially, Black's ire was contained. He wrote Abe a very friendly note after Fortas's first opinion, *United Steelworkers of America v R.H. Bouligny,* was handed down in 1965, writing in part that

I am happy to agree to your first Court opinion. May you write many more like it in *which you lead the Court in sticking to its own business of interpretation rather than yielding to the temptation to make laws either on a legislative or constitutional level.*[151] (my emphasis)

However, Black misspoke prematurely. Shortly after these encouraging words, Black spotted in Abe's behavior an attitude that Hugo reviled in his colleagues: Roam at will to find the meaning and spirit of due process. Very quickly, within his first year on the Court, Fortas was using judicial power in due process and other areas "in all the wrong directions."[152] Fortas "was not afraid to interpret loosely the Fourteenth Amendment due process clause and the rest of the Constitution in order to safeguard the rights of others."[153] The new judge believed—much like his mentor, Douglas, contrary to the constitutional literalist Black—that the "very job of a jurist was to expand the rights of the Constitution in order to protect minorities, the downtrodden, and the oppressed."[154] Given Fortas's experiences with litigation, as well as his firm grasp of constitutional doctrines (he successfully argued the 1962 *Gideon v Wainright* case before the Court), Black failed to convert him to the literalist, nonexpansive school of due process and soon came to "despise [Fortas because] intellectually, he was a due process guy."[155]

Beyond that, Fortas's imperious, know-it-all attitude and continuing advisory relationship with the president enraged the Alabaman. "It was clear from the start that Fortas would not be just another freshman justice, expected to serve out his apprenticeship quietly while he learned the ropes. He knew the ropes well."[156] Further, Hugo intuitively believed that Abe, although a brilliant legal practitioner, was "too much the wheeler dealer, . . . totally unprincipled, and intellectually dishonest."[157] At his advanced age, the Judge had no tolerance for such a person on the Court.

Black's inner feeling, as usually was the case, proved to be correct. While Fortas was a very successful attorney and presidential advisor, he had no commitment to a jurisprudence when he joined the Court in 1965 and was not really interested in developing one after he joined. Abe, believed the Judge, was a very pragmatic, result-oriented jurist who, unlike Hugo, never changed after coming on the Court. As a Justice, Fortas "would listen to the clerks' principled arguments for a particular decision and say, 'Well, yes, in theory, that is where we should come out. But we just can't do that in this case.' "[158] Early on, Black took note of these characteristics and decided that Fortas had to be stopped, for sophists were dangerous to the community, whether in ancient Greece or modern America, and Fortas was a sophist!

Constitutional Disputes

Fortas immediately became a part of the liberal Warren gang of expansionist due process justices, a group that included Brennan, Douglas, and Warren himself. In the name of safeguarding rights and liberties, Fortas would interpret due process as broadly as it needed to be interpreted. For him, "the due process guarantee represented a means of ensuring fairness for defendants in the system."[159] One can imagine the look on Black's face and the early morning talks with Elizabeth after he'd read the Fortas "slip opinions" (drafts of opinions) in due process cases.

Initially, their battles were internal ones. They took place in conference session and in memos to the brethren about pending cases and controversies. Finally, their battles surfaced in the opinions themselves. Some of their major battles involved the scope of free speech (*Tinker v Des Moines School District*),[160] business practices (*United States v Yazell, Fortner Enterprises v U.S. Steel*),[161] criminal justice (*Foster v California*),[162] speech plus conduct (*Gregory v Chicago*),[163] free press (*Time Inc. v Hill*),[164] and civil rights (*Brown v Louisiana*).[165]

These doctrinal differences led, inevitably, to "bitter exchanges" and "open warfare" between the two Southerners.[166] In the *Brown v Louisiana* case, involving blacks who were arrested and convicted of trespassing in a "whites only" section of a public library, Fortas wrote the opinion for the majority setting aside the convictions. Black bitterly dissented, accusing Fortas of prejudice against the South. His criticism was so harsh that Warren, after seeing it, apologized to Abe: "I am somewhat saddened by Hugo's dissent," he said to Fortas. "It does not reflect the better part of his nature."[167] Black had written, in dissent,

> I am deeply troubled with the fear that powerful private groups throughout the Nation will read the Court's action, as I do—that is, as granting them a license to invade the tranquility and beauty of our libraries whenever they have a quarrel with some state policy which may or may not exist. . . . I say once more that the crowd moved by noble ideals today can become the mob ruled by hate and passion and greed and violence tomorrow. If we ever doubted that, we know it now.[168]

Black spoke for over one half hour in announcing his dissent in *Brown v Louisiana*. While his wife Elizabeth described Hugo's oral presentation of the dissent as "magnificent, spine-chilling, and thrilling," with everyone sitting "on the edge of their chairs,"[169] according to "one reporter who heard it, Black's speech 'made his strongly phrased written dissent seem pale by comparison.' "[170]

As Douglas, a friend of both of them, recalled, relations between the two bitter foes "grew worse and worse." According to Douglas's notes, by the time of the *Gregory* case,[171] Fortas "became more and more incensed." A primary reason was the fact that, when Fortas was being considered for the center seat in 1968, Black had persuaded his close Alabama friend and then a U.S. senator, Lister Hill, to "come out against" Fortas.[172]

By 1969, the result of their feud "was an almost unprofessional version of judicial warfare that did nobody any good."[173] Their battles now took place in open court, with both of them participating in bitter, direct criticism of each other's views, "and one of their brethren said, 'I blame that on Black.' "[174]

This state of war continued until Fortas's resignation a year later, in May 1969. At that time, a very sad Fortas again sought Black's counsel, but the Alabaman did not offer any suggestions that would keep him on the Court. As Elizabeth recalled, "Hugo talked to him saying that if he were in that spot, for the good of the Court *he* would resign."[175]

William J. Brennan, Jr.[176]

As Herbert Brownell, President Dwight D. Eisenhower's attorney general, has recounted, during the 1956 election campaign, Ike indicated that he "would like to appoint a Democrat to the Court should the opportunity arise. . . . [He wanted] to demonstrate to the public that partisan politics was not the major consideration in his judicial appointments."[177] After the October 1956 retirement of Sherman Minton, Eisenhower filled that seat with William Brennan, a New Jersey Supreme Court judge that Brownell had met at a U.S. Department of Justice–sponsored National Conference on Delays and Congestion in the Courts. Brennan was a last-minute speaking replacement for his chief, Arthur Vanderbilt, at the conference. As Brownell noted, Brennan's speech "made our conference a success. He and I struck up a friendship at that time."[178]

Associate Justice Minton's retirement, in great part due to his poor health, led to a series of discussions between Eisenhower and Brownell. The president wanted to select someone with state court experience who was a Catholic and a Democrat because, Ike said, Brownell didn't have to worry about party affiliation. "Going into the 1956 election, Eisenhower wanted to be able to say that his Court appointments had been made on a bipartisan basis."[179] Brownell, very comfortable with Brennan, submitted the New Jerseyan's name to the president; after the appropriate checks, including a call to the Catholic leadership, Brennan was nominated by Eisenhower. Ike immediately appointed Brennan to the Court during the congressional winter recess. The appointment was formally presented to the Senate in January 1957 and, after some harsh questioning by Wisconsin's Senator Joseph McCarthy, Brennan was formally confirmed by the Senate in a voice vote in March 1957.

William Brennan was born in 1906 in Newark, New Jersey. He, like Black, was one of eight children. Like Frankfurter, Brennan was also a child of immigrant parents, Brennan's arriving in America from Ireland in the 1890s. His father, a laborer who became a labor leader and a local, social reformist politician in New Jersey, influenced Brennan a great deal. Brennan graduated from Harvard Law School during the Depression and was one of thousands who took a course with Professor Felix Frankfurter while there. He worked in a private law firm after graduation, served in the Second World War, and returned to private practice in New Jersey afterwards. Actively engaged in state court reform, Brennan was appointed to the Superior Court of New Jersey in 1949. He moved to the appellate division and then became a member of the state's supreme court.

Fate intervened when he pinch-hit a speech for the chief justice of the New Jersey Supreme Court, leading to his appointment to the U.S. Supreme Court. William Brennan quickly became the fourth in the quartet of justices on the high bench who acted vigorously to incorporate the Bill of Rights into the due process and equal protection clauses of the Fourteenth Amendment. The group included Brennan, Warren, Douglas, and Black and was derisively called the "Jesus Quartet" by the highly respected but conservative Federal Court of Appeals Judge Learned Hand.

Brennan and Warren hit it off immediately, both personally and jurisprudentially. Brennan very quickly became the Chief's "closest colleague,"[180] and they and their families became warm friends, remaining so until Warren's death. Brennan was one of the last persons to see Warren alive, visiting his beloved "Super Chief" hours before his death to let him know how the Court was going to come down in the 1974 *United States v Nixon* litigation.

This quartet of justices, led by Hugo (although he rejected any suggestion that he was the intellectual leader of the constitutional revolution soon to take place),[181] came together during the 1956 term. Up to that point, Warren had been examining Frankfurter's jurisprudence and joining the Harvard professor in most decisions. Frankfurter, much like he did with every new justice to the Court, "assiduously courted"[182] Warren when the Chief arrived. Included in Frankfurter's "ritual" was the shipment of articles, books, notes, essays, and other reading material on the Court and on constitutional doctrine that he believed new brethren should read.

Felix's courtship waned as Warren, like Black, Douglas, Murphy, and Rutledge before him, began to tire of Frankfurter's pedantic nature. After two terms, the Super Chief rejected Frankfurter's rhetoric about judicial self-restraint and became irritated by him in general. In fact, there were "acrimonious exchanges in open court."[183] During the 1957 term, for example, Warren admonished Frankfurter for "giggling" while he was talking; Frankfurter responded with an explanatory note: "It is one thing to be carrying on a tete-a-tete. It is another thing to be giggling out of disrespect for what is being said. I may appear inattentive, as indeed I must appear, because I do more than one thing at a time. I am subject to criticism for that. It is not my habit to be wanting in respect."[184]

Douglas recorded another clash between Warren and Frankfurter during the 1961 term: "While the CJ was [talking to Stewart], FF was snickering and passing notes to JMH, as is his custom. The CJ stopped and said: 'I am goddam tired of having you snicker while I am talking. You do it even in the Courtroom and people notice it.' FF denied he was snickering—there followed a long harangue in which the CJ said he had reached the limit of his tolerance for FF."[185]

Frankfurter, clearly, was not able to convince Warren to adopt his view of the judiciary. The little professor (so called because of his diminutive stature) was equally unsuccessful, although not without trying, to bring his former law school student Bill Brennan over to his brand of jurisprudence. Brennan rejected both the jurisprudence and Frankfurter's arrogant manner. He "repeatedly complained to [his clerks] of Frankfurter's 'condescending nature.' To another [clerk], Brennan said: 'He makes me so damn mad sometimes.' "[186]

At one point in his futile effort to "educate" Brennan, Frankfurter wrote a letter of frustration to his colleague, John M. Harlan II. In it he said:

> After sleeping on it, I have decided to curb my temperamental spontaneity and not talk to Bill Brennan. . . . Cocksureness begets sensitiveness, and as his erstwhile teacher, I have to be particularly careful with Bill. He was plainly displeased at the thought of my writing anything before what I saw what he will produce, on the assumption that he will take care of all there is to be said. Therefore, I do not think I ought to tell him what I think should be the conception and temper of our opinion.[187]

In rejecting Frankfurter, Brennan naturally moved to the Black-Douglas camp on major constitutional questions. In giving up on him, Frankfurter used the same term of condemnation he used to describe Douglas: Brennan was too damned "cocksure" of himself!

Openhearted Friends

When Brennan first joined the Court, Hugo wrote a letter to his oldest son in which he described his first impressions of the newest justice:

> Up to date I like the new Justice very much indeed. Maybe he has been a labor lawyer for business but so far his approach to cases does not indicate that such lawyers do not have as much desire to do justice as lawyers that represent the labor unions themselves. . . . He has a nice personality, has understood the cases argued, and has expressed himself with reference to those cases in a fine wholesome manner.[188]

Black's first impressions were right on the mark, and the Judge never deviated from this early assessment of his young colleague.

The Judge was gracious when Brennan wrote his first opinion for the Court. Although Black was not too happy with the decision, he was not inclined to write a dissent. As he said, in a note written while on the bench to his friend Harlan:

> I find that the CJ and Justice Douglas are inclined to acquiesce in the lawyers tax case unless someone else writes a dissent. I am inclined that way too because this is Justice Brennan's first case. Still thinking that the case is being decided wrong, I would not acquiesce except for my belief that how the issue is decided is perhaps of less importance than settling the conflict among the circuits. With these feelings I am not inclined to write a dissent, but should someone else write I could probably not resist joining.[189]

Brennan, from the very beginning of their judicial relationship, felt particularly comfortable with the Judge, who, while tough and ornery, was sincerely concerned about his settling into a positive Court routine. Brennan recalled one such instance that showed Hugo's care and concern for a new colleague. He had just circulated his first draft in the 1964 *Malloy v Hogan* case,[190] and Black had written some comments and called him about the draft. Brennan, on the phone with Black, lost his temper and said, "Oh, the hell with it!" Within nanoseconds, according to Brennan, Hugo was in his chambers to tell him that the Court was a pressure place, and that he should go home and get away from things for the day.[191]

Justice Brennan recalled a watershed moment that came a few short months after he joined the Court. At a conference session, he joined the Court majority in the case of *In re Groban*.[192] Almost immediately afterwards, Brennan had second thoughts about his position in the case. The doubts became full blown after he read Reed's draft opinion for the majority and Black's draft opinion for the dissenting justices. For the first time, the question "Does a justice have to stay 'joined'," arose in Brennan's mind. After rereading the opinions, he was persuaded that he had to change his vote. He then spoke with Reed: "I am joining

Black." Reed responded angrily: You *can't* do that!' Asked Brennan: "Why not?" He did not receive an answer. Brennan then informed Black that the dissenters (Black, Douglas, and Warren) had a fourth joiner!

Brennan noted that it was the *Groban* opinion, announced during the 1957 term of the Supreme Court, that initially brought together the "BBD and W" (Black, Brennan, Douglas, and Warren) coalition;[193] with the addition of Arthur Goldberg, and then Abe Fortas and Thurgood Marshall, these four formed a cohesive alliance on many civil rights and civil liberties cases that came before the Supreme Court over the next decade.[194]

Brennan could recall Hugo infrequently getting "flaming mad" about his views on constitutional issues, especially due process cases, but he was a "delightful, warm friend. An absolutely warm friend."[195] When they disagreed, they talked. Brennan recollected that Hugo would come into his office and sit down; then the New Jerseyan would dictate changes in a draft opinion in order to satisfy the Alabaman. And vice versa: "I'd go over there and he'd [write] to try to satisfy me."[196]

There were times when Black's commitment to his set of constitutional values meant that no amount of negotiation with Brennan could succeed in changing Hugo's mind. They disagreed on the extent of the First Amendment in the area of libel. Black was the absolutist, defending free speech and press under all circumstances. In 1964 Brennan wrote an opinion for the majority, *New York Times v Sullivan*,[197] that, while liberal and creating a standard that called for a showing of actual malice in libel proceedings, was not an absolute, categorical commitment to the First Amendment. After reading Brennan's draft, Black called and told him that he couldn't join in the opinion. While it was well written, "you know damn well I can't join you."[198] Black never lost sight of the value of friendship, even when he seriously disagreed with his friends.

Jurisprudential Differences

Brennan freely and gratefully acknowledged, again and again, Hugo Black's leadership role in the effort to incorporate the Bill of Rights into the Fourteenth Amendment so that these protections extended to persons living in the states. "No justice really did more," Brennan said, "or had a greater influence on the evolving constitutional law than Hugo Black, largely because of his role in the incorporation cases. It was an extraordinary revolution in constitutional law and Black was at its core."[199]

While Black respected and appreciated Brennan's views on the Bill of Rights, the Alabaman saw his colleague as a "weigher": "Both Brennan and Harlan want to weigh everything." What concerned Black was that a balancing of right against right would lead to compromise, and the Bill of Rights, especially the First Amendment's guarantees, could not be compromised. "If you start weighing the public interest," he said to a clerk, "against a constitutional right, you might rule against the right."[200] At bottom, however, Black felt good about Brennan's balancing, for Brennan, unlike Frankfurter and Harlan, invariably came down on the correct side, vigorously defending constitutional rights of persons.

Hugo looked on this new grouping of justices, a solid "liberal" majority phalanx that existed from 1962 to 1969, most often led by the pixieish William Brennan, with mixed feelings. He, obviously, saw that his hope for incorporating the Bill of Rights could succeed, although incrementally. Brennan was, as everyone on the Court keenly observed, a master coalition builder, someone able to put together and, for the most part, hold together a group of brethren on any number of civil rights and civil liberties issues.

Hugo, however, also saw a bunch of undisciplined jurists who would use the due process clause to fix everything that needed fixing—even if it meant redefining the meaning of the Constitution's words. He was caught on the horns of a dilemma. His response: Work with them to incorporate the Bill of Rights, while continuing to educate these good men through majority and concurring opinions he would write.

This liberal coalition of brethren differed from the Frankfurter coalition in a number of important ways, including an understanding of the meaning of due process, the primacy of the First Amendment, and, equally important, the rules of judicial abstinence. Brennan, Warren, Goldberg, Fortas, Marshall, and Douglas were committed to the view that "anyone whose life, liberty or property was threatened or impaired by any branch of government—whether the President or one of his agencies, or the Congress, or the Courts (or any counterpart in a state regime)—had a justiciable controversy and could properly repair to a judicial tribunal for a vindication of his rights." [201]

Black, as everyone knew, always had great difficulty with this attitude of his goodhearted but undisciplined brethren because for him the critical element in any judicial action was the discovery and announcement of timeless principles of law that resided in history. But he tried to work amicably, for the most part, with his liberal colleagues despite his misgivings.

William Brennan, until late in his tenure and with respect to the question of the constitutionality of the death penalty, always tried to avoid absolutes in constitutional interpretation. Although he agreed with Black's view that the Bill of Rights was enough to protect persons in America and that the rights should be incorporated as a whole, as the Alabaman suggested in *Adamson* (1948), Brennan was comfortable with a selective incorporation of these rights. For Brennan, as for Black, the underlying proposition was that federal judges, especially the justices of the Court, had to act aggressively to end practices in the states that deprived persons of due process of law.

> Far too many cases come from the states to the Supreme Court presenting dismal pictures of official lawlessness, of illegal searches and seizures, illegal detentions attended by prolonged interrogation and coerced confessions of guilt, of the denial of counsel and downright brutality. Judicial self-restraint which defers too much to the sovereign powers of the states and reserves judicial intervention for only the most revolting cases [read "shock the conscience"] will not serve to enhance Madison's priceless gift of the great rights of mankind secured under this Constitution. For these secure the only climate in which the law of freedom can exist. [202]

Black took heart from Brennan's words, for they expressed a view of judicial role that was closer to his beliefs than to those of the disciple of judicial restraint, not mentioned by name in the essay, Felix Frankfurter.

Black and Brennan, however, did have a fundamental disagreement over the Constitution itself. Brennan referred to the document as an evolving one.

It is the very purpose of a Constitution and particularly of the Bill of Rights to declare certain values transcendent, beyond the reach of temporary political majorities. [Judges] must read the Constitution in the only way that we can: as Twentieth Century Americans. We look to the history of the time of framing and to the intervening history of [constitutional] interpretation. But the ultimate question must be, what do the words of the text mean in our time.[203]

Black clearly rejected such an undisciplined approach to constitutional interpretation, however well meaning and beneficial it might be at the time of the interpretation. Brennan and the others had broken loose from the tethers—and the constraints—of history. As Hugo reminded people, again and again, he knew of different kinds of justices using this approach with the language of due process and equal protection for not such admirable purposes.

There were other disagreements between Hugo and Bill over judicially created "new rights" that were just emerging at the time of Hugo's death in 1971. The two had disagreed, for example, on the question of whether there was a constitutional right of privacy. Brennan and the liberal gang, in *Griswold v Connecticut,* a watershed 1965 opinion, created a right of marital privacy based in the Constitution's "penumbras."[204] Black vigorously dissented in *Griswold,* not because he thought the Connecticut statute was a reasonable one but because he did not believe that justices were empowered to write their views of privacy into the Constitution. Brennan, as a part of his effort to put into operation what he called the evolving Constitution doctrine, had no difficulty creating such new rights, interpreting due process or equal protection in an expansive and substantive manner.

But Brennan was so pleasant and impish; Black and his wife Elizabeth could never get angry with the Brennans.

John M. Harlan II

John M. Harlan II, appointed by President Dwight D. Eisenhower in 1955, was born in 1899 in Chicago. He was the grandson of John Marshall Harlan, the Court's "Great Dissenter." Out of respect for his forebear, the grandson did not spell out his middle initial. Harlan went to Princeton and, after spending three years at Oxford studying jurisprudence, attended New York Law School. For over three decades, until his appointment to the U.S. Court of Appeals in 1954, he was an extremely successful lawyer in the New York law firm of Root, Clark, Buckner, and Howland. Less than a year later, Harlan was tapped for a seat on the Supreme Court.

Harlan, wrote Herbert Brownell, President Eisenhower's attorney general, decades later, "had been a longtime personal friend of mine. . . . I had persuaded Harlan to leave private practice to become a judge of the Federal Court of Appeals, Second Circuit, and privately hoped for his later advancement to the Supreme Court."[205] When Justice Robert Jackson died in October 1954, Brownell, who had known Harlan when the two were partners in the law firm and had also worked for and supported New York Republican Governor Thomas E. Dewey, pushed successfully for Harlan to be nominated as Jackson's replacement on the high bench.

Almost immediately, Harlan became one of Frankfurter's voting allies. However, while he disagreed with Black on doctrinal matters, there never existed the bitterness that characterized Hugo's relationship with Felix. Rather the opposite, for the two men took an instant liking to each other, even before Hugo insisted that they were very distant cousins with common roots in the deep South.

Very Friendly "Enemies"

Harlan was never the pontificating "professor" Frankfurter was and never lectured Black the way the Harvard don did from the moment Frankfurter joined the Court in 1939.[206] By the early 1960s, Hugo and John had become extremely close, "telephoning each other nightly to discuss issues facing the Court,"[207] even though they often disagreed on some significant constitutional issues. The Judge thought very highly of John's grandfather, Justice John Marshall Harlan, who sat on the Court from 1877 to 1911; he was known as the "Great Dissenter" for his dissent in the separate-but-equal case of *Plessy v Ferguson,* the 1896 decision that led to the legalization of Jim Crow segregation in the South. One of Black's law clerks recalled Hugo's comment "that he thought that the first Justice Harlan's dissent in *Plessy v Ferguson* was by far one of the best statements of the law that had ever been written."[208] Doubtless this view of Harlan's grandfather and namesake helped their friendship along.

On occasion, Black would take delight in sending Harlan essays and law review articles critical of his friend's jurisprudence. "Here are the two law review issues I mentioned to you," wrote the Alabaman in September 1968, "containing articles giving something to confirm your sinful constitutional approach!—and some figs. . . . Affectionately, Hugo." Harlan replied, the same day, thanking the Judge and commenting, "I must confess that I prefer the figs to the Law Review articles."[209]

Their families dined together and sent letters and gifts back and forth often. Hugo and Elizabeth always traveled to Florida during the Court's winter recess, and every winter he sent a basket or bushel of oranges, grapefruits, figs, or sugared pecans to the Harlans, who were spending their break in wintry Weston, Connecticut, in what Harlan called their "hilltop" home.

The friendship grew close towards the end of the jurists' lives. After receiving warm birthday greetings from Ethel, John's wife, in February 1970, Black sent a handwritten note to her that showed his grace and his love for her family: "It is my birthday but it would not have been complete without your sweet note. Your radiant smile has made many people happy and I have found this Court a better place to be because the Harlans have been with me. Affectionately, Hugo."[210]

Whenever the Judge and Elizabeth visited the South during recesses or after the Court adjourned for the summer, they always revisited his ancestral homes and family resting places and took joy in gleaning new information about his genealogy. After visiting a small cemetery and finding the Alabama Harlans' burial grounds, Hugo insisted that the two men were related. "All of this comes down to mean," he wrote Harlan, "that while you and I are related only by marriage the Alabama Harlans and their descendents are a part of your Harlan family."[211] In August, 1966, Harlan wrote to the Judge, "I was of course greatly interested in the account of your Alabama trip and your latest discoveries on the Black-Harlan family tree."[212]

They also shared, discreetly, humorous comments about their colleagues. For example, just after Douglas's fourth marriage to Cathy in 1966, Harlan jotted some lines to Hugo: "From the accounts of the great wedding, I gather that you and Elizabeth have met the Court's most recent 'third lady.' [Douglas was the 'third man' on the Court, behind the Chief and Hugo.] It makes me feel like an old man."[213]

There was also great sadness and pathos when the two men, at the same time, ended their tenure on the Court just a few weeks before the opening of the 1971 term. During the preceding term they had "become increasingly infirm, they still could be seen strolling down the Court's corridors, arms around each other."[214]

By July 1971, Hugo had come to the conclusion that his life was about over. Although there was nothing seriously wrong with him physically at that time, he had decided that it was his time for death and therefore gave up. "He is convinced," Jo-Jo told Hugo Jr., "that he is going to die."[215] He had stopped eating, and his weight was down to 115 pounds. By mid-August, working with a former law clerk and sitting U.S. District Court Judge Louis Oberdorfer, Black had written his retirement letter.

He was brought to Bethesda (Maryland) Naval Hospital and assigned a private room in its VIP area, one that was next to Harlan's room. He continued to refuse to eat, although Elizabeth and John—who was in the hospital because of extreme pain in his back, later diagnosed as cancer—tried to shake him out of his depression. But Black was committed to dying and, less than one month after he submitted his retirement letter to Richard Nixon, he passed away. Harlan, who had written his own retirement letter to Nixon, waited a respectable two weeks after Black's retirement before announcing his intentions in order to enable his close friend to remain alone in the national spotlight.

Because of their close friendship, Black did not relish the thought of having to attack Harlan's jurisprudence in written opinions. Of course, the Judge did just that when the two men clashed over doctrine and judicial role. But while Black gave no ground in these battles, there was a significant gentleness in the two men's repartee when they read their opposing opinions in open Court, unlike the angry, sparring episodes the Alabaman had with Fortas and Frankfurter. Elizabeth recalled one such instance when the two friends read their opinions while she watched and listened on December 9, 1969.

> I went to Court and enjoyed John Harlan's lively opinion and Hugo's spirited dissent in *Zuber* . . . which came down. They swear they put on these lively disagreements for my enjoyment. Rather, they write their views and really feel very strong about it, and I am the excuse for their spirited announcements. From the bench, John wrote me: "Dear Elizabeth, The very dull 'milk' case that you

will hear Hugo and me announce (on opposite sides of the fence) is known between me and Hugo as the 'Elizabeth case.' "[216]

Clearly, Black was more comfortable arguing with Harlan in private about their differences than speaking in public about them. As he said to Harlan, in a note, "I enjoyed our conversation last night. In fact, it is better to talk perhaps than it is to write—at least on some subjects."[217] Regularly, Hugo would leave the Harlan household after get-togethers, circle John's house in the car for a few minutes while others in the gathering were departing, then return and continue his conversation with his gentle adversary.

Their relationship also brought out the Alabaman's sense of humor. For example, after Black read Harlan's draft dissent in *Konigsberg*, he wrote that he "note[d] that you regret to find what we say is 'unintelligible'—What's the matter? Are our words too big or something?" And then Black added a P.S., placing things in perspective: "Leffer's says your fig [tree] may not be out for some weeks, and that he will replace it if it does not."[218]

Hugo Black, Jr., recalled the somber yet warm and touching conversations he had with John Harlan during his stay in the Bethesda Naval hospital in the months prior to his death in December 1971. He told Hugo Jr. one evening that

> the biggest difference between your father on the one hand, and me and Justice Frankfurter on the other hand, is the basic assumption we make about judges. Your father believes that you have to keep judges tethered—you can't trust their consciences loose without some kind of bridle. . . . Nobody's judgment ever exceeded his—his is just the best.[219]

Clashes over Doctrine

Harlan's jurisprudence, wrote his biographer, was "decidedly Frankfurtian."[220] There was, at the heart of Harlan's jurisprudence, an acceptance of Frankfurter's belief that judges had to abstain from judicial interposition in political questions. In addition to this bedrock belief, there were three other general components to Harlan's jurisprudence that were to some degree in conflict with Hugo's essential judicial values.

First, Harlan believed that the republic's process of checks and balances, in particular, the two doctrines of federalism and separation of powers, "were more significant safeguards of individual liberty than specific constitutional guarantees [in the Bill of Rights]." Quite obviously the two men disagreed vigorously on this matter. For Black, the First Amendment guarantees were absolutes, placed on a higher plane than all other values. For Harlan, as for Frankfurter, the First Amendment was not the premier protection for individual liberties. At the 1964 dedication of the Bill of Rights Room in New York's Sub-Treasury Building, Harlan's views were clearly announced. He said that while the Bill of Rights

> symbolize the respect for the individual that is the cornerstone of American political concepts, it would be a grave mistake to regard them as the full measure of the bulwarks of our free society. . . . They were indeed not a part of the original

handiwork of the Framers of the Constitution. . . . The men who wrote the Constitution recognized . . . that true liberty can rise no higher or be made more secure than the spirit of a people to achieve and maintain it. Their prime concern was to devise a form of government for the new Nation under which such a spirit might thrive. . . . The Amendments comprising the Bill of Rights followed only after the structure of government had been established by the Constitution proper. . . . [The founders] determined that in a government of divided powers lay the best promise for realizing the free society it was their object to achieve.[221]

Second, Harlan believed that the twin institutional safeguards of federalism and separation of powers protected people's freedoms in a democracy. Third, as a common law jurist, in great part due to his studying law at Oxford for three years, Harlan strongly believed in the constraints of precedent and in the Anglophile notion, preached by Frankfurter, of flexible, evolving standards of constitutional interpretation.[222]

Toward the end of their tenure as justices, beginning in the mid-1960s, the two did work together when the Court substantively expanded the meaning of due process and equal protection. However, other than these substantive cases and the sit-in litigation of the early 1960s, Black and Harlan settled into a permanent battle over the role of the justices of the Court and disagreed on some very fundamental constitutional doctrines.

But it was a friendly battleground, with the two men maintaining respect for each other and, most important, sustaining—with their wives Ethel and Elizabeth—a close friendship up to the moment of Hugo's death in September 1971.

Hugo's Other "Children," His Law Clerks

Helping Black in his battles with friends and enemies were his loyal law clerks, all but one male and all white. He had fifty-four law clerks in his chambers over the thirty-four years he sat on the Supreme Court. They were selected from all parts of the country, although there was a preference given to Alabama natives who graduated from Yale or Harvard Law Schools. Other than signs of superior legal intellect, possibly some prior clerking experience for an appeals court judge, and some interest, if not ability, in tennis, Hugo had no rigid set of criteria for selecting his clerks.[223]

The Judge had a "strong personal relationship with his clerks. 'In a sense,' he once told them, 'you are all my sons.' He . . . arranged their introduction to pretty girls, advised them to get married, advised them to have children, boarded them in his home, and taught them to play tennis."[224]

By the time he interviewed the candidate in his Court office, the Judge had already made the decision to bring the interviewee on board for the following term.

> His clerks were chosen because he liked them as persons—and since he never interviewed clerk-applicants until he had tentatively chosen his new clerks, and since he rarely met a person he didn't like, he would offer the clerkship during his first meeting with the applicant. He admired friendship more than intelligence.[225]

The interview was just a formality for the Judge, although he did use the time to find more about the young person's interests and his personality.

Within a few moments, the interviewee would be absolutely captivated by Hugo, who was, as one of the law clerks said, "one of the most charming, courtly, soft-spoken gentlemen you'll ever meet."[226] A. E. Dick Howard, who was his clerk during the 1962–1963 term of the Court, recalled that he

> went in rather nervous, as one could be in the presence of one of the great justices of the Supreme Court's history, and he promptly put me at ease. I think that within no more than one minute of sitting there with this man, the humanity and the graciousness came across, he told an anecdote or two, and before long we were just having a plain old conversation and I would tend to forget this man was a justice.[227]

Once on board—and the clerks always "reported for duty in summer,"[228] after being given the assignment to read or reread Edith Hamilton's *The Greek Way*—the clerk had two primary responsibilities in Black's office. The first task was the weekly review of the twenty to thirty certiorari petitions received by the Court over the year, followed by the preparation of a one-page (front and back) cert memo by the clerk, describing the key legal issues and facts presented to the Court and recommending a course of action for the Judge when the case was discussed in conference.

The second major task, aside from preparing cert petitions and handling the Judge's social calendar—which meant playing tennis with the Blacks or filling in for bridge with them—was in assisting Hugo in the preparation of opinions assigned to him. This meant, as well, preparing concurring and dissenting opinions. In this chore, the clerk functioned as a "combination research assistant, critic, sounding board, and tenderer of suggestions—occasionally a point of substance but more often matters of punctuation, phraseology or organization."[229]

Black discussed the constitutional issues ceaselessly with his clerks. The Judge also spoke with them on everything else. "Black's clerks got discourses on the Constitution, on English history, on the history of civil rights, on the Greek wars, on Roman government, on seditious libel, on New Deal politics, on tyranny."[230] He spent a great deal of time with them during the quiet summer months, making sure that

> he could rely on your being a good summarizer and not missing anything, because later in the year when cases were argued and opinions started being written, he just didn't have time to read all that and he had to rely on you to correctly summarize what those things [certiorari petitions] coming in were all about.[231]

Once he was assigned an opinion to write for the Court, "the fun begins," as former law clerk George Freeman recollected. The clerks worked in a room adjacent to the Judge's, and he would regularly pop out of his office to chat, give them another book to read, or read over their shoulders as they did their work. Black would review all the paper associated with the case and would, with his two clerks, read and discuss the literature. These discussions, "often turning into lively debate," would begin in his office and would last for hours. Frequently, the talks concluded around midnight in the Judge's Alexandria residence.

After this discussion period, Hugo would draft an opinion in longhand, often writing in the dark hours of the early morning, and then give it to the clerk for review and comments. The dénouement: "Often revisions result; sometimes a clerk can get a word or comma accepted, but the substance and decision are never anything but Black's alone."[232]

The highlight of the week for Black's law clerks was when Hugo came back from the Court's conference sessions.

> About 4 or 5 o'clock Justice Black would come back from the conference and he would then tell us what had happened at the conference—how the cases were decided. He would say, "and Felix said this, and Bill Douglas said this, and the Chief said this, and I said that." Those sessions with the judge were the highlight of the week.[233]

The benefits, the enduring consequences of working with the Judge were felt by all of his clerks. George Freeman carried away the following from his year's work with Hugo: First, "a deeper appreciation for the substance of constitutional law, a commitment to free speech and free exercise of religion." Second, "a better appreciation of the use of the English language, of which Black was a master. A simplicity of style, a directness of style which has helped me ever since." And finally, "the sense of humanity which the man carried with him."[234]

To all the young men and the one woman, Margaret Corcoran, who worked with the Judge, he transmitted his inordinate "fear of judicial power and his belief that the Court was essentially an undemocratic institution that could be checked only by requiring 'strict construction' of the Constitution and legislative acts."[235] At the end of their term as law clerk, they knew the value of judicial self-discipline and learned "the limits of intricate legal analysis as taught in law school and the wisdom of a basic good sense of justice as a tempering factor for any lawyer."[236] Black was, in addition to all his other attributes, an outstanding educator of young persons.

Indeed, Hugo Black was an extraordinary communicator with his brethren too. Everybody knew where his thoughts were on the role and function of judges, and on the primacy of the Bill of Rights, especially the First Amendment, for example. An examination of his jurisprudence follows. It reflects Black's consistent love of the Constitution as well as his great fear of federal judges unleashed and roaming the world of natural law over the thirty-four years he served his nation from the high bench.

CHAPTER EIGHT

Commitment to "Our Federalism" and to the Primacy of Freedom of Expression

Duraing the 1968 term of the Court, Justice John M. Harlan II and Chief Justice Earl Warren were engaged in a heated debate about a case. Warren, who could be as feisty as the Judge, was at his stubborn best and simply refused to accept Harlan's views. In exasperation, and with voice raised, the patrician associate justice said to Warren: "Chief, it is as clear as a goat's ass going up a hill."[1]

Harlan's graphic "barnyardism" just as easily could have been used to describe Hugo Black's jurisprudence for it was just as clearly seen by all who sat on the Court, friend and foe alike. Even though his colleagues might not like Black's constitutional views, they knew them well. As Arthur Goldberg wrote Hugo in 1964, at the end of the 1963 term and at the height of a major, sometimes emotional disagreement between the two men regarding the Court's judgment in one of a number of civil rights demonstration cases that came before it from 1961 to 1963:

> I need scarcely say that while I differ fundamentally with you on the constitutional issue involved [in *Bell v Maryland*] and see it differently from you, nevertheless, in this matter and in all others, *I deeply respect the complete integrity of your views.* It is a source of pride and satisfaction to me that in my short tenure on the Court I have been able in many instances to join in support of your long established and sound views as to fundamental constitutional issues. I regret more than I can say that I am compelled to part company on this one.[2] (my emphasis)

One of Black's law clerks said of the Judge: "He has his own constitutional world where everything falls into a symmetrical pattern." He concluded that Black was never "haunted by the spectre of inconsistency."[3] By the end of his second term on the Court, the Judge's jurisprudence began to congeal, and Black then went about the task of trying to convince his brethren of the correctness of his views regarding the role of the Court in American politics, the roles and functions of its justices, and the Constitution itself.

While he was very good at this kind of activity during the first two-plus decades of his tenure on the Court, by the early 1960s, Black had little patience with brethren who disagreed with him on these matters. He was then a senior associate justice; only three men had served on the Court longer. William Brennan said that the Judge "became absoluter than absolute" regarding constitutional interpretation, while another of the brethren noted that the longer Black sat on the Court, "the less [he] gave."[4] The Alabaman's bitter clashes with Abe Fortas during that decade were symptomatic of his exasperation with justices who acted without the correct jurisprudential anchor.

Always stubborn in defense of his principles, Black refused to join majorities he believed were acting inappropriately. The Judge "began to write more separate opinions and speak less often for the Court, articulat[ing] his own distinctive constitutional jurisprudence."[5] Black wrote close to 1000 opinions (969) during his tenure on the Court. Slightly more than half of them, 479, were majority or plurality opinions. In addition, the Judge wrote 84 concurring opinions and 329 dissenting opinions during his more than three decades on the high bench.[6]

What follows in this and the next chapter is an effort to lay out Black's views on critical constitutional issues and to show how he was able to work with others on the Court—despite some late-career crankiness—in order to get a majority to "join" him in many opinions. Perhaps more important than the decisions he wrote in these important areas were the constitutional concepts put forward by Black— the necessity of a viable federalism, the primacy of the First Amendment in the maintenance of a democratic republic, and the constitutional necessity for absorbing or incorporating the Bill of Rights into the due process language of the Fourteenth Amendment.

There were, of course, many times when he dissented or wrote a concurring opinion. As will be seen, many of these dissents or concurrences led future Court majorities to undertake appropriate, correct interpretations of the nature and limits of power in a constitutional political system.

First, one must examine Black's views regarding federalism and free expression, the subject of this chapter. In chapter 9, Black's sharply held views in the constitutional arenas of criminal justice, civil rights, and, finally, "new rights" created by the justices (such as the right of privacy) will be examined.

An assessment of the litigation brought into the Court in these five substantive and conflict-laden areas of public law provides an understanding of Black's views as well as his reasons for reaching judgment in these cases. In addition, the examination of how the brethren interacted with each other in these cases will highlight the Judge's ability to mold and direct majorities on the Court for three decades. Finally, the examination of these intra-Court interactions will underscore Black's strong commitment to the fundamental axiom that, in his democratic republic, there was a federal judiciary whose actions were always limited to and by the words and phrases of the Constitiution. As will be seen in these cases, Black always believed in a federal judiciary strong enough to protect persons from the unconstitutional actions of other public policy-makers but weak enough, and self-disciplined enough, not to interpose and create judicial remedies to resolve social ills that were not the Court's to fix.

"Our Federalism": Black's Perspective on the Federal-State Relationship in America

From his first day as U.S. senator to his last day on the Court, Black believed in the constraining value of the federal system created in the 1787 Constitution and put into operation in 1789. A federal system has, at its core, the distribution of power between a central and state governments. The Constitution drafters separated powers both vertically (between the national and state governments) and horizontally (within the government between executive, legislative, and judicial branches). The Justice was a citizen of both the national government and of the state of Alabama and was bound by the laws of both jurisdictions. The Constitution makers created this federal system to curb the possibility of tyranny. The more power is fragmented in a political system, the less chance there is for tyranny to emerge.

The justices of the Court have accepted the fact that, in a federal system, both national and the state statutes can overlap so long as they do not conflict with each other. However, given the existence of Section 2 of the supremacy clause, Article VI, in the Constitution,[7] national laws must supercede any state laws that attempt to establish public policy in the same arena but that are in conflict with the central government's legislative enactments.

Black was bitterly opposed to judicial interventions into the economic and social lawmaking activities of the nation and the states. The image of the "nine old men" of the pro Roosevelt Court interposing their laissez-faire, social Darwinistic economic views on the society through substantive, economic interpretations of the phrases "commerce," "tax," and the due process language that included protecting the economic "liberty" and "property" of industrialists haunted the "people's candidate" from Alabama.

"Federalism," the Judge wrote in 1970, "is a system in which there is a sensitivity to the legitimate interests of both state and national governments, and in which the national government, anxious though it may be to vindicate and protect federal rights and federal interests, always endeavors to do so in ways that will not unduly interfere with the legitimate activities of the states."[8] For Black, the Constitution "gave Congress essentially plenary power in the area of commercial regulation. He believed that this power was supreme to any power possessed by the states, but that in the absence of federal action, the states also had essentially plenary power to act in matters of economic regulation."[9] Given this constitutional arrangement, the Court's role was to remain outside the policy-making arena.

Black's belief in the importance of the "federalism" check on political power contained two prescriptive values. He had a lifelong pervasive concern about federal judges interfering with legitimate economic and social activities of national and state legislators. Furthermore, he had a "profound respect for the democratic process." [10] The Alabaman firmly believed "that federal courts should defer to elected legislatures—both federal and state—over a broad array of policy areas." [11]

Short of a confrontation with the prohibitions in the Bill of Rights (or with the few restrictions on state and national legislative behavior that existed in the body of the Constitution itself), popularly elected legislators had the widest latitude to make policy for their constituents. [12] "A state legislature," he used to say, "can do whatever it sees fit to do unless it is restrained by some express prohibition in the Constitution of the United States or of the state." [13] Federal courts, especially the Supreme Court, had to avoid the use of judicial review to interfere with such actions of the legislature—especially economic and social experimentation of governments.

As an early, "orthodox new dealer," Black had "great respect for congressional judgment in the area of commercial activity [as well as a] similar approach to acts of state legislatures involving economic regulation." [14] As he noted, in a 1946 concurring opinion, in *Morgan v Virginia:* "[The commerce clause] means that Congress can regulate commerce and that the Courts cannot." [15] As one of his clerks wrote, Black had "a distrust of the infallibility of judges, coupled with a basic faith in the 'justice and wisdom' . . . of legislatures." [16]

This strongly held belief of Black's, regarding the value of judicial deference "reinforced [his concept of] federalism, since it left the states relatively free from second-guessing courts on commerce, taxation, and other matters. . . . [However, his view of federalism was not an affirmative one;] it was a by-product of his . . . belief in restricting the power of courts that gave states the room to play." [17] Bill Brennan recalled that Black was "frightened to death that if he [started interposing more], he might end up with the same kind of business that led to the nine old men." [18]

In a speech to a law school audience in 1968, Black talked of his fears of an unrestrained federal judiciary. [19]

Black insisted, that "our Constitution was not written in the sands to be washed away by each wave of new judges blown in by each successive political wind that brings new political administrations into temporary power. Rather, our Constitution was fashioned to perpetuate liberty and justice by making clear, explicit and lasting constitutional boundaries." [20] Even in this 1960s era of judicial deference to federal-state litigation in social and economic matters, he was still concerned about judicial interventionism.

National Powers

Black firmly believed that the economic, social, and national security powers of the Congress and the president are plenary ones. The power of the national government to regulate commerce, found in Article I of the Constitution was, for Black, the broadest grant of power given to the national government's policymakers. As his 1945 opinion for the Court in *United States v Southeastern Underwriters Association* clearly stated, if "Congress wanted to go to the utmost extent of its Constitutional power in restraining trust and monopoly agreements," it had the constitutional power to do so. [21]

The federal courts, including the Supreme Court, have accepted the crucial fact that, in time of war (or other national emergencies), the Congress and the executive branch must spring into action to direct the economy and the civilian population towards the clearly defined goal of victory over America's enemies.

During and shortly after the Second World War, the justices announced a variety of decisions that supported the actions of these national authorities in regulating interstate commerce and—through emergency price control mechanisms, for example—the economy.[22] During the war, the brethren strongly supported most of the activities of the president and the Congress regarding the conduct of the war. Indeed, the brethren were as patriotic as any other group of persons working in America during the war; Frank Murphy, resplendent in his army reserve colonel's uniform, had to choose between serving in the military and remaining on the Court. It was, for the Saint, a hard choice but he remained on the high bench.

United States v Southeastern Underwriters Association (1945)
Black for the Court

Black was seen by all his Court colleagues as "Congress' man. Congress has all the power it needs for any national purpose."[23] As the poor people's senator and as a jurist who continued his lifelong hatred of predatory monopoly and monopolistic practices, Black had no qualms about "willingly going as far as a constitutional provision can be taken in construing it."[24] In the effort to restrict corrupt business practices, Congress had passed the 1890 Sherman Anti-Trust Act. It was legislation that prohibited "every contract, combination, or conspiracy" in restraint of interstate or foreign trade or commerce. Black and some of his New Deal colleagues on the Court did all they could to underscore the appropriateness of such legislation and, through their decisions in antitrust cases, to extend the scope of such legislation as far as possible.

Southeastern Underwriters is an example of Black's forcefulness in this area of constitutional law. The question before the justices was whether insurance companies, conducting a large part of their business across state lines, did therefore engage in interstate commerce and, consequently, should come under the regulatory coverage of the Sherman Anti-Trust Act.

Since 1869, when *Paul v Virginia*[25] was decided, the Court had held that such interstate insurance activity was not commerce and therefore could not be regulated by the Congress. The states, however, could not truly regulate these national insurance companies, and so they permitted the creation of regressive "cooperative rate-making" by these companies.[26] Black always opposed unfair, monopolistic economic advantage. As senator, he fought these "economic royalists" by introducing wage-hour legislation and by fierce chairmanship of senate hearings into the corrupt and illegal practices of wealthy corporation owners.

The Roosevelt administration argued that Southeastern, representing about two hundred fire insurance companies, had indeed conspired to restrain interstate commerce and trade by fixing and maintaining arbitrary, noncompetitive insurance premium rates for its customers living in a large number of states. Further, the government argued that insurance business was interstate commerce that could be covered under the Sherman Anti-Trust Act and subject to such regulation by the national government.

Given the existing precedents regarding insurance companies, the lower federal courts held that the Sherman Act did not extend to insurance companies doing business across state lines. And so the case came to the Court. However, it was not a full Court that heard the case. Justices Reed and Roberts had recused themselves and therefore there was only a seven-man Court to decide *Southeastern.*

Chief Justice Stone, was upset for two reasons. First, he was unwilling to have the Court act in such a significant way without a full Court. "Any number of times," he wrote, "I would have been willing to be one of five to overrule a decision, but not one of four." [27] The second reason was that Stone fundamentally disagreed with Black on the substantive question regarding insurance company coverage under national antitrust legislation.

Black, joined by Justices Douglas, Murphy, and Rutledge, considered the Chief wrong on both issues. He said to Stone: "We should not decline to take this case. . . . Since Congress has made six members of this Court a quorum, it undoubtedly contemplated that four should render judgments. Much as I deplore four-to-three decisions, I am not ready to subscribe to a disposition . . . which would thereafter be cited as a precedent to preclude statutory interpretations by a majority of the Court's quorum." [28]

Stone, joined by Black's two principal antagonists, Justices Frankfurter and Jackson, dissented in *Southeastern.* Hugo, however, had his four-man "court" and wrote a decision that extended congressional power to regulate commerce to insurance companies. The business of insurance was national, interstate commerce. Speaking for the majority, the Judge concluded:

> The Commerce power granted Congress is a broad positive power. It is the power to legislate concerning transactions which reach across state lines, affecting the people of more states than one. . . . Our basic responsibility in interpreting the Commerce clause is to make certain that the power to govern intercourse among the states remains where the Constitution placed it. That power is vested in the Congress, available to be exercised for the national welfare as Congress shall deem necessary. No commercial enterprise of any kind which conducts its activities across state lines has been held to be wholly beyond the regulatory power of Congress under the Commerce clause. We cannot make an exception of the business of insurance. [29]

Afterwards, Stone wrote a friend about *Southeastern.* "Unfortunately, Brother Black and his associates take a different view" of the meaning of commerce and of the power of Congress to regulate interstate commerce. [30]

Paradoxically, the Congress responded to Brother Black's plurality opinion by passing the McCarran Act of 1945. It explicitly stated that state regulation of the insurance industry would continue and that no act of Congress, unless specifically targeting the insurance industry, could be interpreted as superseding the states' authority over insurance. [31]

Korematsu v United States (1944)
Black for the Court

The brethren's deferral to the national government's plenary authority in wartime and Black's leadership on this matter were put to the test when the Court dealt with litigation brought to them by Japanese defendants, mostly American citizens, who had been incarcerated by the military during World War II solely because of their race and ancestry. To the end of his life, Black never regretted the firm position taken by him and the majority of the Court in the wartime Japanese exclusion cases.[32]

The sneak attack on Pearl Harbor by the Japanese on December 7, 1941, led to some significant and quite radical defensive actions by the military leadership on the West Coast in early 1942. The person in charge of West Coast military defense was General J. L. DeWitt, a friend of the Blacks for over a decade. On February 19, 1942, seventy-four days after the Japanese attack on Pearl Harbor, President Roosevelt signed Executive Order 9066, authorizing Secretary of War Henry L. Stimson to establish military zones from which certain persons (Japanese-Americans and Japanese aliens living in America) would be excluded.

A month later, Congress passed legislation that, in effect, sanctioned Roosevelt's EO (executive order) by creating criminal penalties for any violations of military orders issued under the authority of the EO. Also, in March 1942, General DeWitt began to issue the initial group of what would turn out to be hundreds of military orders that established curfews for Japanese-Americans, ordered them to assembly centers, and finally, sent over 120,000 persons, including over 70,000 Japanese-American citizens, into relocation camps spread across the western United States and Arkansas.[33]

The constitutional controversy that emerged was a clear one. Could the president, using his "war powers" and supported by national legislation, take away from persons, most of them citizens of America, the due process protection in the Fifth Amendment? Over one hundred thousand men, women, and children of Japanese ancestry were, from 1942 through 1944, forcibly removed from homes, businesses, schools, et cetera, and placed in barren, out-of-the-way relocation centers—without benefit of criminal charges against them, trials, or any hearings at all.

This evident denial of due process "anguished" some of the justices as they struggled with the exclusion cases. Black's friend Douglas raised the following issues for his brethren to consider: "Is it not necessary to provide an opportunity at some stage . . . for an individual member of the [Japanese internees'] group to show that he has been improperly classified? . . . [Isn't it necessary that members of the group have the] opportunity . . . to prove that they are as loyal to the United States as the members of this Court[?]"[34]

However, Black, joined by Frankfurter, was not concerned about these matters. For him, it was clear that the president and his military commanders had plenary power to act to protect the nation in time of national emergency.

In the *Korematsu* case, (1944) Black was able to write an opinion for the Court that reflected his views about presidential and congressional powers in time of war. Fred Korematsu had been charged with failure to report to an assembly center for evacuation from the Western Military Zone to a relocation camp. Korematsu claimed that the military's civilian exclusion order was unconstitutional because it violated the Fifth Amendment: The order was racially discriminatory and American citizens of Japanese ancestry were being incarcerated without benefit of trial or other due process guarantees.

In the conference session of October 16, 1944, there was a sharp five-to-four split on the fundamental issue of whether the military could forceably detain, exclude, and then relocate a racial class of citizens who had not been formally charged with any crime. Five men—Chief Justice Stone, joined by Justices Frankfurter, Black, Rutledge, and Reed—continued to defer to the judgments of the military leaders. Four of the brethren—Justices Roberts, Murphy, Jackson and Douglas—maintained that the actions of the government went beyond the bounds of constitutionality and that the Court had to respond to that reality.

Black was assigned the task of writing the opinion for the Court. He observed that "pressing public necessity may sometimes justify the existence of some restrictions." In modern warfare, "the power to protect must be commensurate with the threatened danger."[35] Procedurally, the Alabaman and his colleagues in *Korematsu* were firmly committed to separating the exclusion order itself from the consequences of that order: relocation.

Although exclusion posed a greater deprivation of freedom than the curfew, argued Black, it had a close and definite relationship to the prevention of sabotage and espionage by America's enemies. The Court accepted at face value the military claim that there could not be a rapid separation of disloyal from loyal Japanese: the exclusion of a class of citizens, based on ancestry, was, the Justice said, a military imperative, not a group punishment based on racial prejudice. Finally, Black defended the narrow scope of the majority opinion:

> It is sufficient here for us to pass upon the [exclusion] order which petitioner violated. To do more would be to go beyond the issues raised, and to decide momentous questions not contained within the framework of the pleadings or the evidence in this case. It will be time enough to decide the serious constitutional issues which petitioner seeks to raise when an assembly or a relocation order is applied or is certain to be applied to him, and we have its terms before us.[36]

Black's opinion validated the actions of his friend, General DeWitt; Hugo evidently did not see the need to recuse himself from the case because of this friendship. None of the brethren knew about the relationship, except Douglas, who, with his wife, had visited the DeWitts, staying at their West Coast residence shortly before the war began.

After the *Korematsu* conference, Douglas circulated a four-page dissenting opinion. For him, Korematsu's case raised the question of the legitimacy of military plans that uprooted 120,000 persons, over 70,000 of them citizens of the United States, without trials or hearings. Douglas jotted down in his conference notes the important issue:

> Was confinement included in the authorization—[there is] no suggestion of enforcement in [the] materials before Congress. . . . By May, 1942, evacuation,

detention in an Assembly Center and detention in a Relocation Center, were but steps in a program which had acquired a unitary character. . . . Korematsu's choice was to go to jail or to submit to an indefinite detention in a Relocation Center. That detention was plainly more than temporary detention as an incident to exclusion. I therefore find no authority for it.[37]

His dissent met with a firestorm of criticism from Frankfurter, Black, and Stone because he had offered loyal Japanese citizens a choice: "stand on their own" or transfer to the relocation center "havens."[38] However, Douglas had changed his mind—which was not unusual for him. He wrote to Black, informing the Judge that, "to lessen the confusion now existing from a multiplicity of opinions," he would be

willing to waive my difficulties and join in the opinion of the Court provided one addition was made. As you know, I think evacuation and detention in an Assembly Center were inseparable. You do not think so. Therefore, I thought an accommodation could be made by adding a new paragraph to your opinion as follows: "A minority are of the view that evacuation and detention in an Assembly Center were inseparable. . . ."[39]

Black incorporated it into the final version of the majority opinion. Douglas filed his dissent away. Understandably, Bill, unlike his colleague Hugo, found that "the evacuation case . . . was ever on my conscience."[40]

Frank Murphy did not change his mind, as he did in an earlier Japanese exclusion case. He dissented from the *Korematsu* majority. Justice Jackson was the second dissenter. Like Murphy, he had been the U.S. attorney general prior to coming on the Court. What was clear in the case to Jackson was a fundamental principle: "guilt is personal and not inheritable."[41] For the Court to validate the contested wartime military orders was to validate "for all time the principle of racial discrimination in criminal procedure and of transplanting American citizens."[42]

Owen Roberts was the third dissenter. He believed that the military action was a "clear violation of constitutional rights."[43] Korematsu was convicted "as a punishment for not submitting to punishment in a concentration camp, based on his ancestry, and solely because of his ancestry, without evidence or inquiry concerning his loyalty and good disposition towards the United States."[44]

In the end, by a six-to-three vote, *Korematsu* validated the actions of the military authorities. Frankfurter wrote a short concurring opinion in which he focused on the nature of the war powers. "To find that the Constitution does not forbid the military measures now complained of does not carry with it approval of that which Congress and the Executive did. That is their business, not ours."[45]

The *Korematsu* decision was, for Black, an easy one and he never anguished over what one critic called the "most Klanlike" opinion the Judge ever wrote.[46] We were at war. The president—and his military commanders—could do whatever was necessary to assure victory against the enemy. If this was an easy judgment, the "steel seizure" case discussed next was, in a way, the opposite kind of case, one where Black wrote an opinion in which President Truman's actions were invalidated by the Court.

Youngstown Sheet and Tube Co v Sawyer (1952)
Black for the Court

The cold war between the West and the Communists, one that started almost as soon as World War II hostilities ended in 1945, turned tragically hot when North Korea invaded South Korea in June 1950. Instantly, American forces were involved, and, shortly thereafter, it became a war between the forces of the United Nations (chiefly American) against the Communist (in particular, the North Korean and Chinese Communist military hordes).

Korea soon became, in America, the nasty little UN "police action" in the Pacific. There was no formal declaration of war by the president and the Congress. It was never a conflict that engulfed the nation as was the case with the recently concluded war against the fascists.

While American soldiers were dying in Korea, those at home watched the new entertainment medium, television, in rapt fascination. Many thousands of Americans went to see and millions more heard or saw on TV the "miracle" 1951 New York Giants, with their great rookie center fielder, Willie Mays, as they won the National League championship over the hated Brooklyn Dodgers in the final inning of the final game with a Bobby Thompson home run. Except for those families whose sons or husbands were doing the fighting, Americans spent little time worrying about the Korean "war." However, this was not the case in Washington, D.C., during these years. President Harry S Truman had the task, as commander in chief, of ensuring that American forces had good leadership in the field and the equipment to bring the battle to the Communists.

During the 1951 term of the Supreme Court, the justices were asked to hear a watershed case involving the power of the president to control the economy in "wartime" using his "inherent" constitutional powers. The constitutional clash between President Truman and the Congress, arbitrated finally by the federal courts, came about due to a "nightmare" that Truman had envisoned: A "dangerous shortage [of ammunition] on the battlefield [in Korea]" would occur if there was a strike of union steel workers in 1952 and no action was taken by the government to prevent the strike.[47]

Wage and price controls were in effect during the undeclared Korean War. The president attempted to control inflation through the Wage Stabilization Board. For political reasons, Truman refused to implement the provisions of the 1947 Republican-inspired Taft-Hartley Act to settle labor-management disputes. Congress of Industrial Organizations (CIO) steelworkers' contracts expired on December 31, 1951. Given a lack of any movement towards a new contract, the unions announced their intent to strike.

Avoiding Taft-Hartley, Truman asked the Wage Stabilization Board to make recommendations on wages and steel prices and, at the same time, asked the steelworkers to remain on the jobs while the board tried to resolve the impasse. The board did recommend an increase in wages, but the recommendation was rejected by management. The unions then agreed upon a new strike date: April 9, 1952. Faced with a strike that would, Truman deeply believed, seriously threaten American armed forces fighting in Korea, he considered a few options: Employ

Taft-Hartley for an additional eighty-day cooling-off period; ask Congress for new legislation; or, consistent with a memo prepared by his former attorney general, Tom C. Clark, a recently appointed justice of the Supreme Court, use the "inherent" powers of the president, with the issuance of an executive order, to seize the steel mills.

On April 8, 1952, a day before the strike was to begin, Truman issued Executive Order 10340 directing the secretary of commerce, Charles Sawyer, to take possession of the nation's steel mills and run them for the government until the labor-management issues were resolved or until Congress acted to resolve the dispute. "Not the least remarkable [in these events] was private encouragement from his close friend Fred Vinson, Chief Justice of the United States. . . . [Vinson] privately advised the president to go ahead with the seizure, basing the recommendation on legal grounds."[48]

With Vinson and Clark advising him, and with other friends on the Court—including Black, who campaigned with and for Truman in Missouri in 1936, and Shay Minton, another Democratic politician who sat with Truman and Black in the Senate and who was now on the Supreme Court—Truman probably felt that his appointees and friends among the justices would validate his actions, just as President Richard Nixon, twenty-two years later, fully expected his four appointees to the Court to side with him on the matter of executive privilege.[49]

The Court took the case from the court of appeals before the lower federal appellate court had rendered a final decision. The federal district court judge, on the motion for a temporary injunction presented by the steel companies, ruled that Truman's action was unconstitutional. The justices heard oral argument a little more than one month after the order was issued (May 9, 1952) and announced their judgment promptly in June. By a six-to-three vote, the justices invalidated the presidential order. After the conference session, Jackson strode into his chambers and announced to his clerks, including Bill Rehnquist, who was to become Chief Justice of the United States. "Well, boys, the President got licked."[50]

Truman, dismayed, wrote his friend Douglas: "I don't see how a Court made up of so-called 'Liberals' could do what that court did to me."[51] After the announcement, Truman was so upset that Black, Truman's old legislative and political friend but the author of the opinion invalidating Truman's actions, gave the president a party that night. According to Douglas, "we all went and poured a lot of bourbon down Harry Truman. He didn't change his mind, but he felt better, at least for a few hours."[52]

When the brethren met in conference on May 16, 1952, the basic question for them to examine was "whether the President was acting within his constitutional power when he issued an order directing the Secretary of Commerce to take possession of and operate most of the nation's steel mills."[53] They took the case on an expedited basis, consistent with Rule 20 of the Supreme Court rules. Because the brethren wanted to quickly resolve the issue, there was very little time for discussion, let alone to produce an institutional opinion of the Court.

Douglas's law clerk had suggested, in a two-page summary of the fact and the law, that "to justify the President's exercise of power in a case where—as here—he has not exhausted those procedures prescribed by Congress could create a dangerous precedent . . . a dictator."[54] He urged the justice to grant certiorari, hear the case, and validate the district court judge's order that stayed implementation of the president's executive order.

At the conference, according to notes taken by Douglas, Chief Justice Vinson strongly defended Truman's actions. "To take the position there is unlimited power or no power is untenable," he said. "History shows there is power [but] must require it by virtue of an act of congress? [Vinson did] not agree."[55] Seizures by presidents in the past have been with and without acts of Congress. Arguing that Truman would have been "derelict" in his duty as commander in chief had he not acted as he did—and as other presidents in the past had done—Vinson urged his brethren to support Truman's actions.

Black strongly, vigorously, disagreed with his Chief. Truman could act under the guidelines of Taft-Hartley or could use the Wage Stabilization Board to try to cool off the CIO. For Hugo, the "question is whether Pres[ident] has the power to seize without a statute. . . . Can the President make laws—here we have labor disputes and law working concerning it—that power under the Constitution is in the Congress. . . . [Black] had one question, should we reach this? He thinks we must—there would be irreparable damage by taking over control of private management—very serious for this Court (which has no army and only prestige) to tell the President what to do."[56]

Since Black believed that the brethren "must reach" the major constitutional question and, since he was senior in the majority on this matter (Vinson being in dissent), he assigned himself the opinion for the Court majority.

Reed, who was to dissent (with Vinson and Minton), was more cautious. He hoped that the Court could avoid the constitutional issue, for it meant ruling against the use of presidential power, but he knew that could not occur. "Perhaps we should rest on the war power and say the president has the power to seize as Commander in Chief." He asked, rhetorically, "Couldn't [a] president seize a railroad to move troops? FDR closed the banks to protect economy."[57]

Frankfurter began his comments by saying that "everyone should write in this case." On the substantive issue of inherent presidential powers, "he agrees with Black [but] he tries to avoid the constitutional issue—the less the court pronounces constitutional doctrine the better—but he thinks here the constitutional question cannot be avoided."[58] Douglas also agreed with Black that the president was bound by the Constitution and that the Court should examine the issue on the constitutional merits and reach judgment.

Justice Robert Jackson, like a few of his brethren, did "not want the Court to pass on whether there is an emergency—the question is what the President can do in an emergency. . . . He would affirm [the district court judgment]." For Justice Harold Burton, another Truman appointee to the Court, the case called for a "decision that requires policy making and therefore it is for Congress to decide [but] the president has no power to seize apart from statutes. [He would] affirm" the district court order.

For Justice Tom Clark, whose memo had been used by Truman's staff to justify the seizure order, the president had acted improperly. He, however, wanted "the decision [to be] limited to this case [for] he was unwilling to say President has no power—*here* the situation could have been averted by two methods not involving seizure." Finally, Sherman Minton spoke. He was the fourth Truman appointee to the Court and, in an earlier period of time, a very close senatorial colleague of Truman's; he was to join Vinson and Reed in dissent. Truman, he urged his brethren, "did everything he could to avoid a strike—there are no vacant spots in power when the security of the nation is at stake—power is the power of defense—it rests in [the] president—there is an emergency now. . . . Truman seized the plants because the defense of the country required it—the President had to act—Minton is very excited about this and pounds the table—[the] President," concluded the agitated Minton, "gets his inherent power from the power to defend the nation in a day of peril—[he would] reverse."[59]

The Court had discussed the issue of presidential power and concluded that the president lacked the power to seize private property. Hugo, the writer of the opinion for the majority, had to write one that held it together. However, because of the lack of time to write such an opinion, every justice in the majority wrote an opinion while joining Black's judgment. Frankfurter's request had been met, for he, Jackson, Burton, Clark, and Douglas wrote separate concurring opinions. Chief Justice Vinson, the person who had assured Truman that the seizure was legal, wrote a dissent, joined by Reed and Minton.

For the Court, Black concluded that "in the framework of our Constitution, the President's power to see that the laws are faithfully executed refutes the idea that he is to be a lawmaker." His opinion stated:

> The President's power, if any, to issue the order [seizing the mills] must stem either from an act of Congress or from the Constitution itself. . . . The Founders of this Nation entrusted the law making power to the Congress alone in both good and bad times. It would do no good to recall the historical events, the fears of power and the hopes of freedom that lay behind their choice. Such a review would but confirm our holding that this seizure order cannot stand.[60]

Black's opinion reflected his view that the Constitution commands all officials to act in certain ways, and if the official went beyond the words of the document, that person was acting unconstitutionally. Given his strongly held belief in the restraining powers of the Constitution, Hugo did not hesitate to rule against his friend, the President of the United States.

Even Frankfurter congratulated Black for holding a "court" and "achieving" the opinion for the six brethren. Frankfurter's own concurrence focused on the separation-of-powers concept, borrowing some words from Chief Justice Hughes: "The duty of the President to see that the laws be executed is a duty that does not go beyond the laws or require him to achieve more than Congress sees fit to leave within his power." While Douglas believed that there was an emergency, "the fact that it was necessary that measures be taken to keep steel in production does not mean that the President, rather than Congress, had the constitutional authority to act." Jackson rejected the inherent-power argument of the president. "The plea is for a resulting power to deal with a crisis or emergency according to the necessities of the case, the unarticulated assumption being that necessity knows no law." Burton, too, discussed the question of inherent powers of the president. "We find no such power available to him under the present circumstances. The present situation is not comparable to that of an imminent invasion or threatened attack."

Clark's concurring opinion was different from the others: Congress has the power to deal with such emergencies and in the absence of legislation, the president may act depending upon the "gravity of the situation confronting this nation." But, noted Clark, the Congress had legislated, and therefore the presidential action was unnecessary and invalid.

Chief Justice Vinson's dissent pointed to the many actions of Congress in the area of foreign policy, e.g., the Truman Doctrine, Marshall Plan, Mutual Security Act of 1951, funding for defense, draft renewal, NATO, UN Charter support, and support for the war in Korea. "The President has the duty to execute [these] legislative programs. Their successful execution depends upon continued production of steel and stabilized prices for steel." If there was a threat to the continued production, he could seize the steel mills. The inherent powers of the president allowed him to so act. However, the majority of six rejected that view at that time.

After the opinion was announced, the archconservative *Chicago Daily Tribune,* on June 4, 1952, editorialized about the Black opinion for the Court. In the editorial entitled "THE CONSTITUTION LIVES," the paper, which had consistently criticized Black from the moment of his appointment to the Court in 1937, lauded the magnificence of Hugo's writing.

> Justice Black's majority opinion in the steel seizure case is a towering landmark of Constitutional interpretation. The opinion will stand as long as the Republic stands; indeed, a contrary opinion would have signaled the death of the Republic. . . . Freedom's greatest enemy in our day has been the expansion of executive power under the pretext of emergency. That is what happened in Germany and Italy and many other lands. . . . The outstanding quality of Mr. Justice Black's majority opinion is its simplicity. . . . There is no wandering off into side issues, no striving for subtleties, no rhetorical ornament. . . . The justices may have diappointed Mr. Truman, but their work has won them the everlasting gratitude of the American people. The Constitution lives.[61]

Douglas, after reading the editorial, and knowing of the paper's long-expressed animosity toward Black, wrote the Justice a brief note and attached it to the editorial: "Dear Hugo: Are you still sure you were right?" The Judge replied the same day: "Not shaken at all. It was just impossible for the *Tribune* to resist the power of my logic!"[62]

Hugo did not lose much sleep over this important opinion. Even Black's critics, in the press and in Congress, believed that the steel seizure case was decided properly.[63] Had there been no such commendation, Hugo would not have been bothered, for he believed that the Constitution commanded the ruling. And, for the Judge, the Constitution's commands were the first and last word on questions of legitimate authority.

States Rights in a Federal System

According to Black, the only constitutional constraints on the power of the local government to enact legislation were found in the First Amendment. So long as the legislation, on its face, was not discriminatory or otherwise in violation of a constitutional prohibition, it was a legitimate exercise of the state's police powers. Even though Hugo might think that the statute was unwise,[64] or his brethren argue that the hidden rationale for the statute was a racially discriminatory one,[65] the statute had to stand unless there were perceived clear and unambiguous constitutional infirmities.

He eschewed all judicial efforts to understand the ulterior motivations of local and state officials. While the Judge always insisted on judicial noninvolvement in this area of federalism litigation—judicial control of the states' powers—the rest of the Court, even after the 1937 turnaround, continued to examine state legislation that was challenged as violative of the Constitution.

Wood v Lovett (1940)
Black dissents

Arkansas legislators, during the Depression, were faced with a fiscal reality: 25 percent of the real property in the state was tax-delinquent. They passed, in 1935, legislation that allowed the state to sell real or personal property for nonpayment of taxes. According to the legislation, there were no procedural ways in which the seizure and sale of the property could be forestalled in the courts.

In 1936, because of nonpayment of taxes, Lovett's land was sold to Wood by the Arkansas commissioner of state lands. A year later, however, the state legislators repealed the statute. In 1939, Lovett brought suit against Wood in state court to recover his property. The Arkansas courts ruled in Lovett's favor, and Wood appealed to the U.S. Supreme Court. He was about to lose prime lands bought for a fraction of their value, and he wanted to prevent that from occurring.

His argument, presented to the brethren in written briefs and in oral argument, was that the 1937 repeal statute impaired the obligation of contract with the state, in violation of Article I, Section 10, of the U.S. Constitution.[66] The Court majority accepted Wood's argument that the repeal legislation conflicted with the Constitution and was therefore unconstitutional. Wood kept the bargain he bought in 1936.

Black was the Court's dissenter, joined by Douglas. Nonpayment of taxes was a national problem during a depression. The repeal legislation was one of a number of actions taken by the states "in an effort to meet the baffling social and economic problems growing out of a nationwide depression." In 1935, legislators believed that selling delinquent lands would solve the problem; the repealing legislation came about because the "legislators became convinced that the law had worked directly contrary to the state's policy of obtaining benefits believed to flow from continuity of possession by home owners and farmers, that it had accomplished inequitable results and it had thereby operated injuriously to the interests of the state and that sound policy dictates its repeal."

The legislators, elected by the people of the state, were trying to solve a very serious problem, wrote the Judge in dissent.

> Without attempting to judge the wisdom or inequities of either act, it is easy to see that both represented attempts, rational and understandable attempts, to

achieve . . . a solution. To hold that the Contract clause of the Federal Constitution is a barrier to the 1937 attempt to restore the distressed landowner the remedy partly taken away by the 1935 Act is, in my view, wholly inconsistent with the spirit and language of *that* Constitution.[67] (My emphasis)

Clearly, Black was speaking for the constituency he represented as U.S. senator from Alabama: poor farmers who stood to lose their land during the Depression. For him, the legislators have a right to respond to such dilemmas, and the courts, staffed by lifetime-appointed, nonelected persons, had no right to interpose their views in these economic and social matters.

As he wrote to his brethren, who were angry at Black's "populism" tendencies in his dissent:

It is a matter of serious moment to any state when 25% of the realty owned by its citizens—homes, farms, and other real property—is in jeopardy of being lost because of inability to pay taxes. Such a manifestation of financial distress indicates a degree of destitution and poverty which calls for the best in legislative statesmanship. . . . To seek to find a rational and fair solution of such a deplorable and perplexing problem was not only the right, but the impressive duty of Arkansas' legislators. To say that the Federal Constitution stands as a barrier to an honest effort to prevent such a wholesale forfeiture of men's property is an attribute to that constitution's qualities which I think is wholly inconsistent with its spirit and not commanded by its language.[68]

Douglas, the Court's newest justice, agreed with Black, writing Hugo that "I agree—with great pleasure. A fine job!" In *Wood,* the Alabaman was speaking for poor Southern people he knew, who were struggling, in the throes of a terrible economic depression, to retain their piece of property. Black believed that state legislators had the task of grappling with the calamity and that they should be given full freedom to try to resolve it. So long as the legislators did not violate a specific prohibition in the Constitution, they were within their authority to try to minimize the impact of the Depression on their constituents.

Ferguson v Skrupa (1962)
Black for the Court

Ferguson involved the legitimacy of the business of "debt-adjusting" in light of the effort by Kansas to proscribe such behavior. Skrupa ran such a business called, appropriately enough, Credit Advisors, Inc. He provided a helpful service, for a fee, to debtors. The debtor gave to Skrupa, on a monthly basis, funds that were distributed by Skrupa to the debtor's creditors. The Kansas statute, however, allowed such a debt-adjusting business to occur only as incident to the "lawful practice of law in this state."

The lower three-judge federal court invalidated the statute as violative of the due process clause of the Fourteenth Amendment. When the Supreme Court heard the case, however, Black, for a unanimous Court, set aside the decision of the lower court. The federal judges had used an outworn jurisprudence to invalidate the Kansas statute. "Under our system of government created by our Constitution, it is up to the legislators, not the courts, to decide on the wisdom and utility of legislation." Although there was a time in our history when judges used the "liberty" in the due process clause to strike down legislation they did not like, "this doctrine has long since been discarded." State legislative bodies "have broad scope" to legislate in this area and "this Court does not sit to subject the state to intolerable supervision."[69]

Black put to final rest the old doctrine of judicial interposition in these matters:

> We emphatically refuse to go back to the time when the courts used the Due Process Clause to strike down state laws regulatory of business and industrial conditions because they may be unwise, improvident, or out of harmony with a particular school of thought. Nor are we able to or willing to draw lines by calling a law "prohibitory," or "regulatory." *Whether the legislature takes for its textbook Adam Smith, Herbert Spencer, or Lord Keynes, or some other is no concern of ours.* The Kansas debt adjusting statute may be wise or unwise. But relief, if any be needed, lies not with us but with the body constituted to pass laws for the state of Kansas.[70] (my emphasis)

Interestingly, an earlier, more emphatic version of his opinion for the Court was tempered somewhat due to concerns voiced by some of Black's brethren. Justice Goldberg wrote to him: "By its many references to the idea that it is no longer this Court's function to pass upon the 'reasonableness' of a state's economic legislation, it implies resolution of some cases about which I am not at all sure and which, in any event, need not be reached in order to decide this case."[71] Goldberg suggested that Black modify the opinion so that Goldberg and other justices would be "free to think in terms of 'unreasonableness' about the merits of conceivable extremes of state economic regulation when such cases arise."[72]

To keep his "Court," Black reluctantly modified the language in *Ferguson v Skrupa*. He was, however, not very happy with the caution expressed by Goldberg. And the Justice wrote, on the margins of the Goldberg memo, that he "agreed to some of these changes with great regret but not to all. With these changes, we fail to administer the final fatal blow to the idea that this Court can overrule a legislature's belief of reasonableness."[73]

Younger v Harris (1970)
Black for the Court

One manifestation of the federalism issue that touched the brethren very closely was the issue of federal judicial intervention in legal proceedings that were already under way in state courts. Given the concept of *abstention,* the federal courts throughout American legal history have been wary of interference while a case was pending in local tribunals. In a 1965 opinion of the Court (with Black not participating),[74] however, the Court majority relaxed its position and ruled that a federal district judge could enjoin state court proceedings that had commenced under a state statute being used to "harass a civil rights organization in the exercise of its First Amendment rights."[75] Only six of the brethren participated in the decision; Goldberg, Stewart, and Black were nonparticipants.[76]

Black was extremely unhappy about that case. *Dombrowski,* for him, was absolutely incorrect. The "normal thing to do when federal courts are asked to enjoin pending proceedings in state courts is *not* to issue such injunctions."[77] When the issue arose again a few years later, in the case of *Younger v Harris,*[78] he was able to command a Court majority to give *Dombrowski* "a very narrow reading and [to reaffirm] its traditional stance."[79]

Black's friend Douglas was his major opponent in these extended deliberations, although, ironically, Douglas did not participate in some of the early formal votes because he had not been present for the oral arguments. For Douglas, there was no reason to abstain if the principal legal issue was a federal constitutional question and so long as no new state issue required interpretation.[80]

John Harris was a "Black Power" leader in Oakland, California, who had passed out pamphlets in 1966 urging that African Americans take justice into their own hands and bring the mayor of Los Angeles, Sam Yorty, to trial because of his racist behavior while in office. Harris, along with other Black Panthers, also was rallying his constituents to "get whitey" and said that the African Americans in Los Angeles had to defend themselves, "if necessary, with force."

He was charged with violating California's Criminal Syndicalist Act, which, among other things, punishes a person who "prints, publishes, or publicly circulates any paper containing teaching of criminal syndicalism." He sought, unsuccessfully, to have California courts prevent his prosecution from proceeding. He then petitioned a special three-judge federal district court to enjoin his continuing prosecution, on the grounds that the act under which he was charged was an unconstitutional infringement of the First Amendment's freedom of speech.

The federal court in California enjoined the prosecution of Harris under California's Criminal Syndicalist Act, pending a review of the statute's constitutionality. Harris had argued that the statute prevented him from using his First Amendment free-speech rights, and the federal court invalidated the statute. The three-judge court held that the traditional doctrine of federal judicial abstention in state cases did not apply in this case. Where the First Amendment is involved, the federal courts could consider the constitutionality of a state criminal statute, even though the state prosecution had not concluded. That court also held that the state's Syndicalism Act was unconstitutional. The state of California appealed from the judgment of the lower federal court that declared the California Act unconstitutional.

The case came to the U.S. Supreme Court during the 1968 term. When the case was debated in conference, five of the eight justices, Douglas not participating this time, said that the three-judge federal court should be reversed. Warren, Brennan, and White disagreed; they were for affirmance of the three-judge federal court order.

However, Black, joined by Justices Harlan and Stewart, was strongly for reversal, along with a dramatic narrowing of *Dombrowski*. Because Chief Justice Warren was in the minority, Black, the senior associate justice in the majority, given his passionate dislike of the *Dombrowski* precedent, took it upon himself to write the opinion for the five-person majority. Marshall and Fortas were the other two justices who had supported reversal, but on much narrower grounds, which meant that Hugo had to write the opinion in a way that held on to their two votes, thereby holding together his "court."

Fortas drifted away from Black's strong draft opinion that reached out to greatly narrow *Dombrowski*. He was prepared to write a concurring opinion, but on narrow grounds. Brennan then announced that he was writing an opinion that would maintain *Dombrowski*'s viability while vacating the three-judge district court ruling in *Younger*.

Before the Court could coalesce around the polar views, during the spring of the 1968 term, Fortas suddenly resigned from the Court due to the discovery of his Wolfson Foundation connections. Additionally, a flare-up emerged among the eight remaining justices shortly thereafter because Douglas had, in a seemingly contradictory manner, concurred with Black's opinion in the case but later joined Brennan's quite different opinion in *Younger*. Evidently, Douglas had promised Black that he would concur in Black's opinion. After reading Brennan's opinion, which stated that, unless a state law had a "chilling effect" upon free speech, federal courts would not intervene via the injunctive relief remedy in state court proceedings, Douglas told Brennan that he would concur in that opinion as well.

Douglas's actions meant that Black's view was a minority, dissenting view and that Brennan had a five-person *Younger* majority: Brennan, Warren, Marshall, White, and now Douglas. During a contentious conference session, after it was pointed out that Douglas's actions were contradictory, he stood up, turned towards Brennan, and said, "Take my name off your opinion." That deadlocked the brethren four to four, on *Younger* and forced the rescheduling of arguments for the next term of the Court.[81]

When these cases were heard again in the next term, Burger had replaced Warren, and Blackmun had replaced Fortas. As a consequence of these two personnel changes on the Court, the conference discussions were quite different. Now all the justices except for Douglas called for reversal of the three-judge federal district court action. Burger thought that there was "no actual case or controversy and the District Court should not have got[ten] into the matter." Even Brennan, according to Douglas's notes, spoke for reversal and rejected Harris's argument "that they have exhausted their state remedies."[82] At the conference of November 20, 1970, all the justices, except Douglas voted to reverse, and Black was, this time, given the task of writing the opinion for the Court by the new Chief.[83]

Black's opinion was a classic defense of federalism, which meant, for him, that federal courts were to stay out of state court cases until appeals were made from the highest state court to the Supreme Court or unless there were very special circumstances, such as actual "bad faith intent to harass" defendants, in the state trial. It was his "Our Federalism" statement in which he stated that only "special circumstances" occurring in a state court proceeding could ever warrant injunctive or declaratory relief from a federal court.

Black had worked hard to get the majority opinion that restricted the reach of federal judges in state court proceedings;[84] when *Younger* was read, in February 1971, Hugo felt "good and peppy, . . . having delivered himself of *[Younger]*, which [has] been hanging fire three years."[85] For Black, "Our Federalism" meant that the federal courts must continue to act in light of the truism that "the national government will fare best if the states and their institutions are left free to perform their separate functions in their separate ways."[86]

> One familiar with the profound debates that ushered our Federal Constitution into existence is bound to respect those who remain loyal to the ideals and the dreams of "Our Federalism." This concept does not mean blind deference to "States' Rights" any more than it means centralization of control over every important issue in our National Government and its courts. The Framers rejected both these courses. What the concept does represent is a system in which there is sensitivity to the legitimate interests of both State and National Governments, and in which the National Government, anxious though it may be to vindicate and protect federal rights and federal interests, always endeavors to do so in ways that will not unduly interfere with the legitimate activities of the States.[87]

Douglas's solitary dissent in the case argued that the Civil War had dramatically changed the relationship of the states to the central government. The central government, after 1865, had assumed a greater responsibility for ensuring that persons were not discriminated against by officials of the states. Douglas's radical views did not trouble his old friend Black in the least. The Judge scribbled on the Douglas draft dissent the following, which stands as Hugo's final comment on the matter:

> I have read and heartedly disagree with this opinion. The civil war Amendments were not written in language designed to change our government into one that abolished state power except with respect to actions against persons on account of race. . . . I do not at this time see anything here that impels me to modify my original opinion.[88]

The *Younger v Harris* case was referred to by Black when he said to Hugo Jr. that "we've got to tie the judges of this Court [down] . . . even if we've got to sacrifice doing some good through the federal courts."

It is understandable why Mrs. Black described her Hugo as "feeling good and peppy" after he delivered the *Younger* opinion. Clearly, on the merits, Black would surely have agreed that the California Criminal Syndicalist Act was an obvious unconstitutional state infringement of Harris's First Amendment rights. But, given his commitment to a viable federalism, one where the states had a significant role to play in providing for the general welfare of state citizens, he dared not validate federal judicial interposition into cases that were ongoing in state courts—unless there was shown, on the face, a bad-faith effort at harassment by the state.

The "Firstness" of the First Amendment

The *Younger* case, in a way, brings the discussion of Black's jurisprudence around to the First Amendment. That amendment, according to the Judge, must never become a "tinkling cymbal."[89] All judges, most especially the justices of the U.S. Supreme Court, must act vigorously to ensure that the constitutional guarantee of freedom of speech remains a vital and viable right of citizens and other persons living in a free nation.

Black, in his own words, always viewed the First Amendment as withdrawing from all governments "all power to act in certain areas—whatever the scope of those areas may be."[90] For the Alabaman, this clearly applied to the First Amendment's free speech guarantee: "Without deviation, without exception, without any ifs, buts, or whereases, that freedom of speech means that government shall not do anything to people or, in the words of the Magna Carta, move against people, either for the views they have or the views they express or the words they speak or write."[91]

Black, like a justice he admired a great deal, Louis Brandeis, believed "with Jefferson that it is time enough for government to step in and regulate people when they do something, not when they say something."[92] In a letter written to noted scholar Alexander Meiklejohn, Hugo wrote that the First Amendment's guarantee of free speech was much more than "an admonition."[93] It was a categorical command to all governments to allow people to express themselves freely, without any interference from the state.

For Black, the right to freedom of speech and press was both an end in itself and a critical variable in making the democratic experiment a successful one. "The power to think, speak, and write freely without governmental censorship or interference is the most precious privilege of citizens vested with power to select public policies and public officials."[94] In a letter to Irving Dilliard, a respected news journalist and friend, Hugo commented on the Alien and Sedition Acts of 1798. Again reflecting Jefferson's thoughts, Black wrote that "the United States was without power to pass laws that abridged discussion of public questions at all." He added that "that view prevailed when Jefferson was elected." And, in a final comment that captured his frustrations about the state of affairs in America when he wrote the letter, he added: "No group seems to be advocating such a view today [1953]."[95]

For the Judge, the "important thing . . . was that the people have an opportunity to hear all sides of [an issue] and to decide freely what laws they want to live by. . . . It was this view that led [him] to place such heavy emphasis upon the First Amendment as the basic law guaranteeing the right of the people to open discussion of public issues."[96] The underlying premise of the First Amendment was that, if the people heard all sides of an issue, however controversial or heretical the ideas might be, they would choose "the better, wiser, more beneficial of alternative courses."[97]

Bridges v California (1941)
Black for the Court

Harry Bridges was a controversial, radical West Coast teamster union leader. He was convicted and fined for contempt of court in 1940, for criticizing a judge outside the courtroom in a telegram he had sent to Secretary of Labor Frances Perkins. Bridges complained about the judge's decision in a lawsuit between the teamsters and another union. Calling it an "outrageous" decision, Bridges threatened to call a strike in the port of Los Angeles if it was enforced.

The case caused a great deal of anger and lengthy debate when it came to the

Court. Argued twice, during the 1940 and 1941 Terms of the Court, the opinion was finally announced on Monday, December 8, 1941, the day after America was attacked by Japan at Pearl Harbor.

When the case was first heard in October 1940, only Black, Reed, and Douglas thought that the conviction should be overturned. Hugo would have set aside the contempt-of-court conviction because such out-of-court comments were protected by the First Amendment's free-speech guarantee.

The comments of Chief Justice Charles Evans Hughes in conference evidently set the tone for a majority of the Court when *Bridges* was first heard. Hughes said that "the facts here transcended the limits of reasonable discussion and I think the lower court should be affirmed." He assigned the task of writing the majority opinion to Frankfurter joining them in the six-person majority for validating Bridge's contempt-of-court conviction were associate justices McReynolds, Roberts, Stone, and Murphy.

Frankfurter sent a copy of his draft majority opinion to retired Justice Louis Brandeis. "Of course," Brandeis wrote back, "you have a unanimous court for your opinion." Frankfurter replied, "Hardly that, I am very doubtful whether I will keep a Court. Black has a fierce dissent." Brandeis responded, according to Frankfurter's account: "Black and Co. have gone mad on free speech."[98]

By spring 1941, however, after the draft opinions were circulated, two events led to a turnabout in the Court's thinking about the First Amendment. First, the archconservative and anti-semitic McReynolds retired from the Court. Second, Justice Murphy, newly arrived on the Court, changed his mind and cast his vote with Black.

Since the vote was now four to four rather than six to three, *Bridges* was carried over for reargument in the 1941 term of the Court. Moreover, by the end of the 1940 term, a third event occurred that further eroded Frankfurter's voting majority: Chief Justice Hughes announced his retirement. By the opening of the 1941 term, James Byrnes and Robert Jackson were appointed by Roosevelt and confirmed by the Senate. While Byrnes sided with Frankfurter in *Bridges,* Jackson joined Black's call for reversal. Hugo's dissent was now the majority view of the Court. Holding his "Court," Black spoke, in December 1941, for a five-person majority in *Bridges*.

In direct opposition to Frankfurter's embracing all of the principles of law that came from England, Black spoke of America's success, in the form of the written Constitution with its all-important amendments, in enhancing liberty for its inhabitants. "No purpose," wrote Black, initially in dissent, "in ratifying the Bill of Rights was clearer than that of securing for the people of the United States much greater freedom of religion, expression, assembly, and petition than the people of Great Britain had ever enjoyed."[99]

Frankfurter believed that the states had the right to punish as contempt of court any out-of-court statement that could possibly interfere with a pending case. A judge's power to punish for contempt was "deeply rooted in history, in the system of administering justice evolved by liberty-loving English-speaking peoples."[100]

The two men strongly disagreed on the place of English law in American justice. "Justice Black saw the First Amendment as something very new and distinctively American." Frankfurter, however, saw the First Amendment "as he saw much of the Constitution—as a natural development of English traditions, a part of a continuum."[101]

Black's opinion in *Bridges* was, as Benno Schmidt said, "a judicial Declaration of Independence for the First Amendment, freeing it from English law."[102] This purely American, populist-style view is clearly seen in the very first paragraph of the Alabaman's draft dissent. While it was language that did not enter the final opinion for the Court written by Black, it was the core of his absolutist commitment to the First Amendment:

> First in the catalogue of human liberties essential to the life and growth of a government of, for, and by the people are those liberties written into the First Amendment to our Constitution. They are the pillars upon which popular government rests and without which a government of free men cannot survive. *History* persuades me that the moving forces which brought about the creation of the safeguards contained in the other sections of our Bill of Rights sprang from a resolute determination to place the liberties defined in the First Amendment in an area wholly safe and secure against any invasion—even by government.[103] (my emphasis)

Black's strong dissent turned into a somewhat-softened majority opinion. While it was couched in the prevailing, still-popular "clear and present danger" language in order to hold his Court, Black's opinion underscored his belief in the absoluteness of the First Amendment freedoms.[104]

The *Bridges* decision triggered the decades-long battle between Black and Frankfurter over the scope and the very primacy of the First Amendment. Black saw the First Amendment rights as the pillars that held up America's democratic republic. Frankfurter's belief, expressed in his dissent, was the conceptual foundation for his future battles with Black: "Free speech is not so absolute or irrational a conception as to imply paralysis of the means for effective protection of all the freedoms secured by the Bill of Rights."[105]

Dennis v United States (1951)
Black dissents

The First Amendment's protections were absolute. For Black, by 1950, there was no compromise with this view. After a few terms on the Court, he became increasingly critical of all "tests" created by his brethren in First Amendment litigation, such as "balancing" and "clear and present danger." The Constitution's words in that amendment were unequivocal. And those words were the guides for the federal judges, not the much weaker, flexible, judicially devised tests. The "clear and present danger" standard was deficient because "it can be used to justify the punishment of advocacy."[106] It was also too easily converted into a "balancing" test because a Supreme Court majority had to determine when a danger from speech was so serious and imminent that it justified governmental proscription of the speech as well as punishment for uttering the words. The "balancing" test, employed by the Supreme Court majorities in both "Red Scare" periods, the 1920s and the 1940s–1950s, was for the Judge totally inconsistent with the command of the First Amendment. It was, he said, "the most dangerous of the tests developed by the justices of the Court." [107]

For a majority of the brethren, especially the Chief Justice Fred Vinson and the archly patriotic Felix Frankfurter and his allies on the Court, it was clear that the Communist "menace" had to be curtailed. This was true whether the case involved the Smith Act's provisions, some aspect of the Internal Security Act of 1950, the scope of a congressional committee's power to investigate Communists and alleged Communist-front persons and associations, or the constitutionality of loyalty-security programs, during the height of the cold war.

Supreme Court majorities, consisting at various times in the 1950s of Vinson as well as Jackson, Frankfurter, Clark, Minton, Burton, Reed, and Harlan, generally supported governmental proscriptions on First Amendment freedoms. Black, joined by Douglas, was always in the minority until the late 1950s when they were joined by Warren and Brennan; when Frankfurter left the Court in 1962, new appointee Arthur Goldberg also sided with them.

The *Dennis* case of 1951 epitomized the direction the conservative Court majority had taken in this area of constitutional interpretation during the height of the cold war. Hugo was very frustrated with his brethren's intolerance toward political deviants as well as by his inability to persuade them that they were wrong and that the First Amendment protected even Communists from arrest and conviction for their thoughts and their words.

The justices of the Supreme Court were deciding these First Amendment issues when, in Bob Jackson's words, "the Communists [were] the current phobia in Washington." [108] Jackson also put words on paper to describe the hysteria that swept the nation at this time. It was, he said, inconceivable that Eugene Dennis, the Communist party leader, and others like him could receive a fair jury trial, given the national mood, the "present atmosphere in Washington." The fear, he wrote, "cast a shadow on the jury box, [with] everybody looking over their shoulder to see who [was] watching. Men [were] destroyed by gossip and smear." [109]

Jackson was so distraught by this vision of a closed, xenophobic America that his friend Frankfurter had to write him a note suggesting that he manage his concern by curtailing some of the language he was planning on using in these Communist conspiracy cases. "This is to ask you," wrote Frankfurter, "to consider whether you could not say what you think you ought to say . . . without giving avoidable reinforcement to the McCarthy's, the McCormick's, and the other exploiters of the irrational in the land." [110]

During the 1950 term of the Supreme Court, the *Dennis* case came to the brethren for review. Eugene Dennis and ten other top Communist party members were convicted in U.S. District Court, Southern District, New York, for violation of Section 3 of the Smith Act (conspiracy to organize the Communist party of the United States as a group to teach and advocate the overthrow of the government of the United States by force and violence). It was a long (nine-month), well-publicized, rancorous trial, one that led to the summary conviction, at the conclusion of the trial, of the petitioners' lawyers for contempt of court—a contempt that was upheld by a Court majority over Black's, Douglas's, and Frankfurter's dissents.[111]

The passions unleashed by *Dennis* were so strong that Frankfurter wrote an unusual memo to his brethren. Dated February 27, 1951, Felix complained about outside interference from two radically different types of groups: the Communist party and the American Bar Association!

> If there are cases that call for undisturbed judicial determination, and therefore from abstention of outside interference, these surely are such cases *[Dennis* and *Sacher]*. . . . I wonder, therefore, whether the Court consults its self-respect in not taking notice of two occurrences as to these cases during the last few days [the Communist party's radio statement and a recommendation of a special committee of the ABA, the former calling for reversal while the latter calling for "disbarment of them and their like"].

Frankfurter's recommendation for the Court was quite dramatic. "As a single judge, I would not hesitate to issue an order to show cause why an attachment for contempt should not issue against the American Bar Association—who certainly should know better—and the Communist Party."[112]

According to Douglas's notes taken at the conference session of December 9, 1950, five days after oral argument in Dennis, there was very little debate or discussion—or even anger—among the brethren.

> The amazing thing about the conference in this important case was the brief nature of the discussion. Those wanting to affirm had minds closed to argument or persuasion. The conference discussion was largely *pro forma*. It was the more amazing because of the drastic revision of the "clear and present danger" test which affirmance requires.[113]

The justices' single focus was whether the Smith Act was constitutional or not, and not whether the convictions were valid ones based on the evidence presented by the Justice Department at trial. Most of them had reached the conclusion, before the conference session, that the Smith Act was valid as it applied to the Communists in America.

Chief Justice Vinson said that he would affirm the convictions, with "practically no discussion," according to Douglas's conference notes.[114] Reed, too, simply noted that he would affirm. Frankfurter spoke next and discussed the "1) status of [the] clear and present danger since *Gitlow*—2) how imminent must the substantive evils be? 3) should the clear and present danger be submitted to the jury? In Holmes and Brandeis' opinions it is a question of fact 4) can we take judicial notice of the evil of the danger? He indicates he would affirm."[115]

Setting aside his feelings about the inability of Communists to receive a fair trial anywhere in America, Jackson's comments in conference reflected his concurrence: "The U.S.," he said, "can protect against activity—can stop some things because they are inherently dangerous without reference to clear and present danger—he has not made up his mind—he passes, but indicates he will affirm."[116] Burton spoke of the need to change the test: "clear and probable rather than clear and present is the test—can take judicial knowledge of the danger [of the Communist menace]." And Shay Minton simply noted, that he too would affirm.[117] Clark, probably because he was the attorney general when the prosecution of the Communists began, did not participate.

Clearly, except for Black and Douglas, the Court was ready to do all that was necessary to affirm the convictions, including taking "judicial notice" of the Communist peril, modifying, or, as Jackson was to recommend in his concurring opinion, even discarding the Holmes/Brandeis "clear and present danger" doctrine. In order to affirm the convictions of the eleven Communist party leaders, the majority had to somehow work around the Holmes/Brandeis doctrine.

In the end, the task of applying some version of the "clear and present danger" test was taken on by the Chief. The effort was a poor one and was roundly critiqued by Black in his characteristic style: pungent marginal annotations. For example, when Vinson wrote: "No one could conceive that it is not within the power of Congress to prohibit acts intended to overthrow the Government by force or violence," Hugo commented in the margin of the slip opinion: "Of course—but these people [were] not convicted for *acts*."[118] And when the Chief Justice referred to the "kind of activity" Dennis and the others were engaged in, Black noted: "What 'activity'?"[119] Again, when Vinson misinterpreted, as he had to do to affirm the convictions, the "clear and present danger" doctrine, the Judge quoted from *Abrams* to show Vinson that Holmes and Brandeis were concerned about "imminent danger" and not, as Vinson stated, "requisite danger."[120] *Abrams v. U.S.*, 250 U.S. 616 (1919) was a case decided after the World War ended. The seven-person Court majority upheld Abrams's convictions under the 1916 Sedition Act. Justice Holmes, joined by Brandeis dissented. And when the Chief, in a jab at Black and Douglas, wrote, "To those who would paralyze our government in the face of impending threat by encasing it in a semantic straitjacket one must reply that all concepts are relative," Hugo responded in the margin: "First Amendment and the Bill of Rights are words but not therefore a 'semantic straitjacket.' "[121] After Vinson put together governmental power to limit speech with its power to protect the people from "armed internal attack," Black commented, "Now [he] puts 'speech' and 'armed internal attack' in [the] same category."[122]

As for the famous Vinson putsch fear, Black noted, acidly, that it was a "ghost conspiracy."[123] When the Chief said it was "impossible to measure the validity [of the damage the Communist party has done] in terms of the probability of success, or the immediacy of a successful attempt," the Associate Justice countered that that was "precisely what clear and present [danger] meant."[124] Clearly unwilling to accept the view put forward by the majority that the Communist party had to be stopped or America would be destroyed, Black commented whenever Vinson made such references: "The goblins'll get you!"

Again and again, he ridiculed Vinson's majority opinion. Indeed, for the Judge, it was child's play. For example, when Vinson wrote about the trial judge: "It is thus clear that he reserved the question of the existence of the danger for his own determination," Black acidly noted, "Is not the capacity to commit the crime always an essential element which, like others, must be found from the facts by the *jury*?"[125] (my emphasis).

Frankfurter's concurring opinion took judicial notice of the danger Communism posed to his beloved adopted country and concluded that Congress acted reasonably when it passed the Smith Act. Jackson discarded the Holmes/Brandeis test entirely and substituted, instead, the doctrine of conspiracy, which turned speech into seditious conduct. As Black accurately noted in his dissent, all the majority opinions in Dennis "show that the only way to affirm these convictions is to repudiate directly or indirectly the established 'clear and present danger' rule."

In their effort to support governmental suppression of free speech, the majority had ignored the "capacity to commit the crime" which, for Black and for Douglas, was for a jury to decide. Hugo became incensed when Vinson, in his effort to affirm, again misstated Brandeis's views as expressed in *Whitney* (1927) regarding the issue of jury review of these kinds of facts. The Chief had written: "No realistic construction . . . could arrive at the conclusion that [Brandeis] intended to state that the question was *only* determinable by a jury." Black's response: "Ridiculous! Of course [Brandeis] meant what he said in both *Whitney v California,* 274 U.S. 337 (1927) and *Pierce v Society of Sisters,* 268 U.S. 510 (1925) that a jury must pass over facts—Maybe he was wrong, but it is unfair to his work to deny that he meant what he said so emphatically." [126]

The Alabaman's criticism, and he knew it, was fruitless. As Douglas had recorded in his notes, the majority's mind was made up. The Smith Act would not be invalidated by them. The convictions of the Communist leaders had to be affirmed. And they were. As Douglas had correctly observed, the Court majority was ready to modify *any* standard in order to affirm the convictions of the eleven Communists. "Five years ago," wrote Black, "few would have thought such convictions possible." [127] But that was before Joe McCarthy and the beginning of the Red Scare! Now even the Supreme Court majority found these "miserable merchants of unwanted ideas" [128] guilty of plotting the overthrow of the government by force and violence—without a shred of evidence ever presented by the government!

Black's dissent in *Dennis* was brief. For him, the indictment for conspiracy to organize was a "virulent form of prior censorship of speech and press." Continuing, he wrote:

> So long as this Court exercises the power of judicial review of legislation, I cannot agree that the First Amendment permits us to sustain laws suppressing freedom of speech and press on the basis of Congress' or our own notions of mere "reasonableness." Such a doctrine waters down the First Amendment so that it amounts to little more than an admonition to Congress. The Amendment as so construed is not likely to protect any but those "safe" or unorthodox views which rarely need its protection. [129]

Closing on a note of sadness, he wrote: "Public opinion being what it now is, few will protest the conviction of these Communist petitioners. There is hope, however, that in calmer times, when present pressures, passions and fears subside, this or some later Court will restore the First Amendment liberties to the high preferred place where they belong in a free society." [130]

The clash of values was prominent in *Dennis.* Opposing Black's view that the

First Amendment had the highest, preferred place in the hierarchy of constitutional values was the Frankfurter/Jackson perception, joined by the Chief Justice, that a national emergency, for example, the international Communist conspiracy, enabled the policy-makers to avoid the restrictive language of the First Amendment. Other than his friend Douglas, few of the Judge's brethren ever contemplated taking his radical position on the question of the absoluteness of the First Amendment; it was, however, one that Black did not change in his tenure on the Court. This is clearly seen in the Judge's last major case before his retirement, also a free-speech case, the Pentagon Papers litigation.

New York Times v United States (1971)
Black concurs

Toward the end of the 1970 term of the Court, his thirty-fourth on the Court, Hugo's health took a turn for the worse. During the latter part of May 1971, the Judge collapsed in the hallway near his chambers, and his clerks carried him, feverish, into his offices. Although he recovered from the fever, Black's "strength was seriously depleted. Disabling headaches plagued him, and his cheerful whistle as he strolled through the marble halls was suddenly missing." [131]

It was at this time in his life that yet another watershed First Amendment case came to the Court. For Black, the litigation started his adrenaline flowing, and he participated fully in what turned out to be his last opinion, *New York Times v United States*. On June 15, 1971, two days after the *New York Times* ran the first two installments of a series of confidential studies of American involvement in Vietnam, the Pentagon Papers, Attorney General John Mitchell obtained a restraining order from a U.S. District Court judge in New York, enjoining the *Times* from publishing additional segments from the RAND study.

Later that week, the *Washington Post* began to publish segments of the Pentagon Papers, but Mitchell also secured a restraining order against that newspaper. The Nixon administration's argument: Revelation of the Pentagon Papers in the media while America was still at war in Vietnam posed a dire threat to the national security. By June 24, the cases were before the U.S. Supreme Court. Less than a day before, the Court had taken the cases on appeal. In twenty-four hours the Court had to prepare the certiorari conference. For Black, the bad precedent had been established: The presses in both papers did not run further installments of the Vietnam study because of the restraining orders issued by federal judges.

Hugo knew that three judges would act, quickly, to restore the First Amendment's freedom of the press to the newspapers. They were Brennan, Douglas, and Marshall, although, as it was uncovered when his papers were released, Marshall initially had some doubt about lifting the restraining orders. Black also concluded, correctly as it turned out, that the Chief Justice, Warren Earl Burger, who had recently been appointed by President Nixon, along with Blackmun and Harlan, would support Nixon's efforts to gag the press. That meant that Black, senior in the majority, had to get and keep either Potter Stewart or Byron White.

On Friday, June 25, 1971, the Court, without Douglas because he had already left for his summer retreat in Goose Prairie, Washington, met to discuss the cases, including whether the Court should hear arguments in an expedited manner. The Alabaman's view was direct: There was no need to even hear oral argument or read briefs, the Court must lift the restraining orders without further delay. Douglas, who had phoned in his view, agreed with Hugo. Brennan and Marshall joined Black. Because it was an expedited Rule 20 appeal to the brethren, there had to be five votes to grant certiorari.

Harlan, White, Blackmun, and the Chief, however, wanted to hear arguments during the October 1971 term of the Court and to restrain the newspapers until then. Stewart's was the key vote: He could not tolerate a restraining order lasting through the October Term; he voted to grant certiorari and to take the case from the district court. Harlan joined in the vote to grant expedited review, and oral arguments were set for the following day.

The order was issued indicating that oral arguments would be heard on Saturday, June 26, 1971, and that the temporary restraints placed on the papers would continue until the Court resolved the matter. Burger's order had a footnote: "Mr. Justice Black, Mr. Justice Douglas, Mr. Justice Brennan, and Mr. Justice Marshall would not continue the restraint, as limited or otherwise, and, treating the application as a petition for certiorari, would deny certiorari."

For Nixon's solicitor general, Erwin Griswold, this timetable was an intolerable one, for he had not looked at any of the forty-seven volumes. Even so, he had to make the case for the "national security" justification for stopping the presses before the nine men the following day. At 11 A.M. on June 26, oral argument commenced for one hour in front of a full courtroom, with Douglas sitting (having flown in from Goose Prairie the evening before).

The government argued, plain and simple, that the publication of the Pentagon Papers would adversely affect national security and that the restraining orders should stand. Alexander Bickel, a Frankfurter law clerk, surrogate, and Yale Law School professor, argued on behalf of the *Times*. His major argument, however, was not the absolutist one. There were occasions when national security could silence free speech and press, he argued before an angry, silent, stern Hugo Black. However, Bickel continued, the Pentagon Papers matter did not rise to such a level of danger to the nation's security, and therefore the restraints should be removed.

After oral arguments ended, the Justice expressed his displeasure at the presentation. He told his clerks: "Too bad the New York Times couldn't find someone who believes in the First Amendment."[132] Felix Frankfurter, speaking through Bickel, seemed to be haunting Hugo from the grave.

The brethren met later that afternoon to reach judgment. From Douglas's notes, it is clear that there was a great deal of heat produced by the brethren. It started when Black "insisted that no notes be taken in this conference as they would be bound to leak out somewhere."[133] Douglas, obviously, ignored Hugo's request and took copious notes of the discussion.

Black could count on only himself, Douglas, and Brennan to argue that the press had an absolute right to publish. Burger, Harlan, and Blackmun would argue for further argumentation in the lower courts, with the restraining order remaining in force. Marshall and White did not accept the absolute freedom argument, but would remove the order if there was no national security threat. Stewart wanted to see the record to determine whether there was a national security danger. Whichever side received two of these three votes would win the case.

The Chief, as with every case discussed in conference session, began the discussion with the argument that the case should be sent back to the lower courts in order to develop the appellate record. According to Douglas's notes, Burger argued that the cases were being heard on a "panic basis" and that, because there was no time to reflect on the constitutional issue, he was "unable to vote on the merits."

Black "disagrees with WEB" and urged immediate publication of the papers. The Judge maintained that "we should not destroy the First Amendment" by approving the use of the courts to restrict the press. Such an action "would be the worst blow to the First Amendment." Douglas simply noted that Black's comments were "my view."

Harlan voted for the government's position, arguing that the "judicial process has been made a travesty—[the judges, including his friend Hugo] have been panicky and hurried." Maintaining that there were "many imponderables in national security and only the judgment of men in the field can be relied upon," the gentle jurist sided with the government. Harlan also insisted that he "wanted to read the documents—he needs the help of the law clerks," and "to write out his views will take time and he'll file [his dissent] later."

Brennan sided with Black and Douglas, arguing that it was a prior-restraint case with the "heavy burden on the U.S." to justify the suppression of the publication. The Nixon administration had not met that burden, and therefore Brennan would lift the restraints immediately.

It was Stewart's turn: He argued that the government had not made the case for suppression of the information. Potter noted that if the publications would "result in immediate grave and irreparable harm to the U.S. or the sentencing to death of 100 young men, this court as a court of equity would have the power to enjoin publication." For Potter, the question was "Is there here any such threat?" Since the Pentagon Papers ended in 1968, he didn't think there was any future threat to national security that would lead to the deaths of young servicemen.

Justices Byron White and Thurgood Marshall also argued for lifting the injunction, although both rejected Black's absolutist perspective. They insisted that the executive branch had broad powers in the national security area, including the right to confidentiality. But, as Thurgood said in the conference, "the First Amendment, when it says 'no law,' applies to all three branches of government. The Executive can't do what Congress can't do. There is no inherent [presidential] power to stop the Times from printing." The junior justice, Harry Blackmun, spoke last, joining Burger and Harlan on the side of the government. He thought there was, in the Pentagon Papers, "dangerous material that will harm this nation." The final tally seemed to be, according to Douglas, six to three in favor of setting aside the restraining orders.

Given the imperative of a quick order, the brethren agreed to a short, unsigned per curiam order, written by Brennan, lifting the restraining orders, followed by opinions written by each of the nine men. Black, who had been very ill, and was, within two months, to retire from the Court and then pass on, had the feeling that this was to be the last opinion he would write. Telling his clerks, angrily, that the Johnson and Nixon administrations "deceived us all this time,"[134] Black set about writing his last major opinion, appropriately enough a First Amendment opinion.

And that opinion was piercing, reaffirming the Judge's view that the First Amendment was framed in absolute terms and was "the very foundation of constitutional government." No governmental agency, least of all a federal court of law, had the legitimate authority to gag free speech or free press. "The First Amendment was offered to *curtail* and *restrict* the general powers granted to the Executive, Legislative, and Judicial branches." (his emphasis)

> For the first time in the 182 years since the founding of the Republic, the federal courts are asked to hold that the First Amendment does not mean what it says, but rather means that the Government can halt the publication of current news of vital importance to the people of this country. I can imagine no greater perversion of history. . . . Both the history and language of the First Amendment support the view that the press must be left free to publish news, whatever the source, without censorship, injunctions, or prior restraints. . . . Only a free and unrestrained press can effectively expose deception in government. And paramount among the responsibilities of a free press is the duty to prevent any part of the government from deceiving the people and sending them off to distant lands to die of foreign fevers and foreign shot and shell.[135]

Frances Lamb, Hugo's secretary and friend, helped him modify some of the initial language used by the Alabaman in his last case. In his initial draft, the Judge's law clerk had drafted—and the Judge had accepted—the following sentence: "the injunctions against these newspapers amounts to a *wanton, flagrant, indefensible, and continuing violation* of the First Amendment" (my emphasis). On the margin she wrote: "HLB, I think we should talk about this. FL." The following passage in the initial draft also troubled her: "And paramount among the responsibilities of a free press is the duty to prevent any part of the government from deceiving the people and tricking them into a war *where young Americans will be murdered on the battlefield.*" Lamb, in the margin of the slip opinion, wrote to the Judge: "and this?"[136] (my emphasis).

On reflection, after conferring with Frances and with Elizabeth, Hugo tempered the language. As Elizabeth recorded it, she also had a few objections to some of Hugo's language, especially the sentence about sending American boys to be "murdered."

> He thought it over all night and this morning at 4:00 A.M. he woke me up and asked, "How would it be if I said, 'Send American boys to die of foreign fevers and foreign shot and shell'?" This I thought great, and the substitution was made. The new line came out of the song 'I am a Dirty Rebel,' which Hugo and the boys used to sing just for fun.[137]

In the first of the two passages objected to by both ladies, the Judge wrote in his final, printed opinion: "I believe that every moment's continuance of the injunctions amounts to a *flagrant, indefensible, and continuing violation of the First Amendment*" (my emphasis). He modified the second passage to read: "from deceiving the people and sending them off to distant lands to *die of foreign fever and foreign shot and shell*" (my emphasis). Needless to say, Black was pleased with the opinion, although extremely angry with the Nixon administration's flagrant use of the judiciary to silence, even for a few weeks, the free press in his beloved republic.

Elizabeth, naturally, was in the audience when the opinions were read by the brethren. She recollected that there was "great tension in the Courtroom, and when it was announced, . . . there were great sighs in the Courtroom, some of despair and some of relief. . . . I went to Hugo's office and told him, 'Honey, if this is your swan song, it's a good one.' He agreed he could be proud of this one."

The Pentagon Papers case turned out to be Black's last opinion from the high bench. Shortly after the announcement of the Court's decision, the Judge found himself, for the final time, in the Bethesda Naval Hospital.

For Hugo, the question in all First Amendment cases that came before the Court was a simply profound one: "Do we have the courage to be free?"[138] He did not fear the consequences of a society that tolerated full First Amendment freedoms; however, a great many of his brethren did. While he was able to persuade some of them, men such as Douglas and Brennan, about the value of an absolute First Amendment in a democratic society, he could never persuade a Court majority. However, the Judge never gave up.

"Speech Plus Conduct" and Other Controversial First Amendment Free-Speech Questions

Henry Abraham, a noted constitutional scholar, has written about the First Amendment in a way that frames the complex questions associated with speech plus conduct that Black and the Court had to resolve. "There is no doubt that picketing, for example, is a vital prerogative of the freedom of expression," writes Abraham. "However, mass picketing; picketing that applies physical force to those who might wish to exercise their equal rights of freedom of expression by disregarding the picket line; or certain kinds of picketing violative of a picketee's property rights or picketing utterly unrelated to a picketee's 'operations'; or picketing in derogation of secondary boycott statutes, is *not*."[139]

Picketing and other types of conduct are particular forms of free expression. The free expression of ideas was, for Black, the bedrock of a democratic republic. Ideas are communicated by the spoken and printed word. However, ideas are also spread by the actions of persons and through symbols that often speak louder than printed and spoken words. And ideas are transmitted, by word, print, and conduct, on the public streets and on private property. Are all these varieties of expression of ideas protected by the First Amendment? If not, where does a judge draw the line when having to decide such a case?

Black was a First Amendment absolutist. He did, however, distinguish between pure speech and conduct associated with or in place of speech. If the speech is a part of unlawful conduct, then it cannot immunize the illegal conduct. "I draw the line between speech and conduct," he said towards the end of his life. "I am vigorously opposed to efforts to extend the First Amendment's freedoms of speech beyond speech, freedom of press beyond press, and freedom of religion beyond religious beliefs. [The First Amendment] does not immunize other conduct in addition to these particularized freedoms."[140] Black insisted that the First Amendment did not "grant a constitutional right to engage in conduct, picketing or demonstrating, whether on publicly owned streets or privately owned property."[141] Although the Justice argued against any kind of balancing-of-rights test when the Court was discussing the scope of the First Amendment rights, he did acknowledge that balancing by the justices could occur "*only* where a law is aimed at conduct and indirectly affects speech"[142] (my emphasis).

There were many times when Black and his colleagues had to grapple with the meaning of freedom of speech in this more complex setting involving speech and some kind of conduct. The judge fought with many of his brethren on cases that involved (1) speech as conduct, such as picketing and sitting down in front of or inside different kinds of public buildings, (2) speech and speech plus action on private property, and (3) symbolic speech, such as the burning of a flag or a draft card to protest a public policy disliked by the demonstrators.

"Speech Plus Conduct" Issues

In July 1964 Black received a letter from Arthur Waskow, at the time a peace research institute fellow at the Institute for Policy Studies in Washington, D.C. Waskow had been studying the uses of "disorderly protest" by civil rights protesters and was angry with Black because of the justice's dissent in an important 1963 civil rights "sit-down" case, *Bell v Maryland*.[143] "The key to your dissent was [your] argument that disorder, especially forcible disorder, leads inevitably to violence and violence to mob conflicts. . . . My research in the history of American racial violence and conflict has suggested to me that certain forms of disorder may act as substitutes for violence and as 'non-lethal equivalents' of rioting." Waskow enclosed three papers discussing his research on the uses and benefits of disorderly protest, hoping that the Justice would be able to use them. He closed by noting how he would "deeply appreciate knowing of any criticisms of them that might occur to you."[144]

Black responded to Waskow almost immediately. Naturally, he had read the pieces carefully but "because we have had and likely will continue to have so many cases involving the questions about which you wrote, I think it would be best if I do not express any comments on your views." The Judge, however, did suggest a strategy for Waskow to use to find out how he would have responded to the research fellow's defense of disorderliness: Read "several of my opinions," Black wrote, citing *Giboney v Empire Storage and Ice Company, NLRB v Fruit and Vegetable Packers and Warehousemen*, the *Ritter* and *Wohl* cases, among others.[145]

Black wrote the opinion for the Court in *Giboney*. Because the Judge was a longtime supporter of trade unionism and the Court had voted to uphold the use of an injunction against a union, Chief Justice Harlan F. Stone assigned it to him.[146] His opinion held that Missouri could enjoin unions from picketing to prevent enforcement of valid state antitrust laws. The case involved the constitutionality of a Missouri injunction and subsequent conviction that halted picketing by members of a Kansas City coal and ice haulers' union.

One local ice company, Empire Storage, refused to comply with the union's demand that the company cease selling ice blocks to nonunion ice peddlers. As a consequence, it was picketed by the union and its business plummeted 85 percent. The company secured an injunction and the Missouri Supreme Court upheld its granting, agreeing that the union's action was a consequence of a combination-in-restraint-of-trade prohibited by the Missouri anti-restraint-of-trade statute.

Black, writing for a unanimous Court, upheld the state court judgments, thereby rejecting the union's First Amendment, free-speech contentions. He maintained, in an argument that found its way into his sit-down decisions of the 1960s, that

> it rarely has been suggested that the constitutional freedom for speech and press extends its immunity to speech and writing used as an integral part of conduct in violation of a valid criminal statute. . . . It has never been deemed an abridgement of freedom of speech or press to make a course of conduct illegal merely because the conduct was in part initiated, evidenced, or carried out by means of language, either spoken, written or printed.[147]

Picketing, he said, "may include conduct other than speech, conduct which can be made the subject of restrictive legislation."[148] The injunction, concluded Black, the former county prosecutor, "did no more than enjoin a felony."[149] Missouri's commitment to end restraint of trade felonies "outweighed any First Amendment interest which the challenged injunction burdened."[150]

While Black joined in the 1940 watershed picketing case *Thornhill v Alabama*[151]—one in which Justice Murphy, for an eight-person majority (with McReynolds dissenting) joined peaceful labor picketing to the free-speech protection—the Alabaman cautioned that the majority opinion was overbroad. In *Thornhill,* while Murphy denied that the First Amendment provided an absolute right to picket, the Court struck down as unconstitutional an Alabama statute that prohibited all labor picketing. Such conduct is educationally sound, informing citizens about economic matters that "were indispensable to the effective and intelligent use of the processes of popular government to shape the destiny of modern industrial society."[152]

Implicit in *Thornhill,* as Black seized on in his later actions in this area of First Amendment speech-plus-conduct jurisprudence, was the idea that picketing could be curtailed if the picketers marched with signs that went beyond the issues in the particular labor dispute. *Ritters* and *Wohl,* decided by the Court two years later, also involved the constitutionality of injunctions issued against union picketers.

In *Ritter,* Black dissented, for "he concluded that the injunction was issued because of the views the picketers were expressing rather than out of concern for free movement on the public streets and walkways."[153] In conference, he argued that the Texas statute's aim was to silence free speech and that was an unconstitutional action of the legislature. In his dissent, Black said that

> it is one thing for a state to regulate the use of its streets and highways so as to keep them open and available for movement of people and property. . . . It is quite another thing, however, to abridge the constitutional liberty of one rightfully upon the street to impart information through speech or the distribution of literature. . . . [The state court, in validating the use of the injunction] directly restricted the petitioners' rights to express themselves publicly concerning an issue which we recognized in the *Thornhill* case to be of public importance.[154]

In the *Wohl* case, decided during the Court's 1942 term, the majority overturned an antipicketing injunction upheld by the trial judge. The judge, using *Thornhill* precedent to guide him, concluded that since the picketing did not involve a labor issue in dispute by labor and management, there were no constitutional rights infringed by the injunction. Black joined Douglas's concurring opinion, which concluded that

> picketing by an organized group is more than free speech, since it involves patrol of a particular locality and since the very presence of a picket may induce action of one kind or another, quite irrespective of the nature of the ideas which are being diseminated. . . . Those aspects of picketing make it the subject of restrictive regulation.[155]

In a Jehovah's Witness case, *Cox v New Hampshire*,[156] decided in the 1941 term of the Court, the brethren upheld an ordinance requiring all those who wanted to use the public streets to do so only after receiving a parade permit from the local law enforcement officer. Because Chief Justice Charles Evans Hughes based the Court's opinion on the "reasonableness" of the permit system introduced by New Hampshire, Black prepared a separate concurrence. His draft opinion rested on the "literal language of the First Amendment," which was "clear, unambiguous, and unequivocal," unlike the murky "reasonableness" standard suggested by Hughes. That standard ultimately relied on subjective assessments by the judiciary, and the Alabaman refused to join such an opinion. "Standards of reasonableness," he wrote, "vary according to individual views. The broad and I might say limitless range within the area of differing concepts of the word 'reasonable' causes me to fear its use in relation to the cherished privileges intended to be guaranteed by the First Amendment."[157]

Black, however, spoke briefly to Hughes, suggesting that if the Chief dropped the "reasonableness" language, he would not file his concurring opinion. To keep his "Court" in *Cox*, the Chief Justice agreed to drop the offensive "reasonableness" concept, and Hugo joined in the majority opinion.[158]

Clearly, reviewing these and other cases involving speech plus conduct,[159] Black always drew back from arguing that the First Amendment directly and clearly included the right to picket in the company of free speech or free press. He never automatically supported litigants who were arrested for conduct that accompanied speech. Anything other than speech, press, peaceable assembly, or religion was not entitled to the absolute protection of the First Amendment and could be subject to governmental controls.

The short answer to Waskow's query to the Judge is that, for Black, disorderly conduct accompanying speech was not immunized by the First Amendment. A town could control such action if it believed that, through such an ordinance, permit system, or regulation—evenhandedly applied to all—it was maintaining societal order. The First Amendment did not provide for the use of any means— here, conduct—to achieve a desired end.

"Speech Plus Conduct" on Private Property Cases

Justice Black believed that if a private town was the absolute equivalent of a public town, then First Amendment activity could be carried out in that private place. In 1945, in *Marsh v Alabama,*[160] writing for the Court majority, Black stated that a person's First Amendment rights in the town of Chickasaw, Alabama, owned by the Gulf Shipbuilding Corporation, could not be denied by the owner of the private property. The town manager had denied Grace Marsh the right to preach on the sidewalks of the town's business block. Arrested by the sheriff, who was paid by the corporation to serve as the town's law enforcement officer, for violating Alabama's trespass statute, Marsh was subsequently convicted for entering and remaining on the premise of another after having been told not to remain.

She appealed her conviction to the Supreme Court. The question for the Court was whether a state can impose criminal penalties on persons who distribute literature on the streets of a company-owned town, contrary to the wishes of the owner, and yet be consistent with the First Amendment.[161] Black wrote the opinion for the Court. Certainly, he said, a public municipality could not completely prevent freedom of expression. Was the private town different? He concluded that if the private town has assumed a "public function," if it has "*all* the characteristics of any other American town," and "if it did not function differently from any other town," then it was the "functional equivalent" of a public municipality and subject to the commands of the First Amendment.[162] (my emphasis)

The sanctity of private property rights, wrote Black, who was from his earliest days in Alabama a defender of the sanctity of the value of private property, does not rise above the free-expression rights in the First Amendment. Property rights arguments, by themselves, wrote Black for the Court, do not "justify a state's permitting a corporation to govern a community of citizens so as to restrict their fundamental liberties and the enforcement of such a restraint by the application of a state statute."[163]

In 1968, in the case of *Amalgamated Food Employees Union Local 590 v Logan Valley Plaza,*[164] the Court faced the question of whether the huge, modern shopping-center mall, a post–World War II business phenomenon that had swept across America, was the functional equivalent of a company town and, therefore, whether all persons entering the private mall retained their free-expression rights enumerated in the First Amendment.

Weis Supermarket in the plaza employed nonunion workers. The owner prohibited union organizers from speaking to his employees through picketing in front of his store in the private mall. After almost two weeks of such picketing, Weis and the owners of the mall enjoined the protesters from picketing on the private property. The union appealed to the Pennsylvania Supreme Court. However, that court upheld the use of the injunction, and the case came to the U.S. Supreme Court.

Justice Thurgood Marshall wrote the majority opinion for a divided Court. Black vigorously dissented. Marshall's argument was that peaceful picketing in a private facility open to the public, assuming no alternative picketing areas available, is protected by the First Amendment. "The shopping center here is clearly the 'functional equivalent' of the business district in *Marsh*."[165] When private property opens to the public, its private character disappears.[166]

Black fumed at this categorical misreading of his opinion in *Marsh*. Dissenting, and joined by White, he pointed to the gross misapplication of the precedent by Marshall and the Court majority. Chickasaw, Alabama, and Logan Valley Plaza, Pennsylvania, were not analogous; they were not even close to being so. The former performed all the functions of a regular town while the latter performed few of the functions of a town, whether private or public. The union protesters, Hugo concluded, did not have a constitutional right to have Weis furnish them a place to protest against Weis's personnel policies. The majority opinion, in effect, took Weis's property; therefore, Black wrote with bitter sarcasm, the Court ought to award Weis compensation for this taking of private property![167] (After his departure from the Court, a much more conservative Burger Court majority greatly narrowed the impact of *Logan Valley Plaza*.)[168]

"Symbolic" Speech

Black argued, in the "speech plus" and "public/private forum" cases, that conduct could be disassociated from the free-expression protections of the First Amendment. Balancing, a concept Black normally hated to use, was appropriate in these cases. The community has the expectation of public orderliness, and its agents can establish protocols, in the form of trespass statutes, breach of the peace ordinances, disorderly conduct statutes, and permit systems, to maintain public order. The First Amendment's liberties are not limited to verbal and printed expression. However, public expression that incorporates some kind of conduct with the speech or press right, whether street demonstrations, handbill distribution, religious record-playing on public street corners, sit-ins, labor or antiwar picketing, and other conduct, must comport with the local ordinances that reflect the values of orderliness and the sanctity of private property.

If there was a conflict between the two sets of values, as was seen in these cases, Black generally selected the "orderliness" value over the countervailing value of discussing public issues through conduct that is disruptive and disorderly and/or presented on private property, against the owner's wishes, that does not have all the attributes of a public forum.

But what about speech labeled symbolic, nonverbal speech? What about a person's freedom to burn a draft card to protest the Vietnam War or to burn an

American flag to protest the assassination of Martin Luther King, Jr? What about a student's right to wear a black armband in order to show her feelings about the war in Vietnam?

The justices heard a number of symbolic-speech cases during Black's tenure on the Court. Three of them—*United States v O'Brien* (1968),[169] *Tinker v Des Moines Independent Community School District* (1969),[170] and *Street v New York* (1969)[171]—are particularly pertinent in developing an understanding of Black's position on symbolic speech. In all three, there was a balancing process implemented by the justices: the symbolic speech arrayed against the government's responsibility to maintain order and prevent harm.

The Vietnam War ripped American society apart. Intense criticism of the war swept the nation in the late 1960s. By the time of the 1968 national conventions, it had become a major fault line in politics and, ultimately, in law. Antiwar protesters generated a number of cases, from mass demonstrations to picketing against the war in private shopping centers to acts of symbolic speech, such as publicly burning their draft cards to protest the Asian conflagration.

In March 1966, David O'Brien and three other protesters, claiming they were "pacifists and as such could not kill," burned their draft cards on the steps of the South Boston courthouse. He was charged with violating a 1965 amendment to the Selective Service Act that made it illegal to "destroy or mutilate" draft cards. A lower federal court ruled that his actions were protected by the First Amendment. The government asked the Court to hear the case, Solicitor General Thurgood Marshall arguing that O'Brien's symbolic actions interfered with the government's legitimate effort to draft men into the nation's armed services. O'Brien's purpose, argued Marshall, was "to influence others to adopt his anti-war beliefs. . . . Terming [his] conduct 'symbolic speech' does not transform it into activity entitled to the same kind of constitutional protection given to words and other modes of expression," concluded the solicitor general.

With one exception, Douglas dissenting, the Supreme Court majority, including Black, agreed with the 1966 legal argument of then Solicitor General Marshall (who was, by 1968, a member of the Court, recusing himself in *O'Brien*). Writing the opinion for the Court, Chief Justice Warren stated that the Court "cannot accept the view that an apparently limitless variety of conduct can be labeled 'speech' whenever a person engaging in the conduct intends thereby to express an idea."[172] A "sufficiently important governmental interest in regulating the nonspeech element," Warren concluded, "can justify incidental limitations on First Amendment freedoms."

A year later, in another Vietnam War–inspired protest case, Black dissented from the Court in *Tinker*. Justice Fortas, for the Court majority of seven, concluded that Christopher Eckhardt, Mary Beth Tinker, and her brother John, high school students who wore black armbands in a "silent, passive expression of opinion, unaccompanied by any disorder or disturbance on the part of petitioners," and who were suspended for their act, were practicing a constitutionally protected symbolic freedom of expression.

Wearing of the black armband, concluded the Court majority, "was entirely divorced from actually or potentially disruptive conduct by those participating in it. It was closely akin to 'pure speech' which, we have repeatedly held, is entitled to comprehensive protection under the First Amendment." Public schools "may not be enclaves of totalitarianism," wrote Fortas. "School officials do not possess absolute authority over their students." [173] So long as the symbolic speech did not lead to disruption, the Court concluded that it was akin to pure speech and therefore protected from infringement, even by school authorities.

For Black, joined by his friend Harlan, the students' action was conduct, not expression, and it could be regulated by school authorities. Indeed, Hugo maintained, even if it were pure speech, school authorities had a legitimate right to control the time, manner, and place of such pure or nondisruptive symbolic speech.

The Judge, in his strong dissent, categorically rejected, in his harshest language, the majority's belief that the wearing of armbands is symbolic speech, which is "akin to pure speech," and the argument that the public school is an appropriate arena in which students can engage in nondisruptive symbolic speech. What concerned Black more than anything was the conclusion reached by the majority "arrogat[ing] to itself," rather than public school officials, "the decision as to which school disciplinary regulations are 'reasonable.' " [174]

> I have never believed that any person has the right to give speeches in demonstrations where he pleases and when he pleases. . . . It is a myth to say that any person has a constitutional right to say what he pleases, where he pleases, and when he pleases. Our Court has decided precisely the opposite.

Clearly, in *Tinker*, Black expressed, once again, his deep-seated fear of what he believed was the natural, inevitable outcome of allowing students the freedom to express themselves whenever they wished, regardless of public school leaders' authority and responsibility for educating students. As he wrote, "groups of students all over the land are already running loose, conducting break-ins, sit-ins, lie-ins, and smash-ins. Many of these student groups, as is all to familiar to all who read the newspapers and watch the television news programs, have already engaged in rioting, property seizures, and destruction." Fortas's decision for the Court, the Justice concluded, as he read his dissent in open Court with bitterness in his voice, is "wholly without constitutional reasons, subjects all the public schools in the country to the whims and caprices of their loudest-mouthed, but maybe not their brightest, students." [175]

"We don't need no damn flag," Sidney Street hollered after hearing that James Meredith had been shot in Mississippi. "I burned it! If they let this happen to Meredith, we don't need an American flag." Thus was the Court confronted with another kind of symbolic-speech issue, the burning of the American flag. The Vietnam War and the civil rights movement in the 1960s forced the justices to examine this issue and make a determination regarding desecration of the symbol of the nation.

The question for the Court, simply put, was this: Was the burning of the flag symbolic speech and therefore protected by the First Amendment? In the 1969 term, the Warren Court had to come to grips with this issue in the case involving Sidney Street, *Street v New York*.[176] After burning the flag, Street was arrested by

New York City police and charged with violating a statute that made it a crime to physically or verbally desecrate the flag.

The justices fought hard on this case, splitting five to four on whether the state could restrict verbal desecration of the flag (it could not) and four to four on whether New York could prohibit the physical desecration of the flag. Black and his friend Harlan disagreed, in this case. Writing for the majority, Harlan insisted that New York had punished Street merely for speaking defiant words about the flag. No state can constitutionally inflict punishment upon one who ventures publicly to defy or cast contempt on the flag by words.[177]

Once again very angry with his brethren, Black bitterly dissented. The conviction rested on Street's conduct, not his words, the Justice maintained. The highest New York appellate court had unanimously concluded that the conviction rested "entirely on the fact that the defendant had publicly burned the flag—against the law of New York State." Writing for three others, Hugo presented a short, blistering dissent to the Supreme Court majority.

> It passes my belief that anything in the Constitution bars a state from making the deliberate burning of the American flag an offense. It is immaterial to me that words are spoken in connection with the burning. It is the *burning* of the flag that the state has set its face against. . . . The talking that was done took place as an integral part of conduct in violation of a valid criminal statute against burning the American flag in public.[178] (his emphasis)

Black, in these "speech plus" cases, was ever careful to tie his judgments to his understanding of the Constitution's phrases and to the plain meaning of the words. He always differentiated between pure speech and speech accompanied by some kind of action, whether picketing, marching in the streets, burning draft cards or flags. His view was that these were actions that could be constrained, lawfully, by the nation, the state, and the locality. Even though speech was a part of the event, the speech aspect did not immunize the event in its entirety. While speech was protected absolutely, conduct with speech was not. The Judge did not deviate from this position, as his opinions over his thirty-four years on the Court clearly indicate.

Black spoke clearly, unerringly, about the necessity of maintaining a working federal system and ensuring that all persons had the wide range of absolute protections of the First Amendment. A viable federal system, "Our Federalism," was necessary to allow the governors to respond creatively to the problems that beset the nation and the states. It is the task of legislators, not justices of the Court, to resolve these economic and social dilemmas.

To do this enormously complex task of governing to resolve societal problems well, there was the equally critical right of the people to be able to express themselves, and to listen to and read what others believe, in an orderly manner, on all issues. Hugo, although personally a Puritan who refused to see *Who's Afraid of Virginia Woolf* with his wife because he thought it was a "dirty" movie,[179] believed in the absolute, but pure, freedoms found in the First Amendment. Conduct was conduct and could be regulated by authorities, whether school board officials, local public safety officers, or the Congress of the United States. A tenuous balance had to be maintained between speaking out and societal orderliness. Black, the reader of history, was ever sensitive to the first inroads to anarchy and disorderliness. He knew so well the consequences of the first loss of freedom in society.

Throughout his tenure on the Court, therefore, the Justice fought vigorously to prevent the American republic from slipping into a tyranny that was the destroyer of freedom. The Founding Fathers were concerned with this historical phenomenon and wrote a Constitution and amendments to try to minimize the possibility of totalitarianism. Hugo Black, the man who in the 1920s joined a band of tyrannical vigilantes, after 1937 was ever the twentieth century's judicially vigilant defender of freedoms and liberty.

Fourteenth Amendment Battles: Incorporation, Due Process, Equal Protection, and "New Rights"

B lack's most extensive battles with his judicial foes—in particular, Felix Frankfurter and his jurisprudential allies—conflicts that were painful and contentious, were those fought over the scope of the Fourteenth Amendment. The Judge believed strongly that the language of the amendment, especially its due process and equal protection clauses, did not give the justices "a blank check to alter the meaning of the Constitution as written so as to add to it substantive constitutional changes which a majority of the Court at any given time believes are needed to meet present-day problems." [1]

It was litigation in these areas that kept the Judge up late at night. On important Fourteenth Amendment cases, as Elizabeth recollected,

> Hugo awakens in the middle of the night thinking about it. Soon he pulls the chain to turn on the light. "Darling," he says to me, "are you awake?" By that time I am, of course, fully awake. "I am bothered about a case." "Tell me about it," I say. "Well, this is what it is all about . . ." Then he recounts in detail and with passion the horrible injustice being perpetrated on a person because of his brethren's failure to see it his way. Sometimes this unwinds him, sometimes not. [2]

Inevitably, Black would soon be sleeping soundly and the following morning would be ready to challenge his colleagues once again. As Elizabeth wrote, so correctly: Hugo "is like a spirited racehorse, held back only by the firm reins of his own self-control, but once on the track and running, giving the race everything he has!" [3]

Black had fundamental jurisprudential disagreements with most of the brethren, liberals and conservatives alike, because of their willingness, in his view, to carelessly redefine the scope of the due process and equal protection clauses of the Fourteenth Amendment. But, while the Judge had very defined views of these clauses, he was also able to work with his brethren to change some of the more onerous court precedents in this area, although not quite the way Black would have changed them if he had had *his* Court.

Should the Bill of Rights Be "Incorporated" into the Fourteenth Amendment?

The Civil War amendments, especially the Fourteenth, have led to some significant and dynamic constitutional interpretations by the men and women who have sat on the Supreme Court. The Fourteenth Amendment consists of a set of prohibitions against state action that would deny a person the privileges and immunities of citizenship, life, liberty, or property without due process and provides all persons with the equal protection of the laws. The clause "privileges and immunities" of citizenship, located in both Article IV and in the Fourteenth Amendment, was thought by Alexander Hamilton and other constiutional-era leaders to be the "basis of the Union" because it prohibited states from discriminating against citizens from other states. However, it has not been given a substantive interpretation by the Supreme Court. The Court has said that the clause "simply . . . require[s] substantial justification for state laws discriminating against persons from other states."[4] As a consequence of such an interpretation of privileges and immunities, civil rights litigators in the Supreme Court since the 1870s have used the due process and equal protection clauses on behalf of their clients. The Justices of the Supreme Court have been consumed with defining and interpreting these two clauses in the Fourteenth Amendment since the amendments were ratified in the years after the Civil War.

Incorporation: The Bill of Rights and the Fourteenth Amendment

Black was absolutely committed to the idea that the Fourteenth Amendment included all of the rights protected by the Bill of Rights. The Bill of Rights was originally added to the Constitution because of the states-righters' fear that the new, central government might tyrannize the citizens of the states. Most of the thirteen colonies already provided protections for their citizens against state intrusions into their liberties. But under the new Constitution of the United States, the central government might abuse citizens through the actions of any one or more of the three new national actors: the executive branch, the Congress, or the brand-new national judiciary, with the U.S. Supreme Court at the apex of the legal process in the new republic. Therefore, many of the states, especially Virginia, demanded the addition of a Bill of Rights, applicable to the central government, before they ratified the 1787 Constitution, with its new "federal" structure of government.

When the Bill of Rights was introduced and passed by Congress in 1789, and ratified by the states in 1791, its First Amendment began with the words "Congress shall make no law . . ." Later constitutional interpretation by the Court effectively narrowed the scope of the Bill of Rights. *Barron v Baltimore* (1833) concerned an allegation by a dock owner that a local government was taking his property without just compensation as required by the Fifth Amendment. Speaking for the Court, Chief Justice John Marshall determined that the Bill of Rights restricted only the actions of agents of the central government "and not . . . the government of the individual states."[5]

Supreme Court majorities after the Civil War maintained that the due process clause did not incorporate the Bill of Rights into the Fourteenth Amendment. *Twining v New Jersey* (1908) was, for Black, the most restrictive—and erroneous—of the Court's decisions.[6] According to the Judge, *Twining* "was the case [involving the scope of the Fifth Amendment's self-incrimination clause] where the Supreme Court took its longest step towards construing the Due Process Clause as a broad permission for courts to substitute their own notions of reasonableness for clear constitutional commands."[7]

Palko v Connecticut, a 1937 decision in which Black participated,[8] addressed the scope of the protection against double jeopardy found in the Fifth Amendment. In an opinion written by Justice Benjamin Cardozo, decided less than three months after Hugo began sitting on the Court, the majority rejected the argument that the protection extended to the states. Cardozo wrote that only a few provisions had been "absorbed" or incorporated into the Fourteenth Amendment because they were the "essence of a scheme of ordered liberty," or because they were "so rooted in the traditions and conscience of our people as to be ranked as fundamental," or because the injury caused by their abuse would create a "hardship so acute and shocking that our polity will not endure it."[9]

Because of his deep respect for Cardozo, Black joined the majority opinion, with its shock-the-conscience rhetoric. He later regretted it. "In Black's early years," commented one of his law clerks, "he had not yet formulated his views completely and . . . was reluctant to dissent too frequently. Thus, for example, *Palko.* In later years, the Judge came to regard *Palko* as one of the worst of all due process opinions."[10] Undeniably, the problem for Hugo with decisions like *Palko* was that the reasoning employed by the majority left the judges free to decide whether a particular right was "essential to a scheme of ordered liberty."

By Black's 1940 *Chambers v Florida* opinion, the Judge was able to observe that, while the "scope and operation of the Fourteenth Amendment have been fruitful sources of controversy in our constitutional history," there had developed a "current of opinion—which the court has declined to adopt in many previous cases—that the Fourteenth Amendment was intended to make secure against State invasion all the rights, privileges and immunities protected from Federal violation by the Bill of Rights (Amendments I to VIII)."[11] From then on, Black asserted this view in his due process decisions until his retirement from the Court in 1971.

Betts v Brady (1941) was the first occasion Hugo had to present his thoughts on incorporation to his brethren—and to the legal community beyond the marble palace. *Betts* concerned a claim to the right to counsel by an indigent defendant in a robbery case.[12] Black dissented from the majority's refusal to require representation by an attorney at public expense on grounds that the Sixth Amendment included a right to counsel and the "Fourteenth Amendment made the Sixth applicable to the states." He wrote: "Discussion of the fourteenth amendment by its sponsors in the Senate and House shows their purpose to make secure against invasion by the states the fundamental liberties and safeguards set out in the Bill of Rights."[13] By 1941, the Alabaman had convinced Douglas and Murphy that the Fourteenth Amendment totally incorporated, or absorbed, the Bill of Rights protections into it. In 1944, Wiley Rutledge became the third justice to join Black's position on total incorporation.

Hugo's antagonist, Frankfurter, just as vigorously disagreed with the Judge's view of the history of the Fourteenth Amendment. For Frankfurter, the incorporation debates raised a critical federalism issue, one that Black was not insensitive to because of his own defense of federalism. Frankfurter asserted that Black's incorporation theory would usurp state control over criminal justice by limiting the development in the states of innovative criminal due process interpretations.

Furthermore, the cautious Frankfurter maintained the view that due process could not be "captured in a neat catch-all rule of thumb."[14] Due process was a phrase sufficiently imprecise that its "vague contours" had to be given shape and definition on a case-by-case basis by the justices of the Supreme Court, creating guidelines for such adjudication. For the professor, these guidelines were those "canons of decency and fairness which express the notions of justice of English-speaking peoples, even toward those charged with the most heinous offenses."[15]

According to Frankfurter, the justices of the Supreme Court were charged with scrutinization of the legal and political history of England and America to find and identify those legal guidelines associated with fairness, decency, and justice, while at the same time restraining themselves in order to "avoid infusing into the vagueness of that constitutional command *one's merely private notions*."[16] At base, Frankfurter's view of due process was based on the dispassionate judge fleshing out in particular cases and controversies the jurist's understanding of the *"English sporting sense of fair play."*[17] (my emphasis)

Felix's subjective due process jurisprudence drove Hugo mad. By 1940, the Judge had clearly rejected that view of due process, for it was based on an extremely "loose interpretation"[18] of the document. "Canons of decency and fairness is not what due process is all about," Black argued. It would permit judges to write the Constitution over from day to day, month to month, year to year, based on what best fits the times."[19]

His view of due process was the exact opposite of Frankfurter's: Due process meant that the people were assured that life, liberty, or property would not be taken from them without a jury trial in line with the laws of the land.

> The clause . . . gives all Americans, whoever they are and wherever they happen to be, the right to be tried by nondiscriminatory procedures and applying valid pre-existing laws There is not one word of legal history that justifies making the term "due process of law" mean a guarantee of a trial free from laws and conduct which the courts deem at the time to be "arbitrary," "unfair," or "contrary to civilized standards."[20]

The Justice, during the 1944 term of the Court, began to show Frankfurter and the other skeptical brethren why he believed in total incorporation. Black wrote the following note to his colleagues:

> Mr. Justice Frankfurter has filed a concurring opinion [in *Malinski v New York*] which construes the Due Process Clause as authorizing this Court to invalidate state action on the ground of a belief that the state action fails to set "civilized

standards." This seems to me to be a restoration of the natural law concept whereby the supreme constitutional law becomes this Court's views of "civilization" at a given moment. Five members of the Court, including Mr. Justice Frankfurter, have expressed their assent to this interpretation of the Due Process Clause. I disagree with that interpretation. Due Process, thus construed, seems to me to make the remainder of the Constitution mere surplusage. This Due Process interpretation permits the Court to reject all of those provisions of the Bill of Rights, and to substitute its own ideas of what legislatures can and cannot do. In the past, this broad judicial power has been used, as I see it, to preserve the economic status quo and to block legislative efforts to cure its existing evils. At the same time, the Court has only grudgingly read into "civilized standards" the safeguards to individual liberty set out in the Bill of Rights. While the case under consideration unquestionably involves the admissibility of compelled testimony, the concurring opinion is careful to point out that this question must not be resolved by reliance upon the constitutional prohibition against compelled testimony. I think this is an improper case to debate this question. The case could be decided without it. When the matter does hereafter arise in a proper case, I shall discuss it and shall also explain why I did not write about it here."[21]

One of Black's law clerks stated the Judge's views starkly. "There were two facets of Justice Black's theory of due process: Facet number one was that due process encompassed all the specific prohibitions of the Bill of Rights. . . . The second facet, equally important, was that due process did not encompass anything else!"[22]

Because of Frankfurter's views, also espoused by other brethren, Black believed that the due process clause, as interpreted by them, was one of the most dangerous provisions in the Constitution. According to him, judges, without any self-discipline, had used and abused the language of due process since the latter part of the nineteenth century. Preventing federal judges from striking down legislation because it offended their sense of justice or their ideas of the freedoms "essential to a scheme of ordered liberty,"[23] meant, for Black, drastically limiting the use of due process to the specific procedural protections found in the Bill of Rights.

Black always insisted that due process was a constitutional phrase severely abused by his colleagues in the federal judiciary. In the hands of roving judges, due process became the instrument for bypassing the legislative process and substituting judicial views for the views of the people's representatives. The continued reference, by Frankfurter and his allies, to the idea that some police or prosecutorial practice "shocks the conscience" was always anathema to Black.

The "Total Incorporation" Concept
Adamson v California (1947)
Black dissents

Black delivered his promised statement on total incorporation of the Bill of Rights into the parameters of the Fourteenth Amendment in the form of a powerful dissent in a murder case, *Adamson v California*,[24] that had wound its way to the high bench during its 1947 term. Adamson was convicted of murder and sentenced to death under California law. In that state, the prosecutor could legally make reference to the defendant's unwillingness to testify at the trial. This occurred at his trial, and Adamson appealed the conviction on the grounds that the Fifth Amendment's privilege against self-incrimination had been violated by California law.

The Court majority admitted that it would assume that the prosecutor's comments "would infringe the defendant's privilege against self-incrimination under the Fifth Amendment if this were a trial in a court of the United States under a similar law."[25] Justice Reed, writing for the majority, relied on the *Twining* precedent for the conclusion that the Fourteenth Amendment did not incorporate the Fifth Amendment ban on self-incrimination into the Fourteenth Amendment's due process clause. He further asserted emphatically that "the due process clause of the Fourteenth Amendment, however, does not draw all the rights of the federal Bill of Rights under its protection."[26] Consequently, because the Fifth Amendment's protections were "secured to him against federal interference," Reed concluded that "a denial of due process does not emerge."

Black's strong dissent, joined by Douglas, made the argument for complete incorporation of the Bill of Rights into the Fourteenth Amendment. He was joined in his dissent by Justices Murphy and Rutledge. They wrote separately because of their willingess to address the privileges and immunities language in the Fourteenth Amendment.

The Judge maintained that the *Twining* approach to due process set the justices free to use "natural law" reasoning to decide whatever the Court majority thought best in any given case at any particular time.

> The *Twining* case was the first, as it is the only decision of this Court, which has squarely held that states were free, notwithstanding the Fifth and Fourteenth Amendments, to extort evidence from one accused of crime. I agree that if *Twining* be reaffirmed, the result reached might appropriately follow. But I would not reaffirm the *Twining* decision. I think that decision and the "natural law" theory of the Constitution upon which it relies, degrade the constitutional safeguards of the Bill of Rights and simultaneously appropriate for this Court a broad power which we are not authorized by the Constitution to exercise.[27]

Black wrote that "my study of the historical events that culminated in the Fourteenth Amendment, and the expressions of those who sponsored and favored, as well as those who opposed its submission and passage, persuades me that one of the chief objects that the provisions of the Amendment's first section, separately, and as a whole, were intended to accomplish was to make the Bill of Rights applicable to the states."[28] He added a thirty-page historical appendix answering Frankfurter's concurring opinion, which was a direct challenge to his reasoning.

Hugo argued that the Court majority had not made a careful analysis of the background and purpose of the Fourteenth Amendment. It was no surprise that the majority was willing to abandon language and history to rely instead on its own "Anglo-Saxon" visions of "natural law" to define due process, but it was time to put that to rest once and for all.

And I further contend that the "natural law" formula which the Court uses to reach its conclusion in this case should be abandoned as an *incongruous excrescence* on our Constitution. I believe that formula to be itself a violation of our Constitution, in that it subtly conveys to courts, at the expense of legislatures, ultimate power over public policies in fields where no specific provision of the Constitution limits legislative power."[29] (my emphasis)

Further, repeated references to *Twining* did not change the fact that the Court had incorporated several Bill of Rights protections against the states through the due process clause, including the right to counsel in capital cases, cruel and unusual punishment limitations, notice requirements in criminal cases, just compensation requirements, and virtually all of the First Amendment guarantees. The *Palko* ruling held that some but not all of the Bill of Rights protections applied. If any part of the Fifth Amendment protections apply to the states, Black insisted, there is no reason under *Palko* why the whole amendment should not.[30]

Frankfurter was sickened by the Alabaman's due process jurisprudence. In *Adamson*, Frankfurter published a concurrence that was really his strong jurisprudential retort to Black's dissent. "After enjoying unquestioned prestige for forty years, the *Twining* case should not now be diluted, even unwittingly, either in its judicial philosophy or in its particulars."[31] He maintained, in direct opposition to Hugo, that the operative question for the brethren was whether or not the trial proceedings "offended those canons of decency and fairness which express the notions of English-speaking people even toward those charged with the most heinous crime." These Anglo-Saxon canons, Frankfurter insisted, were "not authoritatively formulated anywhere as though they were prescriptions in a pharmacopeia."[32]

The professor also stated that

> the scope of that Amendment was passed upon by forty-three judges. Of all these judges, only one, who may respectfully be called an eccentric exception, ever indicated the belief that the Fourteenth Amendment was a shorthand summary of the first eight Amendments theretofore limiting only the Federal Government, and that due process incorporated those eight Amendments as restrictions upon the powers of the States.[33]

Frankfurter insisted that

> those reading the English language with the meaning which it ordinarily conveys, those conversant with the political and legal history of the concept of due process, those sensitive to the relations of the States to the central government as well as the relation of some of the provisions of the Bill of Rights to the process of justice, would hardly recognize the Fourteenth Amendment as a cover for the various explicit provisions of the first Eight Amendments.[34]

In addition, he condemned Black because Hugo's circulated drafts discussed the limited value of a selective incorporation rather than the total incorporation of the Bill of Rights into the Fourteeenth Amendment. Black acknowledged his vulnerability to that attack. Indeed, Bill Douglas sent Hugo a note urging him to remove the one paragraph in which he discussed selective incorporation as an alternative to the total incorporation strategy. "That is a very thorough and impressive job you have done in *Adamson v California*. I join you in it. I would prefer, in page 20, to delete the 'selective process' clause of the last sentence of the first paragraph. I appreciate that you may need it, however, to get the others [Murphy and Rutledge] in. If so, OK. WOD."[35]

Black was torn. He wrote, in still another draft dissent, the following in response to both Frankfurter and Douglas:

> If the choice must be between the selective process of the *Palko* decision applying some of the Bill of Rights to the states, or the *Twining* rule applying none of them, I would choose the *Palko* selective process. But rather than accept either of these choices, I would follow what I believe was the original purpose of the Fourteenth Amendment—to extend to all the people of the nation the complete protection of the Bill of Rights. To hold that this Court can determine what, if any, provisions of the Bill of Rights will be enforced, and if so to what degree, is to frustrate the great design of a written Constitution.[36]

Hugo wrote this segment of his dissent in order to have his views made absolutely clear. He wanted no one to misunderstand his fundamental position on due process.

Douglas joined Black. In his autobiography, Douglas observed, about *Adamson,* that

> in those days we spent many long hours going through the dusty volumes of Civil War history and law trying to ascertain the meanings of the drafters of the Fourteenth Amendment. . . . Murphy and Rutledge, joining Black's opinion in the *Adamson* case, filed a separate opinion that said that they thought that the guarantees of due process were not necessarily limited to the provisions of the Bill of Rights but include other privileges and immunities—a decision with which I, in the years to come, was inclined to agree.[37]

In a handwritten note to Hugo, Justice Murphy joined him in dissent. Murphy wrote in part that "I think you go out of your way—as you always do—to strike down natural law. . . ." He concluded, "Finally, allow me to write that your dissent is exciting reading. It is an excellent historical discussion not attempted before, as far as I know, in the books."[38]

Black's historical account of the meaning of due process drew sharp criticism from some legal scholars, including some of Felix's surrogates in academia.[39] However, Hugo's historical analysis of the Fourteenth Amendment drew praise from others such as Charles Grove Haines, who wrote:

> Your dissent . . . in my opinion deals in a masterful way with an issue that has been one of the major controversies in constitutional interpretation since the Civil War. . . . You have put the matter in its proper historical setting and clearly defined the main issues on which the Court has given divergent opinions for many years. The avowed purpose of section one of the Fourteenth Amendment and the tendency to stray from the path originally proposed and to build up an independent or natural law content for due process of law [have] thus been brought into the open and [have] been subjected to urgently necessary critical analysis. . . .
> There appears to me to be no rational basis for the reasoning the Court has

adopted which puts only a few of the rights guaranteed by the first Eight Amendments within the scope and protection afforded by the Fourteenth Amendment and leaves to the Justices a "roving commission" to determine what rights are thus guaranteed protection from unreasonable or unwise state action.[40]

Adamson laid out the essential disagreement between Frankfurter and Black; these differences were never resolved by the two battlers.

Due Process of Law: The Continuing Clash of Views

At one point in the drafting of his *Adamson* dissent, Hugo wrote and then discarded a sentence. It read: "I think our Bill of Rights should no longer be treated as an *unwanted stepchild*" (my emphasis).[41]

Black eventually won the war he fought on the high bench over the Bill of Rights and due process. By the end of the Warren Court era in 1969, all the significant segments of the Bill of Rights had been made applicable to the states through their selective incorporation into the Fourteenth Amendment's due process language. Moreover, Hugo Black was still around, at the end, to savor the victory. He lived to see his view of due process realized and implemented throughout the nation, although more incrementally than he liked.

Rochin v California (1952)
Black concurs

The Rochins were asleep when three deputy sheriffs burst into their bedroom without a valid warrant. There were two capsules on the nightstand. Mr. Rochin quickly swallowed both of them. The police attempted without success to forcibly remove the capsules from his mouth and throat. They took him to a hospital where his stomach was pumped against his will. The contents were analyzed by the police laboratory and found to be morphine. He was convicted for possession of narcotics and sentenced to sixty days in jail. The California courts upheld the conviction and Rochin appealed to the U.S. Supreme Court, arguing that he was convicted in violation of the Fourth Amendment's prohibition against unreasonable searches and seizures.

The Supreme Court reversed the conviction in a majority opinion written by Felix Frankfurter.[42] The only way to determine whether there was a due process violation, he had said in *Adamson* and repeated in *Rochin,* was to conduct a case-by-case analysis to determine whether the behavior of the authorities "offend those canons of decency and fairness which express the notions of justice of English-speaking peoples . . . so rooted in the traditions and conscience of our people as to be ranked as fundamental."[43]

In the conference session, Douglas noted Frankfurter's conclusion (shared by Justice Reed) that the case "makes him puke."[44] While Black called for reversal on the grounds that the Fourth and Fifth Amendments were violated by California, Frankfurter discussed the case in natural law terms. Felix believed that coerced confessions are not precluded from a criminal trial because they are unreliable (although they often are) but because they "offend the community's sense of fair play and decency."[45] All of the brethren agreed that unlawful coercion was used against Rochin, and all of them, except for Reed, voted for reversal. The debates grew heated, however, when the brethren spoke about the justifcation the Court would present to the legal community.

Frankfurter, writing for the Court, justified the overturn of the conviction because he discovered "conduct that shocks the conscience."[46] Whatever the outer bounds of permissible police conduct may be, in *Rochin* the police clearly exceeded them.

Black concurred in the result, but not because his conscience was shocked by the police actions against Rochin. He argued that self-incrimination was barred because the Constitution's Fifth Amendment said it was, period. "I think a person is compelled to be a witness against himself not only when he is compelled to testify, but also when as here, incriminating evidence is forcibly taken from him by a contrivance of modern science."[47] Then he criticized Frankfurter's "shock the conscience" theory of due process.

> I regret my inability to accept [Frankfurter's] interpretation without protest. But I believe that faithful adherence to the specific guarantees in the Bill of Rights insures a more permanent protection of individual liberty than that which can be afforded by the nebulous standards stated by the majority.[48]

Black went on to argue that "the accordion-like qualities of [Frankfurter's natural law] philosophy must inevitably imperil all the individual liberty safeguards specifically enumerated in the Bill of Rights." In another angry outburst, according to his law clerks, Hugo claimed that Frankfurter's jurisprudence was simply "judicial mutilation"[49] of the Constitution by the unfettered justices of the Supreme Court. Frankfurter's *Rochin* opinion was the paradigmatic representation of the jurisprudence Black so bitterly despised and fought against all his judicial life.

Afterwards, the Judge received a kind letter from one of his correspondents, Alexander Meiklejohn, the noted public law scholar. The professor congratulated Black for his opinion in *Rochin*, saying that his concurrence

> goes straight to the heart of the matter and I'm daring to hope that, sooner or later, what you are saying will have a decisive influence in the direction of better understanding. The philsophy of the majority opinion is, as you say, radically unsound, but it has a very strong appeal to the "American mind," as it now functions.

Hugo answered the letter as soon as it was received, thanking Meiklejohn for his comments and agreeing with him that the "people are going wrong" on the issue by supporting Frankfurter's views of due process.[50] The Judge's task, through his opinions, was to continue to educate not only his brethren but the many publics beyond the courtroom itself, as is evident in the *Katz* litigation.

Katz v United States (1961)
Black dissents

Charlie Katz was under suspicion by FBI agents in Los Angeles for engaging in illegal bookmaking. Without getting a warrant, the FBI wired the *outside* of the public phone he used to transmit bets to Miami and Boston and then convicted him for violating federal criminal law based on the transcripts of his talks.

Charlie's lawyers challenged the use of the tape transcripts as evidence against him, arguing that these were private, constitutionally protected conversations. The solicitor general argued that, so long as there was no *physical* penetration of Charlie's "home," that is, the interior of the phone booth, the transcripts were admissible at trial.

Potter Stewart wrote the opinion for the Court majority. The justices extended the protection and scope of the Fourth Amendment beyond the traditional "property" protections to cover Katz's expected right of privacy from governmental intrusion, even in a public phone booth. A person is protected, under the Fourth Amendment, against unreasonable searches and seizures that intrude into a space the person reasonably expects to be private.

> What a person knowingly exposes to the public, even in his own home or office, is not a subject of Fourth Amendment protection. But what he seeks to preserve as private, even in an area accessible to the public, may be constitutionally protected. . . . What [Katz] sought to exclude when he entered the booth was . . . the uninvited ear. . . . A person in a telephone booth may rely on the protection of the Fourth Amendment. . . . [Katz] is surely entitled to assume that the words he utters into the mouthpiece will not be broadcast to the world. . . . The reach of the Fourth Amendment cannot turn upon the presence or absence of a physical intrusion into any given enclosure.[51]

Black told his brethren that "if I could agree with [you] that eavesdropping carried on by wiretapping constitutes an unreasonable search or seizure of conversation that is forbidden by the Fourth Amendment, I would be happy to agree to [your] opinion."[52] But the aging warrior could not agree, for it would have meant giving the Fourth Amendment a meaning the Framers did not intend to give to the protection against unreasonable searches or seizures. He insisted that the Framers knew of eavesdropping, "and if they had desired to outlaw or restrict the use of evidence obtained by eavesdropping, I believe they would have used the appropriate language to do so in the Fourth Amendment."[53] Pointedly, he concluded his lecture to his brethren by stating that "they [the Founders] certainly would not have left such a task to the ingenuity of *language-stretching* judges." (my emphasis)

"The Fourth protects people, not places," insisted Stewart for the Court majority. This was the key point the Judge could not accept, given his understanding of the history of the constitutional period. Hugo, next to this case-defining sentence, wrote, in the margin of Stewart's slip opinion, *"No!"*

For the Judge, once again a well-meaning majority had—unconstitutionally, he believed—redefined the meaning of the Fourth Amendment in order to remediate perceived misconduct on the part of law enforcement officials, in this case, FBI agents. Rebutting the Stewart presumption, Black wrote, in his draft dissent, that there was

> no general right created by the Amendment so as to give this Court the unlimited power to hold unconstitutional everything which affects privacy. Certainly the

Framers, well acquainted as they were with the excesses of governmental power, did not intend to grant this Court such omnipotent law making authority as that. The history of governments proves that it is dangerous to freedom to repose such powers in Courts.[54]

In Black's view, the majority had once again tampered with the words of the Constitution as well as ignored the intent of the men who wrote the Fourth Amendment. He was highly critical of the Court's transformation of the amendment from one that prohibited unreasonable searches and seizures of tangible items into a judicially altered amendment that, without qualifications, bars a governmental invasion of a person's right of privacy. Conversations, words, maintained the Judge in his dissent, "can neither be searched nor seized. . . . [The Amendment refers to tangible items and to things] already in existence so [they] can be described" in order for a search warrant to be issued by a magistrate.

> I do not believe that it is the proper role of the Court to rewrite the Amendment in order to bring it in harmony with the times and thus reach a result that many people believe to be desirable. . . . Since I see no way in which the Fourth Amendment can be construed to apply to eavesdropping, that closes the matter for me. In interpreting the Bill of Rights I willingly go as far as a liberal construction of the language takes me, but I simply cannot in good conscience give a meaning to words which they have never before been thought to have and which they certainly do not have in common ordinary usage.[55]

For most of his thirty-four years on the Court, Hugo railed against his "language stretching" brethren. While he understood the natural inclination of learned men on the Court to want to interpret the Constitution as they believed it was written, he also saw them do so without reliance on the intent of the Framers, much less an understanding, albeit limited, of the nation's past history. Such carelessness on the part of the justices of the Supreme Court, for the Judge, who was historian as well, was inexcusable. And Hugo was not reluctant to tell his colleagues—enemies such as Frankfurter and Jackson, friends such as Douglas and Brennan—when they were wrong in their interpretation of due process of law.

Equal Protection of the Laws

If the due process clause was a difficult phrase for the justices to deal with, the Judge believed that the equal protection phrase was even worse. Although the Fourteenth Amendment to the U.S. Constitution prohibited states from denying "to any person . . . the equal protection of the laws," the post–Civil War reality was stark, pervasive racial discrimination directed towards the recently freed slaves. It was a discrimination that cut across all forms of social interaction, and the segregation laws that emerged from this environment in the decades after the Civil War formed the basis of Jim Crowism, an apartheid system that lasted well into the ninth decade of the twentieth century.[56]

During the nineteenth century, the U.S. Supreme Court legitimatized the customs and practices of racial discrimination and, in so doing, articulated the notion of two unequal races in America: the superior race (whites) and the inferior ones (blacks). In *Dred Scott v Sanford* (1857),[57] *United States v Harris* (1883),[58] and the *Civil Rights Cases* (1883),[59] the Court majority amplified this racist view of American society. In 1896, the watershed case of *Plessy v Ferguson*,[60] the Court, with one dissenter, Harlan's grandfather, John Marshall Harlan, upheld a Lousiana statute that required railroads to provide for "equal but separate accommodations for white and colored races." The doctrine of "separate but equal" was to remain the law of the land until well after two major civil rights decisions, *Brown v Board of Education* 1954 *(Brown I)* and 1955 *(Brown II)*.

When the Alabaman joined the Court in 1937, he came to an institution that had, since *Plessy*, "seesawed" on the question of civil rights for blacks.[61] Through the middle of the 20th century, the Court continued to reinforce the "equal but separate" doctrine in litigation involving social relations between blacks and whites.

These civil rights cases were extremely important for Black, given the protest at having a Klansman on the Court, including complaints and anguish from close friends such as Walter White and his assistant, Thurgood Marshall, and from others who did not know Hugo at all except for his sordid reputation. However, from his court appointment until his retirement, he always struggled with these cases because of the generality of the equal protection clause and the mischief such generality led to when "language stretching" judges were hearing cases that dealt with very controversial issues.

Early Litigation
Cooper v Aaron (1958)
All sign the opinion

After *Brown* came down in 1954, invalidating *Plessy*'s "separate but equal" doctrine, "the demagogues took over,"[62] as Hugo warned. Without any support from the president and the Congress, the Supreme Court and the federal district court judges[63] who were responsible for passing on desegregation plans submitted by local school boards stood alone at the cutting edge of the legal war on segregation. Black's mail was flooded with hate letters from segregationists across the nation, accusing the Alabaman of being, along with Earl Warren, a "rabid agitator for compulsory racial mongrelization," and of having a sister-in-law, Jinksie, who was a "registered communist."[64]

It was during this time that Hugo's oldest son, found that being the son of a Supreme Court justice who had aggressively supported the end to Jim Crowism was not conducive to a successful legal practice in Alabama. Hugo Jr. recalled that when "Daddy" visited Birmingham after *Brown*, there were always problems. "Invariably, someone would insult him on the street by saying, 'You are a traitor to the South,' or some such nonsense. . . . Then several times during the day and night we would get anonymous phone calls from people who blurted out brilliant things like 'Hugo Black is a nigger lover.' " The Judge was seen as a "hateful renegade" by loyal Southerners.[65]

This bitterness directed towards him lasted almost until the end of his life. For many years after *Brown*, Hugo could not visit Alabama, and his children had to forgo social events in Birmingham and other Southern locales because of the racist animosity that a "Black" family visit always triggered. Hugo was hurt because his family, including Jinksie and Cliff Durr and his oldest son, suffered due to the Court's actions in the area of civil rights; perhaps even more painful to him was the unreasonableness implied in the Black-bashing antics and words of the people in his beloved Southland.

In addition, Hugo Jr.'s family was ostracized, "blackballed," from many local clubs and fraternal organizations because of his father's opinions and his own representation of labor unions in Alabama litigation. Hugo Jr. quite candidly wrote of how he refused to defend black civil rights defendants because of the adverse impact of such clients on his business.

> We were so intimidated by the feeling against Daddy that I knew my partners would be better off without me and I would be more effective somewhere else. I realized I could not keep my self-respect if I kept running from the just side of fights. And I felt that I did not want to live any place where my daddy, who should have been respected beyond all other Alabama public figures, living or dead, could not come home without being treated like a leper.[66]

And so Hugo Jr., the "son of the notorious justice of the U.S. Supreme Court," and his family moved away from Alabama. They "picked up and left town," as the *Alabama Journal* reported, and settled in 1961 in Miami, Florida, where Hugo Jr. established a fine practice and has remained ever since.[67]

The efforts of the school board in Little Rock, Arkansas, to develop a "good faith" desegregation plan, in compliance with the Court's *Brown* decision, quickly led to dramatic confrontation. The school board's May 1955 action, approved by a federal district court judge, which called for integration of Central High School in 1957, was effectively blocked when Governor Orville Faubus called out the Arkansas National Guard to stop the entry of a handful of blacks into that city's secondary school.

The federal district court judge ordered the school board to proceed with the desegregation plans, and black children attempted, unsuccessfully, to enter the high school the next day. The judge then issued an injunction against the governor and the National Guard, enjoining them from any further attempts to intervene with the implementation of the lawful desegregation plan.

The black students once again tried to enter the school, but were quickly rebuffed by the large racist mob that had congregated in front of the institution. Faced with lawlessnesss and action that challenged national supremacy, President Eisenhower sent federal troops to Little Rock in order to enable the federal integration order to be implemented.

Because of the "intolerable" situation in Little Rock, the school board requested a delay of two and a half years in further desegregation efforts. The federal district judge, citing the "unfavorable community attitude," granted the delay but was overturned by the Eighth Circuit Court of Appeals.

The explosive case came to the U.S. Supreme Court on appeal during the summer of 1958. In a special session, held on September 11, 1958, the Court met to examine what was, for Justice Harold Burton, the "first real test of the power of the federal courts to implement the *Brown* decision."[68] The following day, September 12, the full Court affirmed the court of appeals judgment when it ordered the immediate integration of Central High. The opinion for the Court was announced on September 29, 1958.

Cooper v Aaron was a classic confrontation between state and national authority. Chief Justice Warren, at oral argument, pressed the counsel for the local school board, Richard Butler, to address the issue of violence and evasion of legal orders of the federal judiciary by the state. "Can we defer a program of this kind merely because there are elements in a community that will commit violence to prevent it from going into effect?,"[69] the Chief asked.

Black asked the lawyer for the state whether his argument for delaying integration in Little Rock was "based on the premise . . . that it requires a 2½ year period in which state laws purporting to override the *Brown* decision could have been tested in the Courts?" The answer: "Yes, sir, I think that is our position." When Butler told the Court that integration should be postponed until there was an announced, written national policy on the matter, Frankfurter angrily interjected: "Why aren't the two decisions *[Brown]* of this Court a national policy?"[70]

At the conference that immediately followed the oral arguments, the brethren took only a few minutes to uphold the court of appeals decision and issue the short, unsigned order. Brennan was assigned the task of writing the full opinion for the Court. He was, however, helped by Black, who assisted him in the development of the critical opening paragraph, which Brennan grafted onto the body of the opinion without any changes. Wrote Hugo, who always acted to strengthen the workings of "Our Federalism," in longhand:

> As this case reaches us it involves questions of the highest importance to the maintenance of our federal system of government. It squarely presents a claim that there is no duty on state officials to obey federal court orders resting on this Court's deliberate and considered interpretation of the United States Constitution. Specifically, it involves actions by the Governor, Legislature and other agencies of Arkansas, . . . that they are not bound by our holding in *Brown* . . . that the Fourteenth Amendment forbids states to use their governmental powers to bar children from attending schools which are helped to run by public management, funds or other public property. We are urged to permit continued suspension of the Little Rock School Board's plan to do away with segregated public schools until state laws and efforts to upset *[Brown]* have been further challenged and tested in the courts. We have concluded that these contentions call for clear answers here and now.[71]

Black argued that all state officials were bound to obey the law of the land, including the opinions of the Supreme Court. His second modification of the Brennan opinion, labeled Insert B, focused on that perspective: "Article VI of the Constitution makes the Constitution the Supreme Law of the Land; the Fourteenth Amendment is therefore the supreme law throughout this nation, binding on state no less than federal officials."[72]

Justice Harlan suggested and his friend Black "enthusiastically endorsed" a change in the format of the opinion.[73] It was a significant one, calling for an opinion to be signed by all nine justices rather than one delivered by Justice Brennan. Only Douglas and Brennan disagreed with that proposal. Douglas commented that "the new format seemed silly to some of us, particularly Brennan and myself as it seemed to add nothing in substance." [74]

But he readily acknowledged the real reason for the joint opinion, and it was a sensible one: "Some newspaper articles had suggested that perhaps the three new members of the Court who had come on since 1954 had other views on the matter and the Court was being browbeaten by Chief Justice Warren." [75]

After hard work on the opinion, Brennan had a satisfactory draft ready to go within a few weeks. It became the opinion of the full Court and was announced on September 29, 1958. The justices met at least three times, on September 12, 24, and 26, to agree on the language of the opinion. *Cooper* is a classic example of an institutional opinion of the Court, one in which Brennan worked closely with Black, Frankfurter, Burton, and Harlan, in particular, to reach unanimous consensus on this critically important civil rights/federalism controversy. Reading the notes sent back and forth among the brethren, one is impressed with Brennan's willingness to incorporate all kinds of suggestions from his colleagues into the opinion. [76]

Written for all the members to sign, Brennan's opinion began by laying out the constitutional dilemma in stark terms, using Black's words:

> [*Cooper*] necessarily involves a claim by the Governor and the Legislature of a State that there is no duty on state officials to obey federal orders resting on this Court's considered interpretation of the United States Constitution. Specifically it involves actions by the Governor and Legislature of Arkansas upon the premise that they are not bound by our holding in *Brown v Board*. [77]

After determining that such contemplated action was inappropriate in a federal system, Brennan concluded with a strong lecture on federalism, again helped out by his friend's suggestions:

> It is necessary only to recall some basic constitutional propositions which are settled doctrine. Article VI of the Constitution makes the Constitution the "supreme law of the Land." [*Marbury v Madison*, 1803] declared the basic principle that the federal judiciary is supreme in the exposition of the law of the Constitution, and that principle has ever since been respected by this Court and the Country as a permanent and indispensable feature of our constitutional system. . . . Every state legislator and executive and judicial officer is solemnly committed by oath taken pursuant to Article VI, Section 3 "to support this Constitution." [78]

Felix Frankfurter, however, dropped a "bombshell" [79] on the brethren when he announced, in the September 24 conference session, that he was publishing a concurring opinion. Another conference was held on just that matter. "Warren, Black, [Douglas,] and Brennan were furious" [80] with him. The little professor's conservative ally, Harlan, "spent several hours with Frankfurter trying to get him to alter some phraseology but Frankfurter was adamant. . . . He blew up in conference saying it was none of the Court's business what he wrote," noted Douglas in his memo for the file. [81]

The reason he gave for writing separately, said Felix in his typical irritating and imperious manner, was that he had many former students practicing law in the South and his concurrence might persuade them to follow the orders of the federal courts. The Judge, who grew up in the South and certainly knew many more Southern attorneys than did Frankfurter, was initially incensed at Frankfurter's chutzpah.

The professor's concurring opinion, announced a week after the joint opinion was delivered, was a stirring one. The seventy-six-year old jurist insisted that the law must never "bow to force. To yield to such a claim would be to enthrone official lawlessness, and lawlessness if not checked is the precursor of anarchy." Frankfurter also stated,

> The use of force to further obedience to law is in any event a last resort and one not congenial to the spirit of our Nation. But the tragic aspect of this disruptive tactic was that the power of the State was used not to sustain law but as an instrument for thwarting law. . . . We are now asked to hold that this illegal, forcible interference by the State of Arkansas with the continuance of what the Constitution commands, and the consequences in disorder that it entrained, should be recognized as justification for undoing what the [Little Rock] Board of Education had formulated. . . . Violent resistance to law cannot be made a legal reason for its suspension without loosening the fabric of our society. What could this mean but to acknowledge that disorder under the aegis of a State has moral superiority over the law of the Constitution.[82]

Initially Black and Brennan were mad enough to circulate a brief note, drafted by Brennan, to the brethren stating that they "desire that it be fully understood that the concurring opinion filed this day by Mr. Justice Frankfurter must not be accepted as any dilution or interpretation of the views expressed in the Court's joint opinion." After a discussion on the merits of publishing such a critical statement, it was voted down by the brethren, with only Brennan and Black voting to have it formally printed in the *U.S. Supreme Court Reports,* the official record of all Court activity.

In time, however, Hugo came to understand the reasons for Frankfurter's concurrence. At one level, Felix wrote to address the legal community in the South, a community that was alien to him. However, the concurrence did seem to strike a chord, if the letter Felix shared with Hugo was a reflection of Southern reactions to his opinion. It was written by A. F. House, the president of the Arkansas Bar Association, and said in part that Frankfurter's opinion "with eloquence and fitting compassion . . . reminds Americans of some of the duties of citizenship which they seem to have forgotten during these past four years. In my humble opinion it will . . recreate respect for the law and a willingness to act with self-discipline and fairness in facing a new situation which for the time being is not agreeable."[83]

The second reason for the Frankfurter opinion was a much more personal one. Frankfurter, the Jewish immigrant from Vienna, "understood what happened when decency did not intertwine with experience and reasonableness. He had the example of Nazism, when law had been jettisoned by society, the example of his uncle Solomon Frankfurter [who was killed by the Nazis], and of the tragedy of the destruction of six million of his fellow Jews."[84] Black, intuitively, sensed this rationale and, with further reflection, ended his harsh criticism of the Frankfurter action in *Cooper.* As Hugo wrote, after Felix died in February 1965, Frankfurter "loved this country with a passionate devotion and . . . long before I had ever met him, he had dedicated his life to its service."[85]

In *Cooper,* the Court, using Black's strong language, firmly and boldly addressed the question of the constitutional responsibility of all state officials. "No state legislator or executive or judicial officer can war against the Constitution without violating his undertaking to support it."[86]

However, with increasing frequency and with great ingenuity, Southern officials were indeed warring against the Constitution's commands, as stated by the Court in *Brown* and in *Cooper.* Hugo was greatly concerned because desegregation was proceeding at "glacierlike" speed. For the Albaman, it was important to set aside the "all deliberate speed" language, words that had been used by racists to evade, avoid, and delay the end to segregation in the South. However, this would not occur for another decade.

The "Sit-Downs"
Bell v Maryland (1963)
Black for the Court, then Black dissents

The Court was also faced with a very different set of cases that grew out of the *Brown* decision. The civil rights protest movement in the deep South began in earnest in the wake of the black boycott in Mongomery, Alabama, and the death, in 1955, of Emmit Till, a fifteen-year-old black Chicago youth who was killed while visiting relations in Mississippi. (It was alleged that he had flirted with a white woman, whose husband then murdered Till and was subsequently acquitted by an all-white Mississippi jury.) A new strategy was developed by the protesters. It was hoped that the new action plan would lead to an abrupt ending to all the vestiges or badges of slavery in the South. This activist strategy was called the sit-in. It was a tactic initially planned and implemented by civil rights workers in Greensboro, North Carolina, in February 1960.

Sit-in (or "sit-down," as Hugo somewhat derisively called them)[87] demonstrations took place in the South from 1960 to 1964, the year the Congress passed the Civil Rights Act. That act, in part, prohibited any kind of discrimination in places of public accommodation that had some connection, however incidental, with interstate commerce. By the time the national civil rights legislation was enacted in 1964, many thousands of protesters throughout the South had been arrested for sitting in restaurants and other private facilities, open to the public but on a segregated basis, in the effort to force these places to integrate their facilities.

These protesters, both black and white persons and mostly young black high school and college students, were charged with violating local trespass, vagrancy, loitering, or breach of the peace ordinances. The convictions were appealed to the U.S. Supreme Court. The lawyers for the arrested protesters maintained that there had been, in each incident, sufficient "state action" involved with the private discrimination to make the local racial discrimination a "state action" that was in violation of the Fourteenth Amendment's prohibition against such discriminatory behavior.

An earlier Supreme Court majority, in the 1883 *Civil Rights Cases,* had stated that the Fourteenth Amendment was a prohibition against discriminatory actions taken by state agents, that is, police officers, legislators, bureaucrats, judges, and other state officials. The Supreme Court, in the 1948 case of *Shelley v Kraemer,* determined that a state court's enforcement of a private, racially restrictive covenant that banned blacks from purchasing a property and whites from selling to them was a form of "state action" prohibited by the Fourteenth Amendment's equal protection clause.[88] For the lawyers arguing the sit-down cases before the Supreme Court, and for the brethren themselves, the important question was whether or not "the state [or a local subdivision of government] could use its power to help a private owner to discriminate against blacks."[89]

Black was always deeply troubled by the actions of black protesters trying to overcome the evils of segregation in America. While he agreed with them that segregation was evil and had to be eradicated, root and branch, from the community, he believed that the way to make the change was through the rule of law, not marching in the streets or sitting down in libraries and in restaurants. Such action, he believed, would lead to reaction, and such violence in the streets could lead only to anarchy. Though the federal courts were "not as glamorous as the streets," he said to Elizabeth, "nevertheless . . . they are the route by which the only lasting civil rights will come."[90]

Hugo's family suffered a great personal loss in March 1965 as a result of these marches and demonstrations. Black's daughter, Jo-Jo, was married to Mario Pesaresi by a young Unitarian preacher, Jim Reeb. Reeb and many other ministers and rabbis participated in the Selma-to-Montgomery civil rights march to protest voting discrimination in Alabama. One sultry evening, in a small town on the road to Montgomery, Reeb was unmercifully clubbed by four white racists. Taken to a Birmingham hospital, he died two days later, triggering mass protests nationally.

Elizabeth asked Hugo whether they should write a check to help support Reeb's widow and her four children. "I got from Hugo almost a cry of agony and impatience, begging me not to bring it up again [for if they gave a check and it was made known] he will probably have to sit out all those cases. I was contrite."[91] There was no gift, not even an anonymous one from the Blacks. He refused to go to the memorial service for Reeb for the same reason—although Elizabeth did attend the service for the murdered minister at All Souls Church in Washington, D.C.

In addition to his fears that unruly street demonstrations would breed violence and anarchy, Black's views about the sanctity of private property came out strongly in the Court's deliberations about the validity of the arresting protesters. During the discussions involving the 1962 term's sit-in cases, Hugo vigorously defended the sanctity of property rights. In one conference session he argued: "We have a system of private ownership of property and . . . I see nothing in the Constitution which says [that an] owner can't tell people he doesn't want to get out. Therefore, he can call the police to help protect that right. If that right is in the owner, the law must enforce that right."[92]

As clearly as viewing a goat's rear end going up a hill (to paraphrase Justice

Harlan), Black believed that "a store owner as a home owner has a right to say who can come on his premises and how long they can stay. If he has that right, he cannot be helpless to call the police."[93] He refused to accept the argument, based on English common law, that a person doing business with the public had to allow all people into his private establishment.

Black was not without harsh critics, including his once-close friend Bill Douglas, who exclaimed at one point to the Judge: "Retail stores can't discriminate and therefore state proceedings to help them are unconstitutional. . . . I would make the store owner a public utility and I'd overrule the Civil Rights cases."[94] The 1962 term ended with the decades-long friendship between Black and Douglas "under increasing strain"[95] due to these early sit-down cases.

During the 1963 term, the Court heard *Bell v Maryland,* and the clash between Black and Douglas intensified. It was a case involving fifteen to twenty blacks who had sat down at a whites-only lunch counter in Hooper's Department State, in Baltimore, Maryland, in 1960. They refused to leave when asked by the manager and were arrested for violating Maryland's criminal trespass statute, which states that "Any person or persons who shall enter upon or cross over the land, premises or private property of any person or persons in this State after having been duly notified by the owner or his agent not to do so shall be deemed guilty of a misdemeanor."

Bell came to the Court at the very moment the Congress was moving towards closure on a major piece of civil rights legislation, one that had a national public accommodations requirement in it. The justices, very aware of this legislative development that began in earnest after the assassination of President John F. Kennedy in November 1963, were extremely sensitive about the impact of a Court opinion in *Bell* that might adversely affect the actions of the Congress. In his conference notes, Douglas wrote the following:

> The U.S. has filed an *amicus* brief seeking to have us decide the case on the ground of vagueness . . . rather than on the duty of the owner of a business serving the public to serve all—regardless of race. The reason why the Solicitor General has taken that position is that the public accommodations law has not passed Congress and if—as is likely—the majority [led by Hugo Black] will hold that private property is that sacrosanct, the opposition to the public accommodation bill will use that opinion to kill the bill.[96]

For Black, however, the principle of property rights was inviolable, and he wanted the Court to address the constitutional issue head-on, regardless of the possible negative impact on the pending civil rights legislation. Despite the racist or other motivations of the owner of an establishment, if that person was not violating a local statute or the Constitution itself, and if the agents of the state were not directly involved in the discrimination, then there was nothing that could be done by federal judges to change the reality of discrimination. In his conference notes for October 23, 1963, Black wrote: "I deny [contrary to Goldberg's presentation in conference] that people have a constitutional right to trespass or stay on property over the owner's protest."[97] In response to Goldberg's comments that the owner's racially discriminatory action amounts to "indicia of slavery," Black wrote, "I think it is an indicia of slavery to make me associate with people I do not want to associate with."[98]

Douglas also believed in reaching the constitutional merits of the *Bell* sit-down litigation, regardless of the fallout in Congress. For Douglas, as one of his law clerks wrote in the *Bell* mark-up, "This sit-in case . . . presents the question, . . . whether the owner of a restaurant can discriminate on the basis of race and employ the state police and courts, acting through the state trespass statute, to enforce his [private, personal] decision."[99]

Douglas insisted that federal courts, and especially the U.S. Supreme Court, had to intervene—on the constitutional merits—and set aside these convictions because they were manifestations of "state action" that violated the command of the Fourteenth Amendment. By enforcing the trespass ordinances against the black protesters, at the request of the white store managers, the state—specifically, the state courts—was involved in unconstitutional, discriminatory state action.

In a memo circulated to the brethren a couple of days prior to the October 23 conference, Douglas said: "The question in the sit-in cases [is] whether States, acting through their courts, can constitutionally put a racial cordon around businesses serving the public."[100] Affirming the convictions of the black protesters, Douglas concluded, "fastens apartheid onto our society—a result incomprehensible in light of the purposes of the Fourteenth Amendment and the realities of our modern society."[101]

Given the fluidity of choice on the Court, Black's five-person *Bell* majority turned into a minority. He had been afraid he would lose one of his "soldiers" that made up his five-person majority, one he called "scant and scared. . . . Hugo [made] innumerable phone calls and [submitted] many rewrites, both to please his army and to answer the minority dissents," wrote his wife Elizabeth.[102] Although Black believed that Potter Stewart was the weakest of his troops, it was Tom C. Clark who "deserted" Hugo's majority during the spring of 1964[103] and ultimately joined in the majority opinion of the Court[104] written by Bill Brennan. In the end, Black was joined in dissent only by Harlan and White.

The Brennan opinion for a new and extremely fragile majority vacated and remanded the convictions of Bell and his friends on procedural grounds. He said in that opinion,

> We do not reach the questions that have been argued under the Equal Protection and Due Process Clauses of the Fourteenth Amendment. It appears that a significant change has taken place in the applicable law of Maryland since these convictions were affirmed. . . . The judgments must consequently be vacated and reversed and the cases remanded so that the state court may consider the effect of the supervening change in state law.[105]

Contrary to Black and Douglas, in dissent and in concurrence, who did reach the constitutional questions raised in the *Bell* litigation, Brennan was extremely sensitive and aware of the adverse impact a Court decision on the merits might have for the pending 1964 Civil Rights statute. He realized "that Congress under [President] Johnson's leadership was after the Civil Rights Act of 1964. I was so concerned that if we came down with *Bell v Maryland* on constitutional grounds, it would kill the civil rights act. Hugo was just beside himself with me on that. He came storming in saying 'You can't do that.' "[106]

Brennan, however, did just that because of his concern that a constitutionally based opinion of the Court majority would have the effect of providing legal ammunition for the opponents of the civil rights legislation in Congress. He did not want the Court majority to give the opposition what was, in actuality, an advisory opinion as to the constitutionality of public accommodations in light of the value of private property.

Potter Stewart evidently "said something in conference that apparently hit Brennan pretty deep, . . . he implied that Brennan's opinion merely to vacate was an opinion *not of principle but of expediency*" (my emphasis). [107] Brennan's view, that the case be decided on narrow procedural grounds, prevailed. As Douglas noted, in a memo to the file after the opinion was announced, Brennan's opinion "was the product of his plan to keep the Court from deciding the basic constitutional issue of the Fourteenth Amendment." [108]

Afterwards, Douglas wrote an angry letter to Brennan, saying that he had "suffered a real shock when I realized you were in dead earnest in vacating *Bell* and remanding it to the State Court and thus avoiding the basic constitutional question. I guess I underwent a real trauma when I realized that the spirit of Felix still was the dominant force here." [109] Although Brennan did not respond to Douglas's note, it did pain him, as did Potter's "expediency" comment. However, he believed that avoidance of the constitutional question was the appropriate action for the federal judiciary at a time when heated debates in Congress about the constitutionality of the proposed civil rights statute were taking place.

For the Judge, who had come to despise segregation in his beloved South, it was very important for black protesters to know that they "[cannot] continue to break the law in the belief that the Supreme Court will sustain the legality of their claims." [110] His dissenting opinion reflected Black's strongly held belief about property and protest and the importance of reaching judgment on these and other properly presented constitutional issues before the Court:

> The crucial issue which the case does present but which the Court does not decide is whether the Fourteenth Amendment, of itself, forbids a State to enforce its trespass laws to convict a person who comes into a privately owned restaurant, is told that because of his color he will not be served, and over the owner's protest refuses to leave. We dissent from the Court's refusal to decide that question. . . . We think that the question should be decided and that the Fourteenth Amendment does not forbid this application of a State's trespass laws. [111]

Black and his joiners believed that it was "wholly unfair to demonstrators and property owners alike as well as against the public interest not to decide it now." Looking to the substantive issue, he concluded that there was no Maryland law, statute, ordinance, or regulation that "shows the slightest state coercion of, or encouragement to, Hooper to bar Negroes from his restaurant." Absent such state action, the Fourteenth Amendment cannot be used to invalidate the convictions for criminal trespass.

In *Bell,* Black was very consistent in his criticism of brethren who continued to act in an undisciplined manner when interpreting the words of the Constitution or trying to determine the history of the era. He was also very angry with Arthur Goldberg's efforts to read the history of the Fourteenth Amendment's legislative trail as supporting the view that the Fourteenth Amendment, standing alone, prohibits racial segregation. In a letter to Goldberg, in response to Arthur's request to Black to comment on Goldberg's separate opinion in *Bell,* he declined to comment, saying that "I believe the whole tone of your opinion would have to be changed in order to make it the *temperate kind of reasoned argument any opinion of this Court should have in this highly emotional field.*"[112] (my emphasis)

Black's dissent was critical of this type of judicial behavior. Once again he reminded his colleagues that the Constitution provides "no amending power to this Court. Our duty is simply to interpret the Constitution, and in doing so the test of constitutionality is not whether a law is offensive to our conscience or to the 'good old common law,' but whether it is offensive to the Constitution." Justices can only "construe the Constitution," they do not have the authority to "rewrite or amend" the document.[113]

In his *Bell* dissent's closing sentences, he summarized his views about groups taking to the streets, street justice, and the rule of law. Drawing upon his understanding of the ebbs and flows of history, he wrote:

> The experience of ages points to the inexorable fact that people are frequently stirred to violence when property which the law recognizes as theirs is forcibly invaded or occupied by others. Trespass laws are born of this experience. . . . The Constitution does not confer upon any group the right to substitute rule by force for rule of law. Force leads to violence, violence to mob conflicts, and these to rule by the strongest groups with control of the most deadly weapons. . . . At times, the rule of law seems too slow to some for the settlement of their grievances. . . . This constitutional rule of law has served us well. Maryland's trespass law does not depart from it. Nor shall we.[114]

Integrate Now
Alexander v Holmes County, Mississippi **(1969)**
A per curiam opinion of the Court

Almost from the moment *Brown II* was announced, Hugo felt uncomfortable with its implementation order to desegregate public education programs "with all deliberate speed."[115] Knowing his Southern constituents probably better than any of the brethren, the Judge knew that deliberate speed would not work and that there would be both legal and illegal evasion, avoidance, and delay in implementing desegregation plans. And there would be violence because, as he warned his brethren during the early 1950s *Brown* discussions, the demagogues had indeed taken over leadership positions throughout the South after 1954.

The use of "deliberate speed" phrase, wrote an angry Black in 1969, "connotes delay, not speed, and its use in *Brown II* with reference to delay in enforcement of cherished constitutional rights has proven *an unfortunate one.* . . . It is almost beyond belief," he exclaimed, that there had been a fifteen-year delay in desegregating public schools in the South (my emphasis).[116]

By the early 1960s, the justices were continually responding, in a reactive manner, to a variety of ingenious efforts by local Southern racists to outflank *Brown*'s call for desegregation. In their efforts to delay desegregation, local community school boards in the South had developed exotic and distant time transfer plans,[117] threatened to close the public school systems,[118] created "freedom of choice" plans for the local whites,[119] and devised a number of other mechanisms and excuses for delaying the closure of the dual public school system. These included excuses such as needed changes in curriculum, building renovations, faculty and student preparation, redrawn bus routes, teacher reassignment, as well as classroom conversions.[120] An angry and embarrassed Southerner, Hugo Black, had to confess that the "deliberate speed" language "has turned out to be only a soft euphemism for delay."[121]

Ending the dual school system in the South was, as Black had predicted and as his friend Douglas had written, "outrageously sluggish."[122] By 1968, the brethren were clearly venting their frustration at these local efforts to evade implementing *Brown*.

> This deliberate perpetuation of the unconstitutional dual system can only have compounded the harm of such a system. Such delays are no longer tolerable.
> . . . The burden on a school board today is to come forward with a plan that promises realistically to work, and promises realistically to work *now*."[123]

This judicial anger and impatience led the Court, in the 1969 case of *Alexander v Holmes County, Mississippi*,[124] to formally end the era of "all deliberate speed." And Black had the pleasure of forcing, indeed coercing, some of the brethren, including the new Nixon-appointee, Chief Justice Warren E. Burger, to issue an order calling for the immediate integration of Mississippi school districts—without any delay. (Mississippi did not fully comply with *Brown* until 1981, when the last of their school districts were desegregated by federal court order.)

Black was the first of the brethren to review the issues in the Mississippi case because he was the Fifth Circuit judge when the appeal came in the summer of 1969. On July 3, 1969, that court entered an order calling for the submission of desegregation plans from thirty-three Mississippi school districts to be put into effect in Fall 1969. However, at the request of the Nixon Justice Department, the federal appeals court, in late August, postponed the date for the submission of plans until December 1, 1969. (For the first time in these school desegregation cases, the Justice Department sided with the local white school board officials who wanted to delay desegregating the public schools.)

Fourteen black plaintiffs immediately asked Black, in his capacity as Fifth Circuit justice, to vacate the suspension of the July order. Black "wrestled with the Government's and Mississippi's request for a three month delay in integration. The boys [his law clerks]," wrote Mrs. Black, "want him to deny." For three days, Black and his law clerks debated the substance of the case as well as the propriety of one justice acting for the entire Court. "The boys want Hugo to grant the Negro petitioners' request to force integration on September 1. Hugo denied this latter request but is writing an opinion stating his reasons and saying he will vote for immediate full integration when Court reconvenes."[125]

Black's decision not to act unilaterally, although he very much wanted to so act, reflects his great self-control. Although an earlier Court opinion, *Green v County School Board of New Kent County*,[126] decided in 1968, had stated that "the time for mere 'deliberate speed' has run out," that decision contained language that allowed a school district a "transition period" with which to desegregate the public schools. Black wanted a categorical order calling for integration *now,* which meant convening the full Supreme Court for discussion and action on Hugo's remedy. While he felt that there was a "strong possibility that the full Court would agree with my views, I cannot say definitely that they would. . . . Therefore, deplorable as it is to me, I must uphold the [district court] order."[127] Hugo also "suggested to the Petitioners that they bring the cases to the attention of the full Court at as early a date as possible."[128] The plaintiffs immediately petitioned the full Court for a review of the Fifth Circuit action. On September 23, the Court granted expedited certiorari.

The justices discussed the case at their October 9 conference. It was a rancorous exchange. Chief Justice Burger started off the discussion by arguing that, since the school year had begun, the plan could not be put into effect until September 1970.[129] While he claimed to agree with Hugo, Burger insisted that the federal courts could not make the school boards desegregate "between now and next term [September, 1970]."[130] Angry about the fact that the issue was "made a political football by Nixon and others will do the same," the Judge stated emphatically that "there is no chance of getting the colored people into integrated schools unless we eliminate 'all deliberate speed.' . . . the whites in the South will win the battle. [Therefore] . . . [Black] would provide for instant integration."[131]

Douglas would also "reverse summarily" the August circuit court order. However, the others disagreed, except for Thurgood Marshall, who would have issued a summary reversal per curiam because, he noted with bitterness, "argument [with the white racists] is useless." Douglas, however, came to believe, with Black, that arguments were appropriate and that, in Brennan's words, "we should not act summarily."[132] Oral arguments were therefore set for October 23, 1969.

On October 24, the Court had its second conference on *Alexander.* According to Douglas's notes of the discussions, Burger said that he "hoped" the Court would speak "as one voice" in the case. His recommendation: Remand the case to the lower courts so that they could, working with Nixon's Department of Health, Education, and Welfare, develop a plan to "terminate segregation" by December 31. For the Chief, "all deliberate speed" meant getting the task "done," not getting the task "started."

Black again vigorously disagreed with the Chief. For the Alabaman, dual school systems were dead, and integration "should be 'right now.' " To delay, even five weeks, was to give in, again, to the forces of racism. The Court should issue a short order that would mandate integration immediately.

Douglas agreed with his friend, and Brennan echoed these views: " 'Now' means 'now.' " Stewart said that "no more time is available." White would have told the court of appeals to implement the governmental plan immediately. Burger wanted an interim order to come out of the conference for publication the following Monday. Black argued for a final order that "would do away with the dual system. He would not fool around with interim orders." Although Douglas suggested that a committee of three (Burger, Black, and Brennan) draft the opinion, the Chief took it upon himself to write it, with the help of two of the more conservative—and Republican—members of the Court (Harlan and Stewart).

The Burger draft caused instant problems, for it would have given the Fifth Circuit the responsibility for determining the implementation date for school desegregation. After seeing the Chief's draft the evening of October 25 and discussing it with Bill Douglas, Black drafted a dissent at Douglas's suggestion. As the Justice jotted down on Burger's cover letter,

> I began to write after dinner about 8:20 PM and finished at 12:10. Elizabeth wrote out on the typewriter this first draft the following morning (Sunday) and I am taking it to the office where my secretary and two clerks will meet me about 10:30 AM. I hope to get out the opinion and have it crosslisted this afternoon.[133]

Publicly, to the brethren, Black, however, responded sharply. In a letter to them, Hugo indicated that if the Chief's proposed order received a majority vote of the justices and it was issued, he would write a dissent. He closed the short note with the following observation: "The duty of this Court and of the others is too simple to require perpetual litigation and deliberation. That duty is to extirpate all racial discrimination from our system of public schools NOW."[134]

Black spent a good part of the evening writing his eight-page draft dissent. In it, Black reviewed the history of "deliberate speed" and noted that, even for its originator (Mr. Justice Oliver Wendell Holmes), "the phrase connoted delay, not speed." Fifteen years of delay is "almost beyond belief," he wrote. He was dissenting because the Burger order "revitalizes the doctrine of 'all deliberate speed' under . . . euphemisms, in spite of the fact that we have already emphatically repudiated the 'deliberate speed' delay formula at least twice. . . . In my opinion there can be no more disastrous educational consequence than the continuance for one more day of an unconstitutional dual school system such as those in this case. . . . The time has passed for 'plans' and promises to desegregate."[135]

He closed his dissent with an order he would have issued. It began with language that was ultimately incorporated into the final order drafted by Brennan: "Desegregation of segregated dual school systems, according to the standard of 'all deliberate speed,' is no longer constitutionally permissible. The obligation of the federal courts is to achieve desegregation of such systems *now*." His draft order proposed the vacating of the court of appeals order and a remand to that Court "for it to issue a decree and order, to be effective immediately upon entry, declaring that each and all of the schools [were to desegregate facilities immediately]." Given the importance of the task, Black concluded his order with the request that the court of appeals "lay aside all other business . . . to carry out this mandate."[136]

Douglas noted on Black's draft, "I agree." So, too, did Brennan and Marshall.

But Burger, Harlan, White, and Stewart did not. On Monday, October 27, 1969, therefore, a special conference was called by Burger to discuss *Alexander*. There was, in Elizabeth's words in her diary, "a rather sharp interchange of views on the wording of the orders."[137] After the conference ended, there was a flurry of memo writing by most of the brethren,[138] all eager to resolve the matter without Hugo publishing his dissent, which was one that would greatly embarrass the Court.

By Tuesday, October 28, however, Mrs. Black noted in her diary: "Hugo is a winner in the Mississippi cases."[139] Brennan had incorporated Black's draft order into his draft and had that circulated. After some additional changes suggested by Black, the Brennan version was adopted by the Court. The four more conservative jurists gave in to Black's insistence that there had been enough writing but not enough action. They joined the Brennan draft order.

On Wednesday, October 29, 1969, the short per curiam order was issued. Burger, in a letter to the brethren, said that it "resembles the proverbial 'horse put together by a committee' with a camel as the end result. But then even the camel has proven to be useful."[140] The unsigned order was, essentially, the Hugo Black "blackmail" order. The era of "all deliberate speed" had ended. In the final official version, the Court said that "the obligation of every dual school system is to desegregate *now*."

On that same day, Douglas wrote a short memo to his brethren about an article he was recommending to them. He closed with the following observation: "I send this note merely to entertain you, not convince you, which of course make this a most unusual memorandum."[141]

Of course Black was happy that the Court went along with him and that he did not have to print his dissent. Had the votes not been there, the Judge would certainly have published it. However, he was getting tired of waging protracted battle with his colleagues on issues that, to him, were crystal clear.

Creating "New Rights"

Hugo Black believed that the justices of the Supreme Court had no authoritative right to read the Constitution and then to extrapolate from the document "new rights" for the society. He understood well the reality of judicial interpretation of the Constitution. He knew that every time the justices hand down an opinion that is centered on constitutional interpretation, they redefine the words. For the Alabaman, such redefinition had to follow either the intent of the Framers or the correct interpretation of the clause or phrase in the Constitution. In either case, it meant that the justices had to draw upon the realities of history for guidance in a particular case or controversy.

Some constitutional interpretations by the Court are of fairly specific constitutional provisions, such as the free-speech protection in the First Amendment. Then there are some that are much more difficult to interpret, clauses such as "due process" and "unreasonable search and seizure." In recent decades, including the time Hugo sat on the Court, there was another, much more problematic kind of constitutional interpretation that litigants were asking the brethren to engage in:

interpretation of the Constitution to "find" new rights that, it was argued in the briefs, were implied by the language of the Bill of Rights, though the words are found nowhere in the Constitution itself.

Black, the wary, constitutional literalist, was ever on guard against intrusion by the judiciary into what was properly a legislative domain. Throughout his tenure on the Court, Hugo returned again and again to one of his axiomatic principles of adjudication: "it is language and history that are the crucial factors which influence me in interpreting the Constitution—not reasonableness or desirability as determined by justices of the Supreme Court." [142]

To those, on and off the Court, who argued that there was the need for the brethren to interpret the Constitution flexibly to meet the needs of a new age for protection of new rights, Black answered:

> I realize that many good and able men have eloquently spoken and written, sometimes in rhapsodical strains, about the duty of this Court to keep the Constitution in tune with the times. The idea is that the Constitution must be changed from time to time and that this Court is charged with a duty to make those changes. For myself, I must with all deference reject that philosophy. The Constitution makers knew the need for change and provided for it. Amendments suggested by the people's elected representatives can be submitted to the people or their selected agents for ratification. [143]

In this *Griswold* dissent, the Judge also quoted Learned Hand, the well-known conservative federal appellate jurist and close friend of Felix Frankfurter, on at least two occasions. Wrote Hand (and Hugo borrowed the words with pleasure, for he had been conveying the same message for three decades): "For myself, it would be most irksome to be ruled by a bevy of Platonic Guardians, even if I knew how to choose them, which I assuredly do not." [144]

Clearly, for the Alabaman, the brethren were not Platonic Guardians and they ought not to substitute their values for those of the legislators simply because the judges believed that the law was arbitrary or capricious. Hand stated:

> Judges are seldom content merely to annul the particular [legislation] before them; they do not, indeed they may not, say that taking all things into consideration, the legislators' solution is too strong for the judicial stomach. On the contrary they wrap up their veto in a protective veil of adjectives such as "arbitrary," "artificial," "normal," "reasonable," "inherent," "fundamental," or "essential," whose office usually, though quite innocently, is to disguise what they are doing and impute it to a derivation far more impressive than their personal preferences, which are all that in fact lie behind the decision. [145]

Judge Hand, while critical of judges creating disguises for their prejudices, often created his own phrases (as was seen when the Court adopted his "gravity of the evil" test in *Dennis* in 1951). Black was always angered by such license, so frequently taken; indeed, the "catchwords and catch phrases invoked by judges who would strike down under the Fourteenth Amendment laws which offend their notions of natural justice [or implied rights] would fill many pages." [146]

What really raised Black's blood pressure and kept him, and his wife Elizabeth, up late at night were those instances in which the brothers on the bench created new rights rather than merely mauling the meaning of constitutional phrases such as due process (using labels like "shock the conscience"). New rights created by brethren were qualitatively different in that the federal judge was creating a legal value based on the jurist's general definition of justice, and not merely crudely interpreting an existing phrase in the Constitution.

The classic clash between the Judge and the creators of new fundamental rights took place in the mid-sixties when the Court majority discovered, in the Constitution, the "right of privacy."

Griswold v Connecticut (1965)
Black dissents

The *Griswold* case was the litigation in which the Court found that there was a constitutionally based "right to privacy." When the case came to the Court, the judges were ready to reach and create such a right. Although it was clear at the conference that there was a majority for striking the Connecticut law, there was also considerable diversity among the justices on just how to do it.

> The history of the Court is filled with irony, and nowhere is that better illustrated than in the development of the right to privacy. First, there is the fact that what was perhaps Douglas's most important opinion isn't even mentioned in either volume of his autobiography. Then there is the behavior of Felix Frankfurter, one of the Court's most ardent advocates of a broad reading of privacy under the Fourth Amendment. . . . At the same time, the man who (to date at least) has been viewed as the modern Court's most distinguished conservative, John Marshall Harlan II, was one of the most committed advocates of the right to privacy in such sweeping terms that his *Poe v. Ullman* [147] dissent would have suited Justice Frank Murphy, arguably the most liberal of modern justices, very nicely!" [148]

Griswold, the executive director of the Planned Parenthood League of Connecticut, was convicted as an accessory for giving married persons medical advice about avoiding unwanted pregnancy. A Connecticut statute, passed in 1879, made it a crime for any person to use any drug or device to prevent conception. Griswold appealed his conviction, and the Court took the case.

At the conference session after oral argument, according to Douglas's notes, the Chief, Earl Warren, spoke first. His comments indicated that he was puzzled about the litigation. Warren did not believe that the case rested on the First Amendment claims of the doctors, who were called "aiders and abettors." For the Chief, it was clear that the statute "affects the rights of men," but he was perplexed about how the Court could set aside the statute. It wasn't a First Amendment issue and the Chief didn't think the Court could use "balancing," "equal protection," "*shocking* due process," or "privacy" to set aside the statute. (my emphasis) Warren concluded that "this [marital privacy] is [the] most confidential relationship in our society, [it] has to be clear cut and it isn't." He presented, finally, the "void for vagueness" argument, maintaining that the Connecticut statute was unconstitutional because it was "not narrowly enough written."

Black spoke next. The Judge could accept the idea of a use of vagueness as a due process violation but he could find no evidence that the law was vague. Although he was a categorical defender, Hugo could not accept the idea that the case implicated the First Amendment–protected freedom of association because he did not see the statute as "overbroad." With some ironic humor, the Judge indicated that "[the] right of association is for me [a] right of assembly and [the right] of husband and wife to assemble in bed is [a] new right of assembly to me." The Judge said, finally, that "if I can be shown [that the law is] too vague on due process grounds, I can join it." However, he did not see that argument made during the *Griswold* discussions.

Douglas answered his friend:

> the "right of association" is more than a right of assembly. It's a right to join with, to associate with. The right to send child to a religious school is on the periphery. *Pierce* is such a case. We've said the right to travel is in radiation of First Amendment and so is the right of association. [There is] nothing more personal than this [marital] relationship and if [it's] on the periphery it's [still] within First Amendment protection.

Another of the Court's conservatives, Clark, disagreed with Black and joined Douglas's argument. The former attorney general said that there is "a right to marry, maintain a home, have a family. This is an area where [we] have the right to be let alone." Douglas's notes recorded that Clark "prefers that ground for reversal."

Goldberg believed that the state could not regulate intimate marital relationships. He said that there was "no *compelling* state reason in that circumstance justifying the statute." He argued in conference, although his concurring opinion spoke to other reasons, that the overturn could be "related to 1st amendment rights of association. . . ."

Stewart, who was to join Hugo in dissent, countered that he couldn't "find anything in the 1st, 2nd, 4th, 5th, 9th or other amendments [to justify overturn of the Connecticut statute]. So I have to affirm." Both Harlan and White argued for overturn of the Connecticut statute and the setting aside of Griswold's conviction. They were to write concurring opinions that presented a "natural justice" justification for setting aside the conviction.

Douglas, given the assignment to write for the Court, considered the conference session discussions and concluded that the greatest agreement in the Court's position seemed to surround the First Amendment freedom of association claims. Griswold and the married couple had been denied their First Amendment right to associate and to receive information, both spoken and written, about birth control.

His first draft was written to reflect what he thought was a consensus on the issue. The draft began with the court's 1958 proposition that the First Amendment implies a right of freedom of association and privacy in those associations.[149] No association is more fundamental or more important to the society than the marital one.

Douglas sent the draft on to Brennan for comment. Brennan quickly responded with a lengthy note encouraging Douglas to expand his approach and not to argue the case on the First Amendment justification alone. Brennan wrote, interestingly at the urging of his law clerk, a very substantial letter.

> I should like to suggest a substantial change in emphasis for your consideration. . . . I hesitate to bring the husband-wife relationship within the right to association we have constructed in the First Amendment context. . . . I would prefer a theory based on privacy, which, as you point out, is the real interest vindicated here. . . . Instead of expanding the First Amendment right of association to include marriage, *why not say that what has been done for the First Amendment can also be done for some of the other fundamental guarantees of the Bill of Rights?* In other words, where fundamentals are concerned, the Bill of Rights guarantees are but expressions or examples of those rights, and do not preclude applications or extensions of those rights to situations unanticipated by the Framers. . . . The Connecticut statute would, on this reasoning, run afoul of the right to privacy created out of the Fourth Amendment, together with the Third, . . . Taken together, those amendments indicate a fundamental concern with the sanctity of the home and the right of the individual to be let alone. . . . It is plain that, in our civilization, the marital relationship above all else is endowed with privacy. . . . With this change of emphasis, . . . I think there is a better chance it will command a Court.[150] (my emphasis)

Douglas accepted virtually all of Brennan's suggestions and dramatically expanded the opinion to develop the right-of-privacy concept. The Brennan camp was ecstatic. "This is a signal victory," wrote his clerk in a memo to Brennan on April 26, 1965.

> [Your draft] approach is, I think, substantially in accord with your note of April 24. . . . The penumbra stuff can perhaps be explained as interpretation of the Amendments to include things not literally enumerated, to avoid attack by Justices Black and Stewart that "emanations" are as much to be avoided as straight substantive due process.[151]

The finished opinion was more in line with Brennan's note to Douglas, indicating that just as the First Amendment suggested a freedom of association not found in the written Constitution, so there was a constitutionally protected right of privacy, emanating from a number of Amendments (the First, Third, Fourth, Fifth, and the Ninth) in the Bill of Rights. The "specific guarantees in the Bill of Rights have penumbras formed by emanations from those guarantees that help give them life and substance. . . . [V]arious guarantees create zones of privacy."[152] In the final analysis, Douglas agreed with Brennan that the essence of the opinion had to focus on the marital relationship—and he was some kind of expert on that issue for he was to marry four times. Douglas wrote:

> We deal with a right of privacy older than the Bill of Rights—older than our political parties, older than our school system. Marriage is a coming together for better or for worse, *hopefully* enduring, and intimate to the degree of being sacred. It is an association that promotes a way of life, not causes; a harmony in living, not political faiths; a bilateral loyalty, not commercial or social projects. Yet is for as noble a purpose as any involved in our prior decisions.[153] (my emphasis)

Justice Goldberg wrote a concurring opinion that, much like Douglas's, rested on an "implied rights" jurisprudence. Goldberg had originally intended merely to join Douglas's majority opinion, but Earl Warren came to see him and changed his mind.

The Chief and Douglas had been at odds for over a year. It was a personal clash that led to the two men not speaking to each other. Warren was very uncomfortable with the thought of joining Douglas's opinion. In *Griswold* this clash created a problem because there were only four votes for the Court's opinion, although there was a clear majority to strike down the statute. Goldberg offered to write a concurrence in which he could join Douglas, one that would stress the Ninth Amendment argument. Warren agreed to this strategy because it would mean that he would not have to "join" Douglas's opinion.

The Goldberg opinion focused on the Ninth Amendment's Pandoralike words. He argued, with Warren joining him, that the Ninth Amendment "shows a belief of the Constitution's authors that fundamental rights exist [such as the right of marital privacy] that are not expressly enumerated in the first Eight Amendments and an intent that the list of rights included there not be deemed exhaustive."[154] He believed that the judges "must look to the traditions and collective conscience of the people to determine whether a principle is so rooted there as to be ranked as fundamental."[155]

Black, who wrote a stinging dissent in *Griswold,* almost went ballistic over Goldberg's "shocking doctrine," especially the "collective conscience" catch-phrase. He asked, rhetorically, how do we discover this "collective conscience," for "our Court certainly has no machinery with which to take a Gallup Poll in order to determine the 'collective . . . conscience' of our people." Black's dissent had to confront two different yet similar jurisprudential arguments presented by the majority, Justice Goldberg's, and that of White and Harlan. Black's dissent was much more critical of them, especially the latter two, White and Harlan, who used "natural law" reasoning to justify judicial invalidation of the Connecticut statute.

For Black and for Stewart, who joined the Alabaman in dissent, the law was bad and even stupid, but that judgment was not a reason to strike it down as unconstitutional. "I like my privacy as well as the next one," the Judge wrote, "but I am nevertheless compelled to admit that government has a right to invade it unless prohibited by some specific constitutional provision."[156] As he stated in the conference session, Black could not accept the First Amendment argument as the rationale for overturning the statute. The people in the Planned Parenthood clinic were engaged in action. There was conduct that could legitimately be controlled by Connecticut. Speech was not being punished, conduct was. And he thought that the Fourth Amendment "privacy" argument was specious. As he said from the bench when he read his dissent: "The constitutional right of privacy is not found in the Constitution." He wrote

It belittles that [Fourth] Amendment to talk about it as though it protects nothing but "privacy." . . . One of the most effective ways of diluting or expanding a constitutionally guaranteed right is to substitute for the crucial word or words of a constitutional guarantee another word, more or less flexible and more or less restricted in its meaning. This fact is well illustrated by the use of the term "right of privacy" as a comprehensive substitute for the Fourth Amendment's guarantee against "unreasonable searches and seizures." "Privacy" is a broad, abstract, and ambiguous concept.[157]

Again, as in so many opinions Black wrote, his central message was that the Court majority had no business departing from the clear language of the Constitution. "My disagreement with the Court's opinion holding that there is such a violation here is a narrow one, relating to the application of the First Amendment to the facts and circumstances of this particular case. But my disagreement with Brothers Harlan, White and Goldberg is more basic."[158]

White and Black's friend Harlan were guilty of the worst sins of the past, unpardonable jurisprudential errors that Frankfurter had mastered during his tenure on the court: the use of the "natural law" language of the due process clause to strike down duly enacted legislation. "Indeed," Hugo said, "Brother White appears to have gone beyond past pronouncements of the natural law due process theory. . . . [Quoting Justice Iredell in a 1798 case involving another Connecticut statute] The ideas of natural justice are regulated by no fixed standard: the ablest and the purest men have differed upon the subject. . . ."[159]

And Black, with rapierlike deftness, condemned Goldberg's fantastic use of the Ninth Amendment: "The recent discovery that the Ninth Amendment as well as the Due Process Clause can be used by this Court as authority to strike down all state legislation which this Court thinks violates 'fundamental principles of liberty and justice,' or is contrary to the traditions and [collective] conscience of our people.' "

Black did, however, have some final comments about the calls for new rights in order for the brethren to "keep the Constitution in tune with the times." This was, he maintained, a doctrine that lacked constitutional legitimacy and struck at the heart of representative democracy in his republic. "The Constitution makers knew the need for change and provided for it. . . . That method of change was good enough for our Fathers, and being somewhat old-fashioned I must add it is good enough for me,"[160] paraphrasing the concluding lines from the popular song he first began singing in Sunday school some sixty years earlier, "Give Me That Old Time Religion."

After the decision was announced, the *Christian Science Monitor* editorialized about America's "PRICELESS PRIVACY" and lauded the Court decision in *Griswold*.[161] It stated that *Griswold* "strengthen[ed] the right of privacy in general." Black, still fuming over his brethren's jurisprudential sloppiness, saw the editorial and, before he had it filed, wrote on the page, "This shows how even Editors who should know better are satisfied with any constitutional interpretation that may further beliefs of theirs."[162]

Again and again, one has to marvel at the self-discipline of the Judge. While his brethren were striking down statutes they thought "evil," Hugo was reminding them, and the nation, that they were acting in a manner that went beyond the bounds of constitutional legitimacy. But in this area of new rights, Black had been defeated; the Judge would leave the Court six years later having failed to convince the Court majority of its errors.

Harper v Virginia Board of Elections was another contentious 1965 case heard by the Court, one in which Black again dissented from his roving brethren. In this case, the majority broadened, substantively, another clause of the Fourteenth Amendment. In this poll tax litigation, the majority enhanced the scope and operation of the equal protection clause. In an opinion written by his friend Douglas, the Court said that "a State violates the Equal Protection clause of the Fourteenth Amendment whenever it makes the affluence of the voter or payment of any fee an electoral standard." [163]

While Hugo disliked the poll tax as much as he disliked the Connecticut anti-contraceptives statute, "this is not in my judgment a justifiable reason for holding this poll tax unconstitutional." [164] These mid-sixties disputes between Black and the brethren, especially with his once-close colleague Douglas, were very painful for the Judge. Black felt terrible, for these clashes were matters "he felt very strongly on—not just the demise of the poll tax, but of Bill Douglas's splitting with him and 'writing new law' by construing it under the Equal Protection clause. He, Bill, had pushed Hugo unmercifully on this case all week and Hugo was relieved after it came down." [165]

Black had joined the Court in 1937 when a quartet of justices were substituting their social and economic values for those of the elected New Dealers in the White House and in Congress, doing so under the rubric of substantive due process. In his final years on the Court, Black saw another quartet, more liberal and more inclined to defend individual rights against governmental abuses, but nevertheless acting under the rubric of an expansionist "natural law" due process and, "substantive" equal protection jurisprudence.

Adding insult to injury, the liberal majority was creating new rights such as the "right of privacy" in their effort to invalidate what they thought were bad or evil statutes. "Déjà vu all over again" was the Judge's impression, one that he shared with his wife late at night in these last years. And the graceful Elizabeth, more frequently in the final five years of the Judge's tenure on the Court, would suggest a bit of bourbon to try to get her Hugo back to sleep.

CHAPTER TEN

The Enduring Legacy

A s his first law clerk, Buddy Cooper, said, Hugo Black had a brilliant "mind and . . . psyche." When dealing with him, as his wife said, one experienced "the raw, naked force of Hugo's intellect and will, usually concealed beneath [a] kind, gentle exterior."[1] Always intensely focused on the task at hand, whether educating a son or a grandson, attacking a venal corporation owner or a corporate manager in a Senate hearing, or writing the opinion for the Court, Black hardly ever acted incautiously. This was so when he addressed his last problem: his own mortality.

The Death of the Judge

Black had completed his opinion in the Pentagon Papers case in late June 1971. He was happy with what he wrote but he knew it was his swan song. He knew it was time for him to die.

Hugo needed assistance getting around. He was very weak and refused to take nourishment. His weight had plummeted from 145 to 115 pounds in a few months. His eyesight was almost gone. He had temporal arteritis, a very painful inflammation of the arteries in his head; the medication, prednisone, was not working. Black was eighty-five years old, but he was not a healthy old man.

Some time earlier, he had informed Hugo Jr., "I would know when I had to get off the Court." In July, he told his son that "the time has come."[2] After some "deep soul searching,"[3] he concluded that he no longer had the strength and the capability to continue to actively serve on the Court, or even to continue to live. No one could change his mind. Few people ever did.

And so, in mid-July, the Judge wrote a sad letter to Sterling's daughter Ann "in which he virtually announced he was dying."[4] At about this time, Jo-Jo called Hugo Jr. to tell her older brother that Daddy was ready to die.[5]

The son flew up from Florida to see the Judge and tried to get Hugo to snap out of his blue mood. To no avail. " 'Face reality, Son,' " said the father, quietly, to his oldest child. Already, Black, with the help of a former law clerk, Louis Oberdorfer, at the time serving as a federal district court judge, had drafted a retirement letter that was to be delivered to President Richard M. Nixon when Hugo gave the word.

By late July 1971, Black was in and out of the Bethesda Naval Hospital. Elizabeth, caring for her ninety-three-year-old mother who was dying of cancer (and who would pass away in December 1971) as well as her eighty-five-year-old husband, was both physically and mentally exhausted. Two dear persons in her life were dying. She noted, so sadly, that her Hugo was "joyless and apathetic."[6] She also wrote in her diary that her husband was quietly sitting "staring into space, his eyes looking like deep liquid pools. . . . Hugo spent all morning in bed staring starkly into space. . . . He really is morose . . . and blue."[7]

By this time, the dog days of late August, in Washington, D.C., Hugo Jr. was very reluctantly burning the Judge's conference notes at his father's insistence. By the end of August, Hugo was in Bethesda for the last time. The Judge's children were summoned and watched over their father, by then extremely frail and weak, no longer the stern taskmaster of their early and middle years. On September 11, Elizabeth celebrated her fourteenth wedding anniversary in Bethesda sitting next to her nearly comatose Hugo.

Six days later, Elizabeth typed in the date, September 17, 1971, on Hugo's already-prepared letter of retirement, sealed it, and gave it to Hugo Jr. for delivery to President Nixon. Black had her give a copy of the retirement letter to the Chief so that Burger could distribute it to the brethren. During his last days, other than a very brief visit by Burger, who paid his respects to Black and his fellow jurist Harlan (also hospitalized in Bethesda at that time), the Judge did not see any of his colleagues on the Court. He did not want them to remember him in such terrible physical and mental condition.

On Saturday, September 25, 1971, after suffering a small stroke earlier in the week, Hugo Black died at one o'clock in the morning. On Tuesday, September 28, 1971, there was a memorial service for the Judge at the National Cathedral in Washington. Hugo's favorite hymns were sung and his favorite Bible passages read.

Duncan Howlett, a friend of Hugo's who was a Unitarian minister, then read passages from some of the Greek and Roman classics that the Judge loved so much, especially "Virgil's Song." Long before, in 1957, the Judge had told Elizabeth it was " 'one of the most beautiful things I have ever read . . . it expresses my feelings so exactly that I want it read at my own funeral. . . . Should that remote and unlikely event ever occur,' " he said, "in mock seriousness."[8] As the minister read the piece, tears came to Elizabeth's eyes just as they did the first time she'd heard the words, almost twenty years earlier, when the Judge read them, standing at her desk in his chambers.[9]

As Virgil sweetly sings, let the sweet muses lead me to their soft retreats, their living fountains, and melodious groves where I may dwell remote from care, master of myself, and under no necessity of doing every day what my heart condemns. Let me no more be seen in the wrangling forum, a pale and anxious candidate for precarious fame; and let not the tumult of visitors crowding to my levee, nor the eager haste of officious freedmen disturb my morning rest. Let me live free from solicitude, a stranger to the art of promising legacies, in order to buy the friendship of the great. And when Nature shall give the signal to retire, may I possess no more than I may bequeath to whom I will. At my funeral let no token of sorrow be seen, no pompous mockery of woe. Crown me with chaplets, strew flowers on my grave, and let my friends erect no vain memorial to tell where my remains are lodged.

After the memorial service, the Judge was buried in Arlington National Cemetery, next to his first wife, Josephine. (When Elizabeth died almost two decades later, she, too, was buried beside her beloved Hugo.) His favorite Bible passage, I Corinthians 13, was read at the gravesite by Howlett: "And now abideth faith, hope, and charity, these three; but the greatest of these is charity." Howlett, however, did what the Judge often did when reciting I Corinthians 13. He substituted the word "love" for "charity," and so the minister and friend concluded: "And now abideth faith, hope, and love, these three; but the greatest of these is love."

The nation began to mourn the passing of this great American jurist immediately. Black's very familiar fast-paced walk down the Court's corridors would no longer be seen, and the Civil War tunes he whistled would no longer be heard by the clerks, brethren, marshalls, and other members of the Court family. But his legacy to the America he loved remains.

The Enduring Legacy

Do we know what kind of man the Judge was? Yes. Although Hugo Black was an intensely, private person, totally in control of every action, there is enough evidence to be able to put together a portrait of the complex man without getting into psychoanalysis of the dead. The characteristics that contributed to his greatness as a lawyer, senator, and jurist also explained his behavior as a father, husband, and friend.

Hugo loved four women in his life: his mother, Josephine and Elizabeth, and, finally, his daughter, Jo-Jo. Hugo was also a stern father and grandfather to the boys in his life: Hugo Jr., Sterling, and their sons.

The Judge had his shares of prejudices. He accepted, throughout his lifetime, many of the values of his generation growing up in the South. He was a sexist as well as a homophobe, and, living in a Jim Crow society even after he moved to Washington in 1927, Hugo was also a racist. He listened to the traveling Populists when he was five. He attended every political rally held in the Ashland town square. Hugo was not, as he said when he was four years old, a "t'ird partyite," he was always "a Democrat."

Black was also aware of the horror of the crop-lien system, and the Judge knew that his father's comparative wealth was due to the misfortune of others. The crop-lien pattern reflected, for Hugo, the paradox his beloved South had not yet successfully confronted: Rich in resources, both human and material, the South was unable to tap them in positive, creative ways. When that happened, the

Judge predicted, there would emerge a New South, one that transcended the racism and the ignorance of the region as it existed during his life.

Hugo abhorred alcoholics, including his father. And the Judge never took to hippies, unshaven beatniks, and all those young people who actively challenged the war in Vietnam or took to the streets to demonstrate against racism and the continuing evils of segregation. They were ill-mannered and ridiculed what he valued most: the rule of law.

Born and growing up in the South at the very height of Jim Crowism, Ku Klux Klanism, and nativism, Black at first accepted the racist beliefs at the heart of these movements. He didn't really begin to "rebel" against the traditions and customs of the South until after he left Birmingham, Alabama, for Washington, D.C., in 1927 to become a United States senator. Yet, paradoxically, Hugo also knew that institutional inequality was wrong, that it went against every religious precept he cherished, and, in the end, he concluded that the Constitution prohibited such discrimination. He came to believe, vigorously, that every vestige of slavery, all the beliefs in racial inferiority, had to be destroyed in order for the national community to progress. The epitome of a very successful political pragmatist, Black became the archetypal jurist committed to a vision about the future of the American experiment in republicanism.[10]

He always treated women much differently than men; in a fundamental way he treated women as less significant. While Black had fifty-four law clerks, he selected only one woman to be his clerk over his thirty-four-year tenure on the Court, and she was the daughter of an old friend from New Deal days, Tommy Corcoran. As it turned out, the appointment was a mistake, and there were a few times during her year of service when Hugo came close to dismissing her. He never contemplated hiring another female law clerk after his troubles with Margaret during the 1966 term.

He placed the women he loved on pedestals, another Southern habit, and for one of them—his first wife, Josephine—that treatment may have contributed to her inability to deal with the rough-and-tumble political life and with her husband's enormous self-assertiveness. His daughter and his second wife, however, were much stronger and more secure. He wanted his daughter, Jo-Jo, to attend Sweet Briar College, a nice "finishing-school" educational institution that his wife Josephine had attended a generation earlier. However, Jo-Jo graduated from Swarthmore and, to Hugo's muted chagrin, married a Catholic man in a Unitarian service.

The Judge took enormous pride in his writing. He labored mightily, throughout his tenure on the Court, to produce opinions that could be comprehended by the farmer behind the plow. Writing took all the skills of good lawyering. Because of his outstanding record in earlier life as a police court judge, a county prosecutor, and as the most successful lawyer in Alabama, Black had a "genuine [lawyer's] instinct for the heart of the matter, 'what is really involved.' "[11] Hugo would read his opinions to two laypersons whenever he could. He always asked them, " 'Were you able to understand what the case was about, and the meaning of every word I used?' " His preferred audience? His wife Elizabeth and Spencer Campbell, Black's African-American messenger.[12]

When Roosevelt won the 1932 presidential election, handily trouncing Hoover, Black was ecstatic. His friend William O. Douglas, who joined Roosevelt's New Deal administrative agency team in the early 1930s, described that era in glowing terms, recalling that "these were . . . heady days . . . when Washington, D.C., teemed with brave dreams and bold experiments." [13] Hugo agreed with Douglas's remembrance of that period. After the conservative Coolidge and Hoover administrations, the new Democratic leadership brought to Black, and millions of others, visions of progress after the dark era of the Depression. For the Alabaman, FDR's New Deal provided the hope that average Americans needed.

Paradoxically, the new administration did not think highly of Senator Black's talent and energy at first. Although he was bright, decisive, and innovative, the Alabaman, throughout his life, was constantly underrated by his peers when they first met him. These early perceptions of the Judge were very quickly set aside only to reappear again when he entered a new political arena.

What, then, was the legacy of this man, Hugo Black, who died on September 25, 1971? He developed a jurisprudence that, drawing upon history as the resource, was both literalist and absolutist in nature. Although he did not persuade others on the Court to join him fully in accepting his jurisprudence, he always insisted that his judicial opponents grapple with his thoughts and respond to them, and to him.

Further, the Alabaman was never frightened of raising serious questions and taking principled stands on important issues. During the height of McCarthyism, which began in the late 1940s and lasted for over a decade, in the midst of the national hysteria about Communism and its agents, Black courageously stood firm on behalf of First Amendment freedoms.

Much as Black loved the South, he nevertheless overcame his past to a significant extent. He spoke and wrote about the evils, legal and ethical, of racial segregation. He fought hard to keep the Court moving forward on this issue, even though it meant, as in *Alexander,* threatening the brethren with a sharp dissent if they did not issue the order for the immediate desegration of Mississippi school districts *now!* Sadly, his outspokenness on the suject brought grief to his own family.

Black's jurisprudential views about the centrality of the Bill of Rights and its protection of every person in the nation against unlawful actions in any governmental operation helped shape our law at a critical moment in American history. His efforts led to the "incorporation," or absorption, of most of the rights therein into the Fourteenth Amendment. Another significant legacy was his perception of the First Amendment as the foundation for all liberties; when persons can take advantage of those liberties to explore and choose among ideas and ideologies, human progress is the result.

Judges and Judging

Judges, whether working in the federal or the state judicial systems, had the solemn responsibility for determining the constitutionality of laws and other governmental actions when challenges to them were properly brought before the judges by parties alleging some concrete injury. Black always felt comfortable with, and often used in his own writings, Chief Justice John Marshall's words that "it is emphatically the province and the duty of the judiciary department to say what the law is."[14]

The Constitution-makers provided the republic with a general outline of governmental powers for both the central and the state governments, as well as building into the document curbs on the use of those powers. There is the constitutional need for governmental powers to enact legislation to reach the constitutional goal of "a more perfect union." The legislators create public policy based on their understanding and their interpretation of the powers granted to them in the Constitution. Its first article provides the national legislature with a host of powers. Congress must legislate in light of its interpretation of, say, the power "to regulate Commerce with foreign Nations, and among the several States, and with the Indian Tribes."[15] A law is passed, based on Congress's interpretation of the commerce power.

But the Constitution also provides that a person who has alleged some kind of real injury because of the law can challenge its validity in a court of law. The argument: Congress did not have the constitutional power to require a segregated barbeque "family" restaurant to end its racial discrimination through the use of the commerce clause.[16]

In America's history, ever since *Marbury v Madison,* the federal courts, especially the U.S. Supreme Court, have acted as mediators in such conflicts. In so acting, consistent with the grant of judicial power in Article III of the Constitution,[17] these nonelected federal judges play an important, at times critically important, role. Through interpretation of the Constitution, drawing upon precedent and an understanding of the meaning and intent of the Constitution's words and phrases, the federal judge typically resolves the problem through her rulings and orders.

Judicial review, then, is a critical political instrument in America's governing process. Using their powers of judicial review, judges determine whether the action of the legislature or the executive branch is consistent with the grant of power to the elected policy-maker in the Constitution or whether the policy-maker acted without constitutional authority. The Judge wrote, "the very government which must be made strong to deal with economic questions must be kept too weak to curb free expression."[18] That task, in the final analysis, was a judicial task of the utmost delicacy.

A lifelong student of constitutional history, Black was ever wary of nonelected federal judges exercising their power of judicial review in a democratic Republic.[19] As senator and as justice of the Supreme Court, he was critical of federal judges employing their own extra-constitutional and very subjective values to adjudge actions of a legislature, whether Congress[20] or a state legislature,[21] to be unconstitutional.

Black had seen reactionary majorities on the Supreme Court, led by the notorious Four Horsemen, overturn Roosevelt administration legislation because these New Deal statutes ran afoul of the "liberty" found in the due process clause.[22] As a justice of the Court, Black continually cautioned his brethren about substituting their values for those of the elected representatives of the people. He deeply feared life appointed judges declaring unconstitutional a law passed by Congress or a state legislature because they thought the law to be 'unreasonable.'[23]

Sensitive to the criticism that the Court, an oligarchic institution, had the power to nullify actions of popularly elected officials, Hugo always insisted that his brethren carefully use their power of judicial review lest the capacity of the Court to serve as mediator of the federal system be reduced, either through legislation curtailing its appellate powers or through loss of respect from a public resentful of another, nonelected policy-maker.

A Restrictive Jurisprudence

Black was consistent in his call for a federal judiciary that practiced self-restraint when employing judicial review. All legislators, whether in the Congress or in statehouses, "have power to legislate against what are found to be injurious practices in their internal commercial and business affairs, so long as the laws do not run afoul of some specific constitutional prohibition."[24] As he said in a watershed 1963 case, for a unanimous Court,

> Legislative bodies have broad scope to experiment with economic problems, and this Court does not sit to subject the state to intolerable supervision. . . . *We refuse to sit as a superlegislature to weigh the wisdom of legislation.* . . . Whether the legislature takes for its textbook Adam Smith, Herbert Spencer, Lord Keynes or some other is of no concern of ours.[25] (my emphasis)

Black's restrictive jurisprudence called for the brethren to aggressively use judicial review to preserve the liberties of the people against atrophy due to clearly perceived unconstitutional governmental actions. At the same time, the brethren had to abstain from ruling against governmental public policy decisions unless the legislation clearly ran afoul of constitutional words and phrases. Performing this delicate legal balancing task well meant that a judge had to draw on history, had to be a jurisprudential literalist when interpreting the Constitution, and, finally, had to accept the absoluteness of some of these constitutional phrases, especially those found in the First Amendment in the Bill of Rights.

Above All, the Constitution

Orderliness and symmetry, for Hugo, were very attractive, very functional characteristics of America's constitutionalism. Process was as important as the outcome—public policies—of the process. The Constitution was the fundamental law for governing the republic, not Plato's utopian society, but America's successful experiment in representative government. Black, as one of his law clerks said— and as all of them might have said,—"had a true passion for the Constitution."[26] Indeed, his worn copy of the U.S. Constitution was placed inside Black's coat pocket when he was laid to rest in September 1971.

Hugo Black, in his last term on the Court, got to know and like Harry Blackmun, the federal court of appeals judge who took Abe Fortas's Court seat in May

1970.[27] Harry was having a particularly hard time writing an opinion for the Court when Hugo came upon him and observed the freshman jurist's pain. "Harry," said the Judge, "never display agony in public in an opinion. *Never display agony.* Never say that this is an agonizing, difficult decision. Always write it as though it's clear as crystal!"[28] (my emphasis).

Indeed, Black's public persona was almost always subdued; he seemed almost immune to vexation. Only once did he respond publicly to criticism. That was the evening of October 1, 1937, when he went on national radio to respond to the Ku Klux Klan stories about him. His eleven-minute statement ended public discussion of the Klan issue.

Supreme Court justices, he told Elizabeth many times, had to be like Caesar's wife, absolutely above reproach. Jackson's incendiary 1946 telegram to Truman about Black, Douglas's marital problems and his ties with the Parvin Foundation, and Abe Fortas's 1969 resignation under siege tarnished the image of the Court, which saddened the Alabaman.

When it came time to retire, although Hugo was distressed because "so much was happening, and there were so many things he wanted to do before it was time to go,"[29] he knew the alternative was much worse: the public image of a feeble, senile justice of the Supreme Court incapable of performing his duties. He had to retire *now!*

Black did all he could to maintain the integrity and independence of the Court in the face of shifting tides of public opinion and political ideology. It is ironic that Hugo, who was chastised by his brethren for being too political, will be remembered for his efforts to take politics out of the Court's business and to decide cases on the basis of historical understanding and the absoluteness of the first principles found in the Constitution.

While Black was ever the Democratic party loyalist—and he truly loved the battles and the excitement of party politics—he avoided introducing his partisan political views into the Court. He did not even accept the president's invitation to attend the joint session of Congress in March 1965 to hear Lyndon B. Johnson introduce his Voting Rights Act. Hugo knew that there would be litigation, and he didn't want to give any impression of bias or wrongdoing. His wife wrote: "Hugo . . . said he was not going, that he, John Harlan, and Potter Stewart thought it inappropriate to go because the bill would soon be in their laps."[30]

The Judge was fond of telling a story about the time he was campaigning in Alabama and became lost on a country road on the way to Andalusia. He stopped a child to ask directions. " 'Andalusia, or Montgomery—which way is which?' The child didn't know. Finally Hugo said, 'You don't know much, do you, son?' The boy replied, 'No, but I hain't lost.' "[31]

Other than his experience on the road to Andalusia, Alabama, Hugo Black, in his entire life, was never lost.

Notes

Abbreviations

AFSCP   Abe Fortas Supreme Court Papers, Yale University Archives, New Haven, CT
EWP   Earl Warren Papers, Library of Congress, Washington, D.C.
FDRP   Franklin Delano Roosevelt Papers, Franklin Delano Roosevelt Presidential Library, Hyde Park, N.Y.
FFP   Felix Frankfurter Papers, Library of Congress, Washington, D.C.
HFSP   Harlan Fiske Stone Papers, Library of Congress, Washington, D.C.
HLBP   Hugo L. Black Papers, Library of Congress, Washington, D.C.
HSTP   Harry S Truman Papers, Harry S Truman Presidential Library, Independence, Missouri
JMHP   John M. Harlan II Papers, Mudd Library, Princeton University, Princeton, New Jersey
NAACPP National Association for the Advancement of Colored People Papers, Library of Congress, Washington, D.C.
RHJP   Robert H. Jackson Papers, Library of Congress, Washington, D.C.
TMP   Thurgood Marshall Papers, Library of Congress, Washington, D.C.
WJBP   William J. Brennan, Jr., Papers, Library of Congress, Washington, D.C.
WODP   William O. Douglas Papers, Library of Congress, Washington, D.C.

Introduction

1. Quoted in John T. Noonan, Jr., "Hugo Black and the Judicial Revolution," 9 *Southwestern University Law Review,* no. 4 (1977), pp. 1127, 1139.

2. Hugo Black to Jinksie Durr, 26 February 1971, HLBP, Box 7.

3. Hugo Black to Howard Ball, 21 January 1969.

4. Jerome Cooper to Howard Ball, 8 May 1985, p. 2.

5. Fred Rodell, "A Sprig of Laurel for Hugo Black at 75," 10 *American University Law Review,* 1, 1961.

6. Interview, Josephine Black Pesaresi, 16 June 1995, Durham, N.C.

7. Quoted in Roger K. Newman, *Hugo Black: A Biography* (New York: Pantheon Books, 1994), p. 26.

8. Tinsley Yarbrough, *John M. Harlan* (New York: Oxford University Press, 1990), p. 333.

9. Hugo Black to Frances Lamb, 25 July 1966, HLBP, Box 464.

10. Quoted in Newman, *Hugo Black,* p. 129.

11. Gerald T. Dunne, *Hugo Black and the Judicial Revolution* (New York: Simon and Schuster, 1977), p. 24.

12. See, generally, Howard Ball and Phillip J. Cooper, *Of Power and Right: Hugo Black, William O. Douglas and America's Constitutional Revolution* (New York: Oxford University Press) 1992.

13. Quoted in David Margolick, "Enigma of Justice Black Is Examined," *New York Times,* 13 April 1985.

14. Ibid.

15. HLBP, n.d., Box 53. Black wrote, in part, in response to the "freedom of choice" argument made by the writer, that "government is bound to deny citizens freedom of choice at some time, to some extent, and on certain subjects. . . . We have a country of law and order instead of one of anarchy and not riot, and I believe in having the former kind of country as I always did back in the days when you were in my Sunday School class in Birmingham."

16. Hugo L. Black to Edna Street Barnes, 14 November 1962, HLBP, Box 1. He said in part, "I only wish that more people who were born in the South, . . . would realize, as I am sure you do, that this is a great country because instead of having a Constitution that fosters slavery, hatred and a caste system, it is a country that proudly boasts of its dedication to the principle of 'Equal Justice Under Law.' "

17. See, for example, his speech to University of Georgia Law School students and faculty entitled "There is a South of Union and Freedom," 2 *Georgia Law Review,* 1 (1967).

18. See, for example, Tinsley Yarbrough, *Mr. Justice Black and His Critics,* Durham: Duke University Press, 1988.

19. Charles A. Reich, reviewing Howard Ball and Phillip J. Cooper, *Of Power and Right,* 38 *Journal of American History,* March 1993.

20. Hugo Black to Hugo Black, Jr., 25 January 1945, HLBP, Box 3.

21. Hugo Black to Sterling Black, 11 April 1944, HLBP, Box 6.

22. Hugo Black to Hugo Black, Jr., 23 December 1943, HLBP, Box 3.

23. Interview, Josephine Black Pesaresi, 16 June 1995, Durham, N.C.

24. John O'Donnell and Doris Fleeson, "Stone Denies Hand in Attack on Black," *New York Daily News,* 12 May 1938, p. 6.

25. Interview, Josephine Black Pesaresi, 16 June 1995, Durham, N.C.

26. Hugo Black to Jerome Cooper, 20 June 1946, HLBP, Box 459.

27. Hugo Black, Jr. to Frances Lamb, 10 December 1971, HLBP, Box 464.

28. Mary Ann Glendon, *A Nation Under Lawyers* quoted in John Leo, "When Judges Feel Romantic," *U.S. News and World Report,* 23 January 1995, p. 20.

29. Ibid.

30. Jerome Cooper, *Sincerely Your Friend, Hugo Black: Letters of Mr Justice Hugo L. Black to Jerome A. Cooper* (University: University of Alabama Press), 1973, p. 4.

31. Interview, Josephine Black Pesaresi, 16 June 1995, Durham, N.C.

Chapter One

1. James F. Simon, *The Antagonists: Hugo Black, Felix Frankfurter, and Civil Liberties in Modern America* (New York: Simon and Schuster, 1989), p. 158.

2. Quoted in Melvin Urofsky, "Conflict among the Brethren: Felix Frankfurter, William O. Douglas and the Clash of Personalities on the United States Supreme Court," 1988 *Duke Law Journal,* 71, 89 (1988).

3. Leonard Baker, *Brandeis and Frankfurter: A Dual Biography* (New York: New York University Press, 1986), p. 335.

4. Robert H. Jackson to Harry S Truman, RHJP, Box 26, 7 June 1946.

5. Hugo Black to Sterling Black, 25 February 1944, HLBP, Box 6.

6. Bernard Schwartz, *Super Chief: Earl Warren and His Supreme Court* (New York: New York University Press, 1980), p. 33.

7. Robert H. Jackson Memo to file *in re:* Hugo Black, 27 November 1949, RHJP, Box 26.

8. Simon, *Antagonists,* p. 158.

9. Hugo Black to William O. Douglas, 11 August 1945, WODP, Box 308.

10. Ibid.

11. Ibid.

12. Jay G. Hayden, "Supreme Court Feud," *Detroit News,* 3 February 1944, Hugo Black file, Federal Bureau of Investigation, Washington, D.C.

13. William Gregory and Robert Rennard, "Hugo Black's Congressional Investigation of Public Utilities," 29 *Oklahoma Law Review* 543, 544 (1976).

14. Harlan F. Stone Memorandum to the Conference (hereinafter referred to as MTTC), 31 August 1945, HLBP, Box 62.

15. Quoted in Howard Ball, "Justice Hugo L. Black: A Magnificent Product of the South," 36 *Alabama Law Review,* no. 3 (Spring 1985), p. 801, fn. 61.

16. Felix Frankfurter, MTTC, HLBP, Box 62.

17. Hugo L. Black to William O. Douglas, 7 September 1945, WODP, Box 308.

18. William O. Douglas to Hugo Black, 13 September 1945, WODP, Box 308.

19. Hugo Black to Harlan F. Stone, 7 September 1945, HLBP, Box 62.

20. Hugo Black to William O. Douglas, 7 September 1945, HLBP, Box 62.

21. Dunne, *Hugo Black,* p. 231.

22. Newman, *Hugo Black,* p. 10.

23. Dunne, *Hugo Black,* p. 21.

24. Ibid.

25. Newman, *Hugo Black,* p. 103.

26. Ibid., p. 87.

27. Ibid., p. 99.

28. Ibid., p. 100.

29. Ibid., pp. 197, 229.

30. Dunne, *Hugo Black,* p. 43.

31. Ibid., p. 20. See also Charlotte Williams, *Hugo Black: A Study in Judicial Process* (Baltimore, Md: Johns Hopkins University Press, 1950), p. 38.

32. Dunne, *Hugo Black,* p. 21.

33. Hugo Black, Jr., *My Father: A Remembrance* (New York: Random House, 1975), p. 46.

34. Correspondence with Howard Ball, law clerk, 1969 term, summer 1972, Hempstead, N.Y.

35. Diary Entry, FFP, n.d. Box 25.

36. Daniel J. Meador, "Mr. Justice Black: A Tribute," 57 *Virginia Law Review,* 1109, 1113, 1971.

37. Vincent Blasi, ed., *The Burger Court* (New Haven, Conn.: Yale University Press, 1982), p. 240.

38. Interview, Josephine Black Pesaresi, 16 June 1995, Durham, N.C.

39. Hugo Black to Harry S Truman, 4 November 1948, HSTL.

40. Hugo Black to Jerome Cooper, 11 January 1952, in Cooper, *Sincerely Your Friend,* p. 7.

41. Hugo Black and Elizabeth Black, *Mr. Justice and Mrs. Black* (New York: Random House, 1986), pp. 84, 99.

42. See, generally, Ibid.

43. Newman, *Hugo Black,* p. 199.

44. Black and Black, *Mr. Justice and Mrs. Black,* p. 112.

45. Black, Jr., *My Father,* p. viii.

46. See, for example, Kim I. Eisler, *A Justice For All* (New York: Simon and Schuster, 1993), p. 120.

47. Hugo L. Black to Hugo L. Black, Jr., 21 March 1945, HLBP, Box 3.

48. HLBP, Family files, Box 3.

49. Quoted in John Medelman, "Do you Swear To Tell the Truth, the Whole Truth, and Nothing but the Truth, . . . He does," in *Justice Hugo Black and the First Amendment,* ed. Everette E. Dennis, Donald M. Gillmor, and David L. Grey (Ames: Iowa State University Press, 1978), p. 64.

50. Black, Jr., *My Father,* p. 123.

51. Ibid., p. 124.

52. Ibid., p. 123.

53. Hugo Black to Hugo Black, Jr., HLBP, n.d., Box 4.

54. Ibid.

55. Black, Jr., *My Father,* p. 92.

56. Ibid., p. 111.

57. Jinksie Durr to Hugo L. Black, 21 June 1962, HLBP, Box 7.

58. Black, Jr., *My Father,* pp. 212, 213, 214.

59. Hugo Black to Hollis Black, n.d., 1944, HLBP, Box 6.

60. Hugo Black to Hugo Black, Jr., 23 December 1943, HLBP, Box 3.

61. Hugo Black to Hugo Black, Jr., 1 April 1950, HLBP, Box 3.

62. Hugo Black to Sterling Black, 2 May 1945, HLBP, Box 6.

63. Hugo Black to Hugo Black, Jr., HLBP, Box 4.

64. Interview, Josephine Black Pesaresi, 16 June 1995, Durham, N.C.

65. Hugo Black to Hazel B. Davis, 30 October 1941, quoted in Hazel B. Davis, *Uncle Hugo: An Intimate Portrait of Mr. Justice Black,* Alabama: privately printed 1965, p. 51.

66. A. E. Dick Howard, "Mr. Justice Black: The Negro Protest Movement and the Rule of Law," 53 *Virginia Law Review,* no. 5 (1967), p. 1050.

67. Edith Hamilton, *The Greek Way* (New York: W. W. Norton, 1942, 1991), p. 75.

68. Correspondence with Howard Ball, law clerk, 1969 term, summer 1972, Hempstead, N.Y.

69. Charles A. Reich, "Forward: Mr. Justice Black As One Who Saw the Future," 9 *Southwestern University Law Review,* no. 4 (1977), p. 853.

70. Black and Black, *Mr. Justice and Mrs. Black,* pp. 90, 112.

71. Black, Jr., *My Father,* p. 135.

72. Quoted in Black, Jr., *My Father,* p. 135.

73. George Freeman and A. E. Dick Howard, "Perspectives: Justice Hugo L. Black," *Richmond, Va. Times-Dispatch,* 12 December 1971, sec. F, p. 1.

74. Hugo Black to Sterling Black, 11 April 1944, HLBP, Box 7.

75. Hugo Black, Jr., to Hugo Black, n.d. January 1945, HLBP, Box 3.

76. Hugo Black to Hugo Black, Jr., 18 January 1945, HLBP, Box 3.

77. Interview with William J. Brennan, Jr., 25 November 1989, Washington, D.C.

78. Hugo Black to Erwin Griswold, 13 March 1963, HLBP, Box 31.

79. Felix Frankfurter to Stanley Reed, 21 December 1954, FFP, Box 93.

80. Quoted in Ball, "Justice Hugo L. Black," pp. 791, 805.

81. Charles A. Wright, "Hugo L. Black: A Great Man and a Great American," 50 *Texas Law Review,* 1, 2, 1971.

82. Ibid., pp. 4, 5.

83. Quoted in Harold Helfer, "How To Stay Young," *Signature,* December 1968, p. 31.

84. Simon, *Antagonists,* p. 159.

85. Sherman Minton to Felix Frankfurter, n.d., 1948–1949 file, FFP, Box 84.

86. Virginia van de Veer Hamilton, "Hugo Black: Road to the Court," 9 *Southwestern University Law Review,* no. 4 (1977), p. 888.

87. Daniel J. Meador, "Mr. Justice Black and His Law Clerks," 16 *Alabama Law Review,* 1963, p. 61.

88. Black and Black, *Mr. Justice and Mrs. Black,* p. 85.

89. See, for example, David Margolick, "Enigma of Justice Black Is Examined."

90. Wallace Mendelson, *Justices Black and Frankfurter: Conflict in the Court* (Chicago: University of Chicago Press, 1961), p. 13.

91. Correspondence with Howard Ball, law clerk, 1969 term, summer 1972, Hempstead, N.Y. "At times, the Judge was obstinate and unwilling to explore contradictory viewpoints. . . . [This was] a result [of] his intense beliefs in certain . . . principles."

92. Anthony Lewis, "Hugo Black—An 'Elemental Force,' " *New York Times,* 26 September 1971.

93. Hugo L. Black, "The Bill of Rights," 35 *New York University Law Review,* 865, 880–881 (1960).

94. Howard Ball, "Hugo L. Black: Twentieth Century Jeffersonian," 9 *Southwestern University Law Review,* no. 4 (1977), p. 1049, 1050.

95. Hamilton, *Greek Way,* p. 215.

96. Ball, "Hugo L. Black," 1050.

97. Joseph Lash, ed., *From The Diaries of Felix Frankfurter* (New York: W. W. Norton, 1974), p. 283.

98. Charles A. Reich, "Forward: Mr Justice Black," p. 853.

99. Hugo Black, Speech, 17 May 1942, HLBP, Box 315.

100. *Milk Wagon Drivers Association v Meadowmoor Dairy,* 312 U.S. 287, 301–302 (1941).

Chapter Two

1. See Black's 1926 standard Senate campaign stump speech where he spoke movingly about his mother, "whose worn and wrinkled hand pointed my way to the truth and light and faith." Hugo L. Black, speech, 20 March 1925, HLBP, Box 82.

2. See generally Virginia van der Veer Hamilton, *Hugo Black: The Alabama Years,* (University: University of Alabama Press, 1982), pp. 5, ff.

3. Black and Black, *Mr. Justice and Mrs. Black,* p. 5.

4. Medelman, "Do You Swear," p. 56.

5. Black and Black, *Mr. Justice and Mrs. Black,* p. 5.

6. Clifford Durr, "Hugo Black: Southerner," 10 *American University Law Review,* 27, 32, 1967.

7. See Mark Silverstein, *Constitutional Faiths: Felix Frankfurter, Hugo Black and the Process of Judicial Decision-Making* (Ithaca, N.Y.: Cornell University Press, 1984), pp. 93, ff.

8. See Tony Freyer, ed., *Justice Hugo Black and Modern America* (University: University of Alabama Press, 1990), p. 17.

9. Silverstein, *Constitutional Faiths,* p. 93.

10. Hamilton, *Hugo Black,* pp. 9–10.

11. Ibid., pp. 10–11.

12. Silverstein, *Constitutional Faiths,* p. 95.

13. Hamilton, *Hugo Black,* p. 15.

14. Reich, "Forward," p. 853.

15. Hamilton, *Hugo Black,* p. 16.

16. Edward L. Ayers, *The Promise of The New South: Life after Reconstruction* (New York: Oxford University Press, 1993), pp. 35, 36.

17. Hamilton, *Hugo Black,* pp. 12ff.

18. Ibid., p. 16. Also, in 1902 the first Jim Crow law was passed and the all-white primary was introduced.

19. Bertram Wyatt-Brown, "Ethical Background of Hugo Black's Career," 36 *Alabama Law Review,* no. 3 (Spring 1986), p. 159.

20. *Newsweek,* "The Newest Justice," no. 8, 21 August 1937, p. 8.

21. Durr, "Hugo Black," p. 32.

22. Black and Black, *Mr. Justice and Mrs. Black,* p. 8.

23. Ibid., p. 178.

24. Wyatt-Brown, "Ethical Background," p. 158.

25. Daniel J. Meador, *Mr. Justice Black and His Books* (Charlottesville: University of Virginia Press, 1974), p. 2. Another scholar wrote that "since Black viewed human nature as changeless, he was particularly attracted to the classics of Greece and Rome and to histories of the ancient world. He was likewise a great admirer of Thomas Jefferson and other founding fathers of the United States and was also a student of the British roots of American thought." Paul M. Pruitt, Jr., "The Return of Hugo Black: The Significance of the Hugo L. Black Collection at the University of Alabama," 43 *Alabama Law Review,* no. 1, 292, Fall 1991.

26. Howard, in Freeman and Howard, "Perspectives: Mr. Justice Black," p. 3.

27. Hugo Black to Hugo Black, Jr., 28 June 1950, HLBP, Box 3.

28. Paul L. Murphy, "The Early Social and Political Philosophy of Hugo Black: Liquor As A Test Case," 36 *Alabama Law Review,* no. 3 (Spring 1986), 101, 114.

29. See *Korematsu v United States,* 323 U.S. 214, 1944, majority opinion.

30. See *Tinker v Des Moines School Board,* 393 U.S. 503, 1968, Black dissenting.

31. See *Bell v Maryland,* 378 U.S. 226, 1964, dissent; *Adderly v Florida,* 385 US 48, 1966, majority opinion.

32. Freyer, *Justice Hugo Black,* p. 5.

33. Ibid.

34. Elizabeth S. Black, "Hugo Black: A Memorial Portrait," *Yearbook: U.S. Supreme Court, 1982,* U.S. Supreme Court Historical Society, Washington, D.C., p. 76.

35. Freyer, *Justice Hugo Black,* p. 5.

36. Hollinger F Barnard, ed., *Outside the Magic Circle: The Autobiography of Virginia Foster Durr* (University: University of Alabama Press, 1990), p. 307.

37. Ibid.

38. Wyatt-Brown, "Ethical Background," p. 161.

39. Freeman, in Freeman and Howard interview, "Perspectives: Mr Justice Black," p. 7.

40. See Black dissenting, *Griswold v Connecticut*, 381 U.S. 475, 1965.

41. Hugo L. Black, *A Constitutional Faith* (New York: Alfred A. Knopf, 1968), p. 9.

42. Ayers, *The Promise*, p. 132.

43. Jack Wheat, "Pepper Recalls Black's Fights in New Deal," *Tuscaloosa, Alabama News*, 13 April 1985.

44. Edna Barnes to Hugo L. Black, Jr., 3 October 1962, HLBP, Box 1.

45. Hugo L. Black, Jr. to Edna Barnes, 14 November 1962, HLBP, Box 1.

46. Quoted in Juan Williams, *Eyes On the Prize Reader* (New York: Viking Press, 1987), p. 8.

47. Ball and Cooper, *Of Power and Right*, p. 158.

48. Black, Jr., *My Father*, p. 212.

49. Silverstein, *Constitutional Faiths*, p. 103.

50. Ibid., p. 102.

51. *Plessy v Ferguson*, 163 U.S. 537 (1896).

52. Martin Luther King, Jr., to Hugo Black, inscription in *Stride Toward Freedom*, Hugo Black Library, University of Alabama Law School, Tuscaloosa, Ala.

53. *Chambers v Florida*, 309 U.S. 227, 1940.

54. *Brown v Board of Education*, 347 U.S. 483, 1954; *Cooper v Aaron*, 358 U.S. 1, 1958.

55. Jinksie Durr to Hugo Black, 5 June 1957, HLBP, Box 7.

56. Jinksie Durr to Hugo Black, 19 April 1962, HLBP, Box 7.

57. Jinksie Durr to Hugo Black, 23 September 1965, HLBP, Box 7.

58. Jinksie Durr to Hugo Black, 18 June 1958, HLBP, Box 7.

59. Hamilton, "Hugo Black," p. 861.

60. See Black, "There is a South of Union and Freedom," pp. 10–15.

61. See James Rhoads to Hugo Black, 12 July 1968; Hugo Black to James Rhoads, 17 July 1968, IILBP, Box 46.

62. Black, Jr., *My Father*, p. 4.

63. Ibid., p. 5.

64. Hugo Black to Barney L. Whatley, 31 May 1963, HLBP, Box 55.

65. Hamilton, *Hugo Black*, p. 10.

66. Ibid., p. 11.

67. Silverstein, *Constitutional Faiths*, p. 95.

68. George Freeman, in Freeman and Howard, "Perspectives: Justice Hugo Black," p. D1.

69. Sheldon Hackney, "The Clay County Origins of Mr. Justice Black: The Populist as Insider," 36 *Alabama Law Review*, 835, 1985.

70. Black and Black, *Mr. Justice and Mrs. Black*, p. 7.

71. Ibid., p. 8.

72. Ibid., p. 7.

73. Ibid., pp. 13–14.

74. Ibid., p. 9.

75. Ibid., p. 10.

76. Ibid., p. 11.

77. George Freeman, in Freeman and Howard, "Perspectives: Justice Hugo Black."

78. Black and Black, *Mr. Justice and Mrs. Black,* p. 12.

79. Ibid., p. 7.

80. Medelman, "Do You Swear," p. 56.

81. Black and Black, *Mr. Justice and Mrs. Black,* p. 22.

82. Quoted in Ball and Cooper, *Of Power and Right,* p. 15.

83. Joseph Alsop and Turner Catledge, *The 168 Days* (New York: Doubleday, Doran and Co., 1938), p. 306.

84. Meador, "Mr. Justice Black and His Law Clerks," p. 61.

85. Freeman, in Freeman and Howard, "Perspectives: Mr. Justice Black," p. 7.

86. Black and Black, *Mr. Justice and Mrs. Black,* p. 22.

87. Ball and Cooper, *Of Power and Right,* p. 15.

88. Hazel Black Davis, *Uncle Hugo,* pp. 5, 27.

89. Black and Black, *Mr. Justice and Mrs. Black,* p. 22.

90. Black, Jr., *My Father,* p. 10.

91. *Newsweek,* 14 March 1936, p. 21.

92. Quoted in Davis, *Uncle Hugo,* p. 81; See also Dunne, *Hugo Black,* p. 42.

93. Black, Jr., *My Father,* p. 116.

94. Davis, *Uncle Hugo,* p. 81.

95. Hamilton, *Hugo Black,* p. 276.

96. Freyer, ed., *Justice Hugo Black,* p. 5.

97. Hazel B. Davis to Hugo Black, 26 February 1964, HLBP, Box 6.

98. Hugo Black to Hazel Davis, 2 March 1964, HLBP, Box 6.

99. Hugo Black to Hugo Black, Jr., 15 February 1951, HLBP, Box 3.

100. Hamilton, *The Greek Way,* p. 30.

101. Ibid., p. 215.

102. Barnard, ed., *Outside the Magic Circle,* pp. 40, 47, 307.

103. Simon, *Antagonists,* p. 137.

104. Jinksie Durr to Frances Lamb, 18 January 1972, HLBP, Box 7.

105. Hackney,"Clay County Origins," p. 77.

106. Ibid.

107. Simon, *Antagonists,* p. 140.

108. Hugo Black, Jr., Remarks made at Hugo Black Centennial Program, University of Alabama Law School, Tuscaloosa, Ala., 18 March 1986.

109. Quoted in Davis, *Uncle Hugo,* p. 5.

Chapter Three

1. Quoted in Newman, *Hugo Black,* p. 69.

2. Ibid.

3. Black and Black, *Mr. Justice and Mrs. Black,* p. 30.

4. Ibid., p. 31.

5. Ayers, *The Promise,* p. 62.

6. Barnard, *Outside the Magic Circle,* p. 43.

7. Newman, *Hugo Black,* p. 69.

8. Hackney, "Clay County Origins," p. 837.

9. Ibid., p. 835.

10. Ibid., p. 921.

11. Silverstein, *Constitutional Faiths,* p. 98.

12. Wyatt-Brown, "Ethical Background," p. 922.

13. Hamilton, "Hugo Black," p. 867.

14. Ayers, *The Promise,* p. 65.

15. Hackney, "Hugo Black: Insider," p.79.

16. Daniel M. Berman, "Hugo L. Black: The Early Years," 8 *Catholic University Law Review,* 103, 108 (1959).

17. Hamilton, *Hugo Black,* p. 29.

18. Ayers, *The Promise,* p. 59.

19. Hamilton, *Hugo Black,* p. 29.

20. Ibid., p. 30.

21. Ibid.

22. Durr, "Hugo Black," p. 30.

23. Barnard, *Outside the Magic Circle,* pp. 40–41.

24. Ibid., p. 306. Hugo, she insisted, loved these common folk and "never gave up his faith in the poor white man of the South." p. 307.

25. Ibid., p. 34.

26. See Black-Whatley correspondence in Hugo Black's files, HLBP, Box 55.

27. Black and Black, *Mr. Justice and Mrs. Black,* p. 35.

28. Ibid., p. 37.

29. Berman, "Hugo Black, Southerner," p. 30.

30. Charles Mandy, "Judge Hugo Black Reduced Fine," *Birmingham Sun,* 26 June 1912, HLBP, Box 512.

31. Charles Mandy, "Evidence of Hospitality," *Birmingham Sun,* n.d., HLBP, Box 512.

32. Quoted in Black, Jr., *My Father,* p. 128.

33. Ibid.

34. Charles Mandy, "Judge Black Has Scare about His Heart Action," *Birmingham Sun,* n.d., HLBP, Box 512.

35. Hamilton, *Hugo Black,* p. 46.

36. Berman, "Early Years," p. 108.

37. Hamilton, *Hugo Black,* p. 45.

38. Black and Black, *Mr. Justice and Mrs. Black,* p. 37.

39. Ibid., p. 39.

40. Hamilton, *Hugo Black,* p. 47.

41. Black and Black, *Mr. Justice and Mrs. Black,* p. 40.

42. Berman, "Early Years," p. 109.

43. Black and Black, *Mr. Justice and Mrs. Black,* p. 42.

44. Hamilton, *Hugo Black,* p. 32.

45. Black and Black, *Mr. Justice and Mrs. Black,* p. 44.

46. Berman, "Early Years," p. 110.

47. Scale Harris to Charles Evans Hughes, 1 October 1937, HLBP, Box 31.

48. Hackney, "Clay County Origins," p. 840.

49. Ibid.

50. Black, Jr., *My Father,* p. 31.

51. Black and Black, *Mr. Justice and Mrs. Black,* pp. 49–50.

52. Black, Jr., *My Father,* p. 37.

53. In the Jewish religion, sitting *shivah* is the traditional seven-day mourning period for the immediate family of the deceased person.

54. William O. Douglas, *Go East, Young Man: The Early Years* (New York: Random House, 1974), p. 447.

55. Black and Black, *Mr. Justice Black,* p. 56.

56. Ibid., p. 58.

57. Ibid., p. 59.

58. *Miniard v Hines, Director General of Railroads,* Circuit Court, Jefferson County, Alabama, 8 October 1919, p. 4, in HLBP, Box 511.

59. Hamilton, "Hugo Black," p. 67, claims the salary was $40,000 annually when he left Alabama for the Senate. Black's son, however, maintains that in Black's last full year of practice, 1925, his income reached $80,000, "which for those days was fabulous money." Black, Jr., *My Father,* p. 45.

60. Black, Jr., *My Father,* p. 45.

61. Ibid., p. 46.

62. Ibid., p. 47.

63. Black and Black, *Mr. Justice and Mrs. Black,* p. 62.

64. Hackney, "Clay County Origins," p. 840.

65. Black and Black, *Mr. Justice and Mrs. Black,* p. 62.

66. Quoted in Black, Jr., *My Father,* pp. 39, 40.

67. Ibid., p. 40.

68. Ibid.

69. Ibid., p. 169.

70. Ibid., p. 170.

71. Ibid.

72. Ibid., p. 171.

73. Interview, Josephine Black Pesaresi, 16 June 1995, Durham, N.C.

74. Hugo Black to Josephine Black, 8 December 1941, HLBP, Box 4.

75. Hugo Black to Hugo Black, Jr., 9 February 1946, HLBP, Box 3.

76. See Hugo Black to Hugo Black, Jr., 17 April 1943; 30 August 1944; and 12 January 1945, HLBP, Box 3.

77. Hugo Black to Hugo Black, Jr., 24 May 1947, HLBP, Box 3.

78. Hugo Black to Hugo Black, Jr., 29 November 1949, HLBP, Box 3.

79. Interview, Josephine Black Pesaresi, 16 June 1995, Durham, N.C.

80. Black, Jr., *My Father,* p. 177.

81. Drew Pearson, "The Washington Merry Go Round," 16 December 1951.

82. Black, Jr., *My Father,* p. 179.

83. Quoted in Hamilton, "Hugo Black," p. 868. She is incorrect about Black's presence. A review of the trial transcript indicates that it was his partner, E. C. Crampton Harris, not Hugo Black, who appeared on behalf of the defendant, Stephenson. See *State of Alabama v Stephenson,* No 6860, 23 August 1921. HLBP, Box 511.

84. Hamilton, "Hugo Black," p. 863.

85. Wyatt-Brown, "Ethical Background," p. 918.

86. He told his son that he'd "bust them into little firms." Black, Jr., *My Father,* p. 140. Hugo Jr categorized his father as a "timeless economic radical."

87. Buddy Cooper to Howard Ball, 8 May 1985.

88. Herbert Mitgang, Review of *Behind The Mask of Chivalry: The Making of the Second Ku Klux Klan,* by Nancy MacLean, *New York Times,* 26 July 1994, p. C18.

89. Ibid.

90. Margolick, "Enigma of Justice Black is Examined," p. A12.

91. Wyatt-Brown, "Ethical Background," p. 922.

92. J. Mills Thornton, III, "Hugo Black and the Golden Age," 36 *Alabama Law Review,* 899, 1985, p. 905.

93. Silverstein, *Constitutional Faiths,* p. 101.

94. Hamilton, *Hugo Black,* p. 108.

95. Ibid., p. 305.

96. Newman, *Hugo Black,* pp. 94, 96.

97. Thornton, "Golden Age," p. 904ff.

98. Black and Black, *Mr. Justice and Mrs. Black,* p. 70.

99. Quoted in Hugo Black obituary, *New York Times,* 26 September 1971.

100. Douglas, *Go East,* p. 455.

101. Thornton, "Golden Age," p. 902.

102. Ibid., p. 901.

103. Ibid., p. 119.

104. Newman, *Hugo Black,* p. 100.

105. Ibid., p. 120.

106. Hamilton, *Hugo Black,* p. 117.

107. Ibid.

108. Ibid., p. 119.

109. Black, Campaign literature, HLBP, Box 90.

110. Newman, *Hugo Black,* p. 106.

111. Hugo Black, Campaign Announcement, n.d., 1925, HLBP, Box 516.

112. Black, Jr., *My Father,* p. 58.

113. Hugo L. Black to M. Pittman, 30 December 1925, HLBP, Box 45.

114. Black, Jr., *My Father,* p. 58.

115. Ibid., p. 59.

116. Hugo L. Black to D. C. Arthur, 18 June 1926, HLBP, Box 12.

117. Black and Black, *Mr. Justice and Mrs. Black,* p. 75.

118. Ibid., p. 77. Black's daughter Jo-Jo recalled that when Hugo was in Bethesda Naval Hospital for medical treatment, he was reading Bertrand Russell, the British philosopher. Soon, all the nurses and doctors in his ward were talking and reading Bertrand Russell. Interview, Josephine Black Pesaresi, 16 June 1995, Durham, N.C.

119. HLBP, Box 50.

120. HLBP, Box 90.

121. Black and Black, *Mr. Justice and Mrs. Black,* p. 68.

122. Ibid.

123. Elizabeth Black, "Hugo Black: The Magnificent Rebel," 9 *Southwestern University Law Review,* no 4 (1977), pp. 891–892.

124. Hamilton, "Hugo Black," p. 872.

125. Hamilton, *Hugo Black,* p. 134.

126. Ibid., pp. 136–37.

127. W. H. Hunt to Hugo Black, 9 August 1926, HLBP, Box 500.

128. *Smith v Allwright,* 321 U.S. 649 (1944).

129. Hamilton, *Hugo Black,* p. 143.

Chapter Four

1. J. L. Thornton to Hugo Black, 16 November 1927, HLBP, Box 81.

2. Hugo Black to J. L. Thornton, December 11, 1926, HLBP, Box 81.

3. Hamilton, *Hugo Black,* pp. 143ff.

4. Berman, "Hugo Black: Southerner," p. 114.

5. Ibid.

6. See for example, letters from S. W. Wright, G. O. Wallace, and Hugh McElderry to Senator Black offering their support. HLBP, Box 91.

7. *Newsweek,* 14 March 1936, p. 14.

8. Hugo L. Black to Ed Nixon of Ozark, Ala. 23 February 1928, HLBP, Box 90.

9. Hugo Black to J. P. Carter, Mumsford, Ala., 2 October 1928, HLBP, Box 90. See also letters from Hugo Black to C. W. Messengale, Birmingham, Ala, 2 October 1928; B. C. Wilson, Jasper, Ala., 29 September 1928; and Leonard Shertzer, Tuskegee, Ala., 4 October 1928, HLBP, Box 90.

10. Hamilton, *Hugo Black,* p. 155.

11. Hubert Baughn to Hugo Black, 20 March 1928, HLBP, Box 90.

12. Hugo Black to Hubert Baughn, 21 March 1928, HLBP, Box 90.

13. Hugo Black to William McAdoo, 16 July 1928, HLBP, Box 90.

14. Letter, Hugo Black to J. P. Morgan, Speigner, Alabama, 27 September 1928, HLBP, Box 90.

15. Hugo Black to John R. McCain, Lineville, Ala., 16 November 1928, HLBP, Box 90.

16. Simon, *Antagonists,* p. 87.

17. Tip O'Neill, *All Politics Is Local* (New York: Times Books, 1994), p. 68.

18. See Charles A. J. McPherson, M.D., Secretary, Birmingham, Ala. Branch, NAACP, to Hugo Black, 16 June 1936, HLBP, Box 200.

19. Hamilton, *Hugo Black,* p. 238.

20. See Black dissenting, *Griswold v Connecticut,* 1965.

21. See Hugo Black's partial dissent in *South Carolina v Katzenbach,* 383 U.S. 302, a 1966 case in which the U.S. Supreme Court validated Section Five of the 1965 Voting Rights Act. See, also, Ball and Cooper, *Of Power and Right,* pp. 259ff.

22. See, generally, James Goodman, *Stories of Scottsboro* (New York: Vintage Books, 1994).

23. See, for example, Sam Wise to Hugo Black, 22 April 1933, HLBP, Box 217.

24. Quoted in Kenneth S. Davis, *FDR: The New Deal Years, 1933–1937, A History* (Random House: New York, 1979), p. 90.

25. Hollis Black to Hugo Black, 30 May 1930, HLBP, Box 1.

26. "Washington: Both Sides of the Curtain," *Barron's, the National Financial Weekly,* April, 1935, p. 4, HLBP, Box 518.

27. Ibid.

28. Black and Black, *Mr. Justice and Mrs. Black,* p. 68.

29. Ibid.

30. Oral History Project, draft of interview with Hugo Black, Lyndon Baines Johnson Presidential Library, n.d. HLBP, Box 520.

31. Hugo Black to C. A. Gaston, 19 August 1935, HLBP, Box 29.

32. Hugo Black, speech, n.d., HLBP, Box 76.

33. Ibid.

34. Davis, *FDR,* p. 98.

35. Ibid.

36. Oral History Project, draft of interview with Hugo Black, Lyndon Baines Johnson Library, HLBP, Box 520.

37. *Schecter Poultry Co. v United States,* 295 U.S. 495, 1935.

38. Senate Report no. 1680. Committee on Interstate Commerce. 75th Congress, 1st Session, 23 February 1937.

39. Hugo Black to William Yerby of Greensboro, Ala., 3 July 1937, HLBP, Box 130.

40. Arthur M. Schlesinger, Jr., *The Coming of the New Deal* (Boston: Houghton Mifflin, 1958), pp. 91–92.

41. 72nd Congress, Second Session, Congressional Record, 1239–1240 (1930).

42. *A Report of the National Power Policy Committee with Respect to the Treatment of Holding Companies,* 74th Cong., 1st Sess., House Doc. 137 (1935).

43. HLBP, Box 90.

44. Schlesinger, *The Coming of the New Deal,* p. 313.

45. Hugo Black to C. B. Fowlkes of Mobile, Ala., 1 August 1935, HLBP, Box 130.

46. Hugo Black, "Inside a Senate Investigation," *Harper's,* February 1936, p. 276.

47. Robert W. Horton, "Senator Black Dons Cloak of Chief 'Ferret,' " *Washington Post,* 31 July 1935.

48. Black, "Inside a Senate Investigation," p. 285.

49. "Senator Black Uncovers Shipping Board Extravagance," *Newsweek,* 7 October 1933, p. 7.

50. Hamilton, *Hugo Black,* p. 222.

51. "Our Ships Will Stay on the Ocean," *Sphere,* June 1934, HLBP, Box 517.

52. See Nicholas Johnson, "Senator Black and the American Merchant Marine," 12 *University of Southern California Law Review,* 439, January, 1967.

53. Quoted in Davis, *FDR,* p. 357.

54. Ibid., p. 356.

55. Johnson, "Senator Black," pp. 448–49.

56. "Postal Chief Reveals Basis of Annulment," *Washington Herald,* 15 February 1934.

57. "Sixth Army Aviator Dead as Plane Falls into Sea," *Washington Herald,* 24 February 1934, p. 1; "Aeronautics," *Time,* 26 February 1934, HLB Papers, Box 110.

58. Davis, *FDR,* p. 361.

59. *Newsweek,* 21 August 1937, p. 8.

60. Schlesinger, *New Deal,* p. 449.

61. Horton, "Senator Black Dons Cloak."

62. George Creel, "Goosekillers," *Colliers,* 9 January 1937, p. 26.

63. Hamilton, *Hugo Black,* p. 247.

64. Davis, *FDR,* p. 535.

65. *Hearst v Black,* 87 F. 2d 70, 71 (D.C. Cir. 1936).

66. Ibid., at pp. 74, 75.

67. Hugo Black to Warren Roberts, 28 March 1936, HLBP, Box 117.

68. Hugo L. Black, *The Utilities Lobby, Radio Address and Speech, 8 August 1935* (Washington: Government Printing Office, 1935), p. 9.

69. "Senator Hugo Black Exposes Public Enemies," *Alabama Herald,* 23 August 1935.

70. David Davis to Hugo Black, HLBP, Box 25.

71. Arthur Schlesinger, Jr., *The Politics of Upheaval* (Boston: Houghton Mifflin, 1960), p. 322.

72. Hugo Black to John Carroll of Chicago, 25 May 1936, HLBP, Box 117.

73. Black, "Inside," p. 286. Black explained his views on the congressional investigation in the following manner: "It has always been my belief that President Wilson was right when he said that pitiless publicity . . . on business throws the light necessary to prevent and correct public abuses."

74. Daniel Willard to Hugo Black, 5 February 1936, HLBP, Box 117.

75. Hugo Black to Daniel Willard, 20 February 1936, HLBP, Box 117.

76. Hugo Black to Sara Eldridge, Sara Eldridge to Hugo Black, 22, 23 March 1936, HLBP, Box 117.

77. *New York Times,* 25 September 1936.

78. A. A. Berle to Hugo Black, 22 April 1936, HLBP, Box 117.

79. W. G. Bruce to Hugo Black, 31 July 1935, HLBP, Box 104.

80. Hugo Black to Jim C. Smith, 12 August 1935, HLBP, Box 104.

81. Harry Witters to Hugo Black, 15 November 1934, HLBP, Box 75.

82. Graham Wilson to Hugo Black, 7 November 1934, HLBP, Box 75.

83. Hugo Black to Hugh Mallory of Selma, Ala., 18 March 1937, HLBP, Box 134.

84. Hugo Black to W. O. Mulkey, Geneva, Ala., HLBP, Box 134.

85. *Congressional Record*, 1935, p. 1979.

86. Hugo Black to Ed McMillan of Brenton, Ala., 9 February 1937, HLBP, Box 134.

87. David McCullough, *Truman* (New York: Simon and Schuster, 1992), p. 226.

88. Ibid.

89. Quoted in Merlo J. Pusey, *Charles Evans Hughes,* vol. II (New York: Macmillan, 1951), p. 754.

90. Ibid., p. 756.

91. McCullough, *Truman,* p. 227.

92. Hugo Black to Hugh Mallory, n.d., HLBP, Box 135.

93. Hugo Black to Franklin D. Roosevelt, 28 January 1937, FDRP, cited in Hamilton, *Hugo Black,* p. 262.

94. Franklin D. Roosevelt to Hugo Black, February 6, 1937, FDRP, cited in Hamilton, *Hugo Black,* p. 262.

95. Letter, Hugo Black to Hugh Mallory, March 18, 1937, HLBP, Box 135.

96. Ibid.

97. Hugo Black, "Should the President's Proposals Regarding the Supreme Court Be Adopted?" *America's Town Meeting of the Air,* 11 February 1937, p. 25.

98. Quoted in Hamilton, *Hugo Black,* p. 263.

Chapter Five

1. Henry J. Abraham, *Justices and Presidents: A Political History of Appointments to the Supreme Court* (New York: Oxford University Press, 1974), p. 161.

2. Katie Loucheim, ed., *The Making of the New Deal: The Insiders Speak* (Cambridge, Mass.: Harvard University Press, 1983), p. 53.

3. In his autobiography, Douglas recalled questions that McReynolds regularly asked him about President Roosevelt (after Douglas joined the Court): " 'The man is really insane, isn't he?' 'Do you think he will ever regain his sanity?' " In William O. Douglas, *The Court Years, 1939–1975* (New York: Random House, 1980), p. 13.

4. In 1922, McReynolds refused to visit Philadelphia with his brethren. He wrote Chief Justice Taft: "As you know, I am not always to be found when there is a Hebrew abroad. Therefore, my 'inability' to attend must not surprise you." Quoted in Abraham, *Justices and Presidents,* p. 167.

5. Douglas, *Go East,* p. 440.

6. Abraham, *Justices and Presidents,* p. 176.

7. Ibid., p. 178.

8. See Howard Gillman, *The Constitution Besieged: The Rise and Demise of Lochner Era Police Powers Jurisprudence* (Durham, N.C.: Duke University Press, 1993).

9. See Holmes, dissenting, *Lochner v New York,* 198 U.S. 45, 1905.

10. Abraham, *Justices and Presidents,* p. 196.

11. Loucheim, *Making of the New Deal,* p. 59.

12. Abraham, *Justices and Presidents,* p. 196.

13. *Panama Refining Corp v Ryan,* 293 U.S. 388 (1935).

14. The Federal Farm Bankruptcy Act was invalidated in 1936.

15. *Railroad Retirement Board v Alton Railroad.,* 295 U.S. 330, 1935.

16. *Schechter Poultry Corp v United States*, 295 U.S. 495 (1935).

17. *United States v Butler*, 297 U.S. 1 (1936).

18. *Carter v Carter Coal Corp.*, 298 U.S. 238 (1936).

19. Alsop and Catledge, *The 168 Days*, p. 296.

20. Ibid., p. 295.

21. Ibid., p. 297.

22. Ibid.

23. Ibid., p. 302.

24. Ibid., p. 303.

25. Oral History Project, Lyndon Baines Johnson Library, HLBP, Box 520.

26. Hamilton, *Hugo Black*, p. 273.

27. William O. Douglas, *The Court Years*, p. 19.

28. Alsop and Catledge, *The 168 Days*, p. 299.

29. Douglas, *Go East*, p. 494.

30. Oral History Project, Lyndon Baines Johnson Library, HLBP, Box 520.

31. Alsop and Catledge, *The 168 Days*, p. 305.

32. Dunne, *Hugo Black*, p. 172.

33. Oral History Project, Lyndon Baines Johnson Library, HLBP, Box 520.

34. Ibid., Also, Alsop and Catledge, *The 168 Days*, p. 307.

35. Ibid.

36. When a historian suggested that Postmaster General James A. Farley, a close political advisor to Franklin D. Roosevelt, would have warned the President about Black's Klan connection, Black wrote to her and said that "[Farley] congratulated me warmly . . . but said that he did not want to mislead me, that he had not known anything . . . until he heard it on the radio. . . . He followed this up with the statement that had he been consulted, however, he would have strongly recommended me and was very happy about my appointment." HLBP, Box 31.

37. Raymond Morley, "An Investigator Comes To Glory," *Newsweek*, no. 8, 21 August 1937, p. 7.

38. Alsop and Catledge, *The 168 Days*, p. 308.

39. Ibid.

40. Morley, "An Inquisitor," *Newsweek*, p. 7

41. "Nominee No. 93," *Time Magazine*, 23 August 1937, pp. 13, 14.

42. Morley, "An Inquisitor," *Newsweek*, p. 40.

43. Raymond Moley, "Whoso Diggeth A Pit," *Newsweek*, 23 September 1937, p. 44.

44. Duncan Aikman, "The Klan on the Court," *Newsweek*, 30 September 1937, p. 10.

45. Quoted in Alsop and Catledge, *The 168 Days*, p. 311.

46. Alsop and Catledge, *168 Days*, p. 309.

47. Richard Spong, "On Supreme Court: Man Who Holds Swing Vote," *Birmingham Sun*, n.d., HLBP, Box 234.

48. Black and Black, *Mr. Justice and Mrs. Black*, p. 69.

49. Quoted in Evan Thomas, "There is Always Something," *Newsweek*, 21 October 1991, p. 33.

50. "Black Scandal," *Time*, 27 September 1937, p. 10.

51. Ibid.

52. Aikman, "The Klan," p. 9.

53. Editorial, "Hugo Black," *Commonweal*, No. 24, 24 September 1937, p. 484.

54. Editorial, "The Case of Mr. Justice Black," *The New Republic*, 29 September 1937, p. 201.

55. Berman, "Early Years," p. 103.

56. Quoted in Hugo Black obituary, "Justice Black, Champion of Civil Liberties for 34 Years on Court, Dies at 85," *New York Times,* 26 September 1971, p. 76.

57. Douglas, *Court Years,* p. 19.

58. Hugo Black to Hugh Grant, 26 October 1937, HLBP, Box 31.

59. Hugo Black to Hazel Black Davis, November, 1937. Quoted in Davis, *Uncle Hugo,* p. 32.

60. Alsop and Catledge, *The 168 Days,* p. 312.

61. Quoted in "Black Scandal," *Time,* 27 September 1937, p. 9.

62. Douglas, *Court Years,* pp. 19–20.

63. *Time,* 11 October 1937, p. 36.

64. See *Time* or *Newsweek,* 11 October 1937, for the text of his statement about membership in the Klan and for comments about its content.

65. Black and Black, *Mr. Justice and Mrs. Black,* p. 230.

66. Hugo Black, note to the file, May 1968, HLBP, Box 31.

67. Quoted in Wheat, "Pepper Recalls," p. 3.

68. J. C. Toland to Hugo Black, 6 December 1938, HLBP, Box 11.

69. HLBP, Box 31.

70. Albert Levitt to Hugo Black, 18 August 1937, HLBP, Box 251.

71. Quoted in *Time,* 11 October 1937, p. 18.

72. HLBP, Box 240.

73. Dunne, *Hugo Black,* p. 56.

74. Walter White, *A Man Called White* (New York: Viking Press, 1948), p. 177.

75. Walter White to Hugo Black, 11 January 1937, HLBP, Box 55.

76. Walter White to Hugo Black, 18 January 1937, HLBP, Box 55.

77. White, *A Man Called White,* pp. 177–178.

78. Ibid., p. 178.

79. J. L. LeFlore to Walter White, 12 August 1937, NAACPP, Box 29.

80. Walter White to Hugo Black, telegram, 16 August 1937, NAACPP, Box 29.

81. Thurgood Marshall to John M. Holmes, 25 August 1937, NAACPP, Box 29.

82. Walter White to Hollis Black, 7 September 1937, NAACPP, Box 29.

83. White, *A Man Called White,* p. 177.

84. Ibid., p. 179.

85. Walter White to Franklin D. Roosevelt, telegram, 16 September 1937, NAACPP, Box 29.

86. White, *A Man Called White,* p. 179–180.

87. Hollis Black to Walter White, 6 October 1937, HLBP, Box 55.

88. Walter White to Max Lowenthal, copy to Felix Frankfurter, 20 August 1937, FFP, Box 79.

89. Hugo Black to Walter White, 21 December, 1948, HLBP, Box 55.

90. Walter White to Hugo Black, 20 May 1954, HLBP, Box 55.

91. *Chambers v. Florida,* 309 U.S. 227 (1940).

92. T. Hughes to Hugo Black, 15 December 1938, HLBP, Box 41.

93. Judge Armstead Brown, Florida Supreme Court, to Hugo Black, 14 March 1942, HLBP, Box 259. Brown informed Black, "As you know, one of the four negroes involved in the Chambers case, Isiah Chambers, broke under the long strain and lost his mind and has been in our state insane hospital for a year or so."

94. *Chambers v Florida,* 309 U.S. 227 (1940), at 235.

95. G. F. Flemmings to Hugo Black, 23 March 1940, HLBP, Box 259.

96. Mary McLeod Bethune to Hugo Black, 24 February 1940, HLBP, Box 259.

97. Rev. G. P. Musselman to Hugo Black, 14 February 1940, HLBP, Box 259.

98. John O. Nute to Hugo Black, 2 March 1940, HLBP, Box 259.

99. James C. McClendon to Hugo Black, 14 February 1940, HLBP, Box 259.

100. Editorial, "Justice Black Comes Through," *Houston Informer*, 24 December 1938, HLBP, Box 257.

101. Ball and Cooper, *Of Power and Right*, p. 88.

102. Harlan F. Stone to Felix Frankfurter, n.d., 1937, quoted in Lash, *From the Diaries of Felix Frankfurter*, pp. 67–68.

103. Quoted in Dunne, *Hugo Black*, p. 196.

Chapter Six

1. Quoted in Black, *A Constitutional Faith*, p. 11.

2. Quoted in Loucheim, *The Making of the New Deal*, p. 96.

3. Ibid.

4. Douglas, *Go East*, p. 319.

5. A. Leon Higginbotham, to Thurgood Marshall, 15 July 1990, TMP, Box 4.

6. See, generally, James J. Magee, *Mr. Justice Black: Absolutist on the Court* (Charlottesville: University of Virginia Press, 1980).

7. Ibid., p. 15.

8. Ibid.

9. Ibid., p. 13.

10. Ibid., p. 14.

11. Ibid., p. 19.

12. Black and Black, *Mr. Justice and Mrs. Black*, p. 104.

13. Correspondence with Howard Ball, law clerk, 1969 term, summer 1972, Hempstead, N.Y.

14. Correspondence with Howard Ball, law clerk, 1961 term, summer 1972, Hempstead, N.Y.

15. See Abraham, *Justices and Presidents*, p. 202.

16. HLBP, Box 53.

17. See Tinsley Yarbrough, "Mr. Justice Black and Legal Positivism," 57 *Virginia Law Review* (1971), p. 387.

18. Black, Jr., *My Father*, p. 234.

19. William O. Douglas, Hugo Black eulogy, 29 September 1971, WODP, Box 888.

20. Ibid., p. 5.

21. George L. Saunders, Remarks in Memory of Hugo Black at Meeting of the Bar of the Supreme Court of the United States, 18 April 1972, Washington, D.C., p. 3.

22. Hugo Black, Foreword, in Lenore Cahn, ed., *Confronting Injustice: The Edmond Cahn Reader*, 1966, p. xi.

23. Hugo L. Black, "Reminiscences," 18 *Alabama Law Review* 1 (1965), p. 10.

24. Black, *A Constitutional Faith*, p. 68.

25. See Berman, "Hugo Black: Southerner," p. 50.

26. Interview, Tinsley Yarbrough with Hugo Black, 6 July 1971.

27. Saunders, Remarks in Memory of Hugo L. Black, p. 3.

28. Douglas, "Hugo L. Black," p. 3.

29. See, for example, Black's dissents in *Rosado v Wyman*, 397 U.S. 397 (1970) and *Wheeler v Montgomery*, 397 U.S. 280 (1970).

30. See Black's majority opinion in *Korematsu v United States*, 323 U.S. 214 (1944). See also *Ex Parte Endo*, 323 U.S. 283 (1944), and *Hirabayashi v United States*, 320 U.S. 81 (1943).

31. *Korematsu,* at 215.

32. "Justice Black," *New York Times,* 26 September 1971, p. 76.

33. Meador, "Mr. Justice Black: A Tribute," p. 1109.

34. Hugo Black, "The Bill of Rights Is Enough," 35 *New York University Law Review,* April 1960, p. 3.

35. Black, *A Constitutional Faith,* p. 43.

36. Hugo Black to Alexander Meiklejohn, 25 July 1962, HLBP, Box 42.

37. Hugo Black, speech on Thomas Jefferson, n.d., HLBP, Box 42.

38. Magee, *Mr. Justice Black,* pp. 99, ff.

39. Hugo L. Black, address, Einstein Memorial Meeting-Town Hall, New York, 15 May 1955, pp. 4, 5.

40. Hugo Black to Irving Dilliard, 7 January 1953, HLBP, Box 317.

41. *Smith v California,* 361 U.S. 147, 1947 at 158–59.

42. Black, *Constitutional Faith,* p. 53.

43. Ibid., p. 44.

44. *Cox v Louisiana,* 379 U.S. 559, 584 (1965), Black dissenting.

45. Ibid., at 577–78.

46. Senator Hugo Black, 81 Congressional Record (1937), p. 1294.

47. Black and Black, *Mr. Justice Black and Mrs. Black,* p. 234.

48. Black, *A Constitutional Faith,* pp. 34, 33.

49. *Gideon v Wainwright,* 372 U.S. 344 (1962).

50. *In re Gault,* 387 U.S. 1 (1967).

51. *Powell v Alabama,* 287 U.S. 45 (1932).

52. See *Griswold v Connecticut,* 381 U.S. 479 (1965), a majority opinion written by Justice Douglas. Note especially Black's dissent in this case in which the majority created the right of marital privacy.

53. Tinsley Yarbrough, "Justice Black and Equal Protection," 9 *Southwestern University Law Review,* no. 4, 1977, 903–908, passim.

54. Tinsley Yarbrough, "Justices Black and Douglas: The Judicial Function and the Scope of Constitutional Liberties," 1973 *Duke Law Review,* 441, at 478 (1973).

55. *Harper v Virginia State Board of Elections,* 383 U.S. 663 (1966).

56. See Kenneth Karst, "Invidious Discrimination: Justice Douglas and the Return of Natural Law Due Process," 16 *UCLA Law Review,* 716, 717 (1969).

57. *Harper,* at 672.

58. Ibid. at 675–76.

59. Black and Black, *Mr. Justice and Mrs. Black,* p. 140.

60. Correspondence with Howard Ball, law clerk, 1969 term, summer 1972, Hempstead, N.Y.

61. Interview, James F. Simon with William J. Brennan, Jr., 23 September 1983, Washington, D.C. In Simon, *The Antagonists,* pp. 74–75.

62. Black, *A Constitutional Faith,* p. 24.

63. John M. Harlan, II, "Mr. Justice Black: Remarks of a Colleague," 81 *Harvard Law Review,* 1, 1 (1967).

64. Black, *A Constitutional Faith,* p. 12.

65. Yarbrough, "Justices Black and Douglas," p. 485.

66. Ibid.

67. Correspondence with Howard Ball, law clerk, 1969 term, summer 1972, Hempstead, N.Y.

68. Black, Foreword to *Confronting Injustice,* p. xii.

69. *Griswold v Connecticut,* 381 U.S. 479 (1965), at 522.

70. Black, *A Constitutional Faith*, p. 24.

71. Harlan, "Mr. Justice Black," pp. 1–2.

72. *Adamson v California*, 332 U.S. 46 (1947).

73. Interview, Tinsley Yarbrough with Hugo L. Black, 6 July 1971, Washington, D.C.

74. *Adamson* at 89.

75. Interview with William J. Brennan, Jr., 29 October 1986, Washington, D.C.

76. Black, *A Constitutional Faith*, p. 11.

77. See his separate opinions in *Coleman v Alabama*, 399 U.S. 1, 11 (1970), *Baldwin v New York*, 399 U.S. 66, 74 (1970), and *Ashe v Swenson*, 397 U.S. 436, 447 (1970).

78. See the dissents of Black and Douglas in *Dennis v United States*, 341 U.S. 494 (1951).

79. Hugo L. Black, commencement address at Swarthmore College, 6 June 1955, p. 12.

80. Ibid., pp. 7, 8, 10.

81. Black, *A Constitutional Faith*, p. 9.

82. Letter, Black law clerk to author, April 17, 1975.

83. *Boddie v Connecticut*, 401 U.S. 371 (1971), at 393, Black dissenting.

84. Robert Woodward and Scott Armstrong, *The Brethren: Inside the Supreme Court* (New York: Simon and Schuster), 1979, p. 62.

85. Interview with Byron White, 18 November 1986, Washington, D.C.

86. Hugo Black, marginal comments in *The Least Dangerous Branch*, Hugo Black Library, University of Alabama Law School, Tuscaloosa, Ala.

Chapter Seven

1. Jeffrey D. Hockett, "Justice Robert H. Jackson, The Supreme Court, and the Nuremberg Trial," in Gerhard Casper, ed., *1990: The Supreme Court Review* (Chicago: University of Chicago Press, 1991), p. 281.

2. Interview with Harry A. Blackmun, 19 November 1986, Washington, D.C. Blackmun said that Black was at his manipulative, political best in the case of *Oregon v Mitchell*, 400 U.S. 112 (1970), involving a challenge to the amended Voting Rights Act, lowering the voting age to eighteen. Black passed on the vote until he saw the junior justice, Blackmun, cast his vote on the issue. At that point, with the Court deadlocked four to four on the case, Black cast the deciding vote and was able to write the opinion for the Court. Blackmun said that Black "thoroughly enjoyed [the manipulation]."

3. Felix Frankfurter to Hugo Black, 15 December 1939, JMHP.

4. See, generally, Walter F. Murphy's classic text on this subject, *Elements of Judicial Strategy* (Chicago: University of Chicago Press, 1961).

5. Douglas, *The Court Years*, p. 25.

6. Felix Frankfurter to Stanley Reed, 5 December 1951, FFP, Box 93.

7. *Bartkus v Illinois* 359 U.S. 121 (1958) involved a defendant who was acquitted of bank robbery charges in federal court. Brought into state court in Illinois, he was found guilty. The case came to the Supreme Court with the focus on the Fifth Amendment's double jeopardy clause and its meaning in a federal system.

8. Quoted in Newman, *Hugo Black*, p. 482.

9. Tom C. Clark to Hugo Black, n.d., HLBP, Box 58.

10. See, generally, Ball and Cooper, *Of Power and Right*.

11. Ibid., p. 243.

12. See, for example, Ball and Cooper, *The U.S. Supreme Court: From the Inside Out*, chap. 3 (Englewood Cliffs, N.J.: Prentice-Hall, 1996), for insights into the politics of selecting a new Supreme Court justice.

13. See generally Howard Ball and Phillip Cooper, "Fighting Justices: Hugo Black, William O. Douglas, and Conflict on the Court," 38 *American Journal of Legal History*, no. 1 (Winter 1994).

14. Quoted in Ball and Cooper, *Of Power and Right*, p. 78.

15. *Boddie v Connecticut*, 401 U.S. 371, 389 (1970). Black, in dissent, wrote that "the only way to steer this country toward its great destiny is to follow what the Constitution says, not what judges think it should have said." at 393.

16. Black, Foreword, *Confronting Injustice*, p. xii.

17. Urofsky, "Conflict among the Brethren," p. 78.

18. Interview with William J. Brennan, 29 October 1986.

19. Ibid.

20. *Alexander v Holmes County, Mississippi*, 396 U.S. 19 (1969).

21. MTTC, 26 October, 1969, HLBP, Box 58.

22. Ibid.

23. See Doris Fleeson's column, in the *Washington Star* of May 16, 1946, entitled: "Supreme Court Feud: Inside Story of Jackson-Black Battle Laid Before a Harassed President," and *New York Times* front-page story of 12 June 1946, entitled: "Jackson's Attack on Black Stirs Talk of Court Inquiry."

24. Jerome Frank to Hugo Black, 12 January 1939, HLBP, Box 28.

25. Ball, "Justice Hugo L. Black," p. 804.

26. HLBP, Box 61.

27. Hugo Black to Bill Douglas, inscription in Black's *A Constitutional Faith*, 19 October 1968, HLBP, Box 59.

28. Interview with Cathleen Douglas-Stone, 14 November 1986, Boston.

29. Black, Jr., *My Father*, p. 239.

30. Hugo L. Black to Alan Washburn, 17 December 1958, HLBP, Box 54.

31. Douglas, *The Court Years*, p. 20.

32. *Connecticut General Life Insurance v United States*, 303 U.S. 77 (1937).

33. William O. Douglas to Hugo L. Black, 4 February 1938, WODP, Box 59.

34. Cathleen Douglas-Stone interview.

35. Ibid.

36. Black, Jr., *My Father*, p. 240

37. Ibid. Justices Arthur Goldberg, Harry Blackmun, William J. Brennan, Byron White, Warren Burger, and Louis Powell all noted Douglas's brilliance, his uniqueness, and his idiosyncratic patterns of behavior. All of the Justices interviewed believed, however, that Hugo Black had a much more profound impact on constitutional jurisprudence in America.

38. Black, Jr., *My Father*, p. 240.

39. Brennan interview, 29 October 1986.

40. Felix Frankfurter to John M. Harlan, II, n.d., February-March, 1957, JMHP, Box 65.

41. Hugo L. Black to William O. Douglas, 11 June 1941, WODP, Box 308.

42. Hugo L. Black to William O. Douglas, 24 July 1941, WODP, Box 308.

43. William O. Douglas to Hugo L. Black, 8 September 1941, HLBP, Box 59.

44. Hugo L. Black to William O. Douglas, 15 September 1941, WODP, Box 308.

45. William O. Douglas to Hugo L. Black, 20 September 1941, WODP, Box 308.

46. See the correspondence between Justice Douglas and President Truman, dated February 23, 1946 and February 25, 1946, in which Douglas was offered and turned down the post of Secretary of the Interior. HSTP, Douglas-Truman Correspondence.

47. See the correspondence between Justice Douglas and President Truman in which

Douglas, writing to Truman from Lostline, Oregon on 31 July 1948, turned down the offer to run with Truman. "Basic in my whole thinking was the thought that politics has never been my profession and that I could serve my country best where I am." Truman's response, on 9 August 1948, was brief: "I was very sorry that you couldn't go along on the Vice-Presidency. Senator [Alben] Barkley, however, will make a good campaign, I am sure." HSTP, Douglas-Truman Correspondence.

48. See Melvin I. Urofsky, ed., *The Douglas Letters* (Bethesda: Adler and Adler, 1987), p. 110, n. 1; See also, Douglas, *The Court Years*, pp. 288–90.

49. Owen Roberts to Felix Frankfurter, 13 July 1948, FFP, Box 97.

50. William O. Douglas to Hugo L. Black, 1947, n.d., WODP, Box 308.

51. William O. Douglas to Hugo L. Black, 7 August 1965, HLBP, Box 59.

52. Black and Black, *Mr. Justice and Mrs. Black*, pp. 120–121.

53. Urofsky, *Douglas Letters*, p. 106.

54. See, generally, Howard Ball and Phillip Cooper, *Of Power and Right* for an examination of this issue.

55. See their essays, published in the *New York University Law Review:* Black's was entitled, appropriately, "The Bill of Rights," 35 *New York University Law Review* 865 (1960) while Douglas's was also appropriately titled "The Bill of Rights Is Not Enough," 38 *New York University Law Review* 207 (1963).

56. WODP, Box 968.

57. HLBP, Boxes 53, 54, 57.

58. Ibid., Box 57.

59. WODP, Box 1289.

60. *Adderley v Florida*, 385 U.S. 45 (1966).

61. *WJBP*, Box 487.

62. *Adderly*, pp. 45, 47, 48.

63. Ibid., pp. 49, 59.

64. Schwartz, *Super Chief*, p. 630.

65. Brennan interview, 29 October 1986.

66. *Breithaupt v Abram*, 352 *U.S.* 432, 442–43.

67. Cathleen Douglas-Stone interview.

68. See Ball and Cooper, *The United States Supreme Court*, pp. 291–93, passim.

69. Quoted in Douglas, *The Court Years*, p. 377.

70. Michael E. Parrish, "Felix Frankfurter, the Progressive Tradition, and the Warren Court," in *The Warren Court in Historical and Political Perspective*, Mark Tushnet, editor (Charlottesville: University of Virginia Press, 1993), pp. 53–54.

71. Hugo Black to Felix Frankfurter, 14 January 1939, FFP, Box 25.

72. In Lash, *From the Diaries*, p. 283.

73. Felix Frankfurter to John M. Harlan, II, 26 March 1957, JMHP.

74. Robert A. Burt, *Two Jewish Justices: Outcasts in the Promised Land* (Berkeley: University of California Press, 1988), p. 88.

75. Ibid.

76. Ibid., p. 40.

77. The case, *Schneiderman v United States*, 320 U.S. 118 (1943), involved an effort by the government to revoke the citizenship of a naturalized American, Schneiderman, because it was alleged that he was a Communist.

78. Burt, *Two Jewish Justices*, pp. 40–41.

79. *McLaughlin v Florida*, 379 U.S. 184 (1964).

80. Felix Frankfurter to John M. Harlan, II, 12 December 1964, JMHP.

81. Felix Frankfurter to Charles E. Whittaker, 9 April 1959, FFP, Box 111.

82. Quoted in Schwartz, *Super Chief,* p. 39.

83. Letter, Felix Frankfurter to William J. Brennan, Jr., 16 April 1959, WJBP, Box 23.

84. Leonard Baker, *Brandeis and Frankfurter: A Dual Biography* (New York: New York University Press, 1986), p. 418. "He often came in with piles of books, and on his turn to talk, would pound the table, read from the books, throw them around and create a great disturbance." Burt has written that Frankfurter had not only the knack of standing alone but also the "compulsion to drive his brethren away." Burt, *Two Jewish Justices,* p. 52.

85. William O. Douglas to David Adkinson, 16 December 1974, WODP.

86. Memo to the conference, Felix Frankfurter, 22 October 1942, WODP, Box 77.

87. Black, Jr., *My Father,* p. 227–28.

88. *Minersville School District v Gobitis,* 310 U.S. 586 (1940), involved the constitutionality of a Pennsylvania school board requirement that school children salute the flag as a condition of attending free public schools. The Court, in an eight-to-one opinion written by Frankfurter, Stone dissenting, concluded that the requirement did not violate the "liberty," found in the due process clause, of Jehovah's Witness children who wanted to avoid participation because of their religious beliefs. Legislators have the power, wrote Frankfurter, "to evoke that unifying sentiment [of national loyalty] without which there can ultimately be no liberties, civil or religious," at 597.

89. Burt, *Two Jewish Justices,* pp. 48–49.

90. Felix Frankfurter to Hugo L. Black, 15 December, 1939, JMHP.

91. Hugo L. Black to Fred Rodell, 5 September 1962, HLBP, Box 47.

92. Felix Frankfurter to Hugo L. Black, 30 September 1950, HLBP, Box 57.

93. Hugo L. Black to Felix Frankfurter, 2 October 1950, HLBP, Box 57.

94. Felix Frankfurter, MTTC, n.d., WODP, Box 329.

95. Felix Frankfurter to Hugo L. Black, 29 October 1942, HLBP, Box 25.

96. Felix Frankfurter to Stanley Reed, 21 December 1954, FFP, Box 93.

97. Quoted in Urofsky, "Conflict Among the Brethren," p. 80–81.

98. *Bell v Maryland,* 378 U.S. 226 (1963).

99. Felix Frankfurter to Hugo L. Black, n.d., May 1963, HLBP, Box 60.

100. Hugo L. Black to Felix Frankfurter, 9 December 1964, HLBP, Box 60.

101. Baker, *Brandeis and Frankfurter,* p. 425.

102. Quoted in Black, Jr., *My Father,* p. 238.

103. *NAACP v Alabama, ex rel Patterson,* 357 U.S. 449 (1958).

104. Felix Frankfurter to John M. Harlan, II, 23 April 1958, JMHP.

105. *Milkwagon Drivers Union v Meadowmoor Dairies,* 312 U.S. 287 (1941).

106. Ball and Cooper, *Of Power and Right,* p. 85.

107. Quoted in *New York Times,* 13 October 1975.

108. Robert H. Jackson, "The Black Controversy," RHJP, Box 26.

109. Ibid., p. 1.

110. Ibid., pp. 4–5.

111. Ibid., p. 4.

112. Ibid., p. 6.

113. Douglas, *The Court Years,* pp. 31–32.

114. Dunne, *Hugo Black,* p. 225.

115. Black, Jr., *My Father,* p. 190.

116. Douglas, *The Court Years,* p. 28.

117. Dunne, *Hugo Black,* p. 226.

118. Ibid., p. 29.

119. Black, Jr., *My Father*, p. 191.

120. Hugo L. Black, MTTC, 5 May 1945, HLBP, Box 25.

121. Quoted in William H. Rehnquist, *The Supreme Court: How It Was, How It Is* (New York: William Morrow, 1987), p. 66.

122. Robert H. Jackson draft, in HLBP, Box 57.

123. Felix Frankfurter to Hugo L. Black, 9 June 1945, HLBP, Box 57.

124. Fleeson, "Supreme Court Feud."

125. Telegram, 7 June 1945, Robert H. Jackson to Harry S. Truman, RHJP, Box 26.

126. Charles Grove Haines to Hugo Black, 26 June 1946, HLBP, Box 32.

127. Hugo L. Black to Charles G. Haines, 2 July 1946, HLBP, Box 32.

128. Hugo Black to Sherman Minton, 15 June 1946, HLBP, Box 61.

129. Douglas, *The Court Years*, p. 31.

130. Quoted in Dunne, *Hugo Black*, p. 247.

131. Robert H. Jackson Memo, RHJP, Box 26.

132. Baker, *Brandeis and Frankfurter*, p. 424.

133. Robert H. Jackson Memo, RHJP, Box 26.

134. *West Virginia State Board of Education v Barnette*, 319 U.S. 624 (1943), at 638, 642.

135. Abraham, *Justices and Presidents*, p. 219.

136. Rehnquist, *The Supreme Court*, p. 76.

137. Lash, *From The Diaries*, p. 209. In 1943, Frankfurter wrote that he had to "really nail Bob Jackson to the wall to prevent him from resigning from the Court. He had all the steps taken to do just that," p. 114.

138. Robert H. Jackson Memo, RHJP, Box 57.

139. Fortas, Quoted in Bruce Allan Murphy, *Abe Fortas: The Rise and Ruin of a Supreme Court Justice* (New York: William Morrow and Co., 1988), p. 93.

140. Ibid., p. 94.

141. Laura Kalman, *Abe Fortas: A Biography* (New Haven: Yale University Press, 1990), p. 320.

142. Jinksie Durr to Hugo L. Black, 23 September 1965, HLBP, Box 7.

143. Black and Black, *Mr. Justice and Mrs. Black*, p. 119.

144. Abe Fortas to Hugo Black, n.d., HLBP, Box 59.

145. Kalman, *Abe Fortas*, p. 320.

146. Black and Black, *Mr. Justice and Mrs. Black*, p. 220–21.

147. Carolyn Fortas to William O. Douglas, 12 August 1965, WODP, Box 309.

148. Kalman, *Abe Fortas*, p. 319.

149. Ibid., p. 322.

150. Ibid., p. 320.

151. Hugo Black to Abe Fortas, 14 November 1965, AFP.

152. Bruce A. Murphy, "Abe Fortas: The Reluctant Supreme Court Justice," paper presented at the Western Political Science Association, Salt Lake City, Utah, 30 March 1989, pp. 8–9.

153. Murphy, *Abe Fortas*, p. 216.

154. Ibid.

155. Benno Schmidt, former law clerk to Earl Warren, quoted in Murphy, *Abe Fortas*, pp. 216–17.

156. Ibid., p. 215.

157. Ibid., p. 219. Murphy concluded that "as harsh an assessment as this seems, any

analysis of Fortas's opinions must conclude that he *did* lack an overarching judicial philosophy. Instead, it was as though he were back in his Interior Department days, . . . playing the role of the ultraflexible technician" (my emphasis).

158. Murphy, *Abe Fortas*, p. 219.

159. Ibid., p. 216.

160. *Tinker v Des Moines School District*, 393 U.S. 503 (1969).

161. *United States v Yazell*, 382 U.S. 341 (1966); *Fortner Ent. v U.S. Steel*, 394 U.S. 495 (1969).

162. *Foster v California*, 394 U.S. 440 (1969).

163. *Gregory v Chicago*, 394 U.S. 111 (1968).

164. *Time, Inc., v Hill*, 385 U.S. 374 (1967).

165. *Brown v Louisiana*, 383 U.S. 131 (1966).

166. Murphy, *Fortas*, p. 537.

167. Earl Warren, quoted in Ibid., p. 223.

168. Black dissenting, *Brown v Louisiana*.

169. Black and Black, *Mr. Justice and Mrs. Black*, p. 135.

170. Murphy, *Abe Fortas*, p. 224.

171. *Gregory v Chicago*, 394 U.S. 111 (1968), concerned black protesters, led by comedian Dick Gregory, who had been arrested for disorderly conduct for demonstrating on the public street in front of Chicago Mayor Richard Daley's home. The Court unanimously set aside the convictions, although there were three opinions written, including one by Black.

172. William O. Douglas, Memo to the File, n.d., October term, 1968, WODP, Box 1431.

173. Murphy, *Abe Fortas*, pp. 539–40.

174. Kalman, *Abe Fortas*, p. 321.

175. Black and Black, *Mr. Justice and Mrs. Black*, p. 220.

176. Hugo Black told his law clerk George Sanders that Bill Brennan is "going to be my heir." Quoted in Kim I. Eisler, *A Justice For All* (New York: Simon and Schuster, 1993), p. 121.

177. Herbert Brownell, with John Burke, *Advising Ike* (Lawrence: University of Kansas Press, 1993), pp. 179–80.

178. Ibid., p. 180.

179. Eisler, *A Justice For All*, p. 84.

180. Schwartz, *Super Chief*, p. 205. "Warren was more comfortable with Brennan than with any of the other Justices, and an intimacy developed between them of a type that never took place between Warren and Black or Warren and Douglas, however close the latters' views may have been to his." Ibid., pp. 205–6.

181. Black, Jr., *My Father*, pp. 228–29.

182. Schwartz, *Super Chief*, p. 146.

183. Ibid., p. 147.

184. Felix Frankfurter to Earl Warren, 11 May 1957, EWP, Box 353.

185. William O. Douglas Conference Notes, *Macharoda v United States*, OT 1961, WODP, Box 1259.

186. Eisler, *A Justice For All*, p. 102.

187. Felix Frankfurter to John M. Harlan, Jr., 12 September 1958, JMHP.

188. Hugo Black to Hugo Black, Jr., 26 October 1956, HLBP, Box 4.

189. Hugo Black to John M. Harlan, II, 15 November 1956, JMHP.

190. *Malloy v Hogan*, 370 U.S. 1 (1964).

191. Brennan Interview, October 29, 1986, Washington, D.C.

192. *In re Groban,* 352 U.S. 330 (1957).

193. The phrase "B,B,D, and W" was coined by *Time Magazine* in its 1 July 1957 issue, p. 12.

194. Conversation with Justice William J. Brennan, Jr., 17 March 1986, University of Alabama Law School, Tuscaloosa, Ala. (on the anniversary of the 100th Birthday of the late Justice Hugo L. Black).

195. Brennan interview, 29 October 1986.

196. Ibid.

197. *New York Times v Sullivan,* 376 U.S. 255 (1964).

198. Brennan interview, 26 October 1986.

199. Ibid.

200. Black, Quoted in Eisler, *A Justice For All,* p. 121.

201. Douglas, *The Court Years,* p. 55.

202. William J. Brennan, Jr., "The Bill of Rights," *New York University Law Review* (1965).

203. Justice William J. Brennan, Jr., Address, Georgetown University, 12 October 1985, reported in the *New York Times,* 13 October 1985, p. A36, column 3.

204. *Griswold v Connecticut.*

205. Brownell, with Burke, *Advising Ike,* p. 179.

206. See Yarbrough, *John Marshall Harlan,* pp. 138ff.

207. Ibid.

208. Freeman and Howard, "Perspectives: Justice Hugo Black," p. 5.

209. Hugo Black to John Harlan, II, and John M. Harlan, II to Hugo Black. 6 September 1968, HLBP, Box 60.

210. Hugo Black to Ethel Harlan, 27 February 1970, HLBP, Box 60.

211. Quoted in Yarbrough, *Harlan,* p. 139.

212. John M. Harlan to Hugo Black, 11 August 1966, HLBP, Box 60.

213. John M. Harlan to Hugo Black, 11 August 1966, HLBP, Box 60.

214. Yarbrough, *John M. Harlan,* p. 333.

215. Black, Jr., *My Father,* p. 247.

216. Black and Black, *Mr. Justice and Mrs. Black,* p. 235.

217. Hugo Black to John M. Harlan, II, 15 July 1969, Box 60.

218. Hugo Black to John M. Harlan II, n.d., 1961, HLBP, Box 60.

219. Quoted in Yarbrough, *John M. Harlan,* p. 331.

220. Yarbrough, *Harlan,* p. 149.

221. John M. Harlan, II, "The Bill of Rights and the Constitution," address at the dedication of the Bill of Rights Room in the Sub-Treasury Building, 9 August 1964, New York, p. 3.

222. Yarbrough, *John M. Harlan,* pp. 149ff., passim.

223. See, generally, Meador, "Justice Black and his Law Clerks," pp. 57–63.

224. John Medelman, "Do you swear," p. 60.

225. Correspondence with Howard Ball, law clerk, 1969 term, summer 1972, Hempstead, N.Y.

226. George Freeman, in Freeman and Howard, "Perspectives: Justice Hugo Black," p. 2. Another clerk noted that "the overriding personal impression of the Judge was one of great humanity, love, warmth, and youth." Correspondence with Howard Ball, law clerk, 1969 term.

227. A. E. Dick Howard, in Freeman and Howard, "Perspectives: Justice Hugo Black," p. 2.

228. Freeman, in Ibid., p. 4.

229. Meador, "Mr. Justice Black and His Law Clerks," p. 59.
230. Medelman, "Do you swear," p. 61.
231. Freeman, in Freeman and Howard, "Perspectives: Mr. Justice Black," p. 4.
232. Meador, "Mr. Justice Black and His Law Clerks," p. 60.
233. Freeman, in Freeman and Howard, "Perspectives: Mr. Justice Black," p. 4.
234. Ibid.
235. Correspondence with Howard Ball, law clerk, 1969 term, summer 1972, Hempstead, N.Y.
236. Ibid.

Chapter Eight

1. Quoted in Jonathan Zasloff, "The Varied Dominion of Thurgood Marshall," *The Boston Globe,* 19 June 1994, p. B27.
2. Arthur Goldberg to Hugo Black, 23 April 1964, HLBP, Box 60.
3. Meador, "Justice Black and His Law Clerks," p. 58.
4. Interview with William J. Brennan, Jr., 29 October 1986, Washington, D.C.; interview with Byron White, 18 November 1986, Washington, D.C.
5. Roger W. Haigh, "The Judicial Opinions of Mr. Justice Hugo Black," 9 *Southwestern University Law Review,* no. 4 (1977), pp. 1069, 1070.
6. Ibid.
7. Article VI reads, in part, as follows: "This Constitution and the laws of the United States which shall be made in pursuance thereof; and all treaties made or which shall be made under the authority of the United States, shall be the supreme law of the land; and the judges in every state shall be bound thereby, anything in the constitution or laws of any state to the contrary notwithstanding."
8. *Younger v Harris,* 401 U.S. 37 (1971), at 44.
9. Correspondence with Howard Ball, Floyd Feeney, law clerk, 1962 term, summer 1972, Hempstead, N.Y.
10. Timothy O'Rourke and Abigail Thernstrom, "Hugo Black and Federalism: Local Control," 38 *Alabama Law Review* 331, 334 (1985).
11. Ibid., p. 333.
12. Black wrote that he "would much prefer to put my faith in the people and their elected representatives to choose the proper policies for our government to follow." Black, *A Constitutional Faith,* p. 11.
13. Ibid., p. 28. Holmes's dissent was *Tyson v Banton,* 273 U.S. 418 (1927) at 446. See also Holmes's opinion for the Court validating state sterilization statutes in *Buck v Bell,* 274 U.S. 200 (1927).
14. O'Rourke and Thernstrom, "Local Control," pp. 343, 341.
15. *Morgan v Virginia,* 328 U.S. 373 (1946), at 387.
16. Correspondence with Howard Ball, Kenneth C. Bass, III, law clerk, 1969 term, summer 1972, Hempstead, N.Y.
17. O'Rourke and Thernstrom, "Local Control," p. 344.
18. Brennan Interview, October 29, 1986, Washington, D.C.
19. Black, *A Constitutional Faith,* p. 24.
20. *Turner v United States,* 396 U.S. 398 (1970), at 426.
21. *United States v Southeastern Underwriters Association,* 322 U.S. 533 (1944), at 558.
22. See, for example, *Case v Bowles,* 327 U.S. 92 (1945); *Hulbert v Twin Falls,* 327

U.S. 103 (1945); *Fleming v Mohawk Wrecking and Lumber Co.*, 331 U.S. 111 (1946); *Testa v Katt*, 330 U.S. 386 (1946); *Woods v Miller*, 333 U.S. 138 (1948).

23. Strickland, p. 72.

24. Ibid., p. 71.

25. *Paul v Virginia*, 75 U.S. 168 (1869). In *Paul* a unanimous Court allowed states to pass regulatory legislation impacting on interstate insurance businesses. The Court concluded that insurance sales were not transactions occurring in interstate commerce and therefore the state could regulate the industry.

26. See Dunne, *Hugo Black*, p. 220.

27. Harlan F. Stone to Edwin W. Patterson, 16 June 1941, HFSP, Box 24.

28. Quoted in Dunne, *Hugo Black*, p. 222.

29. *United States v Southeastern Underwriters*, 322 U.S. 533 (1944), at 552.

30. Stone to Patterson, 16 June 1941, HFSP, Box 24.

31. See generally Kermit Hall, ed., *The Oxford Companion to the Supreme Court* (New York: Oxford University Press, 1992), p. 806.

32. See Black's comments on these Japanese exclusion cases in an interview he gave in 1967 that was published as part of his obituary in the *New York Times*, 26 September 1971.

33. The ten relocation centers, or "concentration camps," as Justice Owen Roberts and others referred to them, were called War Relocation Authority (WRA) camps and were located in California, Arizona, Wyoming, Utah, Idaho, Colorado and Arkansas. In the period 1942–1946, these camps housed a total population of 120,313 internees (including 5,918 children born in these camps).

34. William O. Douglas to Harlan F. Stone, MTTC, 31 May 1943, WODP, Box 92.

35. *Korematsu v United States*, 323 U.S. 214 (1944), at 216, 220.

36. *Korematsu*, at 221.

37. William O. Douglas, Conference Notes, 16 October, 1944, WODP Box 112.

38. William O. Douglas, Draft Dissenting Opinion, 1 December, 1944, WODP Box 112.

39. William O. Douglas to Hugo L. Black, 6 December 1944, HLBP Box 59.

40. Douglas, *Court Years*, p. 281.

41. Jackson dissenting, *Korematsu*, at 243.

42. Ibid. at 246.

43. Roberts dissenting, *Korematsu*, at 225.

44. Ibid. at 226.

45. Frankfurter concurring, *Korematsu*, at 225.

46. John T. Noonan, "Hugo Black and the Judicial Revolution," 9 *Southwestern University Law Review*, no. 4 (1977), p. 1127.

47. Robert J. Donovan, *The Tumultuous Years* (New York: Norton, 1982), p. 385.

48. Ibid., pp. 382, 386.

49. See *United States v Nixon*, 418 U.S. 683 (1974).

50. Rehnquist, *The Supreme Court*, p. 92.

51. Quoted in Donovan, *Tumultuous Years*, p. 390.

52. William O. Douglas interview, CBS-TV.

53. *Youngstown Sheet and Tube Co. v Sawyer*, 342 U.S. 579 (1952), at 582.

54. Cert note, *Youngstown*, n.d., WODP Box 220.

55. William O. Douglas, conference notes, 16 May 1952, WODP Box 220.

56. Ibid.

57. Ibid.

58. Ibid.

59. Ibid.

60. *Youngstown Sheet and Tube Co. v Sawyer,* 343 U.S. 579 (1952), at 585, 589.

61. Editorial, "The Constitution Lives," *Chicago Daily Tribune,* 4 June 1952, HLBP, Box 313.

62. William O. Douglas to Hugo Black; Hugo Black to William O. Douglas, 7 June 1952, HLBP, Box 313.

63. In 1971, Hugo and Sam Ervin met to discuss politics. Ervin, who had been "a number one critic of the Supreme Court . . . finally came up with an opinion he could commend Hugo on, . . . the Steel Seizure case under Truman." Black and Black, *Mr. Justice and Mrs. Black,* p. 231.

64. For example, see Black's dissent in *Griswold.*

65. For example, see Black's opinion for the Court in *Palmer v Thompson* 403 U.S. 217 (1970) which permitted Jackson, Miss. to close all its municipal pools rather than integrate them.

66. Article I, Section 10, states in part that "No state shall . . . pass any . . . Law impairing the Obligation of Contracts."

67. *Wood v Lovett,* 313 U.S. 362 (1940).

68. Hugo Black MTTC, *Wood v Lovett,* n.d., HLBP, Box 265.

69. *Ferguson v Skrupa,* 372 U.S. 726 (1962).

70. Ibid., at 732.

71. Arthur Goldberg to Hugo Black, 8 April 1963, HLBP, Box 372.

72. *Ferguson,* at 732.

73. Hugo Black, marginal comments on Goldberg note to Black, 8 April 1963, HLBP, Box 372.

74. *Dombrowski v Pfister,* 380 U.S. 479 (1965).

75. Schwartz, *Super Chief,* p. 755.

76. William J. Brennan docket notes, *Dombrowski v Pfister,* WJBP, Box 378. Harlan, according to Brennan's notes, would have vacated with directions to the lower federal court to abstain.

77. *Younger v Harris,* 401 U.S. 37 (1971).

78. *Younger* was the lead case; there were a total of four cases that raised this judicial federalism question: *Samuels v Mackell,* 401 U.S. 66 (1971); *Boyle v Landry,* 401 U.S. 77 (1971); *Perez v Ledesma,* 401 U.S. 82 (1971). Black wrote the majority opinions in all four cases.

79. Yarbrough, *Mr. Justice Black,* p. 34.

80. *Wisconsin v Constantineau,* 400 U.S. 433 (1970).

81. Quoted in Schwartz, *Super Chief,* p. 756.

82. William O. Douglas conference notes, 1 May 1970, WODP, Box 1499.

83. William O. Douglas conference notes, WODP, Box 1499.

84. See Black's correspondence to the conference, HLBP, LC, Box 438, 439.

85. Black and Black, *Mr. Justice and Mrs. Black,* p. 257.

86. *Younger v Harris,* 401 U.S. 37 (1971), at 44.

87. Ibid., at 47.

88. Hugo Black's marginal comments on Douglas dissent slip opinion in *Younger,* 14 February 1971, HLBP, Box 438.

89. Hugo L. Black to Edmond Cahn, 19 October 1960, HLBP Box 21.

90. Hugo Black, "The Bill of Rights," p. 874.

91. Hugo Black, *A Constitutional Faith,* p. 45.

92. Ibid., p. 48.

93. Hugo Black to Alexander Meiklejohn, 25 July 1962, HLBP, Box 42.

94. Black, *Constitutional Faith,* p. 43.

95. Hugo L. Black to Irving Dilliard, 7 January 1953, HLBP Box 317.

96. Saunders, Remarks at Meeting of the Bar of the Supreme Court of the United States, p. 5.

97. Cahn, *Confronting Injustice,* p. 103.

98. Felix Frankfurter to John M. Harlan, II, 19 May 1961, FFP, Box 66.

99. *Bridges v California,* 314 U.S. 252 (1941), at 265.

100. Ibid., at 28.

101. Anthony Lewis, "Justice Black and the First Amendment," in Tony Freyer, ed., *Justice Hugo Black,* p. 241.

102. Benno Schmidt, Remarks at University of Arizona, quoted in Lewis, "Justice Black," p. 242.

103. Hugo Black draft dissent, n.d. October 1940, HLBP, Box 258.

104. See, generally, Yarbrough. *Mr. Justice Black,* especially ch. 2, p. 4.

105. Felix Frankfurter, draft majority opinion, n.d., HLBP, Box 258.

106. Black, *A Constitutional Faith,* p. 52.

107. Ibid., p. 50.

108. Robert H. Jackson, draft concurring opinion, *Dennis,* p. 3, n.d. RHJP, Box 24.

109. Robert H. Jackson, notes, n.d., RHJP, Box 24.

110. Felix Frankfurter to Robert Jackson, 25 March 1950, RHJP, Box 24.

111. *Sacher v United States,* 343 U.S. 1 (1951) Douglas, Black, and Frankfurter were the only justices to vote to grant certiorari.

112. Felix Frankfurter, MTTC, 27 February 1951, WODP, Box 206.

113. William O. Douglas, conference notes, 9 December 1950, WODP, Box 206.

114. Ibid.

115. Ibid.

116. Ibid.

117. Ibid.

118. Hugo Black marginal comments on Vinson slip opinion for the majority, n.d., February 1951, HLBP, Box 306, p. 6.

119. Ibid., p. 7.

120. Ibid., p. 9.

121. Ibid., p. 11.

122. Ibid.

123. Ibid., p. 14.

124. Ibid., p. 15.

125. Ibid., p. 17.

126. Ibid., p. 18.

127. Ibid., p. 21.

128. *Dennis v United States,* 341 U.S. 494 (1951), Douglas dissenting, at 589.

129. *Dennis,* Black dissenting, at 580.

130. *Dennis,* Black dissenting, at 580, 581.

131. Woodward and Armstrong, *The Brethren,* p. 160.

132. Ibid., p. 169.

133. William O. Douglas conference notes, 26 June 1971, WODP, Box 1519.

134. Woodward and Armstrong, *Brethren,* paperback edition, p. 171.

135. Black, *New York Times v United States,* 403 U.S. 713 (1971), at 718.

136. See Black file on *New York Times* litigation, HLBP, Boxes 433 and 434.

137. Black and Black, *Mr. Justice and Mrs. Black,* p. 267.

138. Black dissenting, *Barenblatt v United States,* 360 U.S. 109 (1958), at 144.

139. Henry Abraham, *Freedom and the Court: Civil Rights and Liberties in the United States* (New York: Oxford University Press, 1994), p. 166.

140. Black, *A Constitutional Faith*, pp. 53, 44–45.

141. Ibid., p. 54.

142. Ibid.

143. *Bell v Maryland*, 378 U.S. 226 (1963).

144. Arthur Waskow to Hugo Black, 7 July 1964, HLBP, Box 376.

145. Hugo Black to Arthur Waskow, 13 July 1964, HLBP, Box 376. The other cases cited by Black were *Carpenters Union v Ritter's Cafe*, 315 U.S. 722; *Bakery Drivers Local v Wohl*, 315 U.S. 769.

146. Douglas, *The Court Years*, p. 35.

147. *Giboney v Empire Storage*, 336 U.S. 490, at 498, 502.

148. Ibid., at 498.

149. Ibid., at 501.

150. Yarbrough, *Mr. Justice Black*, p. 179.

151. *Thornhill v Alabama*, 310 U.S. 88 (1940).

152. Ibid., at 103.

153. Yarbrough, *Mr. Justice Black*, p. 172.

154. Black dissenting, *Ritter*, at 729–731.

155. *Bakery Drivers Local v Wohl*, 315 U.S. 769 (1942), at 776–77.

156. *Cox v New Hampshire*, 312 U.S. 569 (1941).

157. Hugo Black, draft concurrence, *Cox*, HLBP, Box 262.

158. Yarbrough, *Mr. Justice Black*, p. 173.

159. See, for example, *Carroll v Princess Anne County*, 393 U.S. 175 (1968), and *Dick Gregory v Chicago*, 394 U.S. 111 (1969), as well as other sit-in and sit-down cases heard by the Court in the early 1960s, including *Bell v Maryland*, *Adderley v Florida*, and *Brown v Louisiana*, all discussed in Chapter 9.

160. *Marsh v Alabama*, 326 U.S. 501 (1946).

161. See Howard Ball, "Careless Justice: The U.S. Supreme Court's Shopping Center Opinions, 1946–1976," 11 *Polity* no. 2, Winter 1978, pp. 208–209.

162. *Marsh v Alabama*, 326 U.S. 501 (1946), at 503.

163. Ibid., at 509. Black took note of the fact that the town managers, employees of the corporation, "stood in the shoes of the state," at 508.

164. *Amalgamated Food Employees Union Local 590 v Logan Valley Plaza*, 391 U.S. 308 (1968).

165. Ibid., at 317.

166. Ibid., at 319.

167. Ibid., at 330.

168. See *Lloyd v Tanner*, 407 U.S. 551 (1972), and *Hugdens v NLRB*, 424 U.S. 507 (1976).

169. *United States v O'Brien*, 391 U.S. 367 (1969).

170. *Tinker v Des Moines Independent Community School District*, 393 U.S. 503 (1969).

171. *Street v New York*, 394 U.S. 576 (1969).

172. *O'Brien*, 391 U.S. at 376.

173. *Tinker*, 393 U.S. at 508, 510.

174. Ibid., at 513.

175. Ibid., at 518.

176. *Street v New York*, 394 U.S. 576 (1969).

177. Ibid., at 594.

178. Ibid., at 596.

179. Black and Black, *Mr. Justice and Mrs. Black*, p. 271.

Chapter Nine

1. *Harper v Virginia Board of Elections,* 383 U.S. 663 (1966), Black dissenting.
2. Black and Black, *Mr. Justice and Mrs. Black,* p. 104.
3. Ibid.
4. In its entirety, the first section of the Fourteenth Amendment states:

All persons born or naturalized in the United States, and subject to the jurisdiction thereof, are citizens of the United States and of the state wherein they reside. No state shall make or enforce any law which shall abridge the privileges and immunities of citizens of the United States; nor shall any state deprive any person of life, liberty, or property, without due process of law; nor deny to any person within its jurisdiction the equal protection of the laws.

5. *Barron v Baltimore,* 32 U.S. (7 Pet.) 243, 247 (1833).
6. *Twining v New Jersey,* 211 U.S. 78 (1908).
7. Black, *A Constitutional Faith,* p. 38.
8. *Palko v Connecticut,* 302 U.S. 319 (1937).
9. Ibid.
10. Correspondence with Howard Ball, law clerk, 1968 term, summer 1972, Hempstead, N.Y.
11. Hugo Black, majority opinion, draft, HLBP, Box 258.
12. *Betts v Brady,* 316 U.S. 455 (1942).
13. Ibid., at 473, n.1.
14. Mendelson, *Justices Black and Frankfurter,* p. 64.
15. *Malinski v New York,* 324 U.S. 401 (1945), at 417.
16. *Haley v Ohio,* 332 U.S. 596 (1948), at 602.
17. Mendelson, *Justices Black and Frankfurter,* p. 65.
18. Black, *A Constitutional Faith,* p. 24.
19. Hugo Black, interview with Eric Severeid, CBS Reports, 1968, HLBP, Box 490, for transcript and other material, including letters, from viewers of the telecast.
20. Black, *A Constitutional Faith,* p. 33.
21. Hugo Black, MTTC, re *Malinski v New York,* 23 March 1945, HLBP, Box 274.
22. Correspondence with Howard Ball, law clerk, 1961 term, summer 1972, Hempstead, N.Y.
23. *Palko v Connecticut,* 302 U.S. 319 (1937).
24. *Adamson v California,* 332 U.S. 46 (1947), Black, J., dissenting.
25. Ibid.
26. Ibid.
27. Ibid.
28. Ibid.
29. Ibid., at 87, Black dissenting.
30. Ibid., at 89.
31. Ibid., at 66, Frankfurter, concurring.
32. Ibid., at 68.
33. Ibid.
34. Ibid., at 69.
35. William O. Douglas to Hugo Black, 21 May 1947, HLBP, Box 284.
36. Hugo Black draft dissent, HLBP, Box 284.
37. Douglas, *The Court Years,* p. 54.
38. Frank Murphy to Hugo Black, n.d., May, 1947, HLBP, Box 284.

39. See, for example, Charles Fairman, "Does the Fourteenth Amendment Incorporate the Bill of Rights: The Original Understanding," 2 *Stanford Law Review* 5 (1949).

40. Charles Grove Haines to Hugo Black, 19 August 1947, HLBP, Box 284.

41. Hugo Black dissent, draft, *Adamson v California,* HLBP, Box 284.

42. *Rochin v California,* 342 U.S. 165 (1952).

43. Ibid., at 168–69.

44. William O. Douglas conference notes, 20 October 1951, WODP, Box 215.

45. Ibid.

46. *Rochin,* at 172.

47. *Rochin,* Black, concurring, at 174.

48. Ibid., at 176.

49. Freeman and Howard, "Perspectives: Hugo Black," p. 3.

50. Alexander Meiklejohn to Hugo Black; Hugo Black to Alexander Meiklejohn, 28 January 1952, 10 February 1952, HLBP, Box 42.

51. *Katz v United States,* 389 U.S. 347 (1967).

52. Hugo Black MTTC, n.d., HLBP, Box 400.

53. Black dissenting, *Katz v United States,* 389 U.S. 347 (1967), at 364.

54. Hugo Black, dissent, draft, *Katz,* p. 10, HLBP, Box 400.

55. *Katz,* at 361.

56. See, generally, C. Vann Woodward, *The Strange Career of Jim Crow* (New York: Oxford University Press, 1957).

57. *Dred Scott v Sanford,* 19 Howard 393 (1857).

58. *United States v Harris,* 106 U.S. 629 (1883).

59. *Civil Rights Cases,* 109 U.S. 3 (1883).

60. *Plessy v Ferguson,* 163 U.S. 537 (1896).

61. Baker, *Brandeis and Frankfurter,* p. 472.

62. Ibid., p. 482.

63. For a classic view of the dilemmas that these federal district court judges faced, see Jack Peltason, *Fifty Eight Lonely Men* (Urbana: University of Illinois Press, 1962).

64. Anonymous letters, HLBP, n.d., Box 335.

65. Black, Jr., *My Father,* p. 211.

66. Ibid., p. 214.

67. Quoted in ibid., pp. 215, 216.

68. Quoted in Dunne, *Hugo Black,* p. 349.

69. Quoted in Baker, *Brandeis and Frankfurter,* p. 484.

70. Peter Irons and Stephanie Guitton, *May It Please The Court: Transcripts of 23 Live Recordings of Landmark Cases As Argued Before the Supreme Court* (New York: New Press, 1993), pp. 249–61.

71. Hugo Black to William J. Brennan, Jr., n.d., September, 1958, WJBP, Box 328.

72. Hugo Black, Insert B, WJBP, LC, Box 328.

73. William O. Douglas, Memo to the File, 8 October 1958, WODP, Box 1198.

74. Ibid.

75. Ibid.

76. See William J. Brennan Jr.'s voluminous notes on the interactions between the Justices in the creation of the *Cooper* opinion for the Court, WJBP, Box 328.

77. *Cooper v Aaron,* U.S. 1 (1958).

78. Ibid., at 15.

79. William O. Douglas, Memo to the file, 8 October 1958, WODP, Box 1198.

80. Schwartz, *Super Chief,* p. 302. Brennan said that "we almost cut his throat." Brennan interview, 29 October 1986.

81. William O. Douglas, memo to file, 8 October 1958, WODP, Box 1198.

82. *Cooper v Aaron,* Frankfurter, at 16–17, 19, concurring.

83. A. F. House to Felix Frankfurter, October 7, 1958, HLBP, Box 335.

84. Baker, *Brandeis and Frankfurter,* p. 486.

85. Hugo Black, "Felix Frankfurter," *Harvard Law Review* 1965.

86. *Cooper v Aaron,* at 15.

87. See the justice's reference to "sit down" cases in Black and Black, *Mr. Justice and Mrs. Black,* p. 91.

88. *Shelley v Kraemer,* 334 U.S. 1 (1948).

89. Bernard Schwartz, ed., *The Unpublished Opinions of the Warren Court* (New York: Oxford University Press, 1985), p. 144.

90. Quoted in Black and Black, *Mr. Justice and Mrs. Black,* p. 105.

91. Ibid.

92. William O. Douglas, *Bell,* conference notes, WODP LC, Box 1314.

93. Earl Warren, conference notes, EWP, Box 604. Warren indicated that Black drew differences between a store owner and a home owner but "[the Court] cannot make a constitutional difference."

94. Warren conference notes, EWP, Box 604. See also, WJBP LC, Box 410, Washington, D.C.

95. Schwartz, *Super Chief,* p. 487.

96. William O. Douglas, conference notes, *Bell v Maryland,* WODP, Box 1314.

97. These notes evidently survived the destruction of Black's conference notes after his death (by his son, Hugo, Jr., at the specific request of his father). They were transcribed and/or copied by two of Black's law clerks, A. E. Dick Howard and John G. Kester, and were included in a multi page summary of the 1963 term sit-in cases entitled, "The Deliberations of the Justices in Deciding the Sit-In Cases of June 22, 1964, from the files of Justice Black Compiled by A. E. Dick Howard and John G. Kester Law Clerks," in HLBP LC, Box 376.

98. Ibid., pp. 4, 5. Schwartz noted that Black, in this conference, "delivered an emotional statement . . . declaring that he could not believe that his 'Pappy,' who operated a general store in Alabama, did not have the right to decide whom he would or would not serve." Schwartz, *Unpublished Opinions,* p. 146.

99. Mark-up Sheet, *Bell v Maryland,* 5 June 1963, WODP, Box 1314.

100. William O. Douglas, memo, In re: Sit-In Cases, 21 October 1963, WODP, Box 1299.

101. Ibid.

102. Black and Black, *Mr. Justice and Mrs. Black,* p. 92.

103. Ibid., p. 96.

104. Douglas, in a handwritten note for the file, dated 19 May 1964, indicated that Clark had seen him that day and had told him he was switching his vote. "His [switch] upset HLB very much as HLB had hoped the Court would act promptly. There was considerable speculation as to why TCC [switched, but] it now appears that he has concluded that these cases all represent 'state action.' " WODP LC, Box 1314.

105. *Bell v Maryland,* 378 U.S. 227 (1963), at 228.

106. Brennan interview, 29 October 1986, Washington, D.C.

107. William O. Douglas, Memo to the File, *Bell v Maryland,* 20 June 1964, WODP, Box 1314.

108. Ibid.

109. William O. Douglas to William J. Brennan, 3 June 1964, WODP Box 1314.

110. Black and Black, *Mr. Justice and Mrs. Black,* p. 92.

111. *Bell v Maryland,* 378 U.S. 226 (1963), Black dissenting at 318.

112. Hugo Black to Arthur Goldberg, 23 April 1964, HLBP, Box 376.

113. *Bell v Maryland,* 378 U.S. 226 (1963), Black dissenting at 342.

114. Ibid. at 346.

115. *Brown v Board of Education,* 349 U.S. 294 (1955).

116. Hugo Black dissent, draft (not published), *Alexander v Holmes County, Miss.,* 25 October 1969, pp. 2, 3, HLBP, Box 428.

117. See, for example, *Goss v Board of Education,* 373 U.S. 683 (1963).

118. See, for example, *Griffin v County School Board,* 377 U.S. 218 (1964).

119. See, for example, *Green v County School Board,* 391 U.S. 430 (1968).

120. Hugo Black dissent, draft, *Alexander v Holmes County, Mississippi,* fn 2, HLBP, Box 428.

121. Order, Black, Circuit Justice, *Alexander v Holmes County, September 5, 1969,* denying request to vacate suspension of integration order by Fifth Circuit Court of Appeals, p. 2.

122. Douglas, *The Court Years,* p. 120. " 'All deliberate speed' was used to drag feet. . . . [Opponents] thought up ingenious as well as ingenuous plans to forestall [desegregation] programs."

123. *Green,* at 438–39.

124. *Alexander v Holmes County, Miss.,* 396 U.S. 1218 (1969), Justice Black, In Chambers; 396 U.S. 19 (1969).

125. Black and Black, *Mr. Justice and Mrs. Black,* p. 230.

126. *Green v County School Board of New Kent County,* 391 U.S. 430 (1968).

127. Black, Circuit Justice, Order, HLBP, Box 428, p. 4.

128. Hugo Black, MTTC, 23 September 1969, HLBP, Box 428.

129. William O. Douglas, conference session notes, 9 October 1969, WODP, Box 1480.

130. Ibid.

131. Ibid.

132. Ibid.

133. Hugo Black, margin notes on Burger majority draft opinion, 25 October 1969, HLBP, Box 428.

134. Hugo Black, MTTC, 26 October 1969, HLBP, Box 428.

135. Hugo Black draft dissent, HLBP, Box 428.

136. Ibid.

137. Black and Black, *Mr. Justice and Mrs. Black,* p. 233.

138. See the correspondence, re: *Alexander,* WODP, Box 1480.

139. Black and Black, *Mr. Justice and Mrs. Black,* p. 233.

140. Warren Burger, MTTC, 29 October 1969, WODP, Box 1480.

141. William O. Douglas, MTTC, 29 October 1969, WODP, Box 1480.

142. Black, *A Constitutional Faith,* p. 8.

143. *Griswold v Connecticut,* 381 U.S. 479, 522 (1965), Black, J., dissenting at 522.

144. Ibid.

145. Ibid., n. 4.

146. Ibid.

147. *Poe v Ullman,* 367 U.S. 497 was a 1961 case that involved a Connecticut law prohibiting the use of contraceptives. The Court, with Douglas the sole dissenter, concluded that there was no standing to sue, as the state had not actually enforced the law by arresting and charging someone with violation of the statute.

148. Ball and Cooper, *Of Power and Right,* pp. 283ff.

149. *NAACP v Alabama*, 357 U.S. 449 (1958).

150. William J. Brennan to William O. Douglas, 24 April 1965, WJBP, Box 130.

151. SPP to William J. Brennan, 27 April 1965, WJBP, Box 130.

152. *Griswold*, at 484.

153. Ibid., p. 486.

154. Goldberg, concurring, *Griswold*, at 492.

155. Ibid., at 493.

156. *Griswold*, Black, J., dissenting, at 510.

157. Ibid., at 513.

158. Ibid., at 511.

159. Ibid., n.2.

160. Ibid., at 518–19.

161. "Priceless Privacy," editorial, *The Christian Science Monitor*, 21 July 1965.

162. Hugo Black, marginal comments, *Christian Science Monitor* editorial, 21 July 1965, HLBP, Box 383.

163. *Harper v Virginia Board of Elections*, 383 U.S. 663 (1966), at 666.

164. *Harper*, Black, dissenting at 675.

165. Black and Black, *Mr. Justice and Mrs. Black*, p. 140.

Chapter Ten

1. Jerome A. "Buddy" Cooper to Howard Ball, 31 March 1993; Black and Black, *Mr. Justice and Mrs. Black*, p. 99.

2. Black, Jr., *My Father*, p. 248.

3. Black and Black, *Mr. Justice and Mrs. Black*, p. 269.

4. Black, Jr., *My Father*, p. 246.

5. Ibid., p. 247.

6. Black and Black, *Mr. Justice and Mrs. Black*, p. 267.

7. Ibid., pp. 270, 271, 272.

8. Ibid., pp. 80–81.

9. Ibid., p. 81.

10. See Howard Ball, *The Vision and the Dream of Justice Hugo L. Black* (University: University of Alabama Press, 1975).

11. Meador, "Justice Black and His Law Clerks," p. 60.

12. Black and Black, *Mr. Justice and Mrs. Black*, p. 83.

13. William O. Douglas, "Jerome N. Frank," 10 *Journal of Legal Education* 1 (1957), p. 4.

14. *Marbury v Madison*, 1 Cranch 137 (1803), at 177.

15. U.S. Constitution, Article I, Section 8, Clause 3.

16. *Katzenbach v McClung*, 379 U.S. 294 (1964).

17. Article III of the U.S. Constitution, the judicial article, enumerates the appellate and original jurisdiction of the Supreme Court and other lower federal courts that the Congress creates.

18. Hugo Black, Foreword to *Confronting Injustice*, p. xii.

19. See, for example, Sylvia Snowiss, "The Legacy of Justice Black," in Dennis et al., ed., *Justice Hugo Black and the First Amendment*. She argues (p. 17ff.) that the Judge's "literalism reflected his dissatisfaction with the major attempts to reconcile the exercise of judicial review with democratic responsibility."

20. See, for example, *Hammer v Dagenhart*, 247 U.S. 251 (1918).

21. See, for example, *Lochner v New York*, 198 U.S. 45 (1905).

22. See, generally, Ball and Cooper, *Of Power and Right,* ch. 5.

23. Black, *A Constitutional Faith,* p. 24.

24. *Lincoln Federal Labor Union v Northwestern Iron and Metal Company,* 335 U.S. 525 (1949), at 536.

25. *Ferguson v Skrupa,* 372 U.S. 726 (1963), at 730, 732.

26. Correspondence with Howard Ball, law clerk, 1969 term, Summer 1972, Hempstead, N.Y.

27. Harry Blackmun, then a very close friend of the Chief Justice Warren E. Burger, was recommended to the president by Burger and became Richard M. Nixon's third Supreme Court nominee, almost one year after Abe Fortas resigned from the Court in disgrace. The first two men, both Southerners, Clement Haynsworth and G. Harrold Carswell, were defeated in final Senate votes. Blackmun was confirmed by the Senate, unanimously, ninety three to zero.

28. Quoted in John Jenkins, "A Candid Talk With Justice Blackmun," *The New York Times Sunday Magazine,* 20 February 1983, p. 38.

29. Black and Black, *Mr. Justice and Mrs. Black,* p. 244.

30. Ibid., p. 106. Chief Justice Warren and Justices Brennan, White, Goldberg, and Clark attended. Bill Douglas had a dinner engagement and did not attend.

31. Ibid., p. 93.

Bibliography

Abraham, Henry J. *Justices and Presidents: A Political History of Appointments to the Supreme Court,* New York: Oxford University Press, 1974.

———. *Freedom and the Court: Civil Rights and Liberties in the United States.* New York: Oxford University Press, 1994.

Aikman, Duncan. "The Klan on the Court," *Newsweek,* 30 September 1937.

Alsop, Joseph and Turner Catledge. *The 168 Days.* New York: Doubleday, Doran and Co., 1938.

Ayers, Edward L. *The Promise of the New South: Life After Reconstruction.* New York: Oxford University Press, 1993.

Baker, Leonard. *Brandeis and Frankfurter: A Dual Biography.* New York. New York University Press, 1986.

Ball, Howard. "Careless Justice: The United States Supreme Court's Shopping Center Opinions, 1946–1972," 11 *Polity,* no. 2 (Winter 1978).

———. "Hugo L. Black" Twentieth Century Jeffersonian," 9 *Southwestern University Law Review,* 1049 (1977).

———. "Justice Hugo L. Black: A Magnificent Product of the South," 36 *Alabama Law Review,* 791 (1985).

———. *The Vision And the Dream of Justice Hugo L. Black.* University: University of Alabama Press, 1975.

Ball, Howard and Phillip Cooper. "Fighting Justices: Hugo Black, William O. Douglas, and Conflict on the Court," 38 *American Journal of Legal History,* no. 1 (Winter 1994).

———. *Of Power and Right: Hugo Black, William O. Douglas and America's Constitutional Revolution.* New York: Oxford University Press, 1992.

———. *The United States Supreme Court: From the Inside Out.* Englewood Cliffs, N.J.: Prentice-Hall, 1996.

Barnard, Hollinger F., ed. *Outside the Magic Circle: The Autobiography of Virginia Foster Durr.* University: University of Alabama Press, 1990.

Berman, Daniel. "Hugo L. Black: The Early Years." 8 *Catholic University Law Review*, 103 (1959).

Black, Elizabeth S., "Hugo Black: The Magnificent Rebel." 9 *Southwestern University Law Review*, no. 4 (1977).

———. "Hugo Black: A Memorial Portrait." *Yearbook: U.S. Supreme Court, 1982*, 76.

Black, Hugo L. "The Bill of Rights." 35 *New York University Law Review*, 865 (1960).

———. *A Constitutional Faith*. New York: Alfred A. Knopf, 1968.

———. "Felix Frankfurter." *Harvard Law Review*, 1965.

———. "Inside a Senate Investigation." *Harper's Magazine*, February 1936.

———. "Reminiscences." 18 *Alabama Law Review* (1965).

———. "Should the President's Proposals Regarding the Supreme Court Be Adopted?" America's Town Meeting of the Air, 11 February 1937.

———. "There is a South of Union and Freedom." 2 *Georgia Law Review* (1967).

———. "The Utilities Lobby, Radio Address and Speech," 8 August 1935. Washington: Government Printing Office, 1935.

——— and Elizabeth Black. *Mr. Justice and Mrs. Justice Black*. New York: Random House, 1986.

Black, Hugo L., Jr. *My Father: A Remembrance*. New York: Random House, 1975.

Blasi, Vincent, ed. *The Burger Court*. New Haven, Conn.: Yale University Press, 1982.

Brennan, William, Jr. "The Bill of Rights." *New York University Law Review* (1965).

Brownell, Herbert, with John Burke. *Advising Ike*. Lawrence: University of Kansas Press, 1993.

Burt, Robert A. *Two Jewish Justices: Outcasts in the Promised Land*. Berkeley: University of California Press, 1988.

Cahn, Lenore, ed. *Confronting Injustice: The Edmond Cahn Reader*. Boston: Beacon Press, 1966.

Cooper, Jerome A. *"Sincerely Your Friend": Letters of Mr. Justice Hugo L. Black to Jerome A. Cooper*. University: University of Alabama Press, 1973.

Creel, George. "Goosekillers." *Colliers*, 9 January 1937.

Davis, Hazel Black. *Uncle Hugo: An Intimate Portrait of Mr. Justice Black*. Alabama: private printing, 1965.

Davis, Kenneth S. *FDR: The New Deal Years, 1933–1937: A History*. New York: Random House, 1979.

Donovan, Robert J. *The Tumultuous Years*. New York: W. W. Norton, 1982.

Douglas, William O. "The Bill of Rights Is Not Enough." 38 *New York University Law Review* 207 (1963).

———. *The Court Years, 1939–1975*. New York: Random House, 1980.

———. *Go East, Young Man: The Early Years*. New York: Random House, 1974.

———. "Jerome N. Frank." 10 *Journal of Legal Education*, 1 (1957).

Dunne, Gerald T. *Hugo Black and the Judicial Revolution*. New York: Simon and Schuster, 1977.

Durr, Clifford. "Hugo Black, Southerner." 10 *American University Law Review*, 27 (1967).

Eisler, Kim I. *A Justice For All*. New York: Simon and Schuster, 1993.

Fairman, Charles. "Does the Fourteenth Amendment Incorporate the Bill of Rights: The Original Understanding." 2 *Stanford Law Review*, 5 (1949).

Freeman, George and A. E. Dick Howard. "Perspectives: Justice Hugo L. Black." *Richmond, Va. Times-Dispatch*, 12 December 1971.

Freyer, Tony, ed. *Justice Hugo Black and Modern America*. University: University of Alabama Press, 1990.

Gillman, Howard. *The Constitution Besieged: The Rise and Demise of Lochner Era Police Powers Jurisprudence*. Durham, N.C.: Duke University Press, 1993.

Goodman, James. *Stories of Scottsboro*. New York: Vintage, 1994.

Gregory, William and Robert Rennard. "Hugo Black's Congressional Investigation of Public Utilities." 29 *Oklahoma Law Review*, 543 (1976).

Hackney, Sheldon. "The Clay County Origins of Mr. Justice Hugo Black: The Populist as Insider." 36 *Alabama Law Review*, 835 (1985).

Haigh, Roger W. "The Judicial Opinions of Mr. Justice Hugo Black." 9 *Southwestern University Law Review*, no. 4 (1977).

Hall, Kermit L., ed. *The Oxford Companion to the Supreme Court of the United States*. New York: Oxford University Press, 1992.

Hamilton, Edith. *The Greek Way*. New York: W. W. Norton, 1942.

Hamilton, Virginia van der Veer. *Hugo Black: The Alabama Years*. University: University of Alabama Press, 1982.

———. "Hugo Black: Road to the Court." 9 *Southwestern University Law Review*, no. 4 (1977).

Harlan, John M., II. "The Bill of Rights and the Constitution." Address, 9 August 1964, New York.

———. "Mr. Justice Black—Remarks of a Colleague." 81 *Harvard Law Review*, 1 (1967).

Hayden, Jay G. "Supreme Court Feud." *The Detroit News*, 3 February 1944.

Helfer, Harold. "How To Stay Young." *Signature*, December 1968.

Hockett, Jeffrey D. "Justice Robert A. Jackson, the Supreme Court, and the Nuremberg Trial." In Gerhard Casper, ed., *1990: The Supreme Court Review*. Chicago: University of Chicago Press, 1991.

Horton, Robert W. "Senator Black Dons Cloak of Chief 'Ferret.' " *Washington Post*, 31 July 1935.

Howard, A. E. Dick. "Mr. Justice Black: The Negro Protest Movement and the Rule of Law." 53 *Virginia Law Review*, no. 5, 1050 (1967).

Irons, Peter and Stephanie Guitton, ed. *May It Please The Court*. New York: New Press, 1993.

Jenkins, John. "A Candid Talk With Justice Blackmun." *New York Times Sunday Magazine*, 20 February 1983.

Johnson, Nicholas. "Senator Black and the American Merchant Marine." 12 *University of Southern California Law Review* (January 1967).

Kalman, Laura. *Abe Fortas: A Biography*. New Haven, Conn.: Yale University Press, 1990.

Karst, Kenneth. "Invidious Discrimination: Justice Douglas and the Return of Natural Law Due Process." 16 *UCLA Law Review*, 716 (1969).

Lash, Joseph, ed. *From the Diaries of Felix Frankfurter*. New York: W. W. Norton, 1974.

Lewis, Anthony, "Hugo Black—An 'Elemental Force.' " *New York Times*, 26 September 1971.

———. "Justice Black and the First Amendment." In Tony Freyer, *Justice Hugo Black*.

Louchheim, Katie, ed. *The Making of the New Deal: The Insiders Speak*. Cambridge, Mass.: Harvard University Press, 1983.

MacLean, Nancy. *Behind The Mask of Chivalry: The Making of the Second Ku Klux Klan*. New York: Oxford University Press, 1994.

Magee, James J. *Mr. Justice Black: Absolutist on the Court*. Charlottesville: University Press of Virginia, 1980.

Margolick, David. "Enigma of Justice Black is Examined." *New York Times*, 13 April 1985.

McCullough, David. *Truman*. New York: Simon and Schuster, 1992.

Meador, Daniel J. "Justice Black and His Law Clerks." 16 *Alabama Law Review* (1963).

——. *Mr. Justice Black and His Books*. Charlottesville: University of Virginia Press, 1974.

——. "Mr. Justice Black: A Tribute." 57 *Virginia Law Review*, 1109 (1971).

Medelman, John. "Do You Swear to Tell the Truth, the Whole Truth, and Nothing but the Truth, He does." In Everette E. Dennis, Donald M. Gillmor, and David L. Grey, eds., *Justice Hugo Black and the First Amendment*. Ames, Iowa: State University Press, 1978.

Mendelson, Wallace. *Justices Black and Frankfurter: Conflict in the Court*. Chicago: University of Chicago Press, 1961.

Morley, Raymond. "An Inquisitor Comes to Glory." *Newsweek*, 21 August 1937.

——. "Whoso Diggeth A Pit." *Newsweek*, 27 September 1937.

Murphy, Bruce Allan. "Abe Fortas: The Reluctant Supreme Court Justice." Paper presented at the Western Political Science Association, Salt Lake City, Utah, 30 March 1989.

——. *Abe Fortas: The Rise and Ruin of a Supreme Court Justice*. New York: William Morrow and Co., 1988.

Murphy, Paul L. "The Early Social and Political Philosophy of Hugo Black: Liquor As A Test Case." 36 *Alabama Law Review*, no. 3, 101 (Spring 1985).

Murphy, Walter F. *Elements of Judicial Strategy*. Chicago: University of Chicago Press, 1961.

New York Times, "Justice Black, Champion of Civil Liberties for 34 Years On Court, Dies at 85," 26 September 1971.

Noonan, John T., Jr. "Hugo Black and the Judicial Revolution." 9 *Southwestern University Law Review*, no. 4, 1127 (1977).

O'Donnell, John and Doris Fleeson. "Stone Denies Hand in Attack on Black." *New York Daily News*, 12 May 1938.

O'Neill, Tip. *All Politics Is Local*. New York: Times Books, 1994.

O'Rourke, Timothy and Abigail Thernstrom. "Hugo Black and Federalism: Local Control." 36 *Alabama Law Review*, no. 4 (1985).

Parrish, Michael E. "Felix Frankfurter, the Progressive Tradition, and the Warren Court." In Mark Tushnet, ed., *The Warren Court in Historical and Political Perspective*. Charlottesville: University of Virginia Press, 1993.

Peltason, Jack. *Fifty Eight Lonely Men*. Urbana: University of Illinois Press, 1962.

Pruitt, Paul M., Jr. "The Return of Hugo Black: The Significance of the Hugo L. Black Collection at the University of Alabama." 43 *Alabama Law Review*, no. 1, 292 (Fall 1991).

Pusey, Merlo J. *Charles Evans Hughes*. New York: MacMillan, 1951.

Rehnquist, William H. *The Supreme Court: How It Was, How It Is*. New York: William Morrow, 1987.

Reich, Charles A. "Forward: Mr. Justice Black as One Who Saw the Future." 9 *Southwestern University Law Review*, no. 4 (1977).

Rodell, Fred. "A Sprig of Laurel for Hugo Black at 75." 10 *American University Law Review*, 1 (1961).

Saunders, George. Remarks at the Meeting of the Bar of the Supreme Court of the United States In Memory of Hugo L. Black, 17 April 1972, Washington, D.C.

Schlesinger, Arthur. *The Coming of the New Deal*. Boston: Houghton Mifflin, 1958.

——. *The Politics of Upheaval*. Boston: Houghton Mifflin, 1960.

Schwartz, Bernard, ed. *Super Chief: Earl Warren and His Supreme Court*. New York: New York University Press, 1980.

————. *The Unpublished Opinions of the Warren Court.* New York: Oxford University Press, 1985.

Silverstein, Mark. *Constitutional Faiths: Felix Frankfurter, Hugo Black and the Process of Judicial Decision-Making.* Ithaca, N.Y.: Cornell University Press, 1984.

Simon, James F. *The Antagonists: Hugo Black, Felix Frankfurter, and Civil Liberties in Modern America.* New York: Simon and Schuster, 1989.

Snowiss, Sylvia. "The Legacy of Justice Black." In Everette Dennis, ed., *Justice Hugo Black and the First Amendment.*

Thomas, Evan. "There is Always Something." *Newsweek,* 21 October 1991.

Thornton, Myles III. "Hugo Black and the Golden Age." 36 *Alabama Law Review,* 899 (1985).

Tushnet, Mark, ed. *The Warren Court in Historical and Political Perspective.* Charlottesville: University of Virginia Press, 1993.

Urofsky, Melvin. *The Douglas Letters.* Bethesda, Md.: Adler and Adler, 1987.

————. "Conflict Among the Brethren: Felix Frankfurter, William O. Douglas and the Clash of Personalities on the United States Supreme Court." 1988 *Duke Law Journal* 71 (1988).

White, Walter. *A Man Called White.* New York: Viking Press, 1948.

Williams, Charlotte. *Hugo Black: A Study in Judicial Process.* Baltimore: Johns Hopkins University Press, 1950.

Williams, Juan. *Eyes On the Prize Reader.* New York: Viking Press, 1987.

Woodward, C. Vann. *The Strange Career of Jim Crow.* New York: Oxford University Press, 1957.

Woodward, Robert and Scott Armstrong. *The Brethren: Inside the Supreme Court.* New York: Simon and Schuster, 1979.

Wright, Charles A. "Hugo L. Black: A Great Man and a Great American." 50 *Texas Law Review,* 1, 2 (1971).

Wyatt-Brown, Bertram. "Ethical Background of Hugo Black's Career." 36 *Alabama Law Review* (Spring 1985).

Yarbrough, Tinsley. *John Marshall Harlan: Great Dissenter of the Warren Court.* New York: Oxford University Press, 1992.

————. "Justice Black and Douglas: The Judicial Function and the Scope of Constitutional Liberties." 1973 *Duke Law Review,* 441 (1973).

————. "Justice Black and Equal Protection." 9 *Southwestern University Law Review* (1977).

————. *Mr. Justice Black and His Critics.* Durham, N.C.: Duke University Press, 1988.

————. "Mr. Justice Black and Legal Positivism." 57 *Virginia Law Review,* 387 (1971).

Zasloff, Jonathan Zasloff. "The Varied Dominion of Thurgood Marshall." *Boston Globe,* 19 June 1994.

Cases Cited

Index